Lecture Notes in Artificial I

Edited by R. Goebel, J. Siekmann, and

Subseries of Lecture Notes in Computer Science

Lorcan Coyle   Jill Freyne (Eds.)

Artificial Intelligence and Cognitive Science

20th Irish Conference, AICS 2009
Dublin, Ireland, August 19-21, 2009
Revised Selected Papers

 Springer

Series Editors

Randy Goebel, University of Alberta, Edmonton, Canada
Jörg Siekmann, University of Saarland, Saarbrücken, Germany
Wolfgang Wahlster, DFKI and University of Saarland, Saarbrücken, Germany

Volume Editors

Lorcan Coyle
University of Limerick
Lero, International Science Centre
Limerick, Ireland
E-mail: Lorcan.Coyle@lero.ie

Jill Freyne
CSIRO Tasmanian ICT centre
GPO Box 1538, Hobart, Tasmania, 7001, Australia
E-mail: Jill.Freyne@csiro.au

Library of Congress Control Number: 2010938380

CR Subject Classification (1998): I.2, H.3, H.4, F.1, I.4, I.5

LNCS Sublibrary: SL 7 – Artificial Intelligence

ISSN   0302-9743

ISBN-10   3-642-17079-X Springer Berlin Heidelberg New York
ISBN-13   978-3-642-17079-9 Springer Berlin Heidelberg New York

springer.com

© Springer-Verlag Berlin Heidelberg 2010
Printed in Germany

Typesetting: Camera-ready by author, data conversion by Scientific Publishing Services, Chennai, India
Printed on acid-free paper   06/3180

Preface

This volume comprises the proceedings of the 20th Annual Irish Conference on Artificial Intelligence and Cognitive Science (AICS 2009). AICS 2009 was hosted by the School of Computer Science and Informatics in University College Dublin on August 19–21, 2009. The AICS Conference is Ireland's primary meeting for those involved in the fields of artificial intelligence and cognitive science. The conference has taken place annually since 1988 and provides a forum for the exchange of ideas and the presentation of research conducted both in Ireland and worldwide.

After a rigorous review process, 21 papers were selected for oral presentation, and a further seven for poster presentations. Six shorter submissions were accepted for presentation at a technology demo session. The program covered a large range of topics, with submissions covering classification techniques, biologically inspired computation, natural language processing, and applications of AI techniques for the social web and financial markets. Although traditionally the majority of AICS submissions have come from the island of Ireland, AICS 2009 attracted a couple of submissions from farther afield—Mexico and Bulgaria.

AICS 2009 continued the tradition of inviting high-profile speakers from the fields. We were delighted to have two high-profile speakers give keynote talks: David R. Millen, from the IBM Watson Research Center, in Cambridge, USA, gave a paper entitled "Use of Enterprise Social Software to Support Organization and People Sensemaking"; and John Riedl, Department of Computer Science, University of Minnesota, gave a talk on "Collective Intelligence in the Social Web." We are most grateful to both speakers for taking time out of their busy schedules to come to Ireland and attend AICS.

Finally, it would not be possible to hold the conference without the generous contributions from our sponsors. We are most grateful to the School of Computer Science and Informatics, UCD (http://www.cs.ucd.ie); to CLARITY (http://www.clarity-centre.org), a Science Foundation Ireland Centre for Science, Engineering and Technology (CSET) involving UCD, DCU and the Tyndall National Institute; and to CLIQUE www.cliquecluster.org, a Strategic Research Cluster (SRC) funded by Science Foundation Ireland and involving UCD, DERI at NUIG, IBM, Idiro Technologies and Norkom Technologies.

We hope that you will find the papers in these proceedings interesting and stimulating. Here is to the next 20 years of AICS!

November 2009

Lorcan Coyle
Jill Freyne

Acknowledgment

We would like to thank our Program Committee, and our conference co-organizers John Dunnion and Fred Cummins. We also want to acknowledge the advice received from Barry O'Sullivan, Chair of the AIAI, and other members of AIAI, who organized this conference in recent years. We would like to thank those behind the excellent EasyChair conference system, which helped manage submissions and produce the proceedings, and Paypal, which made it easy to process conference fees. We would also like to thank Alexander Ufimtsev, who helped us greatly with the AICS 2009 website. Finally, we would like to thank our student volunteers, Gavin Horan and Angel Stone, who were always busy behind the scenes keeping the conference running seamlessly.

Conference Organization

Program Chairs

Lorcan Coyle
Jill Freyne
John Dunnion

Program Committee

Michaela Black
Derek Bridge
Ken Brown
Arthur Cater
Fintan Costello
Fred Cummins
Padraig Cunningham
Dara Curran
Sarah Jane Delany
Josephine Griffith
Conor Hayes
Alan Holland
Brian Mac Namee
Michael Madden
Kevin McCarthy
Lorraine McGinty
Paul McKevitt
David McSherry
Diarmuid O'Donoghue
Michael O'Mahony
Colm O'Riordan
Barry O'Sullivan
Ronan Reilly
Barry Smyth
Humphrey Sorensen

Table of Contents

Demo Papers

Use of Enterprise Social Software to Support Organization and People Sensemaking

David R. Millen

IBM T J Watson Research Center
Cambridge, Massachusetts, USA 02142
david_r_millen@us.ibm.com

There has been considerable recent interest in the use of Web 2.0/social software in organizational settings. In this talk, several IBM research projects will be discussed in which social software was tailored for business and deployed within a large global enterprise (IBM). These projects include a social bookmarking service (dogear), a lightweight file sharing application (cattail) and a social network application (beehive). Two important research topics will be discussed. First, we explore various application capabilities that support and encourage social interaction and application adoption. Several incentive systems were tested in field trials and showed sustained increase in user participation levels. Recommender applets were also trialed to understand their ability to support the increased end-user "production" of content. The second topic will be the use of social software to promote sensemaking for people and the organization. In particular, we explore the integration of various social software applications with search tools, and the introduction of non-traditional work content (e.g., personal photos) to signal and support organizational acculturation.

L. Coyle and J. Freyne (Eds.): AICS 2009, LNAI 6206, p. 1, 2010.

Collective Intelligence in the Social Web

John Riedl

GroupLens Research
University of Minnesota
Minneapolis, MN 55455 USA
riedl@cs.umn.edu

Many online communities are emerging that, like Wikipedia, bring people together to build valuable long-lasting artifacts in *peer production communities*. These communities exhibit several forms of collective intelligence, including effective decentralized cooperation within large groups of humans, partnerships between human and computer agents, and interaction effects between the two.

On the one hand, effective cooperation among large groups of humans should not surprise us, since such cooperation has been occuring since at least the time of the pyramids. On the other hand, it is unusual to see cooperation within such large groups without at least some members of the group holding whips! More seriously, the emergent behavior of millions of people working together with only the power structures they can evolve themselves is remarkable. We will seek to understand the causes of the successes and failures of these communities by looking at examples of both.

The individual cognitive processes of the human part of the equation are independently interesting as well. What is the nature of people's participation in peer production systems? What are their motives? In what ways is their behavior destructive instead of constructive? How can computer agents interact with the humans to encourage the positive contribtions, and damp down the negative? We will explore these questions in the context of a wide variety of the most successful Social Web systems.

Partnerships between human and computer agents have been talked about for decades, but are beginning to see full-scale deployment on the Internet. Agents scour the Web seeking information of interest to humans, who react to that information in computer-readable ways, leading in some cases to a positive feedback cycle of increasingly frenzied responses by the agents. The most powerful of these feedback cycles – PageRank – has had powerful and unexpected affects on the structure of the Web itself. What can we predict from past experience about the future evolution of these human/computer partnerships?

L. Coyle and J. Freyne (Eds.): AICS 2009, LNAI 6206, p. 2, 2010.

Robustness Analysis of Model-Based Collaborative Filtering Systems

Zunping Cheng and Neil Hurley

University College Dublin, Belfield, Dublin 4, Ireland
{zunping.cheng,neil.hurley}@ucd.ie

Abstract. Collaborative filtering (CF) recommender systems are very popular and successful in commercial application fields. However, robustness analysis research has shown that conventional memory-based recommender systems are very susceptible to malicious profile-injection attacks. A number of attack models have been proposed and studied and recent work has suggested that model-based CF algorithms have greater robustness against these attacks. In this paper, we argue that the robustness observed in model-based algorithms is due to the fact that the proposed attacks have not targeted the specific vulnerabilities of these algorithms. We discuss how effective attacks targeting factor analysis CF algorithm and k-means CF algorithm that employ profile modeling can be designed. It transpires that the attack profiles employed in these attacks, exhibit better performance than the traditional attacks.

Keywords: robustness, model-based, collaborative filtering, recommender system.

1 Introduction

Recommender systems use automated recommendation algorithms, such as collaborative filtering (CF), to help people discover what they need in a large set of alternatives by analyzing the preferences of other related users. With the rapid proliferation of online businesses, such systems are playing a more and more important role in web-based commercial operations and are attracting more and more users. A recent survey [1] reports that 62% of investigated consumers have made a purchase based on personalized recommendations and 72% of them show great interest in purchasing goods with the help of recommendation engines.

The robustness of recommendation algorithms has been studied for several years, in the context of profile injection or shilling attacks [11]. In such attacks, malicious end-users, motivated to modify the recommendation output of the system, create false user profiles (sometimes called sybils), to distort the recommendation process. As an example of such an attack, a vendor, motivated to promote the ratings of a product in order to boost its sales, might create a set of false profiles that rate the product highly (a so-called *push attack* [11]). Alternatively, a competitor might be motivated to demote the product rating

L. Coyle and J. Freyne (Eds.): AICS 2009, LNAI 6206, pp. 3–15, 2010.

(a so-called *nuke* attack). A number of different attack strategies have been studied and they have been categorized in [9] into several different types. Among these, the *average attack* has been found empirically to be the most effective and this has been supported with an analytical argument in [8]. However, most analyses have been carried out on k-nearest neighbour (kNN) memory-based algorithms and the attack models have been proposed with these recommendation algorithms in mind. It is not particularly surprising therefore that an empirical analysis of these attacks applied to model-based algorithms [9] shows that they are significantly less effective in this context. It is argued that the data abstraction component of model-based algorithms ameliorates the effect of attack profiles. Indeed, as shown in [8], the common model-based strategy of clustering can be effectively applied to attack detection, exploiting the fact that attack profiles tend to be highly correlated.

Clearly the key assumption that the model-based methods depend on is that their data abstraction components ameliorate the effect of attack profiles. In this paper, we will show that it is possible to create effective attacks which are able to affect the model parameters. As we will show, these attacks present new vulnerabilities for model-based algorithms that has not been considered in previous work. The contributions of this paper are summarised as follows:

– **Model-based attacks.** Beyond existing attack strategies, we propose to explore *model-based* attack strategies applied to model-based recommendation algorithms. Experiments show that with specific designs for specific models, theses attacks outperform strategies proposed previously.
– **Implications for Robustness Analysis.** Our work demonstrates the need for a reassessment of attack types and recommendation system vulnerabilities.

2   Related Work

The possibility of biasing a recommender system's rating output by the creation of false profiles was first raised in [11]. Since then, a classification of such *profile injection* attacks has been proposed in [3] and the effectiveness of such attacks has been evaluated on both memory-based and model-based recommendation algorithms [9,7]. The five general attack strategies proposed in [9] are sampling attacks, random attacks, average attacks, bandwagon attacks and segment attacks. In practice, an average attack is much more effective than a random attack. The bandwagon attack is nearly as effective as the average attack. Random, average, and bandwagon attack do not work well against item-based collaborative filtering. Elementary obfuscation strategies and their effect on detection precision are discussed in [13]. Both [12,3] also highlight the relation between domain knowledge and the effects of attacks.

In model-based CF algorithms, a theoretical model is proposed of user rating behavior. Rather than use the raw rating data directly in making predictions, instead the parameters of the model are estimated from the available rating data and the fitted model is used to make predictions. Many model-based CF algorithms have been studied over the last ten years. For example, [2] discusses two probabilistic models, namely, clustering and Bayesian networks. In [10], four partitioning-based clustering algorithms are used to make predictions, leading to better scalability and accuracy in comparison to random partitioning. Privacy preservation is one of the main motivations of decentralized recommender systems. In [4], the EM algorithm is used to train a linear factor analysis model, and a P2P-based architecture is firstly proposed for privacy preservation which was implemented in the Mender system. The probabilistic latent semantic analysis (PLSA) algorithm is introduced to CF recommendation in [6]. Its main idea is to employ latent class variables to learn users' communities and valuable profiles and then make predictions based on them.

In this paper, we will focus on model-based algorithms that use clustering to group users into 'segments' of similar users. Ratings are then formed by matching the *active* user, who is seeking a rating, to the most similar segments. We use the k-means algorithm for clustering and the algorithm is discussed in detail in the next section.

3   Model-Based CF Systems

The framework of model-based CF systems in [4,9] is summarized as Fig 1. In Step 1, model parameters are estimated using a large number of users ratings, and then in Step 2, predictions are made for target users with their past ratings and the parameters as input. We can also describe the two steps more formally in Equation 1 and 2 respectively:

$$(\alpha_1, \ldots, \alpha_k) = f(Y) \tag{1}$$

$$P_T = g(Y_T, \alpha_1, \ldots, \alpha_k) \tag{2}$$

where $\alpha_1, \ldots, \alpha_k$ are model parameters, k is the number of them. f is the function of parameter estimation. Y is the users ratings. P_T is predictions for target users. g is the prediction function and Y_T are past ratings of target users.

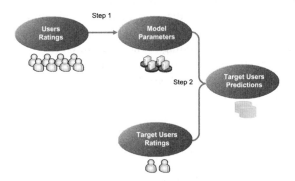

Fig. 1. Model-based CF Framework

In this paper, we will focus on two model-based CF algorithms: factor analysis [4] and k-means [9]. Related model-based attacks would be discussed in next section.

The Mender system is based on factor analysis of a linear model of the user rating process. In the model, it is assumed that there exist some set of underlying hidden categories and that a user's preference for a particular item is a linear combination of how well the item fits into each category and how much the user likes each category. The model is formally defined by the following equation [5]:

$$Y = \Lambda^T X + N, \tag{3}$$

Here, Y, is an $n \times m$ matrix, where n is the number of items and m the number of users. Each component of Y represents a rating for a particular user, item pair. The rating matrix is factorised into Λ, a $k \times n$ where k is the number of hidden categories, and X, an $m \times k$ matrix. N is a $n \times m$ matrix representing noise in the rating process.

The parameters of the model required in order to make predictions are the matrix Λ and the noise variance ψ, which could be computed by

$$(\Lambda, \psi) = f(Y) \tag{4}$$

where f represents the iterative expectation maximization (EM) algorithm. Then, target users with ratings $\mathbf{y}_u$, using Λ and ψ, make predictions $\mathbf{p}$ for given user-item pairs are given by

$$P_T = g(Y_T, \Lambda, \psi) \tag{5}$$

In [9],a model-based CF algorithm is proposed that clusters users-profiles into a set of k clusters or 'segments'. Once segments are identified, a representative profile is calculated for each segment, as the average of the profiles assigned to the segment. We apply k-means clustering to identify the segments. k-means is a clustering method that has found wide application in data mining, statistics and machine learning. The input to k-means is the pair-wise distance between the items to be clustered, where the distance means the dissimilarity of the items. The number of clusters, k is also an input parameter. It is an iterative algorithm and starts with a random partitioning of the items into k clusters. Each iteration, the centroids of the clusters are computed and each item is reassigned to the cluster whose centroid is closest. According to the general form, k-means CF algorithm could be rewritten as:

$$C = f(Y) \tag{6}$$
$$P_T = g(Y_T, C) \tag{7}$$

where C represents the centroids of each segments and f represents the k-means clustering algorithm.

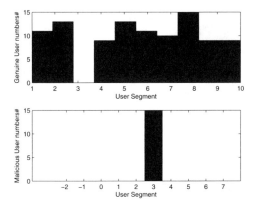

Fig. 2. Users distribution of k-Means CF against Random Attack

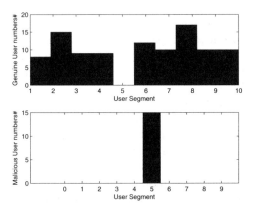

Fig. 3. Users distribution of k-Means CF against Average Attack

4 Model-Based Attacks

In this section, we describe strategies for creating attack profiles targeted at model-based algorithms. Later we will evaluate them in comparison to two of the standard attacks that have been proposed previously - the *random* and *average* attacks. In each attack, the targeted item is given the maximum rating in each of the attack profiles. The attack profiles are then further filled by randomly selecting a set of other items to rate. These items are called *filler* items and the number of items selected is called the *filler size*. The two attacks differ in the way that ratings are assigned to the filler items. In the random attack, ratings are chosen from a normal distribution, with mean and standard deviation set to the mean and standard deviation of the entire set of ratings in the dataset. In the average attack, ratings are chosen from a normal distribution, but with the mean and standard deviation set to the mean and standard deviation of the

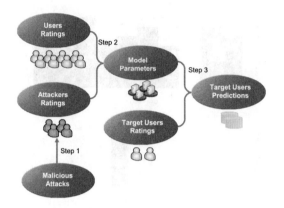

Fig. 4. Attacks Framework on Model-based CF Systems

corresponding item's ratings. Clearly, these attacks require some knowledge of rating statistics in order to be implemented in practice. Figure 2 and 3 show that attackers based on both attack types are clustered together in the k-means CF algorithm. Thus the effect of attackers are limited into a small subset of users. This explains why average attacks do not work well in the k-means algorithm compared with in kNN.

The framework of model-based attacks which are exerted on model-based systems, typically includes three steps, see Fig.5. Obviously, in step 1, the strategies of constructing attackers ratings (malicious profiles) determine how the attackers affect the model parameters and how much the prediction results are changed in step 2 and step 3 respectively. We have investigated two distinct attack strategies that are effective on model-based algorithms. The first reverse-engineers the parameter estimation algorithm in order to obtain attack profiles that cause post-attack parameter estimates to shift the rating output in the required direction. The second is more general purpose and relies on the observation that model-based algorithms collect users with high similarity into the same groups (categories, segments, etc.). Hence, high diversity attacks aim to maximise the influence of attack profiles, by spreading them across the groups as much as possible. We will discuss the details in the following subsections.

4.1   Informed Model-Based Attacks

Model-based algorithms postulate that ratings can be computed using some known formulations like Equation 2. Intuitively, the informed model-based attacks could attack model-based systems by

$$(\hat{\alpha}'_1, \ldots, \hat{\alpha}'_k) = f([Y_P, Y_a]) \tag{8}$$

$$P'_T = g(Y_T, \hat{\alpha}'_1, \ldots, \hat{\alpha}'_k) \tag{9}$$

where Y_a is the malicious user profiles, and P'_T is a set of input ratings which malicious users would like the target item to attain. In practice, Y_P Y_T are

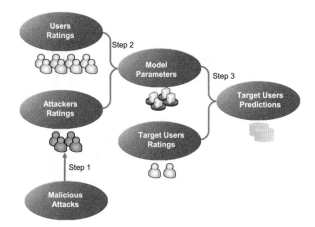

Fig. 5. Attacks Framework on Model-based CF Systems

unknown, so it is required to estimate this as $\hat{Y}'_P$ and $\hat{Y}'_T$, respectively. Thus Equation 8 and 9 could be changed to

$$(\hat{\alpha}'_1, \ldots, \hat{\alpha}'_k) = f([\hat{Y}'_P, Y_a]) \tag{10}$$

$$P'_T = g(\hat{Y}'_T, \hat{\alpha}'_1, \ldots, \hat{\alpha}'_k) \tag{11}$$

Given P'_T, Y_a will be solved from Equation 10 and 11. Apparently, the model parameters are key to the attackers. Usually, it is unrealistic to acquire those parameters for conventional centralized recommender systems. Although, it is possible to estimate them through training users and corresponding predictions, for simplification, we implement this attack on factor analysis system, Mender, by [5]. Mender is a P2P recommender system, in which model parameters have to be shared to public. In our experiments, we discuss model-based attacks in two situations: with full knowledge and with limited knowledge, which mean model parameters and ratings are public or just model parameters are public.

4.2   High Diversity Attacks

The Pearson correlation is the most popularly used similarity formula in recommender systems. However, it is not a transitive relation. That is, if user a is highly similar to user b and c respectively, it doesn't mean there is definitely high similarity between b and c. Therefore, it is possible to generate attack profiles which are similar to target users but dissimilar to each other. This strategy is very easy to be combined with the previous attacks. The algorithm is as follows:

1. Generate traditional attack profiles Y_a, e.g. random, average,...
2. Select profiles Y'_a from Y_a in which the set of common items rated by any two different profiles is not empty and the set of common items rated by any three different profiles is empty

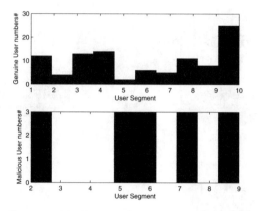

Fig. 6. Users distribution of k-Means CF against High Diversity Random Attack, $d = 5$

3. Diversify any two different profiles $\mathbf{u}, \mathbf{v} \in \hat{Y}'_a$ by

$$\mathbf{u}'_K = 2\overline{\mathbf{v}}_K - \mathbf{v}_K \tag{12}$$

$$\mathbf{u}'_{\overline{K}} = \mathbf{u}_{\overline{K}} \tag{13}$$

where $\mathbf{u}$ is the high diversity attack profile, $\mathbf{u}_K$, $\mathbf{v}_K$ are the ratings of the items rated both by $\mathbf{u}$ and $\mathbf{v}$, $\mathbf{u}_{\overline{K}}$, $\mathbf{v}_{\overline{K}}$ are the ratings of the items not rated by $\mathbf{u}$ and $\mathbf{v}$.

Figure 6 and 7 demonstrate that high diversity random attackers and high diversity average attackers are clustered into different clusters when applying the k-means CF algorithm. This implies that there is greater potential to spread their influence across the database. Therefore, we test it on k-means and find it essentially bias the ratings of representative profiles of segments C for target items. More detailed results could be seen in the next section.

5   Experiments

In order to examine the performance of our model-based FA attack, seven attacks are selected to test. FA attack means FA model-based attack with full knowledge, that is the whole rating data. FA-x attack means FA model-based attack with only the model parameters. H-Random attack means high diversity random attack. H-Average attack means high diversity average attack. Random, Average and Bandwagon attacks are designed according to [3].

5.1   Evaluation Metrics

There have already been several metrics to evaluate malicious attacks. [11] first introduces the prediction shift (PS) metric, which measures the effectiveness

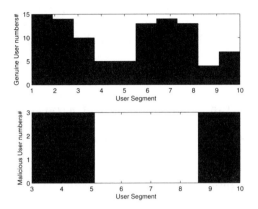

Fig. 7. Users distribution of k-Means CF against High Diversity Average Attack, $d = 5$

of an attack by the difference between predictions before and after the attack. However, just as [9] mentioned, a strong prediction shifts does not always mean an effective attack result. For example, a PS is 1.5, whether it is from 1 to 2.5 or from 3 to 4.5. Obviously, the former doesn't mean that the recommendation results are affected much by attacks. In [9], the Hit ratio is employed to measure the effectiveness on top-N recommendation systems, by examining the shift in the proportion of times that an item appears in the top-N list.

We introduce a new metric to evaluate the attack: high rating ratio (HRR), which shows how much predictions are pushed to high values for an attacked item.

$$H(\rho, i) = \frac{|u \in \mathcal{U}|p'_{u,i} \geq \rho|}{|u \in \mathcal{U}|p_{u,i} \geq \rho|} - 1 \tag{14}$$

where i is the attack item, ρ is the given rating threshold, and $\mathcal{U} \subset \mathcal{R}$ is a subset of users for which predictions are made. In practice, we find it is good measure of the effectiveness of a push attack. For the Movielens dataset, in whic ratings are in the range from 1 to 5, we use $\rho = 4$ in all related experiments.

5.2 Data and Test Sets

The larger data set of MovieLens is adopted in our experiments, which consists of approximately 1 million ratings for 3952 movies by 6040 users. Movies are rated on a scale of one to five. From this dataset, we extract a series of subsets to conduct our tests. Each of them consists of 1220 items. The average sparsity of the selected rating matrices is 10.31%.

To evaluate the attack, we take the following approach. A subset of 200 users is extracted from the Movielens dataset along with 1220 items, which were rated by three or more users. The dataset is divided randomly in a 50:50 ratio into training and test sets, consisting of 100 users each. An item is selected at random on which to apply a push attack. Predictions are made for the attack item for users in the test set. False profiles are then injected into the training set. Predictions are made for the users in the test set and the prediction shift over all users in the test set is calculated. The process of profile injection and prediction shift calculation is repeated 50 times. The average of the 50×100 prediction shifts is calculated as the attack performance.

5.3   Evaluation of Informed Model-Based Attacks

We evaluate the results based on two parameters: attack size and filler size. Attack size means the percentage of the number of attack profiles against the size of the pre-attack training set. Filler size is the percentage of items rated by attackers against the total number of items. For all tests we select 10% as filler size and from 1% to 10% as attack size.

Figure 8 shows FA and FA-x attacks outperform Random, Average and Bandwagon attacks based on the PS metric. The Average attack is similar to the Bandwagon attack. The Random attack is worst against FA-based CF and the prediction shift is very low. This validates the results from [9,7]: model-based CF algorithms are robust to these simple attacks. However, just as expected, the informed attack is most successful. It is interesting to note that the FA-x attack is almost as effective as the FA attack. This indicates that the factor-analysis algorithm does a good job in capturing real user rating behaviour. Thus the synthetic users generated for the FA-x attack, using the parameters learned by the model, are sufficiently similar to real users to guide the creation of effective attack profiles. It is because rating behaviour is well-captured in the model parameters that the public release of these parameters presents a vulnerability to the system robustness. The HRR results in Figure 9 show that the FA attack is > 60% better than the Average attack. FA attack is also better than FA-x attack by HRR, it may be because that FA attack is armed with more precise

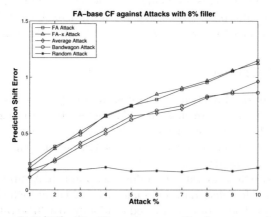

Fig. 8. Prediction Shift(PS): FA, FA-x, Average, Bandwagon, and Random Attacks against FA-based CF algorithm

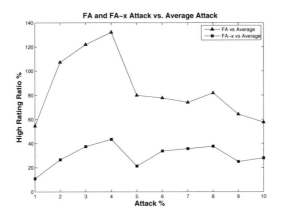

Fig. 9. High Rating Ratio(HRR): FA and FA-x Attack vs. Average Attack against FA-based CF algorithm, r = 4

information and can effectively push items to those unsteady users. FA-x is armed with the model parameters which could indicates the overall distribution, however it doesn't have the precise information for each user. That's why they are similar on PS but different on HRR.

5.4 Evaluation of High Diversity Attacks

We evaluate the results based on two parameters: attack size and diversity size. Attack size means the percentage of the number of attack profiles against the size of the pre-attack training set. Diversity size is the percentage of basis set size against the total number of attackers. For all tests we select 10% as filler size, from 5% to 25% as attack size, and from 10% to 100% as diversity size.

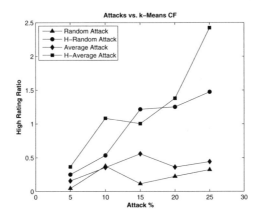

Fig. 10. High Rating Ratio(HRR): Attacks vs. k-Means CF, $d/attacksize = 50\%$

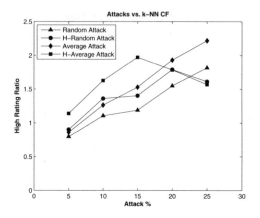

Fig. 11. High Rating Ratio(HRR): Attacks vs. k-NN CF, $d/attacksize = 50\%$

For both kNN and k-means, we apply 10 as the neighborhood size. For k-means, $k = 10$ is being used for user segments generation. In all cases, neighbors are filtered with a similarity value less than 0.1.

Figure 10 depicts HRR for random attack, H-Random attack, average attack and H-Average attack on k-means using attack size 5%, 10%, 15%, 20% and 25%. Apparently, H-Average attack and H-Random attack are much better than the other two. k-Means shows its stability against random attack and average attack. However, it is vulnerable against high diversity attacks. Especially when at 25% attack size, for H-average attack, the value of HRR nearly increases to 2.5 times before the attack on users who gave rating 4 for the target item. This means, for example, if 100 users like the item before the attack, then after the attack, there are 250 users like it.

Figure 11 shows HRR for attacks on kNN with the same parameters setting in Figure 10. We can see that the differences among four attacks are not very large. From 5% to 15%, H-Average outperforms other attacks, however it goes down after 15%. The same situation occurs on H-Random attack which goes down after 20%. This may be because kNN doesn't rely on maximization of the sum of the total similarities. At 25% attack size, average attack also nearly reach 2.5 on HRR. Compared with Figure 10, we could see k-Means against H-Average attack is almost as same vulnerable as kNN against average attack.

6   Conclusion

Recent studies have suggested model-based CF strategies to defend against profile injection attacks. However in this paper, we find that deliberate attacks could make them vulnerable as memory-based algorithms. Experiments show that both informed model-based attacks and high diversity attacks perform much better than traditional attacks on factor analysis and k-means CFs. Therefore, it is wrong to simply conclude that model-based algorithms are more robust than memory-based ones. Attackers can design effective algorithms using knowledge of the underlying recommendation algorithm. Thus, in order to resist varied attacks, we should develop related detection schemes for model-based CF systems.

Acknowledgements

This work is supported by Science Foundation Ireland, grant number 07/ RFP/ CMSF219.

References

1. A|Razorfish, A.: Digital consumer behavior study (July 2007), http://www.razorfish.com/reports/DigConsStudy.pdf
2. Breese, J.S., Heckerman, D., Kadie, C.: Empirical analysis of predictive algorithms for collaborative filtering. In: Proceedings of the 14th Annual Conference on Uncertainty in Artificial Intelligence (UAI 1998), pp. 43–52. UAI (July 1998)
3. Burke, R., Mobasher, B., Bhaumik, R.: Limited knowledge shilling attacks in collaborative filtering systems. In: Proceedings of the 3rd IJCAI Workshop in Intelligent Techniques for Personalization, IJCAI (2005)
4. Canny, J.: Collaborative filtering with privacy via factor analysis. In: Proceedings of the 25th Annual International ACM SIGIR Conference on Research and Development in Information Retrieval, pp. 238–245. ACM, New York (August 2002)
5. Cheng, Z., Hurley, N.: Trading robustness for privacy in decentralized recommender systems. In: Proceedings of the Twenty-First Conference on Innovative Applications of Artificial Intelligence, AAAI, Menlo Park (2009)
6. Hofmann, T.: Latent semantic models for collaborative filtering. ACM Transactions on Internet Technology 22(1), 89–115 (2004)
7. Jeff, R.D.B., Sandvig, J., Mobasher, B.: A survey of collaborative recommendation and the robustness of model-based algorithms. IEEE Data Engineering Bulletin 31(2), 3–13 (2008)
8. Mehta, B.: Unsupervised shilling detection for collaborative filtering. In: Proceedings of the Twenty-Second AAAI Conference on Artificial Intelligence, pp. 1402–1407. AAAI, Menlo Park (July 2007)
9. Mobasher, B., Burke, R., Sandvig, J.: Model-based collaborative filtering as a defense against profile injection attacks. In: Proceedings of the 21st National Conference on Artificial Intelligence and the 18th Innovative Applications of Artificial Intelligence Conference. AAAI, Menlo Park (July 2006)
10. O'Connor, M., Herlocker, J.: Clustering items for collaborative filtering. In: Proceedings of the ACM SIGIR Workshop on Recommender Systems. ACM, New York (1999)
11. O'Mahony, M.P., Hurley, N.J., Kushmerick, N., Silvestre, G.C.M.: Collaborative recommendation: A robustness analysis. ACM Transactions on Internet Technology 4(4), 344–377 (2004)
12. O'Mahony, M.P., Hurley, N.J., Silvestre, G.C.M.: Recommender systems: Attack types and strategies. In: Proceedings, The Twentieth National Conference on Artificial Intelligence and the Seventeenth Innovative Applications of Artificial Intelligence Conference (AAAI), pp. 334–339. AAAI, Menlo Park (July 2006)
13. Williams, C., Mobasher, B., Burke, R., Sandvig, J., Bhaumik, R.: Detection of obfuscated attacks in collaborative recommender systems. In: Proceedings of the ECAI 2006 Workshop on Recommender Systems, ECAI (August 2006)

Phase and Coordination in Speech Production

School of Computer Science and Informatics
University College Dublin
fred.cummins@ucd.ie
http://pworldrworld.com/fred

Abstract. When trying to understand behavioral systems, the measurement of time as phase offers many advantages over conventional clock time. We illustrate this with some experimental results in speech production, in which stable coordinations are evident using phase measurements. These stable coordinations may be related to the abstract constituents posited by linguists, but they are manifest only in the performance of an embodied system. Tying time measurement to the physical system also reveals a large role for individual difference in coordinative structures in speech.

Keywords: speech production, phase, dynamical systems, embodiment.

1 Introduction

Language is conventionally thought of as an abstract domain, relatively independent of its physical manifestation in speech, signing, writing, morse code or semaphore. Linguistic structure is thus typically thought of as removed from, and independent of, physical implementation. However, all language is produced using one physical system or another, and there are many reasons to privilege speech in this regard. Speech is the most common mode of language production. For the vast majority of language users, it is the first form of language experienced and learned. It also long predates all written or coded forms, and may be presumed to be the "natural condition" of a language producing subject[1].

While sequential order is of obvious centrality to all aspects of language, from sound sequencing, through morphology, syntax and semantics, the temporal dimension in speech is characterized by rich patterns of coordination among the speech articulators [14,16]. The coordination of physically embodied articulators places constraints on speech production that serve to both delimit and define the space of possible speech events that can be reliably produced. In what follows, it will be argued that the embodied nature of speech production may allow the identification of hierarchical units in speech. These units are characterized by relatively stable temporal organization when time is measured as phase, rather than as clock time. They arise from well-learned coordination patterns, and

---

[1] The relations between sign, gesture and speech are the subject of much speculation, but little is known about their relative importance in the origins of language.

L. Coyle and J. Freyne (Eds.): AICS 2009, LNAI 6206, pp. 16–25, 2010.
© Springer-Verlag Berlin Heidelberg 2010

exhibit considerable variation across individuals. This empirical approach to the identification of units in language poses challenges and opportunities for theoretical linguistic accounts.

2   Measuring Time as Phase

The "blooming, buzzing, confusion" in which we are immersed is made interpretable in part because we parse the continuous flux into discrete events [13]. Two observable changes in the world may recur together, or at a relatively fixed offset, thus providing evidence that they ought to be considered as components of some larger whole. The identification of a fixed timing relation between two events depends in the first instance on their relation to one another, rather than their separate relations to a fixed temporal scale of reference (clock time). To give a concrete example, the right time for a goalkeeper to have his hands in a particular spot is not to be found on a clock, but is to be identified by using the trajectory of the ball as a referent. The timing of the goalkeeper's movements are intimately connected to those of the kicker and the ball, and are essentially and causally unrelated to the movements of uninvolved players, the referee, spectators, and passing birds. Thus, we will recognize the kick and subsequent save as an event, and distinguish it from a background of simultaneous but unrelated flux.

This insight underlies a long-standing discussion that pits embodied, dynamical models of motor coordination against other forms of computational modeling, such as the identification of putative motor programs. In its clearest form, the debate has been pitched as one of intrinsic versus extrinsic timing [14]. Extrinsic timing refers to models of temporal unfolding in which events are pegged with respect to a clock of some kind. Many models of temporal interval interval production, for example, assume an underlying clock that provides a stable sequence of periods, thus providing other processes with a temporal reference [19,12]. Intrinsic timing, on the other hand. deals with the relative timing of events, where the events themselves serve as reciprocal temporal referents, as in the above example, where the trajectory of the ball provides the appropriate referent for timing the movement of the goalkeeper's hands. Intrinsic timing models thus need a way of expressing when one event component happens, in units that are provided by another event component. Phase measurement is one way this can be accomplished. If the event that is to serve as a referent has a fixed period, other events can be expressed as proportions of that period, thus providing a natural way of expressing temporal coordination that captures invariance across changes in absolute duration[2]. Phase is most readily expressed as the proportion of one period of a sinusoidal or periodic process, however the above arguments seek to emphasize that phase is best intuitively understood as relative timing expressed in intrinsically meaningful units within a specific context. Phase is time made meaningful.

---

[2] Various conventions for describing phase exist, including ranges of 0 to 360 degrees, 0 to 2π radians, -π to π radians, or most simply, as proportions from 0 to 1. We will use the latter form here.

3   Phase Stability as the Hallmark of Meaningful Coordination

When you walk, one foot hits the ground half way through the cycle of the other foot. That is, there is a constant phase relation of 0.5 between the two legs. In fact, all gaits of all animals are characterized by constant phase relations (not necessarily 0.5) among the limbs [10], and different phase relations are the signature of different gaits. Phase relations remain invariant across rate changes within a single gait. This constancy of phase is a clear indicator that the limbs are meaningfully coordinated, one with the other. This can be contrasted with the temporal relationship obtaining between the elements involved in a sequence such as the making of a cup of tea. If we take the sequence to include boiling a fixed amount of water, infusing the tea, and the subsequent drinking, this sequence can also be done at a variety of tempi. However, not all parts of the sequence can be compressed with equal facility. Infusing may be shorter, drinking may be hurried, but boiling a fixed quantity of water will stubbornly resist temporal compression. In this case, if we define an overall cycle that lasts from filling the kettle and ends with finishing the cup of tea, then the phase at which drinking starts, for example, will change as the sequence is executed at different rates. There is a notable absence of temporal coordination between the diverse sub-parts to this action sequence.

Speech is complex sequential action, and it is an open question how that sequencing is achieved. Most linguistic descriptions emphasize serial order. Thus the sequence /pot/ contrasts systematically with the sequence /top/, even though the set of constituents are, at some abstract level of description, the same. Much of the structure of language as conventionally understood lies in the sequencing of elements, and in the grouping of sub-sequences into larger units within an ordered hierarchy. At the level of meaning, the smallest units, morphemes are conventionally assumed to group into larger units, words, which in turn partake in elaborate structural hierarchies such as phrases and sentences.

At the level of sounds, many accounts of speech structure posit atomic units at the level of the phone, with phone sequences organized within containing syllables. Above the syllable, theories of prosodic phonology typically posit several hierarchical layers that help to account for a wide variety of surface features of speech such as lengthening effects at the right edges of supposed constituents, or the blocking of processes such as vowel harmony by constituent boundaries. There has been a marked lack of agreement about the number and nature of levels required to accurately describe the prosodic structure of speech, and there are no effective procedures for the unambiguous identification of many proposed constituents [2,8].

Linguistic theory typically regards the elements that are sequenced as disembodied symbol-like entities, and one of the principal distinctions between phonology and phonetics is that the former is concerned with systematicity in the distribution of symbolic elements (phonemes, syllables, intonational phrases) while the latter is seen as the implementation thereof. The interface between the two thus becomes a challenge for a full account. Some have suggested that the implementation of such sequences within the constraints of the physical vocal tract makes the task of the recovery of the underlying symbol sequences difficult [11] while others have questioned the logic that deduces the presence of this presumed interface [15]. One influential theory that aspires to providing a full account of both linguistic and phonetic phenomena is Articulatory Phonology, in which the units of contrast are also simultaneously units of action, or gestures [3]. Within this approach, the question of how to appropriately coordinate the timing of gestures with respect to one another, or how to phase them, has long been a contentious issue [4]. It has recently been suggested that a suitably embodied instantiation of the theory may allow the discovery of physically optimal coordinative relations among gestures, but this work is still at an early stage [17]. Unfortunately, neither conventional articulatory phonology, nor the recent embodied task dynamic extension, can deal appropriately with the coordination of units much larger than individual gestures within syllables.

In the spirit of this embodied approach to the elements of phonology and phonetics, it is possible to ask if meaningful coordination of larger units than the syllable might be revealed by an appropriate experimental methodology that looked for evidence of phase stability across tempo variation. Rather than positing abstract underlying symbolic units that arise from the grammar of a language, and then seeking to uncover these units in the noisy signal that is the physical speech signal, one could adopt an alternative stance that starts with the physical signal, and looks for invariance across tempo change to uncover meaningful units of coordination. This experimental approach diverges from conventional strategies in several fundamental ways. Firstly, when we look at coordinated movement, we find that individuals differ, and these differences matter. We can readily identify an individual by their handwriting, their prosody, or their gait, because each individual has achieved a behavioral goal in an idiosyncratic manner. Skilled movement is the imposition of constraints upon a very high dimensional system, such that behavioral goals are fulfilled. This produces underspecified solutions, with the result that movement patterns are idiosyncratic [18]. We might not find a single grammar of movement for speakers of a language, but we might find individual structures that are demonstrably meaningful constituents in the speech of an individual. Secondly, coordinative units might be a function, not only of speaker, but also of speaking condition. Where linguistic theory tends to posit invariant underlying structures, a performative, embodied approach might uncover stable units of coordination in some speaking conditions that are simply not present in others, evan as word sequence is held constant.

One example of the identification of large units of prosodic structure that are specific to a speaking condition was provided by a series of speech cycling experiments [7]. In the canonical speech cycling experiment, speakers repeated a short phrase, such as "big for a duck" in time with a repeating sequence of alternating high and low tones. They were instructed to attempt to align the onset of the phrase with the high tones, and the onset of the final stressed syllable ("duck") with the low tones. The experimental variable was the phase of the low tones within the repeating cycle of high tones. In one experiment,

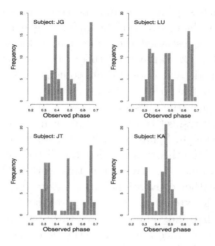

Fig. 1. Left: Distribution of phases of a medial stressed syllable onset within the overall phrase repetition cycle. Right: Schematic representation of the nesting of feet within the phrase cycle corresponding to the three phases that subject reliably produced.

target phases drawn from a uniform distribution ranging from 0.3 to 0.7 were employed. On each trial, one phase was drawn randomly from this range, and subjects attempted to match it. The distribution of produced phases (i.e. the relative timing of the onset of "duck" with respect to the overall phrase repetition cycle) is illustrated in the left panel of Figure 1.

It is immediately apparent that some phases are produced with greater frequency than others. In fact, three and only three phases are produced reliably, and each of these corresponds to the integral nesting of one unit within the overall phrase repetition cycle. The unit that is so nested is produced with a stable temporal relationship or phasing with respect to the containing cycle. This unit is, in fact, well known within phonology and corresponds to the stress foot as defined by Abercrombie [1] (the interval from the onset of one stressed syllable to the next). Within the strict constraints of the speech cycling task, the relative phasing of stress foot onsets within a containing repetition cycle is stable, and points to a meaningful unit of coordination.

In what follows, some new data from a repetition task are presented. The experimental goals are exploratory: we seek to ask whether units of coordination in speech production might be identified by phase stability. In contrast to the speech cycling experiment just described, we here vary articulation rate, and examine the relative constancy of selected phase relations across a range of tempi. Many speech experiments make use of qualitative differences between normal speech and fast speech. In the present experiment, we treat articulation rate as a continuous variable and go to some lengths to ensure that data are obtained at a wide range of rates for each subject. Furthermore, we wish to inquire to what degree any stable coordinative patterns observed are specific to an individual speaker, or to a speech elicitation context, and to ask whether speakers are capable of varying phase as context varies.

4   Methods

Four subjects took part, two males and two females, all from the Eastern part of Ireland. Each read a short narrative text containing a target phrase. They were then instructed to repeat the target phrase again and again, and to vary their rate of speech as indicated by the experimenter's hand level. As they repeated the phrase, the experimenter raised or lowered his hand every four or five repetitions, encouraging the subjects to explore their range of potential articulatory rate variation. Every effort was made to ensure that the repetitions obtained spanned the range from the fastest to the slowest that the subjects could reliably achieve. Articulation rate was then indexed as the reciprocal of the interval duration from the first to the last stressed syllable onset. A similar procedure was then employed to obtain speech at a variety of amplitudes, but those data will not be reported here. The entire process was repeated for a second set phrase taken from a second text.

Each subject completed a second session which was structured as above, but this time all readings and repetition were done in synchrony with a matched subject (male with male, female with female) [6]. The synchronous repetition condition imposes strong temporal constraints upon subjects, and we wished to see to what degree any stable properties of phase variables were specific not only to an individual, but also to the conditions under which speech was elicited.

The two phrases employed were *Diving Deep Down in the Bay of BomBay* and *Big Dinosaurs and Bigger Daleks in Battle*. These were designed so as to provide a series of strong stresses that are separated by varying numbers of unstressed syllables. Vowel onsets for the capitalized syllables were measured by hand, and a variety of phase variables were explored by examining the variation in the proportion of one large interval occupied by some smaller interval, across a wide variety of articulation rates. For example, one could look at the phase of the onset of *Deep* within the containing interval delimited by the onsets of *Diving* and *Down*.

5   Results

Figure 2 shows the observed phase of *Deep* as defined above, collapsed across all rates for the two female speakers. In the central panel, it can be seen that the two speakers produce qualitatively different timing patterns for this small sub-phrase when they speak on their own. All phases observed were stable across rate variation, as evidenced by the low R^2 values arising from correlation of the observed phase with tempo of articulation. The R^2 values obtained were 0.03 (F1, solo), 0.00 (F2, solo), 0.18 (F1, synchronous) and 0.14 (F2, synchronous). Although both are native speakers of closely matched dialects, their coordinative patterns in repeated speech belie highly individual solutions to the behavioral

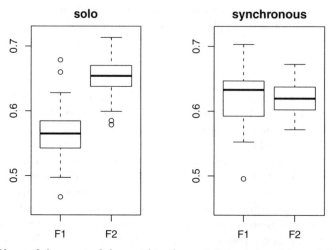

Fig. 2. Phase of the onset of *deep* within the containing interval bounded by the onsets of *diving* and *down* in the phrase *Diving deep down in the bay of bombay*. Data are from two subjects (F1, F2) speaking alone ("solo") or in synchrony with one another ("synchronous").

task of producing an acceptable utterance, just as their individual handwritings would also be found to differ. The right panel of Fig. 2 shows that when they are constrained to speak in synchrony, this particular difference can be overcome, as they produce similar coordinations, with a phase value lying intermediate between the two phases in the middle panel.

Phase stability is common, but not ubiquitous. In Fig. 3, two closely related phase variables are plotted as a function of articulation rate for speaker F1 speaking alone. As evident in the top half of the figure, the onset of *Bom* within the sequence *Bay of BomBay* is invariant across rate change. (Rate is indexed by the reciprocal of the period from the first to the last stressed syllable onset, with fast rates on the right of the figure.) This is in stark contrast to the related variable which indexes the relative timing of the onset of *Bay* within the subsequence *Down in the Bay of Bom*. The latter variable has a straightforward linear relationship to articulation rate. As the speaker speaks more rapidly, the unstressed syllables (and perhaps the initial stressed syllable) in the initial stress foot compress to a greater extent than those in the subsequence *Bay of*. These data strongly suggest that the sequence *Bay of Bombay* is a meaningful, embodied, production unit in the speech of this person under these circumstances, while the syllables in *Down in the* do not form part of any such constituent.

However, these observations are not easy to square with conventional linguistic accounts, as the same phase variables, measured on the other female subject, yield R^2 values of 0.32 and 0.02 where subject F1 had 0.05 and 0.63, respectively. Thus phase stability here reveals a unit of coordination in the speech of an individual that is tied to that person, and quite probably also to the elicitation conditions. It is both embodied and performative. (For comparison, in the synchronous condition, subject F1 had corresponding R^2 values of 0.01 and 0.39, respectively, which are qualitatively similar to those seen in the solo condition, F2 had 0.38 and 0.05, again substantially the same as in the solo condition).

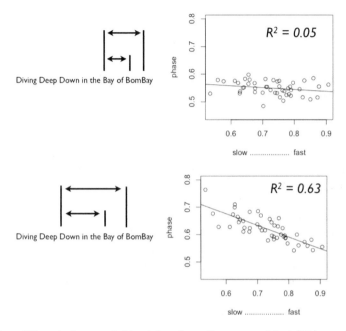

Fig. 3. Two different phase variables taken from the same subject (F1) speaking alone. The x-axis is tempo, with fast utterances on the right.

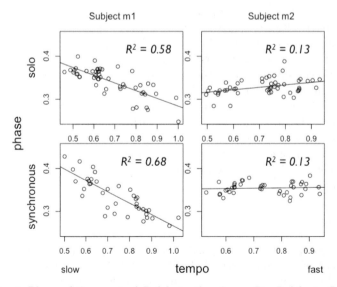

Fig. 4. Phase of the onset of *Daleks* in the phrase *Big Daleks in Battle*

One further example will serve to further illustrate the character of coordinative structure as evidenced by phase stability. Fig. 4 shows the phase of the onset of *Daleks* in the subsequence *Big Daleks in Battle*, for two male subjects in both solo and synchronous conditions. Although the two subjects had no overt difficulty in synchronizing with one another, their phase data clearly reveal coordinative differences between the two subjects that are invariant across speaking conditions. Where subject M1 exhibits a strong linear relationship between this phase variable and rate, M2 produces almost constant phase values.

6   Discussion

The experimental methodology employed here reveals that phase measurements that index the proportional duration of one interval within a larger containing interval may reveal much about coordinative strategies in speech production. Speakers may differ in their coordinative strategies in uttering the same text (Fig 2). This seems to be akin to individual differences found in other forms of motor activity that are highly skilled and that satisfy behavioral goals within a system that can potentially achieve those goals in many ways. There are thus direct parallels to be drawn between coordinative patterns in speech production and individual characteristics of handwriting, gait, etc. Similar phase-based variables have previously been shown to reliably index individual speakers better than speech elicitation circumstances [5]. However in the present case, qualitative difference in phase values were not always invariable. The phase variable shown in Fig. 2 changed for both speakers in the synchronous speaking condition, whereas that observed in Fig. 4 remained invariant across speaking condition, despite behaving quite differently for the two male subjects.

The clear evidence of phase stability across a wide range of articulation rates serves to identify some units (e.g. *Bay of BomBay*) as meaningful wholes that are distinct from those subsequences that display variable phases across tempo change. The units so identified do not stand in any simple correspondence to prosodic units within any conventional linguistic theory. They are functions of embodied speech production in the performance of specific individuals under specific circumstances. It may not be the case that all syllables of any given utterance lie within such units. They thus pose a challenge to conventional analytical accounts. Some recent developments within phonology, such as optimality theory, have opened up room for consideration of individual phonologies that may differ even among speakers of matched dialects [9]. Perhaps there is room here then to bridge the gap between embodied accounts of behaviour and formal linguistic models.

References

1. Abercrombie, D.: Elements of general phonetics. Aldine Pub. Co., Chicago (1967)
2. Beckman, M.E., Pierrehumbert, J.: Positions, probabilities and levels of categorization. In: Proceedings of 8th Austrlian International Conference on Speech Science and Technology, pp. 2–18 (2000)

3. Browman, C.P., Goldstein, L.: Articulatory phonology: An overview. Phonetica 49, 155–180 (1992)
4. Byrd, D.: A phase window framework for articulatory timing. Phonology 13, 139–169 (1996)
5. Cummins, F.: Speech rhythm and rhythmic taxonomy. In: Proceedings of Speech Prosody 2002, pp. 121–126. Aix en Provence (2002)
6. Cummins, F.: Practice and performance in speech produced synchronously. Journal of Phonetics 31(2), 139–148 (2003)
7. Cummins, F., Port, R.F.: Rhythmic constraints on stress timing in English. Journal of Phonetics 26(2), 145–171 (1998)
8. Ferreira, F.: Creation of prosody during sentence production. Psychological Review 100(2), 233–253 (1993)
9. Gafos, A.I., Benus, S.: Dynamics of phonological cognition. Cognitive Science 30, 905–943 (2006)
10. Grillner, S.: Control of locomotion in bipeds, tetrapods, and fish. In: Brooks, V.B. (ed.) Handbook of Physiology, Motor Control. Williams and Wilkins, Baltimore (1981)
11. Hockett, C.: A Manual of Phonology. University of Chicago, Chicago (1955)
12. Ivry, R.B., Richardson, T.C.: Temporal control and coordination: the multiple timer model. Brain and Cognition 48, 117–132 (2002)
13. James, W.: The Principles of Psychology, vols. 1&2. Holt, New York (1890)
14. Scott Kelso, J.A., Saltzman, E., Tuller, B.: The dynamical perspective in speech production: Data and theory. Journal of Phonetics 14, 29–60 (1986)
15. Ohala, J.J.: There is no interface between phonology and phonetics: a personal view. Journal of Phonetics 18, 153–171 (1990)
16. Port, R.F., Cummins, F., Devin McAuley, J.: Naive time, temporal patterns and human audition. In: Port, R.F., van Gelder, T. (eds.) Mind as Motion, pp. 339–437. MIT Press, Cambridge (1995)
17. Simko, J., Cummins, F.: Sequencing of articulatory gestures using cost optimization. In: Proceedings of INTERSPEECH 2009, Brighton, U.K. (2009)
18. Thelen, E., Smith, L.B. (eds.): A Dynamic Systems Approach to the Development of Cognition and Action. Bradford Books/MIT Press, Cambridge (1994)
19. Wing, A.M., Kristofferson, A.B.: Response delays and the timing of discrete motor responses. Perception and Psychophysics 14(1), 5–12 (1973)

The Effect of Query Length on Normalisation in Information Retrieval

Ronan Cummins[1] and Colm O'Riordan[2]

[1] Department of Computing Science, University of Glasgow
[2] Department of Information Technology, NUI Galway
ronanc@dcs.gla.ac.uk, colm.oriordan@nuigalway.ie

Abstract. Document length normalisation is known to be a difficult problem in IR, as tuning is often needed to overcome the collection dependence problem known to affect many normalisation schemes. Furthermore, it has been shown in various studies that the most optimal level of normalisation to apply is correlated with query length. In this paper, we confirm this correlation and present experiments which investigates and explains the effect of query length on normalisation.

1 Introduction

Information Retrieval (IR) systems deal with natural language documents and queries and attempt to limit the problem of information overload by returning only those documents that are relevant to a user's need (query). This represents a difficult problem given the presence of synonmy and polysemy in natural language. IR systems typically have to deal with large quantities of potentially semantically ambiguous information.

Many models have been adopted in the information retrieval domain including Boolean models and extensions, vector space models [5] and variations and also probabilistic models [9]. Irrespective of the model adopted, the ability to correctly identify important terms that capture the content of documents and queries is of utmost importance. Much research has been undertaken in the development of good *weighting schemes* that assign suitable weights to terms in the collection. The motivation is to assign low weights to those terms that contain little semantic power (or resolving power) while attaching high weights to those terms that help correctly capture the meaning of documents and queries. There have been many approaches to correctly developing these weighting schemes ranging from heuristic based approaches coupled with empirical analysis to more modern approaches which attempt to learn optimal combinations of sources of evidence [8,3].

Many, if not all, of the developed or learned weighting schemes can be represented as follows:

$$S(Q, D) = \sum_{t \in Q \cap D} (ntf(D) \cdot gw_t(C) \cdot qw_t(Q))$$

L. Coyle and J. Freyne (Eds.): AICS 2009, LNAI 6206, pp. 26–32, 2010.
© Springer-Verlag Berlin Heidelberg 2010

where the similarity ($S()$) between a query Q and document D in a collection C is a function of a normalised term frequency component (a within document score), a global term score (across the collection) and a query-term score (a within query score).

This paper deals with the issue of document normalisation and, in particular, how normalisation is influenced by query length. Document length normalisation is known to be a difficult problem in IR, as tuning is often needed to overcome the collection dependence problem known to affect many normalisation schemes. Furthermore, it has been shown in various studies that the most optimal level of normalisation to apply is correlated with query length [1,2]. In this paper, we confirm this correlation and present experiments which investigates the effect of query length on normalisation. In these experiments, properties of the document collection (such as average document length, standard deviation of document length) are controlled so as to allow experimentation regarding normalisation.

The remainder of the paper is as follows: in the following section, a brief review of some approaches in document normalisation in IR is presented. Details of the properties of the returned set for queries of different length are discussed in Section 3. In Section 4, we describe our experiments which show how the characteristics of the returned sets affect the performance of the weighting scheme adopted. The final section provides some conclusions.

2   Related Work

Document length normalisation is used to help correctly retrieve documents of various lengths. Normalisation is necessary as long documents can otherwise be unfairly promoted. Singhal *et al* discuss two reasons for incorporating normalisation [7]. For long documents, there will be increased probability of repeated occurrences of terms. Hence, the term frequency values will be increased thereby increasing the relevance score of long documents. There is also an increased probability of any given query term being present.

There have been many approaches to normalisation. In the weighting schemes presented by Salton and Buckley [6], a term's frequency in a document is normalised by the frequency of the maximally occurring term in that document. This penalises terms that occur frequently because of the length of the document. A stronger form of normalisation is the cosine normalisation which normalises the score with the normalisation factor of $\sqrt{(w_{t1}^2 + w_{t2}^2 + \ldots + w_{tn}^2)}$ where n is the number of terms in the document.

The $BM25$ scheme defines similarity between query and document according to:

$$BM25(Q, D) = \sum_{t \in Q \cap D} \left(\frac{tf_t^D \cdot log(\frac{N - df_t + 0.5}{df_t + 0.5}) \cdot tf_t^Q}{tf_t^D + k_1 \cdot ((1 - b) + b \cdot \frac{dl}{dl_{avg}})} \right) \tag{1}$$

where tf_t^D denotes the frequency of a term in a document, tf_t^Q denotes the frequency of a term in a query, N is the number of documents, df_t is the documents containing a term, k_1 and b are constants, dl is the document length and dl_{avg} is the average document length. In the $BM25$ scheme, the b parameter varies the amount of normalisation used (a higher b value leads to a greater penalisation).

The pivoted normalisation approach [7] defines similarity as:

$$PIV(Q, D) = \sum_{t \in Q \cap D} (\frac{1 + log(1 + log(tf_t^D))}{(1 - s) + s.\frac{dl}{dl_{avg}}} \cdot log(\frac{N + 1}{df_t}) \cdot tf_t^Q)$$

where s is a normalisation tuning factor. Simlarly to $BM25$, $\frac{dl}{dl_{avg}}$ is the normalisation factor. Chowdhury *et al* show that tuning the normalisation parameters for $BM25$ and the pivoted normalisation scheme can improve performance considerably [1]. In other words, by maintaining the default values, a serious degradation in mean average precision (MAP) can occur. They show that there is a need to tune the normalisation factor for individual collections.

Recent work advocates a normalisation approach which does not require a tuning parameter and achieves high MAP by using $\frac{dl}{\sqrt{dl_{avg}}}$ as the normalisation factor [4].

3   Query Length and Normalisation

In this section, the relationship between the characteristics in the returned set and the length of a query is explored. In order to investigate this relationship a number of queries of different lengths are created and compared against a number of collections. Short, medium and long queries are used and the properties of the returned sets are measured.

For the subsets of the TREC collections used in these experiments (Table 1), we use topics 301 to 450 and create a short query set (title field only), a medium length query set (title and description), and a long query set (title, description and narrative). We use the standard $BM25$ scheme but it should be noted that many term-weighting schemes show similar trends with regard to query length [1,2].

We measured the performance (MAP) of $BM25$ using 9 values of b (0, 0.125 0.25, 0.375, 0.5, 0.625, 0.75, 0.875 and 1) on the collections. Table 1 shows the optimal value of b for each collection for short, medium and long queries for the $BM25$ scheme. It can be seen that in most cases the optimal level of normalisation increases as the query length increases as has been previously reported [1,2].

Table 1. Optimal b per collection for schemes

				$BM25$	
Collections	#Docs	Topics	short	medium	long
LATIMES	131,896	301-450	0.125	0.625	0.875
FBIS	130,471	301-450	0.125	0.25	0.75
FT	210,158	301-450	0.375	0.375	0.625
FR	55,630	301-450	0.75	0.625	0.625

Average document lengths in returned set of
documents for different length queries

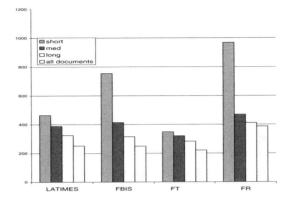

Fig. 1. Average length of returned documents

Std. dev of doc lengths in returned set of documents
for different length queries

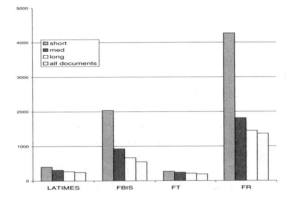

Fig. 2. Standard deviation of returned documents

An analysis of the characteristics of the *entire* returned set of documents for each set of queries (short, medium and long) on the collections shows that short queries return longer documents on average, while medium and long queries return documents that are closer to the average length document in the entire collection (Figure 1). Furthermore, Figure 2 shows that the standard deviation of document length for the returned set of documents is also greater for the shorter queries, indicating that there is a greater variation in the lengths of the documents returned. When the queries are longer, the sets of returned documents become such large samples of the document collections, that the average document length and standard deviation are very similar to those of the documents in the entire collection. The fact that the deviation in document length in the returned set is higher for shorter queries is an important factor in the normalisation to be applied and is investigated next.

4   Experiment: Deviation in Document Length

The normalisation function in many term-weighting schemes (and in the $BM25$ scheme) is comprised of a ratio of a specific document length to the average document length $(\frac{dl}{dl_{avg}})$. However, this ratio gives us relatively little information about the distribution of document lengths in the collection or the expected deviation of a document length from the average document length. For collections with a high deviation of document length, this ratio $(\frac{dl}{dl_{avg}})$ will vary considerably from very low values (for the shorter documents) to very high values (for the longer documents). Furthermore, from the previous experiment, it was determined that short queries (which return documents sets with a high standard deviation) require a smaller value of b for optimal performance. Therefore, when this ratio varies considerably (short queries), we need a low level of normalisation (otherwise this ratio would be overly influential with regard to the retrieval of documents). Ultimately, this suggests that the optimal value of b may be inversely related to the deviation in the length of the documents in the collection.

To test this hypothesis, we devise an experiment which changes the properties of a collection while keeping the queries constant. A small sample of documents from the LATIMES collection is used with the medium length topics (301-350). A small collection of 8,598 LATIMES documents with an average document length of 28 and a standard deviation of 10 (i.e. low deviation given the average document length) is created. The performance (MAP) for various values of b on this collection is measured. The characteristics of the collection is then modified by adding a small sample of extremely long documents (526 documents). This dramatically changes the properties of the collection by adding only a few documents. The collection now consists of 9,124 documents with an average document length of 95 and a standard deviation of 272 (i.e. high deviation given the average document length). The performance (MAP) for the same values of b is recalculated. From Figure 3, it can be seen that when the standard deviation is low (little variation in document length) normalisation is less important (an expected result) but still has a benefit at higher levels of b. When the standard deviation increases, the optimal level of b drops sharply because using a high value of b severely penalises the longer documents (some of which are relevant to at least one of the topics). For the ad hoc retrieval task if any part of a longer document is relevant to the topic, the entire document is deemed relevant. Usually, a high standard deviation indicates a number of very long documents, due to a lower bound (of zero) on the distribution of document lengths.

Figure 4 shows the results from a similar experiment using a different 3,710 LATIMES documents with an average length of 151 and standard deviation of 12. A further 48 longer documents are added changing the average documents length to 184 and the standard deviation to 287. The keys in both figures show

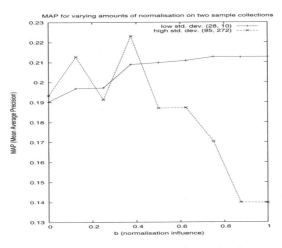

Fig. 3. Δ of deviation with varying b

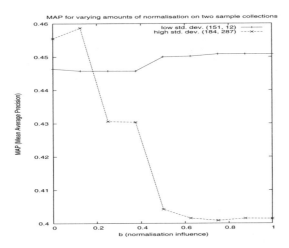

Fig. 4. Δ of deviation with varying b

the average document length and standard deviation respectively in parentheses for each collection. It can seen that this phenomenon is the same (albeit contrived and exaggerated in these cases) as that which was observed when using different length queries. It is important to note that in these experiments the same medium-length queries are being used. Therefore, the effect of query length is not responsible for the change in the optimal level of normalisation to apply. For short queries (which return a set with a higher deviation in document length), a lower level of b is beneficial. Hence, we argue that these two phenomena are actually related and ultimately, it is the deviation of documents lengths that influences the normalisation parameter in term-weighting schemes.

5   Conclusion

Some approaches have attempted to incorporate query length into the term-weighting function [2] and, given the preliminary studies, this would seem a logical approach. However, as these experiments have shown, query length only brings about the change in the returned document set distribution, which is the underlying reason certain collections need different normalisation parameter settings.

Acknowledgements

The first author of this work is funded by an IRCSET-Marie Curie International Mobility Fellowship in Science, Engineering and Technology.

References

1. Chowdhury, A., Catherine McCabe, M., Grossman, D., Frieder, O.: Document normalization revisited. In: SIGIR 2002: Proceedings of the 25th Annual International ACM SIGIR Conference on Research and Development in Information Retrieval, Tampere, Finland, pp. 381–382. ACM Press, New York (2002)
2. Chung, T.L., Luk, R.W.P., Wong, K.F., Kwok, K.L., Lee, D.L.: Adapting pivoted document-length normalization for query size: Experiments in Chinese and English. ACM Transactions on Asian Language Information Processing (TALIP) 5(3), 245–263 (2006)
3. Cummins, R., O'Riordan, C.: Evolving local and global weighting schemes in information retrieval. Information Retrieval 9(3), 311–330 (2006)
4. Cummins, R., O'Riordan, C.: Evolved term-weighting schemes in information retrieval: an analysis of the solution space. Artificial Intelligence Review, 51–68 (November 2007)
5. Salton, G., Wong, A., Yang, C.S.: A vector space model for automatic indexing. Commun. ACM 18(11), 613–620 (1975)
6. Salton, G., Buckley, C.: Term-weighting approaches in automatic text retrieval. Information Processing & Management 24(5), 513–523 (1988)
7. Singhal, A., Buckley, C., Mitra, M.: Pivoted document length normalization. In: SIGIR 1996: Proceedings of the 19th Annual International ACM SIGIR Conference on Research and Development in Information Retrieval, Zurich, Switzerland, pp. 21–29. ACM Press, New York (1996)
8. Trotman, A.: Learning to rank. Information Retrieval 8, 359–381 (2005)
9. Turtle, H., Croft, W.B.: Inference networks for document retrieval. In: SIGIR 1990: Proceedings of the 13th Annual International ACM SIGIR Conference on Research and Development in Information Retrieval, pp. 1–24. ACM, New York (1990)

An Evolutionary Neural Network Approach to Intrinsic Plagiarism Detection

Dara Curran

Cork Constraint Computation Centre (4C)
University College Cork
d.curran@cs.ucc.ie

Abstract. Intrinsic Plagiarism Detection attempts to identify portions of a document which have been plagiarised without the use of reference collections. This is typically achieved by developing a classifier using support vector machines or hand-crafted neural networks. This paper presents an evolutionary neural network approach to the development of an intrinsic plagiarism detection classifier which is capable of evolving both the weights and structure of a neural network. The neural network is empirically tested on a corpus of documents and is shown to perform well.

1 Introduction

Intrinsic plagiarism detection is a method of determining whether a document is written by a single author and if not, which portions of the document do not fit the writing style of the whole. Given a document D made up of P portions of text, intrinsic plagiarism detection attempts to identify all portions that deviate sufficiently from the writing style of the whole document. The problem is well suited to a binary classification strategy.

There are a number of approaches employed to generate classifiers, including Support Vector Machines [11], Neural Networks [16], k-NN [7], Bayesian network [18] and others. Some of these techniques have been previously employed to attempt to generate intrinsic plagiarism detection systems with some degree of success [35].

While there is a great deal of research on the automatic generation of neural networks, this research is rarely harnessed by the classification community to develop classifiers. The contribution of this paper is two-fold. One, it demonstrates the utility of employing evolutionary neural network techniques to the problem of generating classifiers and two, it presents this approach as applied to intrinsic plagiarism detection which to the authors' knowledge has not been attempted previously. Experimental results show that the approach is capable of improving upon existing intrinsic plagiarism detection methods and thus has significant potential.

The remainder of the paper is organised as follows. Section 2 presents related topics including plagiarism detection and evolutionary neural network research.

L. Coyle and J. Freyne (Eds.): AICS 2009, LNAI 6206, pp. 33–40, 2010.

Section 3 describes the approach employed to develop the neural network classifier system. Section 4 discusses the experiment conducted to evaluate the evolved neural network. Section 5 provides a conclusion.

2   Related Work

2.1   Plagiarism Detection

The four main techniques developed for plagiarism detection are Substring Matching, Keyword Similarity, Fingerprint Analysis and Intrinsic Plagiarism Detection.

Substring Matching firstly divides test documents into strings and then attempts to identify matches between strings in the test document and those in a collection of reference documents [2,15].

Keyword Similarity approaches first extract topic-identifying words from each document in a document collection. Then, keywords are extracted from a test document and compared to those of the document collection being employed [26].

Fingerprint Analysis breaks a document into portions according to a selection strategy (such as frequency-based or positional substring selection). The portions are then processed to produce uniquely identifying digital signatures (a set of integers representing each portion), called fingerprints. Each fingerprint is then compared with those in the document collection being used [5,9,28].

Each of these three techniques requires extensive pre-processing of the reference document collection against which the test documents are being compared. This may severely limit the number of documents that can be feasibly contained within a collection. In addition, the reference document collection is likely to exclude new or less popular topics as well as online materials written by non-professionals.

Intrinsic plagiarism detection is a recent technique developed by Eissen et al. [35] which detects suspicious passages within a document with no need for a reference collection. This approach is useful in that it identifies potentially plagiarised passages but since these are not compared to a set of reference documents, there is no guarantee that the identified passages have been plagiarised. The technique essentially identifies the writing style of the document's author thanks to a number of stylometric features including:

- Text statistics (e.g. number of commas, question marks, word lengths, etc)
- Syntactic features (e.g. sentence length, use of function words, etc)
- Part-of-speech features (e.g. number of adjectives, pronouns, etc.)
- Closed-class word sets (e.g. number of stop-words, foreign words, etc.)
- Structural features (e.g. paragraph lengths, etc.)

Based on these features, it is possible to identify passages of text within a single document which appear to deviate from the author's writing style.

2.2   Evolutionary Neural Networks

The evolution of neural networks combines two artificial intelligence tools: evolutionary computation (in particular, genetic algorithms) and neural networks.

Genetic algorithms attempt to apply evolutionary concepts to the field of problem-solving, notably function optimisation, and have proven to be valuable in searching large, complex problem spaces [12].

Neural networks are highly simplified models of the working of the brain. A neural network consists of a combination of neurons (or nodes) and synaptic connections (or connection weights), which are capable of passing data through multiple layers. The end result is a system which is capable of generalisation, pattern recognition and classification [16].

In the past, algorithms such as back propagation have been developed to refine one of the principal components of neural networks: the connection weight. The approach has worked well, but is prone to becoming trapped in local maxima and is incapable of optimisation where problems lie in a multi-modal (i.e. the solution landscape contains more than one peak) or non-differentiable problem space [30]. In addition, it has been shown that back propagation is sensitive to the initial condition of the neural network causing additional problems[19].

Genetic algorithms and neural networks can be combined such that a population of neural networks compete with each other in a Darwinian 'survival of the fittest' setting. Networks which are deemed to be fit are combined and passed onto the next generation producing an increasingly fit population, so that following a number of iterations, an optimized neural network can be obtained without resorting to trial and error manual tweaking of the neural network architecture and weights.

In order to evolve a neural network using a genetic algorithm it is necessary to devise a suitable mechanism to convert a neural network structure into the chromosome structure required by the genetic algorithm. This process is known as the *encoding* problem. There have been many approaches including the evolution of weights [25,32,3,22,8,4,6], structure [1] and both combined [33,8,20,13,17,31,21,34,24]. One of the most successful approaches, which combines the evolution of weights and architectures is the Neuro-Evolution of Augmenting Topologies (NEAT) algorithm [27].

Neuro-evolution of Augmenting Topologies (NEAT). The NEAT system evolves both neural network structure and weights by incrementally increasing the complexity of a neural network[27]. A NEAT genotype is made up of connection genes, each describing connections between two nodes, including weight and node labels. In addition, layer information is also encoded into the genome. The main innovation of NEAT is that the system keeps track of the historical origin of each gene and ensures that genes that do not have common ancestors do not compete against each other. This means that NEAT eliminates the problem of competition between neural network architectures that are fundamentally different.

3   Evolutionary Neural Networks for Intrinsic Plagiarism Detection

The evolutionary neural network approach employed in this paper consists of two parts: document pre-processing and neural network evolution.

3.1   Document Pre-processing

The documents being evaluated by the neural network must be processed and delivered to the neural network in a format suitable for training. The success of an intrinsic plagiarism detection system relies on the identification of text passages which appear to deviate from the remainder of a document. In order to achieve this, a document is partitioned into portions and a number of stylometric features are extracted and compared to the features of the entire document.

A number of stylometric features were chosen for this intrinsic plagiarism detection system:

- Number of punctuation marks
- Sentence length (number of characters)
- Sentence word frequency class
- Number of prepositions
- Number of syllables per word
- Average word length
- Number of stop-words
- Gunning Fog index
- Flesch index
- Kincaid index

Most of the above measures are self explanatory but there are a number which require explanation.

Word frequency class. The word frequency class (WFC) measure developed by Eissen and Stein [35] attempts to define a word's customariness by examining its frequency in texts compared to the frequency of other words. The more a word is used in a text, the higher its frequency class. The word frequency class of a document can give an indication of the size and complexity of an author's vocabulary.

Readability indexes. The Gunning Fog [14], Flesch [10] and Kincaid [23] indexes attempt to estimate the readability of a text by calculating the ratio of multi-syllabic words and sentence length. The resulting value gives an indication of the level of education that is required to read the text.

For each document to be examined, a number of pre-processing steps are then carried out:

- Individual sentences are first identified and extracted from the document.
- Stylometric analysis if carried out on each sentence in the document.

- An average document-wide value for each stylometric feature is calculated.
- The differences between each sentence's stylometric features and the average document-wide value is calculated for each stylometric feature and stored as a vector for each sentence.

The resulting difference vector gives an indication of the divergence of a particular sentence from the average and is employed as the input for the neural network. Each difference measure is normalised to between 0 and 1.

3.2   Neural Network Evolution

The evolutionary neural network framework employed for this paper is the NEAT encoding, in the form of the ANJI neural network Java library (http://anji. sourceforge.net/). The NEAT neural network encoding allows the evolution of both architecture and weights simultaneously, giving a great deal of freedom to the evolutionary process to find suitable networks.

The neural network consists of 10 input nodes (one for each of the stylometric measures) and one output node (where an output of 0 indicates no plagiarism and 1 indicates plagiarism). The intermediary connections and hidden nodes are determined by the evolutionary process. An initial population of random neural networks is generated and for each individual neural network is presented with a number of plagiarised and non-plagiarised difference vectors taken from the pre-processed corpus.

The fitness function of the neural network examines the output of the network and calculates the mean square error. In addition, precision and recall measures were recorded but did not form part of the fitness function. This was decided after a number of preliminary runs showed that mean square error proved to be the most successful in terms of evolving useful networks.

4   Experiments

The evaluation of an evolutionary neural network for the intrinsic plagiarism detection problem described in this paper employs a test corpus of artificially plagiarised documents developed for the PAN'09 workshop on plagiarism detection.

The corpus contains 3,091 documents which are a mixture of non-plagiarised texts and documents containing sections of plagiarism. Documents vary in length from paper size to book size and the plagiarised content in each document varies from 0%-100%. Plagiarised passages also vary in length from a few sentences to many pages. Finally, some plagiarised passages are obfuscated, meaning that a random text operation (such as shuffling a word, deleting a word or replacing a word with a synonym, antonym, hypernym or homonym) is applied. The documents are annotated showing which sections are plagiarised.

The corpus is pre-processed to calculate the document and sentence stylometric statistics described in Section 3.1. This generated approximately 100,000 plagiarised and more than 1.5 million non-plagiarised sentences. A sample of

10,000 plagiarised sentences and 10,000 non-plagiarised sentences was employed to evolve the neural network.

A population of 400 neural networks was evolved for 500 generations. Crossover was set at 0.6 and mutation at 0.05. A number of experimental runs were conducted and from these, the overall best neural network was selected for testing.

The testing phase employed a new sample of 10,000 plagiarised sentences and 10,000 non-plagiarised sentences which had not been previously employed for the training phase. The evolved neural network was given the 20,000 sentences to classify and the results recorded. The evolved neural network scored 83% accuracy on the non-plagiarised class (meaning that it correctly classified a sentence as non-plagiarised 83% of the time). The neural network scored 60% accuracy for the plagiarised class (meaning that 60% of plagiarised sentences are recognised as being plagiarised).

A direct comparison with the results obtained by Stein and Eissen is not possible because their experiments employed a different dataset. However, it is worth noting that their system achieved an accuracy of between 80-85% [29] for the non-plagiarised class and 55% accuracy on the plagiarised class.

5   Conclusion

This paper presented an evolutionary neural network approach to intrinsic plagiarism detection. A corpus of documents is pre-processed to obtain a number of stylometric statistics and a neural network classifier is evolved using the NEAT algorithm. The classifier is tested empirically on the test corpus and is shown to perform as well as the current most successful classifier on the non-plagiarised section of the corpus. More significantly, the classifier is shown to perform considerably better on the plagiarised sections of text. In the future, we hope to test the classifier on a corpus of actual examples of plagiarism.

Acknowledgements

This work is supported by an Enterprise Ireland Proof of Concept Commercialisation grant (grant code PC/2008/0180).

References

1. Angeline, P.J., Saunders, G.M., Pollack, J.P.: An evolutionary algorithm that constructs recurrent neural networks. IEEE Transactions on Neural Networks 5(1), 54–65 (1994)
2. Baker, B.S.: A program for identifying duplicated code. Computing Science and Statistics 24, 49–57 (1992)
3. Belew, R.K., McInerney, J., Schraudolph, N.N.: Evolving networks: Using the genetic algorithm with connectionist learning. In: Langton, C.G., Taylor, C., Doyne Farmer, J., Rasmussen, S. (eds.) Artificial Life II, pp. 511–547. Addison-Wesley, Redwood City (1992)

4. Branke, J.: Evolutionary algorithms for neural network design and training. Technical Report No. 322, University of Karlsruhe, Institute AIFB (1995)
5. Brin, S., Davis, J., Molina, H.G.: Copy detection mechanisms for digital documents. In: Proceedings of the ACM SIGMOD Annual Conference, pp. 398–409 (1995)
6. Chellapilla, K., Fogel, D.B.: Evolving neural networks to play checkers without relying on expert knowledge. IEEE Transactions on Neural Networks 10, 1382–1391 (1999)
7. Dasarathy, B.V.: Nearest neighbor (NN) norms: NN pattern classification techniques. IEEE Computer Society Press, Los Alamitos (1990)
8. De Garis, H.: Genetic programming: building artificial nervous systems using genetically programmed neural network modules. In: Porter, B.W., Mooney, R.J. (eds.) Machine Learning: Proceedings of the Seventh International Conference, Austin, TX, June 21-23, pp. 132–139. Morgan Kaufmann, Palo Alto (1990)
9. Finkel, R.A., Zaslavsky, A., Monostori, K., Schmidt, H.: Signature extraction for overlap detection in documents. Aust. Comput. Sci. Commun. 24(1), 59–64 (2002)
10. Flesch, R.: A new readability yardstick. Journal of Applied Psychology 32, 221–233 (1948)
11. Fradkin, D., Muchnik, I.: Support vector machines for classification. In: Discrete Methods in Epidemiology. DIMACS Series in Discrete Mathematics and Theoretical Computer Science, vol. 70, pp. 13–20 (2006)
12. Goldberg, D.E., Richardson, J.: Genetic algorithms with sharing for multimodal function optimization. In: Proceedings of the Second International Conference on Genetic Algorithms and their Application, pp. 41–49. Lawrence Erlbaum Associates, Inc., Mahwah (1987)
13. Gruau, F.: Neural Network Synthesis using Cellular Encoding and the Genetic Algorithm. PhD thesis, Centre d'etude nucleaire de Grenoble, Ecole Normale Superieure de Lyon, France (1994)
14. Gunning, R.: The technique of clear writing. McGraw-Hill, New York (1952)
15. Gusfield, D.: Algorithms on Strings, Trees, and Sequences: Computer Science and Computational Biology. Cambridge University Press, Cambridge (January 1997)
16. Haykin, S.: Neural Networks: A Comprehensive Foundation, 2nd edn. Prentice-Hall, Englewood Cliffs (1999)
17. Hussain, T.S., Browse, R.A.: Genetic encoding of neural networks using attribute grammars. In: CITO Researcher Retreat, Hamilton, Ontario, Canada, May 12-14 (1998)
18. Jensen, F.V.: Bayesian artificial intelligence: Kevin b. korb, ann e. nicholson, Chapman & hall, 354 pages (2004); Pattern Anal. Appl. 7(2), 221–223 (2004)
19. Kolen, J.F., Pollack, J.B.: Back propagation is sensitive to initial conditions. Advances in Neural Information Processing Systems 3, 860–867 (1991)
20. Koza, J.R., Rice, J.P.: Genetic generation of both the weights and architecture for a neural network. In: International Joint Conference on Neural Networks, IJCNN 1991, Seattle, WA, July 8-12, vol. II, pp. 397–404. IEEE Computer Society Press, Los Alamitos (1991)
21. Maniezzo, V.: Searching among search spaces: Hastening the genetic evolution of feedforward neural networks. In: Albrecht, R.F., Reeves, C.R., Steele, N.C. (eds.) Artificial Neural Nets and Genetic Algorithms, pp. 635–643. Springer, Heidelberg (1993)
22. Montana, D.J., Davis, L.: Training feedforward neural networks using genetic algorithms. In: Proceedings of the Eleventh International Joint Conference on Artificial Intelligence, pp. 762–767. Morgan Kaufmann, San Mateo (1989)

23. Kincaid, J.P., Fishburne, R.P., Rogers, R.L., Chissom, B.S.: Derivation of new readability formulas (automated readability index, fog count and flesch reading ease formula) for navy enlisted personnel. In: Research Branch Report 8-75, Naval Technical Training, Millington, TN, U. S. Naval Air Station, Memphis, TN (1975)

24. Richards, N., Moriarty, D., McQuesten, P., Miikkulainen, R.: Evolving neural networks to play Go. In: Proceedings of the 7th International Conference on Genetic Algorithms, East Lansing, MI (1997)

25. Sasaki, T., Tokoro, M.: Evolving learnable neural networks under changing environments with various rates of inheritance of acquired characters: Comparison between darwinian and lamarckian evolution. Artificial Life 5(3), 203–223 (1999)

26. Si, A., Leong, H.V., Lau, R., Va, H., Rynson, L., Lau, W.H.: Check: A document plagiarism detection system. In: Proceedings of ACM Symposium for Applied Computing, pp. 70–77. ACM Press, New York (1997)

27. Stanley, K.O., Miikkulainen, R.: Evolving neural networks through augmenting topologies. Evolutionary Computation 10(2), 99–127 (2002)

28. Stein, B.: Fuzzy-fingerprints for text-based information retrieval. In: I-KNOW 2005: Proceedings of the 5th International Conference on Knowledge Management, pp. 572–579 (2005)

29. Stein, B., Eissen, S.M.z.: Intrinsic plagiarism analysis with meta learning. In: Stein, B., Koppel, M., Stamatatos, E. (eds.) PAN. CEUR Workshop Proceedings, vol. 276, CEUR-WS.org (2007)

30. Sutton, R.S.: Two problems with backpropagation and other steepest-descent learning procedures for networks. In: Proc. of 8th Annual Conf. of the Cognitive Science Society, pp. 823–831 (1986)

31. White, D.W.: GANNet: A genetic algorithm for searching topology and weight spaces in neural network design. PhD thesis, University of Maryland College Park (1994)

32. Whitley, D., Starkweather, T., Bogart, C.: Genetic algorithms and neural networks - optimizing connections and connectivity. Parallel Computing 14(3), 347–361 (1990)

33. Yao, X.: Evolving artificial neural networks. Proceedings of the IEEE, 1423–1447 (1999)

34. Zhang, B., Muhlenbein, H.: Evolving optimal neural networks using genetic algorithms with occam's razor. Complex Systems 7(3), 199–220 (1993)

35. Eissen, S.M.z., Stein, B.: Intrinsic plagiarism detection. In: Lalmas, M., MacFarlane, A., Rüger, S.M., Tombros, A., Tsikrika, T., Yavlinsky, A. (eds.) ECIR 2006. LNCS, vol. 3936, pp. 565–569. Springer, Heidelberg (2006)

Investigation of Localised Centrality Metrics for Collaborative Networks: What Can They Reveal?

Elizabeth M. Daly

IBM, Dublin Software Lab
IBM Software Group
Elizabeth_Daly@ie.ibm.com

Abstract. Collaborative web 2.0 applications, such as blogs, collaborative bookmarking, file sharing etc., have increased significantly in popularity. In these user-centric applications users are not only consumers, but also contributors. By contributing content to the system, users become part of the network and relationships between users and content can be derived. Social network metrics can be used to identify key users, however, evaluating network metrics for a large scale network can be expensive. For this reason this paper explores the utility of localised network metrics. Experimental results and analysis are presented on a large collaborative IBM bookmarking network called Dogear to investigate the ability to identify central users.

1 Introduction

Web 2.0 is a new medium where users are not just consumers, but are also contributors. By contributing content to applications, such as CiteULike, Delicious or Digg, users become part of the network and relationships between users can be derived forming a social network. The corporate world has started to deploy these types of collaborative applications in order to promote connectivity and, by extension, encourage innovation and productivity. In an organisation, an employee's connections can represent resources they have access to. Evaluating the network of user relationships can aid in determining what role the user plays in knowledge networks. By doing so organisations could better learn how to identify succession candidates, potential bottlenecks and over dependencies, improve cross boundary communication and collaboration. Importantly, the structure of these informal knowledge networks may bare little resemblance to an organisational hierarchy [12].

Cross and Parker define three key roles in an organisational network [4]. First, *central connectors* who have a large number of contacts and can represent people who may play an important connecting role with access to a large number of resources. Highly connected users can potentially become overloaded bottlenecks, if too many people depend on them in terms of information flow, or in contrast, the important role these users play may have gone unnoticed. The network may be heavily dependent on these users for connectivity and what happens if these people retire or leave? Second, *boundary spanners* who provide crucial links between groups of people that may be separated through functional roles, geography etc. The diversity of a user's type of contacts can also be

L. Coyle and J. Freyne (Eds.): AICS 2009, LNAI 6206, pp. 41–50, 2010.

seen as a user having access to a larger set of non-redundant social resources. Finally, *information brokers* who play a vital role in disseminating information. These types of people were highlighted by Granovetter who argued the utility of using weak ties for information flow in social networks [9]. He emphasised that weak ties lead to information dissemination between groups. He introduced the concept of 'bridges', observing that 'those who are weakly tied are more likely to move in circles different from our own and will thus have access to information different from that which we receive' [9].

Various centrality metrics exist to aid in identifying these different types of users, however collaborative networks can consist of thousands if not millions of users, as networks become larger the computation of global network metrics becomes increasingly expensive. In such cases, the option of exploring local networks can be beneficial [5]. For this reason, this paper explores the utility of localized network metrics in a collaborative network. Experimental results are presented on a collaborative IBM bookmarking network called Dogear investigating what these metrics reveal.

2   Related Work

Due to the interactive nature of web 2.0 applications, they provide a rich source for analysing user behaviour and interrelationships. The social networks that arise have been the subject of much recent research on mining social relationships. Relationships between users can be explicit such as friending in Facebook, or implicit through users having similar interests, content and tagging behaviour.

Lewis et al. use Facebook data limited to a group university students in order to gain insights into different user online behaviour based on features such as gender and ethnicity [13]. Additionally, they also examine the different types of online ties such as friendship ties, shared photo ties and college housing ties. Kolari et al. examined the structure and utility of an IBM internal blog network [11]. The authors investigate network structure, cross domain interaction and impact metrics taking into account corporate hierarchy. Bakshy et al. use second life data to model the transfer of user generated content and that adoption is related to whether the content comes from a friend, or whether the content is adopted by those in a user's social circle [1]. Leydesdorff applies betweenness centrality as an indicator of the 'Interdisciplinarity' for scientific journals in a scientific citation network [14]. Golder and Huberman provide analysis of the tagging behavior and tag usage in online communities [8]. The authors provide an overview about the structure of collaborative tagging systems. Based on a small subset of the Delicious corpus, they investigate what motivates tagging and how tagging habits change over time. Chi and Mytkowicz investigate the dynamics of tags related to documents and shows that the information gained from a tag becomes less useful as the proliferation of use increases [3]. Bhattacharyya et al. use similarity of keywords in profiles to build a social graph in order to create a synthetic social graphs [2].

Anaysis of the social structure of collaborative applications can provide key insights into user behaviour, the influence users have on each other and the role of users and their relationships in these networks.

3   Localised Centrality Metrics

Node centrality is used to identify important nodes in a network. Centrality in graph theory and network analysis is a quantification of the relative importance of a vertex within the graph (e.g., how important a person is within a social network). A central node, typically, has a stronger capability of connecting other network members. There are several ways to measure centrality. The three most widely used centrality measures are Freeman's degree, closeness, and betweenness measures [6,7].

Freeman's centrality metrics are based on analysis of a complete and bounded network which is referred to as a sociocentric network. These metrics require evaluation of the entire network resulting in computationally expensive operations, which has motivated the introduction of 'ego networks'. An ego network can be defined as a network consisting of a single actor (ego) together with the actors they are connected to (alters) and all the links among those alters. Consequently, ego network analysis can be performed locally by individual nodes without complete knowledge of the entire network. Marsden introduces centrality measures calculated using ego networks and compares these to Freeman's centrality measures of a sociocentric network [15].

'Degree' centrality is measured as the number of direct ties that involve a given node [7]. A node with high degree centrality maintains contacts with numerous other network nodes. Such nodes can be seen as popular nodes with large numbers of links to others. As such, a central node occupies a structural position (network location) that may act as a conduit for information exchange. In contrast, peripheral nodes maintain few or no relations and thus are located at the margins of the network. Degree centrality for a given node p_i is calculated as:

$$C_D(p_i) = \sum_{k=1}^{N} a(p_i, p_k) \tag{1}$$

where $a(p_i, p_k) = 1$ if a direct link exists between p_i and p_k and $i \neq k$. Degree centrality can easily be measured for an ego network where it is a simple count of the number of contacts.

'Closeness' centrality measures the reciprocal of the mean geodesic distance $d(p_i, p_k)$, which is the shortest path between a node p_i and all other reachable nodes [7]. Closeness centrality can be regarded as a measure of how long it will take information to spread from a given node to other nodes in the network [18]. Closeness centrality is uninformative in an ego network, since by definition an ego network only considers nodes to which the ego node is directly related to and then by definition the distance from the ego node to all other nodes considered in the ego network is 1 and so is not included in this paper.

'Betweenness' centrality measures the extent to which a node lies on the shortest paths linking other nodes [6,7]. Betweenness centrality can be regarded as a measure of the extent to which a node has control over information flowing between others [18]. A node with a high betweenness centrality has a capacity to facilitate interactions between the nodes that it links. In our case it can be regarded as how well a node can facilitate communication to other nodes in the network. Betweenness centrality is calculated as:

$$C_B(p_i) = \sum_{j=1}^{N} \sum_{k=1}^{j-1} \frac{g_{jk}(p_i)}{g_{jk}} \qquad (2)$$

where g_{jk} is the total number of geodesic paths linking p_j and p_k, and $g_{jk}(p_i)$ is the number of those geodesic paths that include p_i.

'Bridging' centrality has been more recently introduced as a measure of how much a node is located between highly connected regions [10]. The authors define a 'bridging coefficient' to capture the bridging behaviour of the nodes' neighbourhood. The aim is to capture nodes where a high amount of information may flow through, due to the density of the information available versus the number of contacts. The 'bridging coefficient' $BC(p_i)$ is given as:

$$BC(p_i) = \frac{\frac{1}{C_D(p_i)}}{\sum_{k=1}^{N} \frac{1}{C_D(p_k)}} \qquad (3)$$

where N is the neighbourhood contacts of node p_i. Bridging centrality is then calculated as the product of the 'betweenness' centrality and the 'bridging coefficient'.

$$C_{Br}(p_i) = C_B(p_i) \times BC(p_i) \qquad (4)$$

Betweenness centrality in ego networks has shown to be quite a good measure when compared to that of the sociocentric measure. Marsden calculates the egocentric and the sociocentric betweenness centrality measure for the network shown in figure 1 [15]. A more recent analysis extended this work by measuring an egocentric bridging centrality, which is also included in figure 1 .

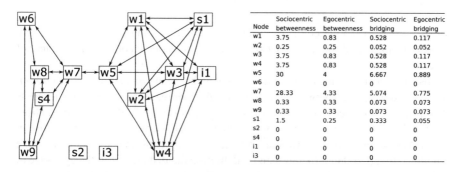

Node	Sociocentric betweenness	Egocentric betweenness	Sociocentric bridging	Egocentric bridging
w1	3.75	0.83	0.528	0.117
w2	0.25	0.25	0.052	0.052
w3	3.75	0.83	0.528	0.117
w4	3.75	0.83	0.528	0.117
w5	30	4	6.667	0.889
w6	0	0	0	0
w7	28.33	4.33	5.074	0.775
w8	0.33	0.33	0.073	0.073
w9	0.33	0.33	0.073	0.073
s1	1.5	0.25	0.333	0.055
s2	0	0	0	0
s4	0	0	0	0
i1	0	0	0	0
i3	0	0	0	0

Fig. 1. Bank Wiring Room network sociocentric and egocentric betweenness

The betweenness centrality $C_B(p_i)$ based on the egocentric measures does not correspond perfectly to the sociocentric measures. However, it can be seen that the ranking of nodes based on the two measures of betweenness are identical in this network. In effect, the betweenness value captures 'how much a node connects nodes that are themselves not directly connected'. Marsden compared sociocentric and egocentric betweenness for 15 other sample networks and found that the two values correlate well in all scenarios [15]. Similarly, analysis by Nanda and Kotz found correlation between sociocentric and egocentric bridging centrality [17].

4   Experimental Results

In order to investigate the potential of localised centrality metrics a real world data set is analysed in order to determine what types of users these metrics uncover. IBM's collaborative bookmarking solution Dogear [16] is popularly used by IBM employees and the data set contains an extensive network of users and contributed URLs, shown in table 1. Egocentric betweenness is calculated for a symmetric relationship matrix using the computationally efficient method presented by Everett and Borgatti [5].

Table 1. Dogear dataset

Number of Users	Number of Bookmarks	Number of URLs
10259	505472	317362

4.1   URL Relationship Network

To gain an initial understanding of the structure of the collaborative bookmarking network, we first derive a simple URL relationship network. Users are linked through overlapping URLs contained in their document collection, if two users share a URL in their collection, then an edge exists between those users. Figure 2 a) shows a log-log plot of the distribution of the number of URLs users have in their collection. As expected the distribution follows the power law with a large number of users who only have a small number of bookmarks and a small group of power users. Figure 2 b) shows a log-log plot of the degree centrality distribution which similarly follows the power law.

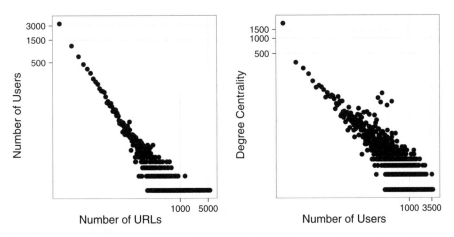

Fig. 2. URL relationship network - a) distribution of URLs per user b) degree centrality

Next we examine the relationship between the number of bookmark URLs a user has in their collection and the degree centrality. This demonstrates that the more a user participates in the network, the more links between other nodes are created.

4.2 Subscription Network

The URL relationship network could be useful to infer implicit relationships, however, the Dogear dataset provides a subscription network where users subscribe to specific users' bookmark collections. Through this subscription service, a 'subscribed to' user has now become a source of information for others in the network, contributions made by the user may potentially flow to the subscribing users as a form of knowledge transfer. This can be seen as an explicit identification of interest and can be used to validate whether the localised centrality metrics can identify important users in the network. A total of 1727 users participate in the subscription network either as subscribers or users that are subscribed to. In addition to the subscription information, the user's email was available to determine the domain each user belongs to. Therefore we can see when a user is highly connected within their domain, or whether their connections span geographic boundaries.

Betweenness Centrality. Figure 3 a) shows the degree centrality versus the number of domains the user spans. The node sizes represent the egocentric betweenness centrality. Egocentric betweenness is calculated for a symmetric relationship matrix using the computationally efficient method presented by Everett and Borgatti [5]. From the plot it seems clear that a high egocentric betweenness (shown as size of dot) results from a high number of contacts spanning a large number of domains. However, upon inspection, two nodes, node A and node B have a similar number of contacts, a similar betweenness value, and yet differ greatly on the number of domains they span. This can be explained when examining the variance of the social properties of each node shown in table 2. Out of the 46 contacts in node A's network, nearly 70% are bi-directional reciprocated links. In the subscription network the average percentage of a user's contacts that are reciprocated is less than 7%. When mapping the user back to an email domain, it turns out node A is in the Japanese mail domain where arguably the language barrier causes a higher inter-connectivity. Node B has a similar number of contacts, however, it is connected to a large number of domains. In contrast to node A, this node has relatively few reciprocated contacts. From this, we can infer that one user is important for connecting users within their domain, and the other node is structurally important for connecting users across domains. Upon investigation, the user represented by node B has since left the company and was involved in strategy and enabling business partnerships. Node C has a high value across all measures and spans 18 domains where the global average is less than two. Additionally, 97% of the user's contacts are out-links where users have subscribed to their bookmark feed, meaning this node may potentially influence many users. It turns out this user is a well respected research fellow within IBM. Node D has also since left the company and played a key role in educating customers and employees about collaboration software. Node E has a large number of incoming and outgoing links and connects users across many domains. This user is well known in IBM as a prolific blogger who specialises in knowledge management.

Table 2. Selected metrics related to betweenness of subscription network

Node id	degree centrality	domains	ego betweenness	out-degree	in-degree	reciprocated
A	46	1	749	41	39	32
B	49	11	771	42	10	3
C	192	18	14833	188	17	10
D	160	23	10985	148	26	9
E	134	25	8007	77	82	25
average	4.1	1.6	38.5	2.28	2.26	0.4

The important aspect to note, is that the betweenness metric captures users that have a useful social network either through the domains they span, the strength of their ties, or the extent to which they are followed by others spanning domains. Additionally, two out of the five users identified of interest have since left the company. This highlights the importance of uncovering the roles different users play in the social graph in order to identify potential gaps their departure could create.

Bridging Centrality. Figure 3 b) shows the same graph as figure 3 a), however, the sizing of the nodes are determined by node bridging centrality. As can be seen nodes with a high bridging centrality, have an inverse relationship to the number of contacts and number of domains they span. Nodes with a high bridging centrality span very few domains and have relatively few contacts in their social graph.

Bridging centrality highlights 4 nodes, node F and three other nodes with the same bridging centrality value 26.66, only node F is visible due to the overlap. Node F is shown in figure 4 and has only two contacts, node D and node G, the degree centrality of the neighbouring nodes are shown in table 3 which have a degree centrality of 160 and 80 respectively. As can be seen these two nodes represent nodes with a high be- tweenness value and these two nodes are ranked 2nd and 6th in the network in terms of

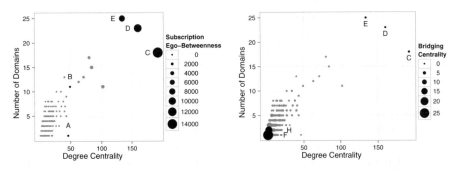

Fig. 3. Subscription network - Number of domains in user's network vs number of contacts (degree centrality) a) Betweenness centrality node sizing b) Bridging centrality node sizing

betweenness centrality. Interestingly, the other three nodes with the same betweenness centrality all link to the same two nodes. Upon inspection of the users, all four users are involved in technical sales and consulting roles. Node H has 3 contacts where 1 relationship is reciprocated. Table 3 shows that the neighbouring nodes have a degree centrality of 160, 134 and 40 respectively. Interestingly, Node H is involved in learning development and identifies themselves as an early adopter of technology in their company profile. Bridging centrality has identified users with a small number of contacts that are connected to nodes with a high betweenness centrality. These nodes potentially have access to a dense amount of information using a relatively small number of contacts.

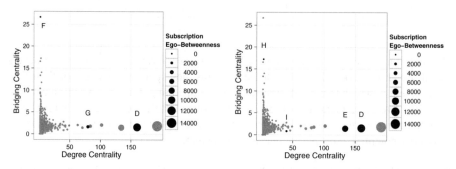

Fig. 4. Subscription network - Bridging centrality vs Degree centrality a) Node F's contacts b) Node H's contacts

Table 3. Selected metrics related to betweenness

Node id	degree centrality	domains	bridging centrality	in-degree	contacts degree centrality
F	2	1	26.66	2	160,80
H	3	2	17.22	3	160,134,40

4.3   Discussion

The advent of web 2.0 collaborative applications encourages users to interact and participate in online networks. Users tend to have different roles in the network, some are innovators and leaders, some are early adopters that closely follow new trends, others are highly focused and are only interested in a small subset of users and content. Many applications benefit from being able to identify a user's roles in the network. In corporate environments that can span many geographic boundaries, enabling collaboration is important for knowledge transfer as contacts to individuals can represent access to knowledge. Betweenness centrality has been shown to be able to identify users that are key to the network graph in terms of information flow, linking many different users. Bridging centrality focuses on nodes that are not necessarily highly central for information flow, but are connected to highly between nodes and have a more focused, concentrated number of contacts.

5   Conclusion and Future Work

This paper has investigated the types of nodes that are identified in a collaborative bookmarking network using localised centrality metrics. Using real world data from the Dogear collaborative bookmarking application, we constructed two relationship graphs. A URL relationship graph linking users with overlapping bookmarks which we consider an implicit relationship, and a subscription relationship graph which we consider an explicit relationship. The analysis showed that betweenness centrality identifies users that have a rich social network either through the domains they span, the reciprocated nature of their ties, or the extent to which they are followed by others spanning domains. The subscription network is a small subset of the application users, as a result, other relationships must be used to provide a more complete insight into the network. The URL relationship network is one example, however the graph presented in this paper is symmetric, where there has been no identification of link directionality. One solution may be to assign direction to the links based on the date when the user adds the bookmark, in an attempt to identify the contributor and the consumer in the relationship. Another potential relationship is one based on overlapping use of tags in order to take into account the different types of relationships.

References

1. Bakshy, E., Karrer, B., Adamic, L.: Social influence and the diffusion of user-created content. In: 10th ACM Conference on Electronic Commerce. ACM, New York (July 2009)
2. Bhattacharyya, P., Garg, A., Wu, F.S.: Social network model based on keyword categorization. In: ASONAM 2009: Proceedings of the International Conference on Advances in Social Network Analysis and Mining (July 2009)
3. Chi, E.H., Mytkowicz, T.: Understanding the efficiency of social tagging systems using information theory. In: HT 2008: Proceedings of the Nineteenth ACM Conference on Hypertext and Hypermedia, pp. 81–88. ACM, New York (2008)
4. Cross, R.L., Parker, A., Cross, R.: The Hidden Power of Social Networks: Understanding How Work Really Gets Done in Organizations. Harvard Business School Press, Boston (June 2004)
5. Everett, M., Borgatti, S.P.: Ego network betweenness. Social networks (Soc. networks) 27(1), 31–38 (2005)
6. Freeman, L.C.: A set of measures of centrality based on betweenness. Sociometry, 35–41 (1977)
7. Freeman, L.C.: Centrality in social networks conceptual clarification. Social networks(Soc. networks), 215–239 (1979)
8. Golder, S.A., Huberman, B.A.: Usage patterns of collaborative tagging systems. J. Inf. Sci. 32(2), 198–208 (2006)
9. Granovetter, M.S.: The strength of weak ties. The American Journal of Sociology 78(6), 1360–1380 (1973)
10. Hwang, W., Cho, Ramanathan, M.: Bridging centrality: Identifying bridging nodes in scale-free networks. Technical Report (March 2006)
11. Kolari, P., Finin, T., Lyons, K., Yesha, Y., Yesha, Y., Perelgut, S., Hawkins, J.: On the structure, properties and utility of internal corporate blogs. In: International Conference on Weblogs and Social (2007)

12. Krebs, V.: Managing the 21st century organization. International Association for Human Resource Information Management Journal XI (2007)
13. Lewis, K., Kaufman, J., Gonzalez, M., Wimmer, A., Christakis, N.: Tastes, ties, and time: A new social network dataset using facebook.com. Social Networks (2008) (in press) (accepted manuscript)
14. Leydesdorff, L.: "Betweenness centrality" as an indicator of the "interdisciplinarity" of scientific journals. Journal of the American Society for Information Science and Technology (2007)
15. Marsden, P.V.: Egocentric and sociocentric measures of network centrality. Social networks(Soc. networks), 407–422 (2002)
16. Millen, D.R., Feinberg, J., Kerr, B.: Dogear: Social bookmarking in the enterprise. In: CHI 2006: Proceedings of the SIGCHI Conference on Human Factors in Computing Systems, pp. 111–120. ACM, New York (2006)
17. Nanda, S., Kotz, D.: Localized bridging centrality for distributed network analysis. In: Proceedings of 17th International Conference on Computer Communications and Networks, ICCCN 2008, pp. 1–6 (2008)
18. Newman, M.E.J.: A measure of betweenness centrality based on random walks (September 2005)

Practical Development of Hybrid Intelligent Agent Systems with SoSAA*

Mauro Dragone[1], Rem W. Collier[2], David Lillis[2], and Gregory M.P. O'Hare[1]

[1] CLARITY: Centre for Sensor Web Technologies
School of Computer Science and Informatics
University College Dublin
{mauro.dragone,gregory.ohare}@ucd.ie
[2] School of Computer Science and Informatics
University College Dublin
{rem.collier,david.lillis}@ucd.ie

Abstract. The development of intelligent Multi Agent Systems (MAS) is a non-trivial task. While much past research has focused on high-level activities such as co-ordination and negotiation, the development of tools and strategies to address the lower-level concerns of such systems is a more recent focus. SoSAA (Socially Situated Agent Architecture) is a strategy for the integration of high-level MASs on one hand with component-based systems on the other. Under the SoSAA strategy, a component-based system is used to provide the lower-level implementation of agent tasks and capabilities, allowing for the agent layer to concentrate on high-level intelligent co-ordination and organisation. This paper provides a practical perspective on how SoSAA can be used in the development of intelligent MASs, illustrating this by demonstrating how it can be used to manage backchannel transport services.

1 Introduction

Multi Agent Systems (MAS) are often advocated as a method of leveraging new and existing Artifical Intelligence techniques in order to build large-scale intelligent software sytems. In this type of system, autonomous software entities are tasked with reasoning about themselves and their environment in order to achieve individual or system-wide objectives and goals.

To date, a large body of research on MASs has been carried out on developing solutions to such problems as agent co-ordination, negotiation and reasoning, along with the development of standards governing agent communication [1]. However, less attention has been paid to the practical implementation of such systems. Agents have tended to be developed purely from an agent standpoint, with little regard to the underlying apparatus of the system.

In recent years, new research has emerged that deals with the lower-level aspects of intelligent systems in more detail. The CArtAgO framework makes use

---

* This work is supported by Science Foundation Ireland under grant 07/CE/I1147.

L. Coyle and J. Freyne (Eds.): AICS 2009, LNAI 6206, pp. 51–60, 2010.
© Springer-Verlag Berlin Heidelberg 2010

of the Agents and Artifacts meta-model in the creation of *artifacts*: resources and tools to be utilised by agents in the satisfaction of their objectives [2]. Other work has focused on the environment within which agents are situated [3], arguing that the environment is an integral part of the MAS. The creation of an exploitable design abstraction of the environment is considered a key step in the design and implementation of a MAS. Both of these approaches emphasise the separation of concerns between the intelligent intentional layer on one hand, and the low-level actions on the other.

This trend is continued by the introduction of the Socially Situated Agent Architecture (SoSAA) framework. SoSAA is an open source framework that combines the concepts of Agent Oriented Software Engineering (AOSE) and Component-Based Software Engineering (CBSE) in the development of MASs[1]. There is a clear separation of concerns between the intelligent functionality of the agents, developed using AOSE concepts, and their lower-level actions, which are encapsulated by components. The background, motivations and underlying low-level functionality of SoSAA have been presented in previous papers [4,5].

In contrast to this prior work, the key contribution of this paper is to demonstrate the practical usage of the framework to integrate a component-based system and intelligent agents to develop a Transport Manager that facilitates communication between low-level components. A brief overview of the framework is provided in Section 2. Section 2.1 outlines a number of improvements that were necessary so as to integrate the SoSAA approach into the underlying Agent Factory framework [6]. This integration is implemented via the SoSAA Adaptor, which is discussed in Section 2.2.

The implementation of the Transport Manager, which implements a hybrid backchannel communication strategy, is presented in Section 3. Finally, our conclusions and ideas for future work are outlined in Section 4.

2   SoSAA

Popularised by their use in robotics (e.g. in [7]), hybrid control architectures are layered architectures combining low-level behaviour-based systems with intelligent high-level, deliberative reasoning apparatus. The solution implemented in the SoSAA framework is to apply such a hybrid integration strategy to the infrastructure of a MAS, as illustrated in Fig. 1. SoSAA combines a low-level component-based infrastructure framework with a MAS-based high-level infrastructure framework. This section provides only a brief overview to the SoSAA framework. A more complete complete discussion can be found in [4].

The low-level framework allows for the development of functional components that encapsulate simple system behaviours and facilitate interaction with the agents' environment. These components are designed so as to be assembled into a system architecture. A run-time environment is provided to the high-level

---

[1] SoSAA may be downloaded from http://www.sourceforge.net/projects/agentfactory

framework, which then contributes its multi-agent organisation, interaction using Agent Communication Languages (ACL), and goal-oriented reasoning capabilities to intelligently perform this system assembly. Agents may also alter the system architecure and/or configuration to reflect changing goals and environmental circumstances. By interacting with the component layer, intelligent agents can access the system's resources, coordinate the components' activities and resolve conflicts. While the high level can be programmed according to different cognitive models, domain and application-specific issues can be taken into account in the engineering of the underlying functional components.

The SoSAA high-level framework provides meta-level perceptors and actuators that collectively define an interface (delivered as a SoSAA Adaptor Service, discussed in Section 2.2) that can be used to sense and act upon elements and mechanisms of the low-level framework by loading, unloading, configuring and binding components.

Fig. 1 shows the multi agent organisation in a typical SoSAA node. The low-level framework provides the interface for operating both at the application and the infrastructure level. Depending on their interests, SoSAA component agents can be categorised as either application or infrastructure agents. Such a clear separation is fundamental for promoting not only the efficiency and the portability of the resulting systems, but also for separating the different concerns at design time to facilitate the use of a modular development process.

The current implementation of SoSAA is based on two open-source toolkits: the Agent Factory (AF) multi-agent toolkit, which is described briefly in Section 2.1, and the Java Modular Component Framework (JMCF) [2]. JMCF comes with a package of built-in component types and base-class implementations. Further details on JMCF can be found in [5].

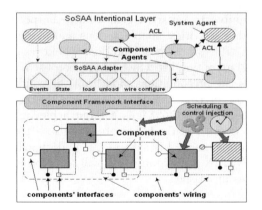

Fig. 1. SoSAA Hybrid Integration Strategy

---

[2] Agent Factory and JMCF can be downloaded from http://www.sourceforge.net/projects/agentfactory

2.1 Improvements to Agent Factory

Agent Factory is a modular, extensible, open source framework for the development of Multi Agent Systems [6]. The key components of this framework are a Run-Time Environment (RTE) consisting of a FIPA-compliant agent platform along with a number of agent system architectures and a set of development kits that contain implementations of agent interpreters and architectures.

One of the more important features offered by the Agent Factory RTE is the support of platform services. These are shared services that are offered to all agents residing on a particular agent platform. Examples include communication services, such as services that enable agents to exchange FIPA-compliant messages using HTTP, UDP or local message passing. In the context of the work presented here, the SoSAA Adaptor is implemented as a platform service that can be accessed by all agents on a platform. Support is also provided for the Agent Factory Agent Programming Language (AFAPL2) [6], an agent oriented programming language that has been successfully applied in a number of significant problem domains [8]. AFAPL2 employs a commitment-based mental state, whose core components are *beliefs*, *plans* and *commitments*. Beliefs represent an agent's view of the world, according to information gathered by its *perceptors*. Plans combine primitive actions (implemented by *actuators* or *effectors*) into complex activities that may be carried out by the agent. This is done by way of certain plan operators that are made available to agent developers. Commitments represent the activites that an agent has resolved to perform, according to its own reasoning mechanism.

A recent addition to AFAPL2 has been the introduction of goal-based reasoning. This implementation is based on the goal mechanism found in the Procedural Reasoning System [9]. Specifically, this involved the introduction of two new operators specifically designed for goals: ADOPT and MAINTAIN. Whenever an agent is required to satisfy a goal, firstly the postconditions of each of the agent's available activities (simple actions and more complex plans) are examined. Those activities whose postconditions would result in the goal being achieved are put into an option list. Once this option list has been created, the agent then examines the preconditions of each of the candidate activities and chooses the first whose precondition is satisfied by the state of the world as it is currently perceived. If an activity fails without achieving the specified goal, the agent will select another of the candidate activities. If an agent is required to ADOPT a goal, once the goal is achieved, it is dropped. In contrast, when attempting to MAINTAIN a goal, an agent will attempt to re-adopt the goal every time it becomes unsatisfied.

2.2 SoSAA Adaptor

The SoSAA Adaptor bridges the low-level component framework and the higher-level agent programming language. In the context of Agent Factory, support for this is implemented through a combination of a platform service, an agent module, a set of actuators and perceptors and a partial agent program that links

```
PERCEPTOR sosaaEventMonitor { ... }
LOAD_MODULE sosaa sosaa.module.ComponentStore;

ACTION create(?id, ?type) { ... }
ACTION remove(?id) { ... }
ACTION bind(?id1, ?iface1, ?id2, ?iface2) { ... }
ACTION configure(?id, ?param, ?value) { ... }
ACTION de/activate(?id) { ... }
ACTION focus(?id) { ... }
ACTION lookup(?id) { ... }
```

Fig. 2. SoSAA Adaptor Code

together all the pieces and provides a basis for developing SoSAA agents. Specifically, the platform service encapsulates the underlying component framework and provides an interface through which that framework may be manipulated, including the loading/unloading, activation/deactivation, binding, inspection, monitoring, and configuration of components.

Access to these operations is supported through the provision of a set of actuator units. Fig. 2 illustrates their declaration as part of a partial AFAPL2 agent program that can be reused as a basis for creating SoSAA agents. As can be seen in this figure, this partial agent program also makes use of an agent module. Agent modules are provided by AFAPL2 to support the creation of resources that are private to a given agent. In this case, the module provides a mechanism for the agent to keep track of the components that it is interested in and also a way of accessing the events and properties that are generated by those components. To achieve this, the sosaaEventMonitor perceptor has been created. This perceptor converts events and properties into beliefs that can be used at the agent level.

3   Example: Transport Manager

To showcase how SoSAA can be used to construct intelligent software, this section focuses on the design and implementation of a hybrid backchannel management infrastructure service [4]. This service provides support for the transmission of diverse types of data between internal systems nodes using heterogeneous transport mechanisms, such as raw TCP-IP, RMI, JMS, and CORBA.

The idea of intelligent backchannel management using agents is not new, and was previously proposed for the RETSINA architecture [10]. Backchannels are designed to allow the flow of low-level data between agents or components. The motivation behind this type of communication is that it does not affect the decision-making of agents and as such, the use of expensive ACL communication is undesirable. In SoSAA, backchannels allow components to pass data between one another. In certain situations (e.g. the failure of a line of communication), components may raise events to inform agents of the circumstances. Thus, since the processing of backchannel data does not require any deliberation on the part of an agent, it can be separated from the intentional layer of the agent.

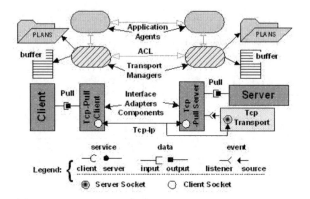

Fig. 3. SoSAA Backchannel Management

Using SoSAA, we have designed and implemented a backchannel management service that consists of an infrastructure agent, known as the *Transport Manager (TM)* and a set of *adaptor components* that implement the data transfer functionality for various transport mechanisms. As illustrated in Fig. 3, a TM is deployed on each node (agent platform) of the distributed system. Application agents, upon agreeing to make use of a backchannel, contact their local TM and request that two components (on different nodes) be wired together using a backchannel. Details of which transport mechanism to use and the setup and configuration of the associated adaptor components that implement that backchannel is delegated to the TMs.

Our backchannel management service supports two types of backchannel: (1) *push* backchannels, wiring remote components where the component that generates the data controls when the next unit of data is transmitted; and (2) *pull* backchannels, wiring components where the component that receives the data controls when the next unit of data is transmitted. Fig. 3 shows a pull type of backchannel that has been set up based on a raw TCP-IP transport mechanism.

Fig. 4(a) provides a high-level view of the four protocols that are required to implement the service. Here, we ignore the application-level protocol as it is not part of the backchannel management service, but rather represents the application-level interaction that results in the agreement to set up of a backchannel.

Once this decision is made, the two application agents contact their local TM using the *setupRemoteConnection* message. This begins the connection protocol shown in Fig. 4(b). In making the initial request, the application agents include the information necessary to set up the backchannel, namely the name of the local and remote components; the interfaces that are to be bound together; and the name of the platform on which the remote component resides so that the TM can locate it. As can be seen in the partial AFAPL2 code outlined in Fig. 5 the TM responds to this request by looking up local component. The *lookup(...)* action is a generic action that is part of the SoSAA adaptor described in Section 2.2. Once invoked, it generates beliefs indicating whether or not the given component implements a client or a server interface. Based on this, the agent adopts a

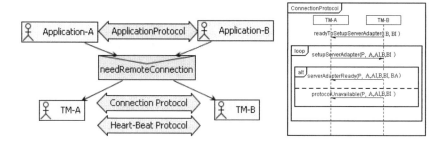

Fig. 4. (a) Interaction Diagram (left), and (b) AUML TransportManager's setupRe-moteConnection protocol (Legend: P: Communication Protocol;A: Name of component A; AI: Name of interface for component A; B: Name of component B; BI: Name of interface for component B; BA: Name of network adapter for component B) (right)

```
BELIEF(platformName(?lP)) &
BELIEF(message(request,?s,setupRemoteConnection(?lC,?lI,?rC,?rI,?rP))) =>
COMMIT(?self,?now,BELIEF(true), SEQ(achieve_goal(GOAL(platform(?rP, ?a))), lookup(?lC),
    OR(DO_WHEN(BELIEF(clientInterface(?lC, ?lI, ?type, ?jI, ?m, ?ib, ?mb, ?b)),
        MAINTAIN(GOAL(clientConnection(?jI, ?lP, ?lC, ?lI, ?rP, ?rC, ?rI, ?a, ?p)))),
    DO_WHEN(BELIEF(serverInterface(?lC, ?lI, ?t, ?jI)),
        MAINTAIN(GOAL(serverConnection(?jI, ?lP, ?lC, ?lI, ?rP, ?rC, ?rI, ?a, ?p)))))))));
```

Fig. 5. Partial *Transport Manager* AFAPL2 code: Handling Backchannel Connection Requests

maintenance goal to set up a backchannel. The parameters associated with this goal include the Java interface (?jI) of the component; the local platform name (?lP), component name (?lC), and interface name (?lI); and the remote platform name (?rP), component name (?rC) and interface name (?rI); the adaptor name (?a); and the transport protocol (?p) (for example TCP, RMI, or JMS). The latter two parameters are not set when the maintenance goal is adopted (i.e. they are unbound variables). This allows the goal to be satisfied for any given protocol and its associated adaptor.

Ultimately, the specific belief that satisfies the goal is adopted once the relevant adaptor has been set up, as is shown in the setupClientConnection(..) plan in Fig. 6. This plan implements the client side of the interaction protocol presented in Fig. 4(b). Here, TM-A is the *Transport Manager* responsible for the client side while TM-B is responsible for the server side. The plan forces TM-A to wait for a readyToSetupServerAdaptor(...) inform message from its counterpart. Upon receipt of this message, TM-A requests the setup of the actual server-side adaptor and waits to be given connection details. When the second message is received, TM-A generates a unique name for the client-adaptor which it then uses to create to adaptor. The adaptor is then bound to the local component; configured based on the information given; and monitored, via the focus action for events, such as transport failures. Finally, the plan activates the local

```
PLAN setupTcpClientConnection(?jI, ?lP, ?lC, ?lI, ?rP, ?rC, ?rI) {
  PRECONDITION BELIEF(platform(?rP, ?a)) & BELIEF(transport(?lP,TCP)) &
      BELIEF(transport(?rP,TCP)) & !BELIEF(transportFailure(?rP,TCP));
  POSTCONDITION BELIEF(clientConnection(?jI, ?lP, ?lC, ?lI, ?rP, ?rC, ?rI, ?a, ?p));
  BODY setupClientConnection(TCP, ?jI, ?lP, ?lC, ?lI, ?rP, ?rC, ?rI);
}

PLAN setupClientConnection(?p, ?jI, ?lP, ?lC, ?lI, ?rP, ?rC, ?rI) {
  BODY
    DO_WHEN(BELIEF(message(inform, ?agentID, readyToSetupServerAdapter(?lC, ?lI))),
      PAR(request(?agentID, setupServerAdapter(?p,?rC, ?rI)),
        DO_WHEN(BELIEF(message(inform,?agentID,serverAdapterReady(?p,?rC,?rI,?nRA,?rip)))),
          PAR(createPullClientName(?lC, ?nRA),
            DO_WHEN(BELIEF(uniqueName(?cAN, ?self)),
              FOREACH(BELIEF(clientTransportAdapter(?p, ?jI, ?aC, ?i)),
                SEQ(create(?cAN, ?aC), bind(?cAN, ?i, ?lC, ?lI), focus(?cAN),
                configure(?cAN, list(SERVER(?rip), SERVER_CONNECTION(?nRA))),
                ADOPT(ALWAYS(BELIEF(clientConnection(?jI,?lP,?lC,?lI,?rP,?rC,?rI,?cAN,?p)))),
                  activate(?lC)))))))));
}
```

Fig. 6. Partial *Transport Manager* AFAPL2 code: Client-Side Adaptor Creation

component, causing the backchannel connection to be established. These final steps are achieved through the use of SoSAA adaptor (see Section 2.2) actions. The decision as to which adaptor should be created is based on knowledge that is stored in a set of clientTransportAdapter(...) beliefs, which map a given protocol (e.g. TCP) and Java Interface (e.g. a pull client) to a component type (i.e. a Java component implementation) and an interface. A similar plan exists for the server-side of the connection protocol.

Finally, the intelligent selection of which transport protocol to use is achieved through a set of custom plans that deal with each potential transport protocol. For example, Fig. 6 shows the setupTcpClientConnection(...) plan, which simply calls the setupClientConnection(...) plan with the protocol parameter (?p) bound to TCP. In AFAPL2, all plans whose post-condition matches the given goal are selected as options, and the first plan whose pre-condition is satisfied is chosen from the set of options. Here, the precondition states that: (1) both the local and remote platforms should have the transport protocol, and (2) that the transport protocol should not have previously failed. Failure of a given transport mechanism is detected through the monitoring of the adaptor, and the raising of error events. This results in the activation of a plan that: (1) records the failure of the transport mechanism; and (2) causes the original goal to become unsatisfied, kicking off a new attempt by the agent to satisfy the goal.

Fig. 7 illustrates the results of a simple benchmarking test in which we measured the reaction time required by the TransportManager agent to switch between a TCP-IP connection to one based on JMS once we injected a failure in TCP-IP network adapter. This simple experiment is based on the core workflow that underpins the HOTAIR Information Retrieval test-bed [11]. The figure shows the rate of fixed-length messages exchanged between two components deployed on the same machine over time. Over 10 runs, the system was able to recover from failure with an average of 312ms.

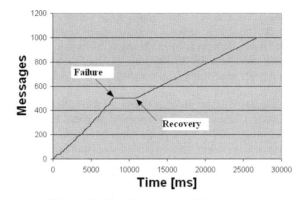

Fig. 7. SoSAA Backchannel Management

4   Conclusions and Future Work

In this paper, we have presented an overview of ongoing work aimed at leveraging the benefits and strengths of both AOSE and CBSE in a way that promotes the development of high-quality applications. We have described both the rational behind our approach and its current incarnation in the SoSAA software framework, based on a combination of the Agent Factory and the JMCF component frameworks. In particular, we have attempted to demonstrate how SoSAA can be used to effectively construct intelligent software. By way of illustration, we have presented the design and implementation of an intelligent backchannel management service that has been developed using SoSAA, and showed how this service can provide a separation of concerns between infrastructure and application-level aspects. The service has been already used in a number of practical systems, including an agent-based information retrieval test-bed [11] and in a multi-agent robotics scenario [12].

Future work will investigate how an agent's plan-selection, plan-abortion and meta-level reasoning can be employed to implement an intelligent transport selection strategy addressing Quality of Service optimisation and system adaptation in response to changing environmental conditions. The first step will be to cache the transport manager usage statistics concerning the adapter components, such as the total number of interfaces established toward each collaborating node, their latest throughput, and the last time they were successfully (or unsuccessfully) used. The HOTAIR test-bed [11] will continue to be used to demonstrate the effectiveness of our approach to a large scale, dynamic system.

References

1. Wooldridge, M.: Introduction to multiagent systems. John Wiley & Sons, Inc., New York (2001)
2. Ricci, A., Piunt, M., Acay, L.D., Bordini, R.H., Hubner, J.F., Destani, M.: Integrating Heterogeneous Agent Programming Platforms within Artifact-Based Environments. In: International Joint Conference on Agents and Multi Agent Systems (AAMAS 2008), Estoril, Portugal (2008)

3. Weyns, D., Omicini, A., Odell, J.: Environment as a first class abstraction in multiagent systems. Autonomous agents and multi-agent systems 14(1), 5–30 (2007)
4. Lillis, D., Collier, R.W., Dragone, M., O'Hare, G.M.P.: An Agent-Based Approach to Component Management. In: Proceedings of the 8th International Conference on Autonomous Agents and Multi-Agent Systems (AAMAS 2009), Budapest, Hungary (May 2009)
5. Dragone, M., Lillis, D., Collier, R.W., O'Hare, G.M.P.: SoSAA: A Framework for Integrating Agents & Components. In: Proceedings of the 24th Annual Symposium on Applied Computing (ACM SAC 2009), Special Track on Agent-Oriented Programming, Systems, Languages, and Applications, Honolulu, Hawaii, USA (March 2009)
6. Collier, R., O'Hare, G., Lowen, T., Rooney, C.: Beyond Prototyping in the Factory of Agents. In: Mařík, V., Müller, J.P., Pěchouček, M. (eds.) CEEMAS 2003. LNCS (LNAI), vol. 2691, p. 383. Springer, Heidelberg (2003)
7. Gat, E.: Integrating planning and reacting in a heterogeneous asynchronous architecture for controlling real-world mobile robots. In: Proceedings of the National Conference on Artificial Intelligence, pp. 809–809. John Wiley & Sons Ltd., Chichester (1992)
8. Collier, R.W., O'Hare, G.: Modeling and Programming with Commitment Rules in Agent Factory. In: Handbook of Research on Emerging Rule-Based Languages and Technologies: Open Solutions and Approaches. IGI Publishing (2009)
9. Ingrand, F., Georgeff, M., Rao, A.: An architecture for real-time reasoning and system control. IEEE Expert 7(6), 34–44 (1992)
10. Berna-Koes, M., Nourbakhsh, I., Sycara, K.: Communication efficiency in multiagent systems. In: Proceedings of 2004 IEEE International Conference on Robotics and Automation, ICRA 2004, vol. 3 (2004)
11. Lillis, D., Collier, R., Toolan, F., Dunnion, J.: Evaluating Communication Strategies in a Multi Agent Information Retrieval System. In: Proceedings of the 18th Irish Conference on Artificial Intelligence and Cognitive Science (AICS 2007), pp. 81–90. Dublin Institute of Technology, Dublin (2007)
12. Dragone, M.: SoSAA: An Agent-Based Robot Software Framework. PhD thesis, University College Dublin (2007)

Genetic Repair Strategies Inspired by *Arabidopsis thaliana*

Amy FitzGerald, Diarmuid P. O'Donoghue, and Xinyu Liu

National University of Ireland, Maynooth, Co. Kildare
{amy.fitzgerald,diarmuid.odonoghue,xinyu.liu}@nuim.ie

Abstract. Recent advances in genetics controversially suggest that the model plant *Arabidopsis thaliana* performs genetic repair using genetic information that originates in the individual's grandparent generation. We apply this ancestral genetic repair strategy within an Evolutionary Algorithm (EA) to solve a constraint based optimisation problem. Results indicate that the grandparent based *genetic repair* strategy outperforms the parent alternative. Within this framework, we investigate the impact of storing only the fittest ancestors for use as a repair template. The influence of performing repair in a fixed direction is compared to randomly varying the direction in which error detection proceeds. Finally we explore the impact of varying the direction of repair on the results produced. All results seem to support the non-Mendelian inheritance process suggested by Lolle *et al*.

1 Introduction

This paper attempts to strengthen the parallels between evolutionary algorithms and recent advances in genetics, within the framework of naturally inspired computation. We explore a recent controversy in biology that centres on a non-Mendelian inheritance mechanism that has been supposedly identified in the model plant *Arabidopsis thaliana* [1]. The mechanism that has been controversially [2] suggested by Lolle *et al* involves the transfer of genetic information from a grand-parent's genes into an offspring - apparently by-passing the parents'genes. This non-Mendelian inheritance process was suggested not as part of the plants normal inheritance process, but in response to specific genetic errors that were apparently corrected by a grandparent-based genetic repair process. Specific mechanisms for carrying out this non-Mendelian repair process include an RNA based archive [1] and a form of "archival"DNA [3].

In this paper we examine the proposed non-Mendelian inheritance mechanism from the perspective of an evolutionary algorithm. This repair strategy is adapted to operate with a constrained optimisation process. This approach allows us to examine the performance of Lolle *et al*'s proposed non-Mendelian inheritance based genetic repair process. In particular, this strategy will be compared against simpler alternative approaches.

The structure of the paper is as follows. First we compare the performance of the ancestral based, template driven, GeneRepair process against the alternative

L. Coyle and J. Freyne (Eds.): AICS 2009, LNAI 6206, pp. 61–71, 2010.

penalty function system. Next, we compare the performance of the parent and grandparent repair templates. In the third set of experiments, we manipulate GeneRepair by using fitness as a selection criterion on the stored repair templates. In the fourth set of experiments, we manipulate the direction in which the error detection phase of GeneRepair proceeds, examining its impact on the fitness of the population. Finally we compare the earlier results against the use of great-grandparent based GeneRepair, examining the impact of using even more ancient genetic data to guide the repair process.

2   Constraint-Based Optimisation with Evolutionary Optimisation

Evolutionary algorithms (EA) has been successful in exploring complex solution spaces, but EA are ill-suited to supporting constraints on these search spaces. For the purposes of this paper, we see both natural and simulated evolution focusing on a highly constrained optimisation problem, where a minimal change to a feasible solution is very likely to generate an unfeasible solution [4]. Evolutionary optimisation (EO) is the term given to the subset of EA that addresses constraints. We investigate if these EO can be improved so that they can handle constraints in a reasonable manner by incorporating a genetic repair process that reflects recent biological findings.

Four distinct approaches have been adopted to enforce constraints on evolutionary searches [5]. Firstly, crossover and mutation operators are modified to ensure that all solutions obey the constraints. This can also take the form of problem specific representations in which invalid solutions cannot be generated. This is not only a biologically implausible approach, it also limits the evolutionary algorithm to solving one (or just a few) problem types. The second approach to dealing with constraints is to use a penalty function (including the death penalty). This method ensures that valid genotypes have the greatest influence on subsequent generations by restricting the reproduction of invalid individuals. (The "death penalty"completely eliminates the influence of invalid individuals on subsequent generations). The biological plausibility of this approach rests in the fact that invalid individuals do not form viable phenotypes and thus can not influence subsequent generations. The penalty inflicted can range from a light penalty for constraint violation to the death penalty [6] being placed on erroneous individuals. The third constraint enforcement method is to adopt a pareto-optimal approach [5]. The final method of enforcing constraints is through a genetic repair operator and it is this 'GeneRepair'[7], [8] approach that is explored in this paper.

A number of techniques for genetic repair have been explored, including: use of heuristics [9], the template approach [10] and the harmonisation operator [11]. This paper explores biologically inspired variants of the GeneRepair approach, that overcomes the problem dependence associated with many constraint enforcement techniques [12]. The GeneRepair approach offers the advantage of using an unmodified evolutionary engine to explore the problem space.

Significantly the genetic repair process presented in this paper uses ancestral genomic data which can always be made available for any problem domain.

The results in this paper were produced using a simple experimental setup described in section 5. For this paper we have used the TSPLIB eil51 51 city Travelling Salesman Problem (TSP) to evaluate our hypothesis and compare results. This is a combinatorial optimisation problem where each individual in the EO represents a tour of all of the cities in the TSP, and each element represents a city. The number of possible solutions for the TSP is n!, where n is the number of cities on the tour. However, the total space that can be explored by an un-constrained EO is n^n where $n^n >> n!$ for large values of n.

Thus, an un-constrained EO will explore not just the search space required by the TSP but will also generate a large number of invalid solutions. The genetic repair operator modifies invalid solutions that lie outside the valid solution space and converts them back into valid members of the solution space. The biological process that inspired our approach shall now be described.

3   Genetic Repair in *Arabidopsis thaliana*

Arabidopsis thaliana (thale cress) is a model plant used for a wide variety of detailed studies and it was the first plant genome to be fully sequenced. Lolle *et al* (2005) investigated *A. thaliana* plants with an organ fusion mutation on the Hothead gene (*hth*) [13], which resulted in an abnormal formation of the plant's flower. The studies of Lolle *et al* revealed that two plants with the *hth* mutation can produce offspring without this abnormality. The resultant offspring have the normal form of the hothead gene (HTH), even though this information was present in neither of the parent genomes. Surprisingly, approximately 10% of the offspring of two mutant plants were found to revert to the normal form of the hothead gene [14]. This rate of reversion is far higher than can be explained by random mutation of these specific alleles, which would be of the order of 1 per billions [15] per allele per generation. It is thought that this phenomenon is not exclusive to the *Arabidopsis thaliana* but occurs in a range of organisms including flax.

It was found that these revertant genomes all appeared to inherit genetic information from their grand-parents genomes, which had the normal (*HTH*) form. Thus, genetic information appeared to skip a generation, reappearing in a subsequent generation. This has been referred to as a *parallel path of inheritance*, which appears to occur in addition to standard Mendelian inheritance. In essence, a corrective template is used to correct broken or damaged sequences of DNA, possibly in response to stress placed on the plant due to the presence of the genetic mutation. While Lolle *et al*'s (2005) controversial explanation relies on a cache of RNA inherited from previous generations, our approach is more similar to the explanation offered by Ray (2005) that is compatible with Lolle *et al*'s findings. Rays explanation relies on an archival form of DNA that serves to store the ancestral DNA, but which is not detected by the processes used to sequence the regular encoding of DNA.

In this paper we examine the efficiency of this "parallel path of inheritance" using the TSP as our benchmark problem for generating and comparing results. There were two main objectives behind these experiments: first to evaluate the efficiency of grand-parent based genetic repair, comparing it to a variety of alternative strategies. Secondly, these experiments attempt to assess if there is any reason to believe that Lolle *et al*'s controversial findings might, in fact, find some support in the analogous domains of evolutionary algorithms.

4   Ancestor Based Genetic Repair Strategies

The GeneRepair operator used in this paper is modelled on that of the model plant *Arabidopsis thaliana*, ensuring that each individual maintains its own archive of ancestral genetic information. Thus, each individual in the population has its own repair template based on its ancestors genetic information. These repair templates are called upon when an invalid individual is produced by the evolutionary process.

Each allele in our EO encodes a single city and each city is uniquely encoded within the fixed length representation. Therefore there is a 1-to-1 association between cities of the TSP problem and the city's representation within the EO. Solutions to the TSP (tours) are formed as an ordered list of cities and the entire population is composed of a fixed number of individual tours (see Figure 2). So, the relative order of cities determines their position within a tour.

The constraints of the TSP problem require that each city must be visited exactly once. Our fixed length genetic representation resulting in two types of genomic error, which are found in pairs. Firstly, duplication errors occur when a city is repeated within a tour (individual). Secondly, omission errors occur when a city is absent from a candidate solution. Thus, an omission error always has a corresponding duplicate error. As can be seen in Figure 1 duplication of the "1"causes omission of "6"from the genetic sequence. The GeneRepair operator identifies all duplicate alleles and replaces each one with the corresponding element in the repair template.

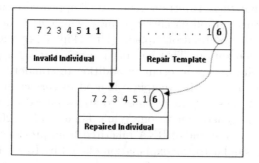

Fig. 1. GeneRepair using a Fixed Template

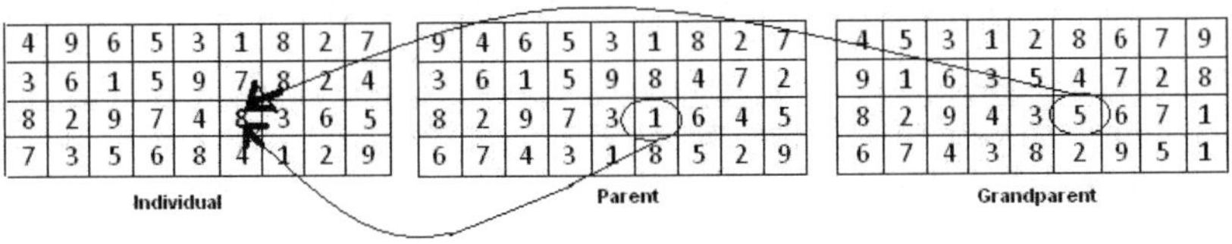

Fig. 2. GeneRepair using an Inherited Template

Ancestral repair templates are stored as independent archived populations. For efficiency only the required template type is stored (See Section 5.3).

In the next section we investigate the relative efficiency of the *parent* and the *grandparent* templates.

5   Results

All of the following experiments use the same experimental setup. Our EO was written in Java and incorporates the MersenneTwister PRNG [16]. This random number generator differs to that used in our previous work [8]. The EO uses the following experimental setup; single point crossover, swap mutation at 2%, rank selection, a population size of 500 and each experiment was run for 500,000 generations. The data below was generated for the eil51 problem set from TSPLIB [17]. Due to the stochastic nature of EO, each experimental condition was tested 26 times.

In this section we report on the effectiveness of the grandparent based genetic repair strategy, as applied to the TSP. First, grandparent based repair is compared with the alternative "death penalty" strategy. In this strategy, invalid individuals are subject to the "death penalty" and so are removed from the population and do not influence subsequent generations.

5.1   Grandparent GeneRepair Template and the Death Penalty

The results detailed in Table 1 indicate that grandparent based genetic repair produces significantly better results than the alternative "death penalty" strategy, for our sample problem of the TSP. Thus the grandparent strategy produces far fitter individuals for this minimisation task.

Table 1. Template Inheritance and the Penalty Function

	Min	Mean
Penalty Function	1486.4	1584.094
Grandparent Template	483	519.81

5.2   Parent and Grandparent Repair Template Results

In our second experiment we compare the performance of grandparent based repair against the simpler parent based strategy. Parent based repair uses the genetic information from each individual's parent as a template to repair genetic errors in the child generation, while grandparent based repair uses the individual's grandparent as the template.

The following table summarises the results across three directions of repair (right to left, left to right and random) and two inheritance selections (fittest and random). All of these experimental conditions are investigated further in the following sections. Grandparent based repair generates the fittest individual (minimum tour length) and also generates the lowest mean result. As grandparent repair produced the lowest average and standard deviation this suggests that the grandparent is the superior repair template. Repeated trials have shown that the best overall result generally originates from the grandparent repair strategy (Mann-Whitney P=0.1423). These findings combined seem to suggest that the grandparent strategy introduces greater diversity into the population and that this diversity can yield the best result across repeated trials. These results support the controversial findings of Lolle *et al* [1].

5.3   A Comparison of Template Fitness

While the most plausible interpretation of genetic repair in *A. thaliana* involves recording randomly selected parent or grandparent information, we next explore the impact that fitness might have on the results produced. The next results compare the performance of storing the fittest parent or grandparent against a randomly selected template of the appropriate ancestry.

The results detailed in Table 3 show that using a randomly selected template produces better results than selecting the ttest of the available templates (MANN-WHITNEY P=0.1894)The results detailed in Table 3 show that using

Table 2. Effect of Ancestry on GeneRepair

Template	Min	Mean
Parent	463	519.49
Grandparent	453	516.60

Table 3. Template Fitness

Template	Min	Mean	Standard Deviation
Fittest Parent	469	524.5	34.72
Random Parent	463	516.15	27.87
Fittest Grandparent	458	519.62	33.72
Random Grandparent	455	517.04	29.75

a randomly selected template produces better results than selecting the fittest of the available templates (Mann-Whitney P=0.0764). This was a relatively surprising result, as it was felt that the fitter template would produce fitter results. However, this result also seems to lend support to Lolle's theory as the random selection process appears to produce the best results (and no mechanism for favouring the fittest ancestor would appear to be naturally available).

5.4   The Effect of Repair Direction

In this section we explore the impact of varying the direction in which GeneRepair operates. GeneRepair has two stages; the first **error detection** phase is followed by a distinct **error correction** phase. Errors are the elements of the individual that violate the problem constraints. When multiple errors are detected, the order in which errors are corrected can impact on the resultant individual. In this paper, the order in which the errors detection operates is dictated by the repair template.

Error correction is then carried out in one of three different directional strategies: randomly changing direction, fixed Left-to-Right and fixed Right-to-Left. Duplicates are identified using a fixed replacement strategy. Error detection always begins at one end of the genome and proceeds along until a genetic error is detected. For the TSP, an error is detected when a duplicate city is found. This erroneous genetic item is then dispatched to the error correction phase. Error correction examines the ancestral genomic data to identify the missing data, using a fixed replacement strategy. Thus, the repaired information originates in the ancestral genome, as proped in *A. thaliana*.

We compare these three repair directions to further investigate the use of GeneRepair. Table 4 outlines the results created when a random grandparent template was used as a repair template and repair was carried out in the three directions listed. These results show that repair acting in a randomly changing direction produces the best minimum result and this is upheld by the fact that it also produces the lowest mean. This can be explained by the fact that repairing in a random direction increases the diversity in a solution as opposed to repairing in a fixed direction.

These early results in Table 4 also show that repairing in a right to left direction outperforms repairing in a left to right direction. This suggests that our fixed replacement strategy favours right to left repair and opens the door to further experiments where the error correction phase is also driven by the ancestral template. First, the random-varying direction was compared to the fixed Left-to-Right detection strategy (P = 0.1762) indicating that the random direction reliably produced better results. Similarly, a comparison between the random and fixed Right-to-Left directions P = 0.0384, again indicating that the random-varying direction produced the better results. These results are compounded further when we compare all four experimental sets, that is fittest and random parent and grandparent. We see that overall, repair carried out in a randomly changing direction produces the minimum lowest result and this is supported by the fact that it also has the lowest mean (Table 5).

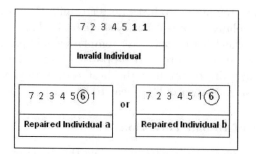

Fig. 3. Effect of Different Repair Directions

Table 4. Repair Direction - Random Grandparent and Random Great-grandparent

Template	Direction	Min	Mean	Standard Deviation
Random Grandparent	Left to Right	483	514.15	22.95
Random Grandparent	Right to Left	464	525.12	35.82
Random Grandparent	Random	453	505.54	26.37

Table 5. Repair Direction - Parent and Grandparent

Direction	Min	Mean
Left to Right	473	519.32
Right to Left	458	520.96
Random	453	515.30

5.5   Great-Grandparent Repair Template

We expanded our investigation to look at whether extending the ancestry of our repair templates produces better results. We ran experiments to look at the results produced the great-grandparent template. For this experiment we used the superior algorithmic parameters found in the results above, that is random inheritance acting in a random direction.

The minimum result produced by the great-grandparent template is lower than that produced by the parent template but the mean of the great-grandparent results is highest. The grandparent appears to produce results superior to that of the great-grandparent which leaves the door open to further investigation into the benefit of retreating further in generations versus the cost on memory. This result seems to suggest that grandparent repair introduces just the right amount of diversity, while great-grandparent produces too much diversity in the repaired populations(at least for the algorithmic parameters discussed above). This result may suggest that *A thaliana* (or other organisms) may be unlikely to access ancestral information that extends back more that two generations.

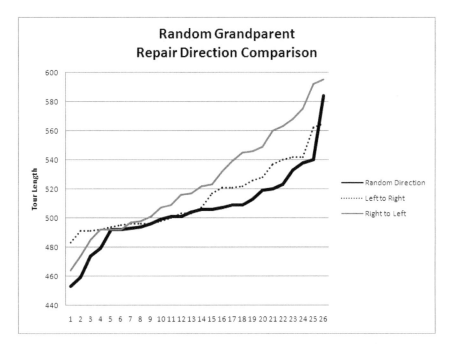

Fig. 4. Grandparent Repair Direction Comparison

Table 6. Random Grandparent and Random Great-grandparent

Template	Direction	Min	Mean
Random Parent	random	470	514.76
Random Grandparent	random	453	509.96
Random Great-grandparent	random	461	518.33

6   Conclusion

Recent advances in the study of the model organism *Arabidopsis thaliana* suggest that this plant uses a novel strategy for repairing errors to its own DNA. Lolle *et al* [1] controversially suggest that *A. thaliana* uses genetic information from the grandparent generation to repair errors that occur in the grandchild generation.

   In this paper we present a new (and largely domain independent) strategy for enforcing constraints on the search space of an Evolutionary Optimisation process. The new evolutionary optimisation is inspired by the phenomenon of non-Mendelian inheritance contentiously witnessed in nature [1] by using stored genetic information from previous generations. .This is a broadly applicable strategy, unlike many approaches to enforcing constraints on evolutionary searches. This strategy repairs genetic errors using ancestral data to repair constraint violations, so that all problem constraints are obeyed. We explored a total of twelve different methods for GeneRepair in the experiments outlined above.

We began by comparing grandparent based genetic repair to the death penalty system to enforce constraints. The grandparent GeneRepair showed itself to produce significantly better results than the death penalty. In fact the result produced by the death penalty was almost four times the size of the result produced using the grandparent template GeneRepair. We went on to compare the relative performance of the following repair templates: parent, grandparent and great-grandparent. The results show that parent is the weaker template, which is in support of Lolle et al [1].

Next, we explored the influence of fitness on the results produced, based on the intuition that storing the fittest parent or grandparent would produce better results. Results showed that using a randomly selected template constantly outperforms selecting the fittest template from the appropriate ancestry. This surprising result seems to suggest that increasing the diversity of the population might play a role in grandparent based repair. We feel that this results again provides indirect support for Lolle et al.

Up to this point experiments had been carried out using repair in a constant left to right direction, so we investigated other possible directions of repair. The experiments showed that repairing in a randomly changing direction produced superior results to repairing from right to left or from left to right.

In summary, our results show that it is possible to adapt an evolutionary strategy to handle constraints in a biologically plausible manner, by amending the algorithmic parameters to repair mechanisms found in biology. This paper shows that using a grandparent or great-grandparent repair template to enforce constraints can outperform the use of a parent template (for our selected problem domain). This supports the findings of Lolle et al that non-Mendelian inheritance of genomic information can lead to stronger individuals and populations.

References

1. Lolle, S.J., Victor, J., Young, J., Pruitt, R.: Genome-wide non-mendelian inheritance of extra-genomic information in arabidopsis. Forensic Science International 434(1), 505–509 (2005)
2. Peng, Chan, Shah, Jacobsen: Increased outcrossing in hothead mutants. Nature 443(E8), 28 (2006)
3. Ray, A.: Plant genetics: Rna cache or genome trash? Nature 437(E1-E2) (2005)
4. Colorni, Dorigo, Maniezzo: Genetic algorithms and highly constrained problems: The time-table case. In: Schwefel, H.-P., Männer, R. (eds.) PPSN 1990. LNCS, vol. 496, pp. 55–59. Springer, Heidelberg (1990)
5. Coello, C.C.: Theoretical and numerical constraint handling techniques in evolutionary algorithms: A survey. Computer Methods in Applied Mechanics and Engineering 191, 1245–1287 (2002)
6. Kalanmoy, D.: An efficient constraint handling method for genetic algorithms. Computer Methods in Applied Mechanics and Engineering 2-4(186), 311–338 (2000)

7. Mitchell, G., O'Donoghue, D.P.: Generepair-repair operator for genetic algorithms. In: Cantú-Paz, E., Foster, J.A., Deb, K., Davis, L., Roy, R., O'Reilly, U.-M., Beyer, H.-G., Kendall, G., Wilson, S.W., Harman, M., Wegener, J., Dasgupta, D., Potter, M.A., Schultz, A., Dowsland, K.A., Jonoska, N., Miller, J., Standish, R.K. (eds.) GECCO 2003. LNCS, vol. 2724, pp. 235–239. Springer, Heidelberg (2003)
8. FitzGerald, A., O'Donoghue, D.P.: Genetic repair for optimization under constraints inspired by arabidopsis thaliana. Parallel Problem Solving From Nature, 399–408 (2008)
9. Arroyo, C.: A parallel repair genetic algorithm to solve the unit commitment problem. IEEE Transactions on Power Systems 17(4) (2002)
10. Mitchell, G.: Evolutionary computation applied to combinatorial optimisation problems. Dublin City University (2007)
11. Nakano, R., Yamado, T.: Conventional genetic algorithm for job shop problems. In: Proc. 4th International Conference on Genetic Algorithms, pp. 474–479 (1991)
12. Michalewicz, Z., Fogel, D.B.: How to solve it: modern heuristics, 1st edn. Springer, Heidelberg (2000)
13. Frugoli, J.: Medicago truncatula handbook. Clemson University (November 2006)
14. Coghlan, A.: Rogue weeds defy rules of genetics. New Scientist 2492, 8 (2005)
15. Weigel, Jurgens: Hothead healer. Nature 434, 443 (2005)
16. Matsumoto, M., Nishimura, T.: Mersenne twister: A 623-dimensionally equidistributed uniform pseudo-random number generator. ACM Transactions on Modeling and Computer Simulation 8(1), 3–30 (1998)
17. Reinalt, G.: Tsplib - a travelling salesman problem library. OSRA Journal of Computing 3, 376–384 (1991)

A Machine Learning System for Identifying Hypertrophy in Histopathology Images*

Ross Foley, William Gallagher, Sean Callanan, and Pádraig Cunningham

University College Dublin
ross.foley@ucd.ie

Abstract. A substantial shift is occurring in the field of histopathology towards the digital domain with the increasing adoption of digital microscopy and large image databases. There is a growing need for image analysis tools that can efficiently and objectively analyse this wealth of digital image data. This paper presents preliminary results on the development of a suite of such tools for the measurement of toxic effects in the liver. We present an automated procedure for the measurement of one toxic effect, centrilobular hypertrophy, and present an evaluation of the components of this process. Centrilobular hypertrophy is a condition whereby liver cells in the region of central veins expand in response to a toxin. Our classification process has three stages. The first stage involves detecting the central veins using an interest point detection technique. In the second stage, the interest points are re-ranked to reduce the incidence of false positives. The third stage entails training a classifier to score the tissue in the regions of the putative central veins as hypertrophic or normal.

1 Introduction

As computing technology advances at a rapid pace worldwide, the impact is starting to be seen in the field of histopathology. Digital imaging offers a wealth of advantages over traditional microscopy procedures, including storage of image data for later use, automation of image analysis tasks, and the application of novel image processing and machine learning techniques.

Automated image analysis approaches can serve as a valuable aid to clinical pathologists and systems biology researchers in the domain of histopathology generally and in the domain of toxicology and drug discovery specifically by offering high throughput, reliable and quantifiable analysis of data.

In histopathology, pathologists traditionally analyse each slide under a microscope which is a labour intensive and time consuming process. Due to increasing numbers of images being created, this method is rapidly becoming unfeasible as it represents a substantial bottleneck in the analysis procedure. Furthermore, Inter- and intra-observer repeatability studies have shown that fatigue as a result of increased work loads, along with subjectivity and basic human error can lead to considerable reduction in the accuracy of results[1, 2].

* This research was supported by the IRCSET funded PhD programme in Bioinformatics and Computational Biomedicine bioinformatics.ucd.ie/phd/.

L. Coyle and J. Freyne (Eds.): AICS 2009, LNAI 6206, pp. 72–81, 2010.
© Springer-Verlag Berlin Heidelberg 2010

A suite of tools that carry out some of the more time consuming analysis tasks and those tasks that require exact quantification would be of great benefit in addressing these challenges. We are working on the development of such a suite of tools for a number of toxic effects in the liver. Although there is evidence of solutions developed for individual pathologies in the liver[3, 4], to the best of our knowledge, a platform such as the one proposed here does not exist. As a first step, we undertook the task of developing a system for the accurate detection and quantification of one effect, centrilobular hypertrophy in the liver.

2   The Challenge: Quantification of Hypertrophy

The liver is a vital organ in human beings and indeed all vertebrates. One of the primary functions of the liver is to serve as the bodies blood filtration system. Blood passes through the liver and is detoxified in the process. The liver consists of a very large number (typically hundreds) of roughly hexagonal shaped regions known as lobules shown in Fig. 1(a). Each lobule consists of a central vein and a number of portal regions dotted around its perimeter as shown in Fig. 1(b). Each portal region consists of a portal vein, a hepatic artery and one or more bile ducts. Blood containing various toxins enters the liver through the central veins and is filtered through the hepatocytes (liver cells), which remove toxins. The filtered blood leaves the liver through the portal veins.

Hypertrophy is a condition whereby the liver cells, known as hepatocytes, expand in response to a toxin or otherwise (starvation can also cause this effect). The condition is called centrilobular hypertrophy when the effect is only seen in the region immediately surrounding the central vein, also known as the centrilobular region. It is characterised by increased cell area and a breakdown of the sinusoidal architecture, seen in Fig. 2(b) as a reduction in whitespace between hepatocytes. An important property of hypertrophy, from a drug discovery perspective, is that it is an adaptive response to a toxin and is therefore one of the very first effects that is observed. The detection of hypertrophy in a drug discovery study can lead to its discontinuation at an early stage with considerable savings of both time and

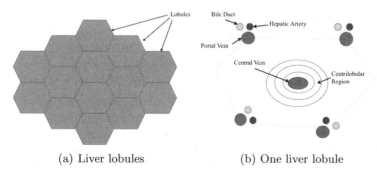

(a) Liver lobules   (b) One liver lobule

Fig. 1. Structure of the liver

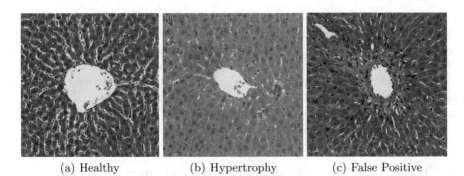

(a) Healthy   (b) Hypertrophy   (c) False Positive

Fig. 2. Centrilobular hypertrophy

money. A system that can accurately and reliably detect and quantify centrilobular hypertrophy is therefore very desirable.

3   Automated Hypertrophy Classification

The long term objective is to automate the process of accurately quantifying the level of hypertrophy in liver images. Such a system would be of considerable value as it would formalise a process in histopathology that is quite subjective and thus subject to the effects of inter- and intra-rater variation discussed in section 1. However, for the purposes of this preliminary investigation our objective is to implement a binary classification system between hypertrophic and normal liver images.

The procedure we are developing towards this binary classification consists of three steps

1. Extract putative central vein regions using an interest point detector.
2. Re-rank the results of the interest point detector so as to remove false positives, an example of which, a portal region, can be seen in Fig. 2(c).
3. Perform a binary classification on each of the re-ranked central vein regions.

3.1   Evaluation of Interest Point Detectors

Interest point detectors are operators that discover maxima and minima in an image based on some criteria such as intensity or texture. Many different interest point detectors exist, each with a different interpretation of what defines a point as "interesting" in an image. As a precursor to Step 1 of the procedure outlined above, an evaluation of three different interest point detectors was carried out.

Harris Corner Detector. Returns maxima at points where a patch of pixels centred on that point is highly different from other shifted overlapping patches close by. It therefore finds points of high change[5].

Difference of Gaussians (DoG). Approximates a second derivative of intensity and therefore discovers points of high intensity change within the image[6].

Fast Radial Symmetry (FRS). Returns maxima at bright radially symmetric (circular) points[7].

3.1.1 Fast Radial Symmetry Interest Point Detector

Loy and Zelinsky [7] proposed a transform that utilises local symmetry to determine points of interest in an image. Major advantages of this transform are the low-computational complexity and fast run-time. The transform is calculated at one or more radii $n \in N$, where N is a set of preselected radii. For each radius n an *orientation projection image* O_n and a *magnitude projection image* M_n are calculated. These images are generated by first calculating the intensity gradient $\mathbf{g}$ at each point $\mathbf{p}$ in the image, using a Sobel filter. Fig 3 shows that for each $\mathbf{p}$ a corresponding *positively-affected pixel* $\mathbf{p}_{+ve}(\mathbf{p})$ and *negatively-affected pixel* $\mathbf{p}_{-ve}(\mathbf{p})$ can be determined from the direction of the gradient vector $\mathbf{g}(\mathbf{p})$. The *positively-affected pixel* is defined as the pixel that $\mathbf{g}(\mathbf{p})$ is pointing to, a distance n away from $\mathbf{p}$, and the *negatively-affected pixel* is the pixel a distance n away that the gradient is pointing directly away from.

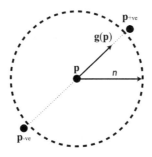

Fig. 3. Pixels $\mathbf{p}_{+ve}(\mathbf{p})$ and $\mathbf{p}_{-ve}(\mathbf{p})$ affected by the gradient $\mathbf{g}(\mathbf{p})$ for the radius n. The circle shows all possible pixels that can be affected by the gradient of $\mathbf{p}$ for radius n.

The coordinates of the positively and negatively affected pixels are

$$\mathbf{p}_{+ve}(\mathbf{p}) = \mathbf{p} + \mathrm{round}\left(\frac{\mathbf{g}(\mathbf{p})}{||\mathbf{g}(\mathbf{p})||^n}\right), \tag{1}$$

$$\mathbf{p}_{-ve}(\mathbf{p}) = \mathbf{p} - \mathrm{round}\left(\frac{\mathbf{g}(\mathbf{p})}{||\mathbf{g}(\mathbf{p})||^n}\right) \tag{2}$$

respectively, where "round" rounds each vector element to the nearest integer.

The orientation and projection images are initially zero. For each $\mathbf{p}$ the corresponding point $\mathbf{p}_{+ve}$ in O_n and M_n is incremented by 1 and $||\mathbf{g}(\mathbf{p})||$ respectively, while the corresponding point $\mathbf{p}_{-ve}$ is decremented by the same values in O_n and M_n. Mathematically

$$O_n(\mathbf{p}_{+ve}(\mathbf{p})) = O_n(\mathbf{p}_{+ve}(\mathbf{p})) + 1 \tag{3}$$

$$O_n(\mathbf{p}_{-ve}(\mathbf{p})) = O_n(\mathbf{p}_{-ve}(\mathbf{p})) - 1 \tag{4}$$

$$M_n(\mathbf{p}_{+ve}(\mathbf{p})) = M_n(\mathbf{p}_{+ve}(\mathbf{p})) + ||\mathbf{g}(\mathbf{p})|| \qquad (5)$$

$$M_n(\mathbf{p}_{-ve}(\mathbf{p})) = M_n(\mathbf{p}_{-ve}(\mathbf{p})) - ||\mathbf{g}(\mathbf{p})|| \qquad (6)$$

O_n and M_n are then combined in the symmetry measure function F_n

$$F_n(\mathbf{p}) = \left(\frac{\tilde{O}_n(\mathbf{p})}{\kappa}\right)^{\alpha} \left(\frac{M_n(\mathbf{p})}{\kappa}\right) \qquad (7)$$

where

$$\tilde{O}_n(\mathbf{p}) = \begin{cases} |O_n(\mathbf{p})| & \text{if } |O_n| < \kappa \\ \kappa & \text{otherwise} \end{cases}$$

κ is a normalisation parameter and α is a radial strictness parameter. A low value for α (e.g. $\alpha = 1$) accepts features with bilateral symmetry whereas higher values (e.g. $\alpha > 2$) ensure strict radial symmetry. We have chosen $\alpha = 2$ as a reasonable compromise. A smooth symmetry measure function S_n is produced by convolving F_n with a two-dimensional Gaussian filter A_n

$$S_n = F_n * A_n$$

The full transform is then computed as the sum of the symmetry contributions of all of the preselected radii,

$$S = \sum_{n \in N} S_n \qquad (8)$$

3.2   Evaluation of Classifiers

Similar evaluations were carried out for both the re-ranking process and the hypertrophy versus normal classification. These evaluations are fully detailed in sections 4.2 & 4.3. The use of discriminate features is of vital importance when carrying out a classification task. Two sets of texture features, Haralick and multiwavelet, are used in both of the classification processes in this paper. These features are described in detail below.

3.2.1   Haralick Features

A common approach to analysing texture in histological and other images is based on features computed from the graylevel co-occurrence matrix (GLCM) of an image[8, 9]. One element of the GLCM, $G_{i,j}$, is calculated by counting how often pixels of some intensity, i are found in a specified spacial relationship with pixels of some other intensity, j. The GLCM is constructed by repeating this process for all pairs of intensities i and j. Each element in the GLCM, therefore, represents the probability $p(i,j)$ of a pixel with gray-level intensity i having a neighbouring pixel with gray-level intensity j. Because features computed from the GLCM consider the values of two neighboring pixels, they are termed second-order texture features, in contrast to first-order measures of textures such as mean and standard deviation, which do not specifically account for relationships between pixels. Two GLCMs with different spatial relationships were produced for the purposes of this research, recording both horizontal and vertical adjacency.

Harlick [10] introduced a number of commonly used second order texture features, four of which have been used in our analysis.

$$\text{Contrast} = \sum_{i,j} |i - j|^2 p(i,j) \tag{9}$$

$$\text{Correlation} = \sum_{i,j} \frac{(i - \mu i)(j - \mu j) p(i,j)}{\sigma_i \sigma_j} \quad \text{where} \quad \begin{array}{l} \mu = \text{mean} \\ \sigma = \text{standard deviation} \end{array} \tag{10}$$

$$\text{Energy} = \sum_{i,j} p(i,j)^2 \tag{11}$$

$$\text{Homogeneity} = \sum_{i,j} \frac{p(i,j)}{1 + |i - j|} \tag{12}$$

3.2.2 Multiwavelet Features

Wavelets are mathematical functions that cut up a signal, in this case an image, into different frequency components and then study each component with a resolution matched to its scale. They have advantages over traditional Fourier analysis where the signal contains spikes or discontinuities[11]. While a scalar wavelet transform uses only one scaling function, a multiwavelet transform uses multiple scaling functions. Multiwavelets have important advantages over scalar wavelets. Multiwavelets, unlike scalar wavelets, can possess important signal processing properties such as short support, orthogonality and symmetry simultaneously[12]. Multiwavelets have been found to outperform scalar wavelets in medical image analysis[13, 14].

In multiwavelet analysis, the multiscaling function

$$\mathbf{\Phi}(t) = [\phi_1(t), \ldots, \phi_r(t)]^T$$

satisfies a two-scale dilation equation

$$\mathbf{\Phi}(t) = \sqrt{2} \sum_k L_k \mathbf{\Phi}(2t - k) \tag{13}$$

where L_k is an $r \times r$ matrix of low-pass filter coefficients and r is known as multiplicity. A multiplicity of $r = 2$ is used in this paper. Similar to the multiscaling function, the multiwavelet function

$$\mathbf{\Psi}(t) = [\psi_1(t), \ldots, \psi_r(t)]^T$$

must satisfy the two-scale wavelet equation

$$\mathbf{\Psi}(t) = \sqrt{2} \sum_k H_k \mathbf{\Phi}(2t - k) \tag{14}$$

where H_k is an $r \times r$ matrix of high-pass filter coefficients.

(13) and (14) can be represented by a multiwavelet filterbank such as that shown in Fig. 4.

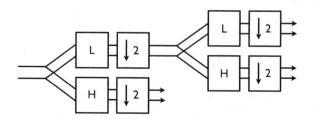

Fig. 4. Tree structured multiwavelet filterbank performing two levels of decomposition

Since both the high- and low-pass filter coefficients are matrices they must multiply vectors (instead of scalars). This brings about the need for a preprocessing step where the input signal is vectorised. There are a number of different approaches taken for this preprocessing step[12, 15, 16] but in this paper we incorporate *critical sampling* as it has been shown to yield better classification results on histology images[14]. In this approach the input signal is preprocessed such that a critically sampled representation is maintained. Since $r = 2$ in this case, we require two input streams. If the signal enters at rate R the preprocessing step provides two streams of rate $\frac{R}{2}$.

Strela et al. [12] proposed a method for performing the multiwavelet transform on images whereby the one-dimensional algorithm is carried out separately on the horizontal (row) and vertical (column) dimensions. Fig. 5 shows the resulting submatrices after each step in the process. Each entry of the matrix after one level of decomposition shown in Fig. 5(c) represents one subband, corresponding to low-pass (L) or high-pass (H) filters in the horizontal (*letter to the right*) or vertical direction (*letter to the left*) and taking the first (1) or second (2) output channel. The second level of decomposition is carried out by applying the same process to the four low-low-pass submatrices in the upper-lefthand quadrant of the matrix in Fig. 5(c). The result of this is shown in Fig. 5(d). This process is repeated for each subsequent level of decomposition. The number of submatrices produced is equal to $4 + 12l$ where l is the number of levels of decomposition.

Jafari-Khouzani and Soltanian-Zadeh [14] demonstrated that the second level of decomposition is less sensitive to noise and yields more robust features. We therefore use features computed from the second level of decomposition in this paper. The following two features are computed from each of the 28 submatrices of the second level of decomposition and are used in the classification process

$$\text{Energy} = \frac{\sum_i \sum_j x_{ij}^2}{N \times N} \tag{15}$$

$$\text{Entropy} = \frac{-1}{\log N^2} \sum_i \sum_j \left[\frac{x_{ij}^2}{\text{norm}^2} \right] \log \left[\frac{x_{ij}^2}{\text{norm}^2} \right] \tag{16}$$

where $\text{norm}^2 = \sum_i \sum_j x_{ij}^2$ and N is the dimension of each submatrix.

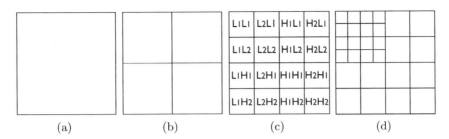

Fig. 5. Decomposition of Image. (a) Original image. (b) After preprocessing of rows and columns. (c) First level of decomposition. (d) Second level of decomposition.

4   Evaluation

Three distinct evaluations are detailed in this section, the evaluation of the interest point detectors, the evaluation of the re-ranking process and finally the evaluation of the hypertrophy vs normal classifier.

4.1   Evaluation of Interest Point Detectors

As part of this evaluation, all central vein regions were annotated in five liver images. This totaled approximately 80 - 90 regions per slide. The interest point detectors were then applied to these slides and the interest points detected by each were recorded. A detection was deemed to be correct if it lay within a specified pixel distance of the centre of an annotated region, otherwise the detection was deemed to be a false response. *Precision* and *Recall* rates were calculated for each detector given by

$$Precision = \frac{TP}{TP + FP} \quad Recall = \frac{TP}{TP + FN}$$

where TP, FP & FN are the numbers of true positives, false positives and false negatives respectively.

For the purposes of our system, the more important attribute is precision, since we do not need to retrieve all of the central vein regions in the image, but we should be highly confident that the regions that we do retrieve are indeed central vein regions. The results of the evaluation are given in Table 1.

Table 1. Evaluation of Interest Point Detectors

Interest Point Detector	Precision	Recall
Fast Radial Symmetry	82%	48%
Harris Corner Detector	49%	92%
Difference of Gaussians	41%	89%

The FRS detector achieved the highest precision with more than acceptable recall and was therefore chosen as the interest point detector for our system.

4.2 Evaluation of the Re-ranking Process

Even with the high precision of 82% achieved by the FRS detector, we are still left with 18% false positives. A subsequent classification of the returned set of regions would help to increase the precision by removing these false positives. In order to carry out an evaluation of the re-ranking process, 40 regions returned from the FRS detector from a range of images were labelled, 20 as central vein regions and 20 as false responses. For each region, 4 patches were extracted from the area immediately surrounding the central white space (above, below, left and right) and assigned the same label. The texture features described in sections 3.2.1 & 3.2.2 were then calculated for each of the 160 patches and an SVM classifier with a linear kernel was used to classify each of the patches. A 5 fold cross validation technique was incorporated so that none of the patches used in the training process originated from the same images as the patches in the test set. The classification scores for each 4 constituent patches were aggregated to classify each region. An overall accuracy of 75% was achieved.

4.3 Preliminary Classification Results

An evaluation of a hypertrophy versus normal classifier was carried out using 20 images labelled by a pathologist, 10 hypertrophy and 10 normal. 5 regions returned from the FRS detector were selected from each of the 20 images. As in section 4.2 features were extracted from 4 patches in each region giving a total of 400 patches to be classified. Again an SVM classifier was used and the same 5 fold cross validation technique was utilised. The classification scores for the 4 constituent patches in each region were aggregated to give a classification score for the region. Additionally, the classification scores for the 5 constituent regions within each image were aggregated to give an overall classification score for the image. An overall accuracy of 80% was achieved.

5 Conclusions and Future Work

It is clear from the results achieved in the classification evaluations that the Haralick and multiwavelet features are suitable for distinguishing between the classes in both cases. We will combine these two steps with the output of the FRS detector to create a system for the accurate detection of centrilobular hypertrophy. The long term goal is not only the detection but also the quantification of centrilobular hypertrophy. We will use the results of the detection system to develop a metric for the accurate quantification of hypertrophy within an image.

References

[1] Cross, S.S.: Grading and scoring in histopathology. Histopathology, 99–106 (August 1998)
[2] Cross, S.S.: Observer accuracy in estimating proportions in images: implications for the semiquantitative assessment of staining reactions and a proposal for a new system. J. Clin. Pathol. 54(5), 385–390 (2001)

[3] O'Brien, M.J., Keating, N.M., Elderiny, S., Cerda, S., Keaveny, A.P., Afdhal, N.H., Nunes, D.P.: An assessment of digital image analysis to measure fibrosis in liver biopsy specimens of patients with chronic hepatitis c. Am. J. Clin. Pathol. 114(5), 712–718 (2000)

[4] Matalka, Ismail, I., Al-Jarrah, Omar, M., Manasrah, Toqa, M.: Quantitative assessment of liver fibrosis: a novel automated image analysis method. Liver International 26(9), 1054–1064 (2006)

[5] Harris, C., Stephens, M.: A combined corner and edge detection. In: Proceedings of the Fourth Alvey Vision Conference, pp. 147–151 (1988)

[6] Wilson, H., Giese, S.: Threshold visibility of frequency gradient patterns. Vision Res. 17(10), 1177–1190 (1977)

[7] Loy, G., Zelinsky, A.: Fast radial symmetry for detecting points of interest. Pattern Analysis and Machine Intelligence 25(8), 959–973 (2003)

[8] Hamilton, P.W., Bartels, P.H., Thompson, D., Anderson, N.H., Montironi, R., Sloan, J.M.: Automated location of dysplastic fields in colorectal histology using image texture analysis. The Journal of Pathology 182(1), 68–75 (1997)

[9] Diamond, J.: The use of morphological characteristics and texture analysis in the identification of tissue composition in prostatic neoplasia. Human Pathology 35(9), 1121–1131 (2004)

[10] Haralick, R.M.: Statistical and structural approaches to texture. Proceedings of the IEEE 67(5), 786–804 (1979)

[11] Graps, A.: An introduction to wavelets. IEEE Computational Science & Engineering 2(2), 50–61 (1995)

[12] Strela, V., Heller, P.N., Strang, G., Topiwala, P., Heil, C.: The application of multiwavelet filterbanks to image processing. IEEE Transactions on Image Processing 8(4), 548–563 (1999)

[13] Soltanianzadeh, H.: Comparison of multiwavelet, wavelet, haralick, and shape features for microcalcification classification in mammograms. Pattern Recognition 37(10), 1973–1986 (2004)

[14] Jafari-Khouzani, K., Soltanian-Zadeh, H.: Multiwavelet grading of pathological images of prostate. IEEE Transactions on Biomedical Engineering 50(6), 697–704 (2003)

[15] Xia, X.G., Geronimo, J.S., Hardin, D.P., Suter, B.W.: Design of prefilters for discrete multiwavelet transforms. IEEE Transactions on Signal Processing 44(1), 25–35 (1996)

[16] Hardin, D.P., Roach, D.W.: Multiwavelet prefilters. 1. orthogonal prefilters preserving approximation order p⩽2. IEEE Transactions on Circuits and Systems II: Analog and Digital Signal Processing 45(8), 1106–1112 (1998)

Creating Visualizations: A Case-Based Reasoning Perspective

Jill Freyne[1] and Barry Smyth[2,*]

[1] CSIRO Tasmanian ICT Center
GPO Box 1538, Hobart, 7001, Australia
jill.freyne@csiro.au
[2] CLARITY: Centre for Sensor Web Technologies
School of Computer Science and Informatics
University College Dublin,
Dublin, Ireland
barry.smyth@ucd.ie

Abstract. Visualization is among the most powerful of data analysis techniques and is readily available in standalone systems or components of everyday software packages. In recent years much work has been done to design and develop visualization systems with reduced entry and usage barriers in order to make visualization available to the masses. Here we describe a novel application of case-based reasoning techniques to help users visualize complex datasets. We exploit an online visualization service, Many Eyes and explore how case based representation of datasets including simple features such as size and content types can produce recommendations of visualization types to assist novice users in the selection of appropriate visualizations.

1 Introduction

Manipulating complex data is now a familiar part of our everyday lives. and to help us there are a wide range of data analysis tools, from general purpose spreadsheets to more complex statistical analysis packages. Visualization is among the most powerful of data analysis techniques and is readily available either as standalone systems or as key components of common software packages such as spreadsheets. Great strides have been made in bringing a wide range of visualization options to the masses. For example, Microsoft's Excel offers 11 different types of chart (bar, line, pie etc.) and a total of 73 basic variations on these charts. Apple's Numbers spreadsheet is similarly well equipped and even Google's free Spreadsheets programme offers access to about 25 different variations of 6 different chart types.

Surely all of this puts sophisticated visualization within reach of the average user? The problem, of course, is that the average user is not a visualization expert

---

* This work was supported by the Australian Government through the Intelligent Island Program, CSIRO and Science Foundation Ireland through Grant No. 07/CE/I1147.

L. Coyle and J. Freyne (Eds.): AICS 2009, LNAI 6206, pp. 82–91, 2010.

and producing the right sort of visualization for a given dataset is far from trivial. Previous work in the area of visualization recommendation includes research into articulated task-orientated systems [4], early data property based systems [9,8], hybrid task and data based systems which examine both user intent and the data at hand [11,2] and more recent work which aims to discover patterns in user behaviour in preparation of a dataset in order to predict visualization requirements [6]. This work returns to the early data property based research as we exploit case-based reasoning techniques to make visualization recommendations. We believe that case-based reasoning [1] is very well suited to providing useful assistance in this type of task and in this paper we describe a case-based recommender system that is designed to do just this.

The starting point for this work is a Web based "social" visualization platform called *Many Eyes* that was created by the Visual Communication Lab in IBM Research's Collaborative User Experience group [10]. In brief, Many Eyes is a web-based visualization platform that allows users to upload datasets, chose from a wide variety of visualizations, and make the results available to others. To date over 33,000 datasets have been uploaded by nearly 8,000 users, creating 24,000 different visualizations. These "visualization experiences" encode important visualization knowledge in terms of the decisions taken by a user about how to visually represent a given dataset. In this way each visualization can be viewed as a *case*, with features of the dataset providing the *case specification* and the resulting visualization configuration providing the *case solution*. In this paper we propose that these visualization cases can be reused in the context of a new dataset, to make suggestions about appropriate visualizations.

2   Many Eyes

Many Eyes (http://manyeyes.alphaworks.ibm.com)is an online browser based visualization tool designed specifically to make sophisticated visualization easily accessible to web users but also to make the process of visualization a social one, where people can come together to discover and share what they see in publicly visualized data [10]. Many Eyes differs from other visualization software in its privacy constraints. All human contributed data is visible to the public, all datasets, visualizations and comments are publicly accessible. As Many Eyes is an experimental system the visualization options vary from the ordinary (histograms and pie charts) to experimental (word trees and matrix charts) and users have little assistance other than small graphics and a short textual description when choosing a visualization for their dataset.

Many Eyes has three core processes, data upload, visualization creation and social discovery and discussion. Due to the system's open access policy each process can be undertaken independently, for example any user can create a visualization on any data set contributed or comment on any data set or visualization created. This platform creates an ideal online environment for collaboration, cooperation and communication around a set of data and its visualizations.

2.1 Data Upload

Raw data uploaded to ManyEyes an be freeform text or tab-delimited data. In an effort to keep entry barriers to using Many Eyes low the system has the capability to recognise and process tab-delimited data, allowing users to copy data directly from Microsoft Excel or Open Office. Many Eyes carries out initial analysis on all tabular data at upload time and makes assumptions as to the type of data, textual or numeric, contained in each column. All datasets are accompanied by metadata. Uploaders are required to provide textual information such as a title for the dataset and encouraged to provide other relevant information such as the source and description of the data. The system appends further metadata including the creation date and creator's details before making it public.

2.2 Visualization Creation

Many Eyes has 6 categories of visualizations, containing a total of 16 visualization types some of which can be further sub-categorized. Maps for example can be broken down into country specific maps. Users are shown a predefined list of visualization categories and types (see Fig. 1). Sample category titles include "track rises and falls over time", "analyze text" and "seeing the world" amongst others. Each subcategory or chart type in the option list is accompanied by 1-2 explanatory sentences to guide the user in their decisions. Further information relating to each chart type describing its strengths and weaknesses and its appropriateness for varying data types is available but users must navigate away from their current process in order to locate this information [5]. Understandably not all of the visualization types in Many Eyes are suitable for displaying both unstructured text and tabular data. Six of the 33 visualization types have been used for text data visualization and 31 of the visualization types have been used to chart tabular data. On selection of a chart type Many Eyes automatically generates a visualization, assigning chart parameters etc when only one suitable option is available and asking for user conformation when multiple options exist.

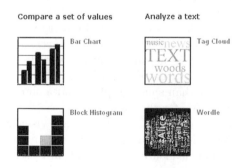

Fig. 1. Selection of category and visualization types in Many Eyes

2.3 Sharing and Discovery

Many Eyes was designed to enable a new kind of social data analysis. Its development team believe that visualization is a catalyst for discussion and collective insight about data and as such they designed Many Eyes as a collaborative visualization tool, providing users with a platform for discovery, sharing and discussion around people, datasets and visualizations. Each registered member has a public profile page which contains personal details, watchlists, topic hubs and details of activity on the site. Users may communicate directly with each other via profile pages or communicate around a specific dataset or visualization.

In the context of the "knowledge worker", the availability of datasets and associated visualizations provides a rich environment from which non expert visualizers can learn. Novice or inexperienced users may discover datasets similar to theirs in order to decide how to effectively uncover the messages contained in their raw data. Many Eyes provides various methods for browsing and searching its repository of data and visualization pairs. We believe that case-based reasoning techniques could automate the process of discovering suitable visualizations for contributed datasets. By creating cases which represent simple dataset features such as the presence of numeric and textual content as well as the size of the dataset we aim to capture the expertise demonstrated by expert visualizers to assist users in selecting the best chart for their data.

3 The Many Eyes Dataset

The dataset used for this work represents approximately 21 months of usage of Many Eyes from January 2007 and covers 33,656 separate dataset uploads and 24,166 unique visualizations from 15,888 registered users. It is worth noting that only about 43% of uploaded datasets are actually successfully visualized. In other words 19,111 datasets are not associated with any visualizations. In turn, just over 60% of users who uploaded datasets went on to store a visualization. This is surely a telling comment on the challenges faced by users when it comes to choosing and configuring suitable visualizations of their data. It seems that in many cases users just did not have the visualization experience (or the time) to select from the many different charting options and configurations that are offered. In general there are two basic types of dataset in Many Eyes. *Text* datasets are a *bag-of-word* type datasets whereas *tabular* datasets are the more traditional column-based datasets, using a mixture of data types. Text datasets can be visualized using a limited set of specialized visualizations (e.g., matrix charts, tree-maps, or tag-clouds). In total 4702 text datasets were visualized resulting in 7090 visualizations (1.5 per dataset). The visualization of 9880 tabular datasets resulted in 16,848 different visualizations (1.7 per dataset). There are 16 core Many Eyes visualization options that are well suited for tabular data.

4 A Case-Based Recommender for Many Eyes

The Many Eyes repository of datasets and visualizations is more than a simple collection of raw dataset and charts. It is reasonable to assume that each combination of dataset and chart is the result of a deliberate visualization exercise. As such it encodes some latent decision making process by which the dataset 'owner' came to settle on a particular visualization option which addressed his/her particular objectives. Of course such objectives may extend beyond the simple need to visually summarise a particular dataset. In many cases it is reasonable to assume, for example, that the user will have considered the aesthetics of particular visualization choices, adding an extra dimension to their decision making.

In short then, the combination of dataset and visualization encodes an *experience*. It is a *case* in the classical view of case-based reasoning. And in this paper we propose to take advantage of this perspective in order to develop a case-based recommender system that is capable of suggesting good visualizations to users based on the characteristics of their particular dataset. This will be of particular interest and benefit to less experienced Many Eyes users, who, in the past, have failed to produce visualizations for their datasets. Of course the recommendations may also be of interest to more experienced users by highlighting alternative visualization options that they may be less familiar with.

To this end we propose to augment the existing Many Eyes system with a CBR component. The role of this component is as follows. When a new dataset is selected the CBR system converts the dataset into a suitable set of features and uses these features to find a set of similar cases from the visualization case base. The visualizations associated with these cases are ranked and returned to the user as a set of recommendations. In the following sections we will summarise the case representation, retrieval, and ranking techniques that are used.

4.1   Case Representation

We will begin by assuming each case represents a single visualization of a single dataset. Thus, each case, c_i is made up of a dataset component, d_i and a visualization component, v_i as shown in Equation 1. In fact there is also additional information that is also sometimes available such as the rating associated with a particular visualization, r_i. In case-based reasoning parlance the dataset component corresponds to the *specification* part of a case, the visualization component corresponds to the *solution* part of a case, and the rating component can be viewed as the *outcome* of the solution. In this paper we will focus on the specification and solution side of visualizations cases, largely because the Many Eyes dataset is very sparse when it comes to the availability of ratings data.

$$c_i = \{d_i, v_i\} \tag{1}$$

The representation of the visualization component is straightforward, at least for this paper, since each case solution is just the type of visualization used, $chart(v_i)$, because we are focusing at the moment on recommending a particular visualization type when faced with a new dataset. Going forward, one can envisage more complex solution features if we wish to reason about particular features of the visualization, such as the axis placement, label usage etc.

Each dataset is characterised by a set of simple features that relate to the type of data contained in the dataset. We distinguish between text and tabular datasets by extracting different features for each. For example, for text datasets we extract features that include the total number of terms (*terms*), the number of unique terms *unique*, and the terms themselves can be used as part of the specification $(t_1, ..., t_{terms})$; see Eq. 2. For tabular datasets we can extract features such as the number of textual columns, col_{txt}, the number of numeric columns, col_{num}, the number of data points (rows), *rows* and a bag-of-words textual description derived from any metadata associated with the dataset, *desc* (e.g., column headings, title etc). In the case of numeric columns we also extract features that reflect the maximum, minimum, average, and standard deviations of the column $(min_i, max_i, avg_i, dev_i)$ and for string columns we extract the number of unique strings, $unique_i$. In this way each case is represented as a feature-based dataset and solution as in Eq. 3.

$$c_i = \{terms, unique, t_1, ..., t_{terms}\}, chart(v_i) \tag{2}$$

$$c_i = \{col_{txt_1}, col_{num_1} rows, desc, type, (min_1, max_1, avg_1, dev_1|unique_1) \tag{3}$$
$$, ..., type_n, (min_n, max_n, avg_n, dev_n|unique_n), chart(v_i)$$

4.2   Similarity and Retrieval

Given a new target case c_T (made up of a particular dataset) the task of the recommender system is to locate a set of similar cases that can be used as a source of visualizations. For the purpose of this paper we concentrate on some tried and tested similarity techniques using simplified versions of the above case representations. For example, to compute the similarity between tabular dataset cases we use the similarity metric shown in Eq. 4 which simply calculates the relative difference between the number of textual and numeric columns and rows between the target dataset and the case dataset; in this instance uniform weighting is used and so $w_f = 0.33$.

$$sim(c_T, c_i) = 1 - \sum_{f \in \{col_{txt}, col_{num}, rows\}} w_f \bullet \frac{|c_T(f) - c_i(f)|}{max(c_T(f), c_i(f))} \tag{4}$$

A similar approach to similarity assessment is used for the text based dataset, by comparing the datasets by the total number of terms and total unique terms. While these similarity techniques are extremely simple, they provide a useful starting point for this work. In the evaluation section we will demonstrate that even these simple techniques work well when it comes to driving high quality recommendations, while at the same time leaving a number of options open for more sophisticated similarity techniques as part of future work. Thus, given a target case c_T we can use the above similarity techniques to produce a ranked list of n similar cases as the basis for recommendation.

4.3   Generating Recommendations

Each of the n cases retrieved will be associated with a single visualization. The same visualization type may occur in more than one case and so we can identify a set of k different visualization types from these n cases. We need a way to rank these visualizations so that those that are associated with more similar cases are preferred over those that are associated with fewer, less similar cases. To achieve this Eq. 5 scores each of the n visualizations, v_i, as the sum of the similarity scores associated with the retrieved parent cases; $chart(v_i, c_j) = 1$ if v_i is the chart used in c_j and is 0 otherwise. The result is a ranked list of visualization recommendations, $v_1, ..., v_k$ in descending order of their aggregate similarity scores as per Eq. 5

$$score(v_i, c_T, c_1, ..., c_n) = \sum_{\forall j=1...n} sim(c_T, c_j) \bullet chart(v_i, c_j) \qquad (5)$$

5   Evaluation

This work is motivated by the fact that less than half (43%) of the datasets uploaded to Many Eyes are actually visualized. We believe that this is at least in part due to the confusion of choice that faced the novice first-time uploader. Our hypothesis is that even a simple form of case-based recommendation will help to improve the visualization rate by making proactive suggestions to the user about which visualization technique might best suit their dataset. In this section we will describe the results of a recent large-scale, off-line, leave-one-out style evaluation using the live Many Eyes dataset.

5.1   Set-up

The core Many Eyes dataset was transformed into a set of 22,935 visualization cases covering 14,582 different unique datasets and 33 visualization types. These cases included 6800 text cases and 16135 tabular cases. For the purpose of this evaluation we are interested in understanding the extent to which our simple CBR strategy can produce useful visualizations, compared with a number of benchmark strategies, which differ in terms of how cases are selected or recommendations are produced. The different techniques are summarised as:

1. *CBR* - the basic CBR approach described above is used to produce a ranked list of the top k visualizations from a set of n similar cases
2. *Popular* - this strategy simply recommends the k most popular visualizations (globally) in Many Eyes.
3. *Exact* - this is a hybrid recommender strategy which identifies a pool of similar cases like the CBR approach but only identifies cases which exactly match the target features. It then calculates the popularity of each visualization type for this pool. Specifically in the case of tabular data the set of similar cases identified match the number of text and numeric columns in the target case and in the text based datasets the word count of similar cases is within a close defined range of the word count of the target dataset.
4. *PopularContext* - similar to *Popular* but it treats textual and tabular visualization types as separately
5. *Random* - recommend a set of k random visualizations.

5.2   Methodology

Our evaluation takes the form of a standard leave-one-out test. For each target case, c_T, we use its specification features to represent a new dataset and generate a set of k visualizations using each of 5 recommendation strategies; note that the k is based on the number of unique visualizations retrieved by the CBR strategy. Our first measure of quality looks at how often the target visualization is present in the set of k recommendations; so an *accuracy* of 60% means that the target visualization is present in 60% of the recommendation sets of size k. The second looks at the average position of the target visualization in the recommendation lists. There are two ways to do this. One is to focus on those recommendation lists that do have the correct target visualization and then compute the average position of the target visualization in the final recommendation list. This so-called *average position* approach ignores recommendation lists that do not contain the correct visualization though, and therefore benefits the less accurate strategies. As an alternative we can compute a position value across all recommendation lists by assigning a $k + 1$ penalty to those lists that do not contain the target visualization *adjusted position*. This is a conservative penalty because it assumes that the correct visualization is actually in position $k + 1$, which may not be, but it serves to at least remove some of the bias associated with *average position*.

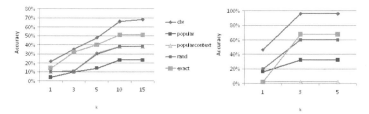

Fig. 2. Accuracy of predicted visualization types (a) tabular and (b) text

5.3   Results

Recommendation Accuracy. Fig. 2(a)-(b) show the accuracy results separately for the textual and tabular cases. These results clearly support the use of the CBR recommendation strategy. Overall CBR is seen to outperform all other techniques with particularly impressive results for the CBR technique in the easier textual case recommendation scenario. There is also a very consistent benefit associated with the similarity-based technique used by CBR compared with the simpler matching used by *Exact*, with the former delivering relative improvements of 25%-50% across a wide range of k values.

Recommendation Position. The results of the positional analysis of the recommendation techniques are presented in Fig. 3 (a)-(b). In terms of the average position statistic the local recommendation techniques such as CBR and *Exact*

are delivering improved performance compared to the global benchmarks, although there are a number of anomalies. For example in Fig 3(a), at $k = 3$, we see that CBR delivers its correct recommendations with an average position of 1.5. However, the popularity-based techniques achieve a better average position of just over 1. But remember, at this setting CBR is recommending a correct visualization among its top 3 recommendations more than 20% of the time versus 5% of the time with popularity-based approaches. By introducing a positional penalty we find that the local techniques do consistently better than all other benchmarks; see Fig. 3(c)-(d).

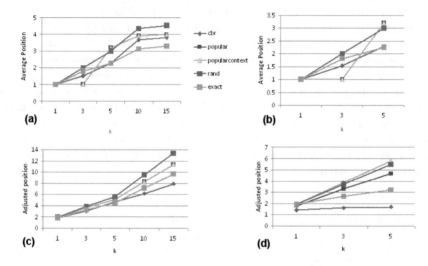

Fig. 3. Average position of the target visualizations (a) tabular, (b) textual and adjusted position of the target visualizations:(c) tabular, (d) textual

5.4   Summary

Even a relatively simple approach to case reuse has delivered useful results which may make a difference to Many Eyes users in practice. In each case we have found the case-based approach to outperform all of the other benchmarks that were tried, consistently producing more accurate recommendations nearer to the top of the recommendation list. Of course these findings need to be validated. They may be based on real-user data but they have not been tested on live users in the field. Nevertheless with these findings we can be optimistic about the prospect of success in such a future trial.

6   Conclusions

The objective is this work is to help users of a Web based visualization system to produce better visualizations by recommending visualizations that have been previously used for datasets that are similar to their own. To that end we have started with a very simple case recommendation technique, but this has performed very well in practice, significantly outperforming a number of benchmarks. However, there remains plenty of room for improvement and as future work a number of obvious next steps present themselves:

1. *More Sophisticated CBR.* Incorporating some notion of semantics into the representation and similarity computation should be possible.
2. *Introducing Adaptation.* Users will benefit greatly from configuration support when it comes to actually using a particular visualization. This includes deciding which fields are associated with which axes, scale settings, etc.
3. *Ratings & Provenance.* The Many Eyes visualization data contains rating information and information about the creator of the particular visualization that could be used to greatly improve the algorithms [3,7].

References

1. Aamodt, A., Plaza, E.: Case-based reasoning: Foundational issues, methodological variations, and system approaches. AI Communications 7(1), 39–59 (1994)
2. André, E., Rist, T.: The design of illustrated documents as a planning task, pp. 94–116 (1993)
3. Briggs, P., Smyth, B.: Provenance, trust, and sharing in peer-to-peer case- based web search. In: Althoff, K.-D., Bergmann, R., Minor, M., Hanft, A. (eds.) ECCBR 2008. LNCS (LNAI), vol. 5239, pp. 89–103. Springer, Heidelberg (2008)
4. Casner, S.M.: Task-analytic approach to the automated design of graphic presentations. ACM Trans. Graph. 10(2), 111–151 (1991)
5. Danis, C.M., Viegas, F.B.: Martin Wattenberg, and Jesse Kriss. Your place or mine? visualization as a community component. In: CHI 2008: Proceeding of the twenty-sixth annual SIGCHI conference on Human factors in computing systems, pp. 275–284. ACM, New York (2008)
6. Gotz, D., Wen, Z.: Behavior-driven visualization recommendation. In: IUI 2009: Proceedings of the 13th International Conference on Intelligent User Interfaces, pp. 315–324. ACM, New York (2009)
7. Leake, D.B., Whitehead, M.: Case provenance: The value of remembering case sources. In: Weber, R.O., Richter, M.M. (eds.) ICCBR 2007. LNCS (LNAI), vol. 4626, pp. 194–208. Springer, Heidelberg (2007)
8. Mackinlay, J.: Automating the design of graphical presentations of relational information. ACM Trans. Graph. 5(2), 110–141 (1986)
9. Roth, S.F., Kolojejchick, J., Mattis, J., Goldstein, J.: Interactive graphic design using automatic presentation knowledge. In: CHI 1994: Proceedings of the SIGCHI conference on Human factors in computing systems, pp. 112–117. ACM, New York (1994)
10. Viégas, F.B., Wattenberg, M., van Ham, F., Kriss, J., McKeon, M.: Manyeyes: A site for visualization at internet scale. IEEE Transactions on Visualization and Computer Graphics 13(6), 1121–1128 (2008)
11. Zhou, M.X., Chen, M.: Automated generation of graphic sketches by example. In: Proceedings of the Eighteenth International Joint Conference on Artificial Intelligence, pp. 65–74. Morgan Kaufmann, San Francisco (2003)

Assessing Context for
Age-Related Spanish Temporal Phrases*

Sofia N. Galicia-Haro[1] and Alexander F. Gelbukh[2]

[1] Facultad de Ciencias
Universidad Nacional Autónoma de México, México, D. F
sngh@fciencias.unam.mx
[2] Centro de Investigación en Computación
Instituto Politécnico Nacional, México, D. F
gelbukh@gelbukh.com

Abstract. This paper reports research on Spanish temporal expressions. The analyzed phrases include a common temporal expression for a period of years reinforced by an adverb of time. We found that some of those phrases are age-related expressions. We analyzed a sample obtained from the Internet to determine the local context where the age-related meaning is unmistakable. We present the results for 21 selected classes.

Keywords: temporal expressions, age of persons, local context.

1 Introduction

Some words or whole sequences of words in a text are temporal expressions: for example, *yesterday*, *Monday 12th*, *two months*, *about a year and a half*; each refers to a certain period of time. Such words or sequences of words mainly share a noun or an adverb of time: *yesterday*, *month*, *year*. This leads to the problem of automatically deciding whether a word or a sequence is a temporal expression. It is an important part of many natural language processing applications, such as question answering, machine translation, information retrieval, information extraction, text mining, etc., where robust handling of temporal expressions is necessary.

Automatic recognition of expressions of time was introduced in the Named Entity Recognition task of the Message Understanding Conferences[1], where temporal entities were tagged as "TIMEX". Since then, researchers have been developing temporal annotation schemes, for example [2] for English, [12] for the much more constrained domain of meeting scheduling.

The authors in [2] produced a guideline intended to support a variety of applications in the performance of some useful tasks. As the authors pointed out, the guideline was not intended to represent all the varieties of temporal information conveyed in natural language communication. They were interested in temporal expressions that

---

* Work partially supported by Mexican Government (CONACyT, SNI, CGPI-IPN, PIFI-IPN).
[1] http://timexportal.wikidot.com/timexmuc6

L. Coyle and J. Freyne (Eds.): AICS 2009, LNAI 6206, pp. 92–102, 2010.
© Springer-Verlag Berlin Heidelberg 2010

reference calendar dates, times of day, or durations. They considered lexical triggers to identify the temporal expressions. A lexical trigger is a word or numeric expression whose meaning conveys a temporal unit or concept. To be a trigger, the referent must be able to be oriented on a timeline, or at least oriented with relation to a time (past, present, future).

In this work, we analyzed other different temporal expressions that do not fulfill the previous trigger characteristics. These phrases are recognized by an initial adverb: for example, *around, still*; and they end with a noun of time such as *year, month*. For example[2]: *aún en los últimos años* "still in the last years", *aún en los setentas* "still in the seventies", *alrededor de año y medio* "about a year and a half", *alrededor de hace 20 años* "about 20 years ago".

We found that this type of phrase presents interesting cases. There is for example a group that describes a person's age. Automatic recognition of a person's age should be useful in question answering and machine translation tasks, among others. For example, considering the following sentence:

El quíntuple retador mundialista Lazarte no claudica en su intención de coronarse campeón del mundo, aún a sus 38 años 'The five-time World Cup challenger Lazarte did no falter in his intention to be crowned world champion, although he is 38 years old'.

Spanish native speakers would understand that the phrase *aún a sus 38 años* denotes Lazarte's age. However, general machine translators give the wrong phrases 'yet his 38 years' or 'although his 38 years'. Also, this sentence would be retrieved by a question answering system to the specific question ¿How old is Lazarte?

In this article, we present a corpus-based analysis carried out to determine the context of such temporal expressions and their automatic determination. In section 2, we present the characteristics of the phrases we are interested in. In section 3 we describe the method we applied to obtain the materials for the analysis. We present the analysis of their local context in section 4. Finally, possible future work and conclusions are presented in sections 5 and 6.

2 Adverbs and Temporal Expressions

Adverbs of time (for example: *before, today, after, tomorrow*) create cohesion and coherence by forming time continuity in the events expressed in texts [8]. They are closely associated with narrative texts but they also appear in newspaper texts, for example: *Senators will approve **today** in the morning a schedule for the debate, **after** the plenary session the coordinators will meet to establish the regulation and **tomorrow** the tribune will be liberated.*

Researchers have been interested in adverbs of time included in temporal expressions, for example [2, 10, 11]. We chose to analyze the Spanish temporal phrases that begin with an adverb of time (AdvT) and end with a noun of time (TimeN), for example:

aún a principios de los años 90 "still at the beginning of the 1990s"
aún en nuestros días "still in our days"
aún hoy día, aún hoy en día "still nowadays"
alrededor de los 20 años "about 20 years"

---

[2] The translations of the Spanish examples are literal.

These phrases present interesting issues. We can observe the relation between the groups of words in the following examples:

1. *A sus 30 años Juan se comporta como niño*
2. *Aún a sus 30 años Juan se comporta como niño*
3. *Hoy a sus 30 años Juan se comporta como niño*

The sentences describe the same main fact: *John, who is 30 years old, behaves like a child*, but they tell us something else when we introduce a modifier [1] (*aún* "still", *hoy* "today") in each one: they argue for different conclusions.

(1) Still, at 30 years old, John behaves like a child $\Rightarrow$ in spite of his age he behaves as if he were a child

(2) Today, at 30 years old, John behaves like a child $\Rightarrow$ today he behaves like a child

The adverbs "still" and "today" make such conclusions obligatory and reinforce the meaning of time in different forms. Both adverbs are related to time duration, one strict reading refers to 24 hours and the other to a longer period of time, but they also imply a direct judgment on the perception of the speaker, on the behavior of the subject or both. Finally, these conclusions are the main scientific objective of this work but here we began by trying to solve the initial step of automatic determination of such phrases.

For the analysis of temporal expressions reinforced by an adverb of time, we use one text collection compiled from a Mexican newspaper that is published daily on the Web in almost its entirety. The texts correspond to diverse sections, economy, politics, culture, sport, etc., from 1998 to 2002. The text collection has approximately 60 million words [3].

We wrote a program to extract the sentences matching the following pattern:

AdvT–something–TimeN

Where:

something – corresponds to a sequence of up to six words[3] without punctuation marks, verbs or conjunctions.

TimeN – corresponds to the following nouns of time: *año* "year", *mes* "month", *día* "day", *hora* "hour", *minuto* "minute", *segundo* "second"

AdvT – adverbs of time, a collection of 51 elements from a dictionary[4].

The extracted sentences were analyzed in [3]. From a subset of these sentences where the adverb corresponds to *actualmente* "at present", *ahora* "now", *alrededor* "around', *aún* "still', and the noun of time corresponds to *año* "year', we found some phrases expressing age of persons.

Usually the age of persons is described by Spanish temporal expressions including the time nouns *años* "years" and *meses* "months" (for babies). They can be recognized in the following ways:

---

[3] A larger quantity of words does not guarantee any relation between the AdvT and the TimeN.

[4] DRAE, Real Academia Española. (1995): *Diccionario de la Real Academia Española*, 21 edición (CD-ROM), Espasa, Calpe.

SEARCH(C)

For each phrase of type ADV-*-NounT or string-*-NounT in C

(1) Obtain 100 examples from the Internet

    (1.1) D = {examples excepting such instances where * includes verbs or punctuation}

    (1.2) Print D

(2) Classify them according to such words retrieved by *

(3) For each group of phrases sharing words retrieved by *, assign a class D_i

    (3.1) F = class D_i

    (3.2) SEARCH(F)

UNTIL no new elements are obtained

Fig. 1. Algorithm to obtain variants of temporal expressions

(1) with a string "*de edad*" ("old" in English) after the word *años*,

(2) a number and years after the person's name, delimited by commas [9],

(3) with the strings: *la edad de, de edad de* (lit. "the age of", "of the age of") before the number of years.

There are, however, other temporal expressions that describe the age of persons: for example, *aún a sus 65 años*, "still at his 65 years", *de alrededor de 20 años*, lit. "of about 20 years". These temporal phrases denote a point in the timeline of a person; it could be a point in the timeline of the events related in the sentence or a point in a tangential timeline.

We manually select one arbitrary example representing what we consider a class: a different combination of an adverb and a preposition before the number of years, the five resulting classes correspond to *aún a, aún con, actualmente de, alrededor de, ahora de*.

3 Searching for More Examples

Since our newspaper text collection contains a subset of all possible temporal phrases expressing the ages of persons, we analyzed a method to obtain a more representative group of phrases. Different possibilities exist for obtaining such variants, and we chose to look for examples on the Internet. This option allowed us to find phrases generated by native speakers more quickly, including the commoner collocations. Nevertheless, we know that searching the Internet has drawbacks, as [7] has already suggested. For example, the searching machines deliver different accounts for repetitions of the same question although this problem does not turn out to be so important in this work. One significant drawback for our work is that the results are classified in accordance with complex and unknown algorithms, so we cannot know what predispositions have been introduced for the order in which results are presented. Despite these considerations, we decided to search the Internet on the basis that we do not know how the results are classified.

The main idea of obtaining more examples from the Internet is based on getting a few examples from the newspaper texts (corresponding to the five classes above mentioned), simplifying them (eliminating determinants, adjectives, etc.) and searching for variants by including Google's asterisk facility [5]. The whole procedure is shown in Figure 1. For example: for the phrase *aún con sus jóvenes 48 años* the string when simplified becomes "*aún con año*" and the search is "*aún con * años*" using the Google search engine tool limited to the Spanish language where the asterisk substitutes for the eliminated words. Google returns hits where there is a string of words initiated by "*aún con*" then a sequence of words, ending with "*años*". The example for the whole procedure in Figure 1 is presented as follows:

SEARCH("*aún con * años*")
Step (1) 100 examples
… y el bachillerato en Lleida, *aún con dieciséis años* entró a trabajar de chico …
aun con tantos años sigo siendo el mismosde siempre**...**
… porque se dio cuenta que *aún con tantos años* encima son capaces de **...**
Un partido, *aún con pocos años* de actuación, inspirado en la Gran **...**
… y menos *aún con Nuestros años* felices (1996) o Tarde (1998)
…
Step (2)   D= { *aún con dieciséis años, aún con pocos años, aun con tantos años, aún con Nuestros años,*   … }
Step (3) For each one of the classes a new process is initiated
      SEARCH("*aún con tantos * años*")
      SEARCH("*aún con pocos * años*")
      …

The process is repeated several times until no new repeated phrases are obtained, determining the sequences of words that appear with higher frequency.

We note that in addition some phrases not corresponding to the temporal phrases we are interested in are picked up: for example, *aún con tecnología 40 años más moderna...* "still with technology 40 years more modern", this type of phrase is eliminated in the manual identification at the end of the whole process.

After this compilation of examples, we manually select 21 classes that appear in the first column of Table 1, where NUM considers numbers represented by digits or letters.

4   Context for Phrases Denoting Age of Persons

We found that some of the 21 classes obtained from the Internet seem to preserve their meaning independently of the context and others require some form of words in context to denote the age of a person. To automatically determine the meaning of these temporal phrases assessing the context is the main issue.

To analyze the context required to preserve the person's age meaning we obtain examples by searching again on the Internet. The quantity of pages automatically obtained was limited to 50, i.e. to obtain 500 snippets.

Context information is considered in this work as two words in a window surrounding the target phrase without consideration of grammatical relations of the whole sentence in an automatic form by means of software. We applied the system for automatic morphological analysis of Spanish [6] to assign parts of speech to the words of the context.

We wrote a program to classify the examples according to the context, to obtain nominal phrases, and to eliminate temporal phrases not matching the pattern AdvT–something–TimeN. We manually performed the general syntactic and semantic analysis of the context in the sentence.

In order to quantify the relations between previous and posterior context we consider:

- the verbs related to the given adverbs
- the prepositional phrases selected by the temporal phrases
- the personal nouns and names in the context, according to [4]
- the punctuation signs, mainly commas

The overall results are presented in Table 1. The second column shows the number of examples obtained, after the elimination of phrases where there is no relation between the AdvT and the TimeN. Since the examples were automatically obtained from the snippet, some of them were not considered because of the lack of text when the sentences are split and context is omitted around the searched phrase. Column 4 gives the number of these eliminated examples because of short snippet. Columns 3 and 5 show the results after syntactic and semantic analysis of the context.

Table 1. Overall results for the examples obtained from the Internet

Type of phrase	# examples	% age-related	# short snippet	# not age
aún a sus NUM años	293	96	7	5
aún hoy a sus NUM años	38	92	2	1
aún a tus NUM años	7	100	0	0
ahora a mis NUM años	182	99	1	1
aún con mis pocos NUM años	1	100	0	0
aún con mis cortos NUM años	2	100	0	0
aún con sus escasos NUM años	4	100	0	0
aún con tus casi NUM años	1	100	0	0
aún con sus casi NUM años	7	57	0	3
aún con sus NUM años	109	86	0	15
ahora de NUM años	352	86	6	45
de alrededor de NUM años	353	44	4	194
actualmente con NUM años	270	80	3	50
actualmente de NUM años	28	36	7	11
actualmente de unos NUM años	16	19	1	12
ahora con casi NUM años	118	67	0	39
ahora con más de NUM años	90	46	7	45
ahora a NUM años	112	0.9	8	103
ahora a los NUM años	132	36	2	82
alrededor de NUM años	242	16	9	194
alrededor de los NUM años	355	84	4	54

Table 2. Results of context analysis for the classes with overwhelmingly age-related meaning

	Age-related		Not age	
	Left context	**Right context**	**Left context**	**Right context**
aún a sus NUM años		**88%** de vida (4) de existencia de edad (44) cumplidos (4) VERB (148) NAMES (6) PUNCT (40)		**100%** de antigüedad de viajar de experiencia de tradición de viuda
aún hoy a sus NUM años	CONJ (23) PUNCT (9)	**35%** de edad (4) VERB (20) PUNCT (11)		**100%** de partida
aún a tus NUM años		**57%** PUNCT (4)		
ahora a mis NUM años	**61%** PUNCT (38) CONJ (72)	de edad (11) PUNCT (39)		**100%** de casada
aún con sus escasos NUM años		**100%** PUNCT (4)		
ahora de NUM años	* N/P-PCT (233) NAM/PN (18)	**86%** *PUNCT (233) de edad (26)	**71%** SER (27) periodo disponer (4)	*ahode* list

We manually analyzed the classified examples. Table 2 summarizes the results for the cases in Table 1 with more than 85% of age-related phrases. The column "Age-related" comprises the right and left context for the phrases denoting age of person; the percentage of phrases where context was identified and classified is shown in the first row. Column "No age" has the same structure. Table 3 summarizes the results for the cases in Table 1 with less than 85% of age-related phrases. The sequences of words and the part of speech appearing in the columns of right and left context correspond to the more general and more interesting patterns; for example, in the class *aún a sus NUM años* there are 34 phrases missing since they require many different patterns. The number of phrases is given in parentheses when it is bigger than one.

In the tables: VERB considers a verb related to the adverb, NAMES correspond to person's name, PUNCT comprises comma, parenthesis, semicolon, CONJ corresponds to conjunctions introducing new phrases, NAM/PN corresponds to name or personal noun, N/P-PCT comprises name or personal noun followed by elements of PUNCT, SER comprises "to be" conjugation, TENER and CONTAR, the "to have" verb. An asterisk (*) means that the left and right context is matched. {< 100} means NUM value lower than 100. {¡} means it excludes context for "No age" cases. Percent marks in bold numbers indicate the quantity of examples in the context descriptions.

Table 3. Results for the classes with age-related meaning depending on context

	Age-related		Not age	
	Left context	**Right context**	**Left context**	**Right context**
aún con sus casi NUM años	PUNCT	**100%** VERB PUNCT (2) de edad		**100%** en el mercado de servicio de vigencia
aún con sus NUM años	**PUNCT (15)	**89%** **PUNCT (42) VERB (21) CONJ (3) *acsus* list		**100%** *No_acsus* list
de alrededor de NUM años	**85%** N/P-PCT (15) NAM/PN (117)	de edad (11)	**51%** *No_dealde* list	*dealde* list
actualmente con NUM años	N/P-PCT (62) NAM/PN CONTAR (27) NAM/PN que CONTAR (13)	**48%** de edad (98) de vida (2) recién cumplidos (3) cumplidos (2)		**70%** *actcon* list
actualmente de NUM años	NAM/PN (5)	**50%** de edad (5)		
actualmente de unos NUM años		**100%** de edad N/P-PCT (2)	**100%** SER (12)	
ahora con casi NUM años	¡ {CONJ, PUNCT} (30)	**37%** PUNCT VERB (21) VERB (34)	de abandono(2)	**74%** {¡} *ahoccasi* list
ahora con más de NUM años		**64%** N/P PCT (8) VERB (16) de edad (4) encima	hasta (4)	**100%** *ahocmas*
ahora a NUM años		**100%** de edad		
ahora a los NUM años	porque (4)	**46%** de edad VERB (21)		**18%** *ahoalos* list
alrededor de NUM años	**72%** {< 100} TENER (28)	{< 100} de edad (4)	**28%** hace (47) durante (8)	
alrededor de los NUM años		**17%** de edad (51)		**41%** {< 100} (22)

We can observe that the classes *aún a sus NUM años* and *ahora de NUM años* are the best examples for context identification. The worst case is *alrededor de los NUM años*, where we notice that almost all phrases indicate an age but in a general form, for example, *el consumo de frutas se da sobre todo alrededor de los 60 años* "the consumption of fruit is mostly seen about the 60 years old".

The class *ahora de NUM años* shows an interesting property: many age-related examples have right and left context matching that includes punctuation, isolating the temporal phrase and giving a context independent meaning.

Contexts for phrases not age-related share prepositional phrases modifying the noun time: for example, *7 años de casada* "married for seven years", *7 años de cárcel* "seven years in jail". In Table 3 two asterisks (**) means that for some examples the left and right context is matched.

Some of the lists indicated in both tables by italics are enumerated in the following paragraphs and the number of cases is given in parentheses when it is bigger than one:

ahode: de antigüedad, de becas, de cárcel, de casados, de duración, más (5)

acsus: encima (3), a cuestas (4), a las espaldas, cumplidos, de edad (14), de vida (5).

No_acsus. de amistad, de aplicación (2), de estudios, de existencia, de experiencia (3), de incapacidad, de profesión, de tradición, promedio (4)

dealde: de antiguedad (15), de duración (2), de evolución, de fallecido, de gobierno (2), de investigación, de investigar, de matrimonio, de persecución, de políticas, de prisión (2), de reformas, de trabajo, luz (9)

No_dealde: una antigüedad (7), datan (19), después (11), distancia (5), duración (2), SER (17), experiencia (3), lapso (2), luego (4), vida media (2), edad media, período (22), vida (3), vida conyugal

Such lists of phrases corresponding to local context presented in Tables 2 and 3 will be the basis for future work on lexical, morphologic, syntactic, and semantic categories for these temporal expressions' structural description. In this work we have used these contexts to automatically determine the temporal phrases reinforced by an adverb that correspond to age-related expressions in a sample taken from a second Mexican newspaper.

We search in this collection for the phrases: *aún a *años*, *ahora de * años*, *ahora con casi *años*, and *actualmente de *años*. We applied the results of context analysis in more than 300 examples and only 3 cases were not detected. The errors were due to false nominal phrase identification that corresponds to the person whose age is mentioned. Although the number of examples is low, we assume that the analyzed context is very similar for these kinds of phrases since the results are very near the 100 percent mark. Also, it should be noted that we used the Google search engine (www.google.com) for Spanish language so the analyzed context in Tables 2 and 3 corresponds to examples where several dialectal variations of Spanish are considered.

5 Possible Future Work

This paper has introduced a context-based method to automatically identify person's age phrases where adverbs make obligatory some conclusions and reinforce the meaning of time in different forms. We suspected that these phrases were not confined to the Spanish language but that both language and culture influence their structures. Therefore a possible future work will consider applying the same method previously described to Italian and French languages where we found very similar examples. The following are some examples obtained from the Internet:

1. For French, we found examples similar to the Spanish phrases *alrededor de* NUM *años*, *aún a sus* NUM *años*, *aún a mis* NUM *años*, *ahora con* NUM *años*, *ahora a mis* NUM *años*, respectively:

*Quand j''avais **autour de dix ans**, je me souviens qu'il y avait trois questions métaphysiques...*
*ça se gâte **encore à ses quinze ans** où il découvre qu'il est homosexuel.... ça promet...*
*En plus du travail, il y a le sourire, la décone, etc... J'adoooooreeee.... je serais chez toi **encore à mes 95 ans**...-)) Bisous*
***Maintenant à quatre-vingts ans**, il faut stopper. — J'ai la moitié de fait. . . la meilleure moitié !*
*Il m'a dit qu'il ne voulait pas compromettre son image en emmenant son frère mineur en boîte, mais **maintenant avec mes 17 ans** c'est un peu comme si je ne ...*
2. For Italian, we found examples similar to the Spanish phrases *aún a mis* NUM *años*, *ahora de* NUM *años*, *alrededor de los* NUM *años* :
*Penso **ancora ai miei tredici anni e ai miei diciassette**, penso a quant'ero sana perché vivevo bene la mia sessualità, perchè scherzavo e ridevo come ...*
*Al punto che, ricorderò sempre una vacanza in Italia di cinque anni fa, quando scoprii che per mio figlio, **allora di otto anni**, una società omogenea era ...*
***Intorno ai vent'anni** ho vinto una borsa di studio per frequentare l'Accademia di giovani autori di Mogol, è stato per me molto importante, ...*

Although we suspect that other languages make use of the same syntactically relevant components, it is possible that they vary in terms of which component takes precedence over another and a manual intensive analysis should be performed. The analysis of other languages in the same way as in this paper will eventually give useful results for machine translation among such languages.

Another possible future work is research on speech language. Since phrases like *aún con mis pocos* NUM *años*, *aún con mis cortos* NUM *años*, *aún con sus escasos* NUM *años* , *aún con tus casi* NUM *años*, *aún con sus casi* NUM *años* are phrases which are used in everyday language and very few examples were obtained from the Internet, examples for these phrases and new examples should be obtained from oral corpora.

6   Conclusions

The variety in the structure of temporal expressions makes analysis of different combinations of classes of words necessary. We analyzed temporal expressions including the noun of time *year* that are modified by an adverb of time and the whole phrase expressing a person's age.

We first present a method to enrich the classes of temporal phrases when only a few examples are compiled. To obtain a more representative sample we compiled examples from the Internet for each class. We manually analyzed the context surrounding them to define the specific context for such expressions in order to automatically identify them. Specific context was obtained for nine of 21 classes.

The automatic identification of these phrases and their interpretation will directly benefit natural language processing tasks including: response to questions; visualization of events in lines of time; generation of phrases; translation, etc.

The temporal expressions considered present very interesting issues. The adverbs make some inferences obligatory and reinforce the meaning of time in different forms. Besides the fact of the time duration involved, they imply a direct judgment on the perception of the speaker, on the subject or both.

References

1. Carbonero Cano, P.: Tiempo y aspecto en el adverbio (a propósito de todavía, aún y ya) Estudios lingüísticos en torno a la palabra. Universidad de Sevilla, Facultad de Filología, 59–69 (1993)
2. Ferro, L., Gerber, L., Mani, I., Sundheim, B., Wilson, G.: TIDES 2003 Standard for the Annotation of Temporal Expressions, MITRE Corporation (2004)
3. Galicia-Haro, S.N.: Using Electronic Texts for an Annotated Corpus Building. In: 4th Mexican International Conference on Computer Science, ENC 2003, Mexico, pp. 26–33 (2003)
4. Galicia-Haro, S.N., Gelbukh, A., Bolshakov, I.A.: Recognition of Named Entities in Spanish Texts. In: Monroy, R., Arroyo-Figueroa, G., Sucar, L.E., Sossa, H. (eds.) MICAI 2004. LNCS (LNAI), vol. 2972, pp. 420–429. Springer, Heidelberg (2004)
5. Gelbukh, A., Bolshakov, I.A.: Internet, a true friend of translator: the Google wildcard operator. International Journal of Translation 18(1–2), 41–48 (2006)
6. Gelbukh, A., Sidorov, G.: Approach to construction of automatic morphological analysis systems for inflective languages with little effort. In: Gelbukh, A. (ed.) CICLing 2003. LNCS, vol. 2588, pp. 215–220. Springer, Heidelberg (2003)
7. Kilgarriff, A.: Googleology is Bad Science. Computational Linguistics 33, 147–151 (2007)
8. Llidó, D., Berlanga, R., Aramburu, M.J.: Extracting temporal references to assign document event-time periods. In: Mayr, H.C., Lazanský, J., Quirchmayr, G., Vogel, P. (eds.) DEXA 2001. LNCS, vol. 2113, pp. 62–71. Springer, Heidelberg (2001)
9. Mark, M., Walter, C.: Pautas para la anotación del Tiempo para Lenguas poco enseñadas (basado en los estándares de TIMEX2) Versión 1.0 Consorcio de Datos Lingüísticos (2006)
10. Saquete, E., Martinez-Barco, P.: Grammar specification for the recognition of temporal expressions. In: Proceedings of Machine Translation and multilingual applications in the new millennium, MT 2000, Exeter, UK, pp. 21.1–21.7 (2000)
11. Saquete, E., Martinez-Barco, P., Muñoz, R.: Recognizing and tagging temporal expressions in Spanish. In: Workshop on Annotation Standards for Temporal Information in Natural Language, LREC 2002 (2002)
12. Wiebe, J.M., O'Hara, T.P., Ohrstrom-Sandgren, T., McKeever, K.J.: An Empirical Approach to Temporal Reference Resolution. Journal of Artificial Intelligence Research 9, 247–293 (1998)

Using Shallow Natural Language Processing in a Just-In-Time Information Retrieval Assistant for Bloggers

Ang Gao[*] and Derek Bridge

Department of Computer Science,
University College Cork, Ireland
ang.gao87@gmail.com, d.bridge@cs.ucc.ie

Abstract. Just-In-Time Information Retrieval agents proactively retrieve information based on queries that are implicit in, and formulated from, the user's current context, such as the blogpost she is writing. This paper compares five heuristics by which queries can be extracted from a user's blogpost or other document. Four of the heuristics use shallow Natural Language Processing techniques, such as tagging and chunking. An experimental evaluation reveals that most of them perform as well as a heuristic based on term weighting. In particular, extracting noun phrases after chunking is one of the more successful heuristics and can have lower costs than term weighting. In a trial with real users, we find that relevant results have higher rank when we use implicit queries produced by this chunking heuristic than when we use explicit user-formulated queries.

1 Introduction

No longer is the Web a place where we do little more than browse and search; it is a place where we increasingly author content too. In some cases, we are authoring traditional content, in the form of essays and reports, creating them through our browsers and storing them 'in the cloud', e.g. using GoogleDocs.[1] But the Web 2.0 era has brought new forms of user-authored content too, of which wikis and blogs are popular examples. For instance, in June 2009, the English Wikipedia contained nearly 3 million content pages;[2] and as of April 2007, the blogosphere contained over 72 million blogs, originating about 17 posts per second.[3] However, an information-seeking/information-authoring dichotomy is a false one. We frequently engage in both activities in tandem. When creating a blogpost, for example, we may interleave search with writing: we seek information to deepen the content; and we seek multimedia resources that we can embed or link to.

Switching between these two tasks (search and writing) and the different tools for accomplishing them (search engines and editors) both wastes time and imposes

---

[*] Supported by Science Foundation Ireland Principal Investigator Grant, 07/IN.1/I977
[1] http://docs.google.com
[2] http://en.wikipedia.org/wiki/Special:Statistics, accessed 04/06/2009
[3] http://www.sifry.com/stateoftheliveweb/, accessed 04/06/2009

L. Coyle and J. Freyne (Eds.): AICS 2009, LNAI 6206, pp. 103–113, 2010.

an extra cognitive load on the user [8]. Tools that offer integrated search and editing functionality can reduce the disruption. In particular, when a user edits her document, an integrated tool can proactively extract queries from the document, send them to search engines, and display the results alongside the document. In fact, this is the idea of Just-In-Time Information Retrieval (JITIR): information is retrieved proactively by the JITIR agent, based on queries that are implicit in, and formulated from, the user's current context, without the user formulating explicit queries [1,8,4]. The user's current context might be documents that the user has opened for reading or editing, the user's Web browsing history, or even aspects of physical context such as location and nearby people [7].

In this paper, we present experiments with the Blogoduct system, a JITIR agent for bloggers and other authors of short documents. The contribution of the paper is its consideration of different heuristics by which the agent can select terms to include in the implicit queries that it creates from the document that the user is editing. We propose and compare several heuristics that, to the best of our knowledge, do not feature in existing JITIR agents. Each of the heuristics that we compare uses some relatively lightweight techniques from the field of Natural Language Processing (NLP).

In Section 2, we review other JITIR agents, focusing on the way they create implicit queries. Section 3 describes our Blogoduct system and the heuristics that we have implemented for creating implicit queries. Section 4 reports an experimental comparison of our heuristics and results from a live user trial.

2   Related Work

The literature contains many descriptions of JITIR systems [1,8,6]. They may differ in several respects: the type of system (e.g. standalone desktop systems, plug-ins, etc.); the files over which they search (e.g. a user's local files, the Web, etc.); how they aggregate results from multiple sources or cluster the results; and how they present results to the user (e.g. separate result panes, transparent pop-up windows, etc.). But for the purposes of this paper, the difference we focus on is how implicit queries are created from the user's document.

The most common technique is to use weights based on term frequency (tf) within the document that the user is editing and inverse document frequency (idf) over the document collection. In fact, the way tf-idf weights are computed and used will depend on the operation of the search engine. Consider the situation where the search engine operates on a repository of local files. In this case, each document in the repository and the document that the user is editing can be represented by a term vector of tf-idf weights; the most similar documents according, e.g., to cosine similarity can be retrieved. This is the default technique used in Savant, which is the back-end of the Remembrance Agent, although Savant is also capable of parsing documents to discard mark-up and to extract special fields on which domain-specific similarity measures can be defined [8].

There is an alternative technique that uses tf-idf weights to create implicit queries, but does not use them during retrieval. Consider the situation where retrieval is done by an Internet search engine. The agent does not supply the search engine with a term vector of tf-idf weights; instead it supplies just a set of keywords, like what any one of us would type into a search box. The search engine uses its matching and ranking algorithms to find the set of results. But how can the JITIR agent select terms from the user's document to include in the implicit query? An obvious approach is to use those with highest tf-idf weights. The complication comes in calculating idf: without access to the documents we cannot compute document frequencies. To overcome this, the search engine is queried with each individual term and the engine's estimate of the number of results is used as a proxy for the true document frequency, e.g. [3]. This is not the true document frequency because it fails to count multiple occurrences of the term in the same document, and it fails to eliminate double-counting that results from indexing duplicate copies of a document.

Watson, one of the best-known JITIR agents, is an example of this kind of system: it computes term weights to choose what to include in a query [1]. However, it has a bespoke term weighting algorithm that assigns higher weights to words that appear more frequently in the document, that appear earlier in the document, that are emphasized in the document (e.g. in italics, in a section heading), and so on. A subsequent version of Watson was also built that creates queries in a *task-specific* way; for example, for someone who is writing arguments for and against a point, domain knowledge is used to create two queries, a similarity query and an opposing query [2].

A rather different approach is taken by the system reported in [6]. It attempts to identify a document's topics, where candidate topics are WordNet word senses. It computes topic probability based on occurrences of on- and off-topic words in the document, relative to their occurrence under WordNet senses. It can create queries in one of two ways: either it creates one query per topic, where the query comprises all the words for the topic, or it creates a single query using tf-idf weights while ensuring that at least two topics are covered.

In the next section, we describe our system, Blogoduct, which uses shallow NLP to create implicit queries.

3   The Blogoduct System

Figure 1 shows, in simplified form, the architecture of Blogoduct, the Just-In-Time Information Retrieval system that we have built. While aimed at bloggers, it can support authors of other forms of content too. It proactively provides aggregated search results from Google and Yahoo!, along with image search results from flickr.[4]

Blogoduct is a client-server webapp. A screenshot of the client is shown in Figure 2. The client is an AJAX application, written in Java and compiled to optimized JavaScript using the Google Web Toolkit.[5] In her browser, the user sees a pane that contains a rich-text editor for creating her document, and a

---

[4] www.google.com; www.yahoo.com; www.flickr.com
[5] http://code.google.com/webtoolkit/

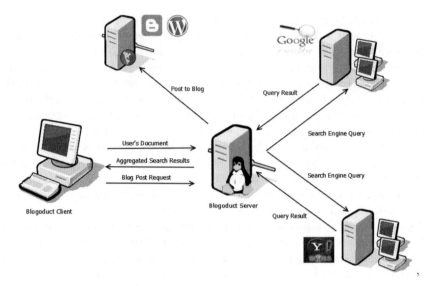

Fig. 1. The Blogoduct architecture (simplified)

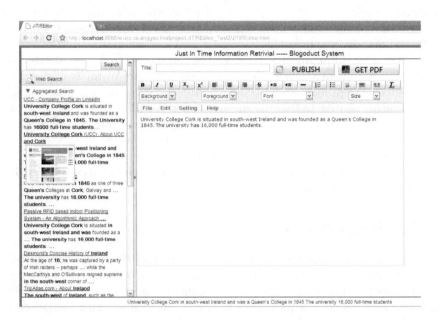

Fig. 2. A screenshot of the Blogoduct client

pane in which search results are listed. Other functionality includes a standard search box, and a button for publishing to the user's blog.

Server-side, Blogoduct is implemented as a Java servlet. The client communicates with the Blogoduct server using GWT Remote Procedure Calls. The server receives a copy of the user's document, from which it can extract search engine queries. The client handles the server's responses asynchronously.

Ordinarily, the Blogoduct server uses Internet search engine APIs to obtain search results, in which case queries will be sets of keywords. Presently, we have implemented interfaces to the Google, Yahoo! and flickr search engines. The Google and Yahoo! results are aggregated; the flickr results are kept separate. However, for running off-line experiments, we can run the server software as a standard application, allowing access to local files. In this case, we can use the Lucene search engine,[6] and queries will be represented as term vectors of tf-idf weights. We exploit this possibility in the experiments we report in Section 4.1.

We experiment with five ways for Blogoduct to decide which terms from the user's document to include in a query. Each of the first four of these heuristics uses shallow NLP techniques available in the OpenNLP toolset:[7]

N: OpenNLP's part-of-speech (POS) tagger identifies the syntactic category (e.g. determiner, noun, verb) of each word. Our heuristic is then to extract all nouns, and create the query from these. The motivation for this is that nouns often carry a lot of the semantic content of a sentence.

Open Class: Our second heuristic also uses POS tagging, but this time we extract all 'open class' words. In linguistics, an open class is one that accepts the addition of new words, e.g. nouns, verbs, adjectives and adverbs but not prepositions, conjunctions, etc. In its effect, this strategy is not much different from simply removing stop-words.

NP: For this heuristic, we use chunking. Chunking is a form of lightweight parsing. In terms of depth of analysis, chunking sits somewhere between POS tagging and full parsing. It finds phrases within a sentence, but it does not aim to find a complete syntactic analysis. We use it to extract all noun phrases, and we use the union of the words in the noun phrases as the query. The chunker we use is OpenNLP's maximum-entropy-based chunker.

Name Detection: Name detection is the identification of the names of entities in a sentence, such as names of people, locations, dates, and so on. These will often be among the most important noun phrases in a sentence. We use OpenNLP's maximum-entropy-based name finder for this.

TFIDF: For comparison purposes, the final heuristic does not use OpenNLP tools. In the fashion described in the previous section, we compute tf-idf weights for each word in the user's document (using Google's estimates of result set size as proxies for document frequencies), and we take the highest scoring 50% of the words to be the query.

In fact, we tried five other heuristics, some of which were combinations of those shown above. Space limitations prevent us from including them in this paper. Their performance in the experiment, in any case, lay somewhere between that of the other heuristics.

The queries produced by the first four of our heuristics for a sample sentence are shown in Table 1.

---

[6] http://lucene.apache.org
[7] http://opennlp.sourceforge.net/

Table 1. The queries that the different heuristics produce for the sentence *"The Irish construction industry lurched downwards again in May"*

N	*construction industry May*
Open Class	*Irish construction industry lurched downwards again May*
NP	*The Irish construction industry May*
Name Detection	*May*

4   Experimental Evaluation

Evaluation of JITIR systems up to now has either required human users to judge a single version of the system (e.g. [1,8]) or, where comparisons of system variants has been done, it is done over a small number of variants and on very small document collections (e.g. [6]). We report a system trial with human users and Internet search in Section 4.2. But first we report a precision-recall evaluation, based on two medium-size document collections and using Lucene as our back-end search engine.

4.1   Comparison of Query Extraction Heuristics

The CISI document collection consists of 1460 documents from the Institute of Scientific Information and has 76 statements of information-needs with relevance judgments; the CACM document collection consists of 3204 documents and 52 statements of information-needs with relevance judgments. Note that, for the most part, the statements of information-needs are short paragraphs. We used these as if they were the document that the user was editing.

Our experimental methodology must simulate the idea of a user whose document grows as she authors it, and we have to repeatedly obtain search engine results from Blogoduct as the document grows. We did this at the sentence level. So, for example, if a statement of information-needs contains n sentences, then we invoke Blogoduct on ever larger prefixes of the information-needs: we begin by invoking it on the first sentence; we invoke it again on the first two sentences; then the first three sentences; and so on, until we have invoked it n times. Each time we invoke it, Blogoduct takes the latest prefix of the information-needs, extracts a query using one of the heuristics, and retrieves results from the document collection using Lucene. Of course, different information-needs contain different numbers of sentences (n), and so they do not necessarily invoke Blogoduct the same number of times.

We report 11-point interpolated average precision [5]. For each of 11 recall levels $(0.0, 0.1, 0.2,\dots,1.0)$, this involves computing the mean over a set of queries of the interpolated precision at that recall level. Interpolated precision at recall level r, $p_{interp}(r)$, is defined as the highest precision found for any recall level:

$$p_{interp(r)} = \max_{r' \geq r} p(r') \tag{1}$$

with the usual definitions of precision and recall [5].

Figures 3 and 4 show plots of interpolated average precision for the CISI and CACM document collections respectively. We see that Name Detection is the least successful heuristic for both CISI and CACM. It is also one of the more computationally expensive, taking as much as 1 second to extract the names from a document. Extracting just nouns (N) is slightly worse than the other heuristics in the case of the CACM document collection. The other heuristics perform similarly to each other: chunking to extract noun phrases (NP) performs best and especially at low recall values, which implies that documents it retrieves to which it assigns high rank are good, but the differences are not significant. Note that TFIDF, while competitive, also has the disadvantage of high costs: recall that document frequencies for each term are obtained from Google.

4.2   User Evaluation

On the basis of the experimental results from the previous section, we decided to adopt the NP heuristic (i.e. chunking to extract noun phrases) for a trial with human users and Internet search engines. We prepared two systems. One is the full Blogoduct; in the other we disabled proactive querying, so a user who wants search results must resort to entering explicit queries through the standard search box. Below, we refer to these respectively as *Implicit* and *Explicit*.

As already mentioned, we adopted the NP heuristic in the Blogoduct system. However, Internet search engines treat keywords conjunctively; if a query to a search engine comprises the text of too many NPs, there may be few, if any, search results. This is not generally the case when queries are represented by term vectors and presented to Lucene. Hence, when Blogoduct is used with Internet search engines, it works in the following way: (a) queries comprise only the text of a maximum of the 10 most recent noun phrases, and (b) if there are fewer than 8 results, we repeatedly reduce the number of noun phrases by one, in first-in-first-out fashion.

We recruited 20 University College Cork students from different departments; each had different levels of search engine experience. We prepared a list of topics (e.g. a recent research result in Physics; Banff National Park), and we asked each participant to pick two topics about which they knew little. We asked ten of the students to write a paragraph on the first topic using full Blogoduct (Implicit), and a paragraph on the second topic using the other version of the system (Explicit). The other ten students did the same but using the systems in the opposite order.

In tasks that were completed using Implicit, users clicked on a total of 73 search results, with the average per task being 3.65. When using Explicit, users clicked on a few more results: 77 in total; 3.85 on average. But what is interesting is the position in the search results of the items being clicked on. This is shown in Figure 5. It seems that relevant web pages are ranked higher on average by

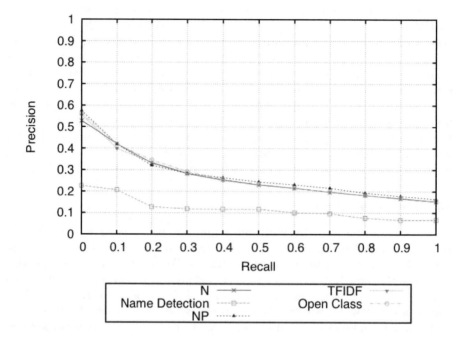

Fig. 3. Interpolated average precision for the CISI document collection

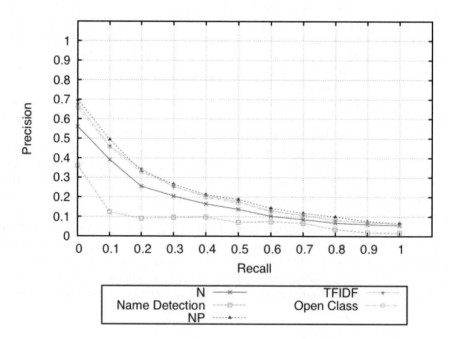

Fig. 4. Interpolated average precision for the CACM document collection

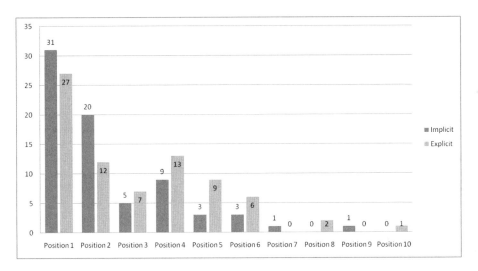

Fig. 5. Click History

Implicit than Explicit (average position of 2.342 compared with 3.0), implying that the queries that Blogoduct automatically creates are better than those that users create explicitly. We also recorded task times (from first click on a search result to final click on a search result), and they were better for Implicit: the average task time for Implicit was 21 minutes, whereas that for Explicit was 24.75 minutes. A follow-up survey seemed to confirm these results. Responses to two of the questions that we asked are given in Figures 6 and 7.

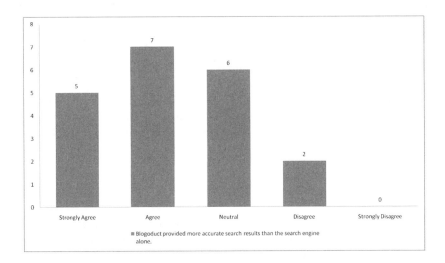

Fig. 6. Survey Responses: Accuracy

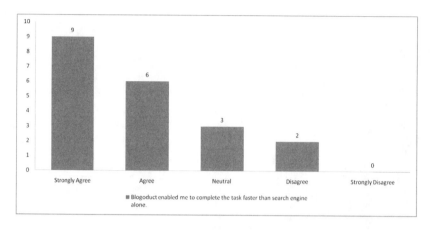

Fig. 7. Survey Responses: Time

5   Conclusions and Future Work

Blogoduct is a JITIR system that is unusual in that it uses shallow NLP techniques to form its implicit queries. In particular, we adopted a strategy of chunking and extracting recent noun phrases, which was competitive in an experimental evaluation on two document collections. In a trial with real users, Blogoduct's automatic, implicit queries produced result lists where relevant items tended to be more highly-ranked than they were when users formulated queries explicitly.

There are many lines of possible future inquiry. First, we would like to take the kind of comparisons that we performed using Lucene and repeat them in the case where the back-end uses Internet search. This, however, raises problems about getting relevance judgments. Second, we would like to compare the NLP techniques with more of the techniques found in systems such as Watson. Third, we believe that JITIR is an ideal scenario to incorporate personalization: users should not see the same results for the same queries. And fourth, we would like to see whether shallow NLP can be used to improve proactive recommendation of blogpost tags.

JITIR systems are seeing real use. For example, Zemanta[8] is a Firefox extension that retrieves ideas for blogpost enrichment from 16 common web services. We hope that in the future ideas from our research can be incorporated into systems such as Zemanta.

References

1. Budzik, J., Hammond, K.: Watson: Anticipating and contextualizing information needs. In: Procs. of the 62nd Annual Meeting of the American Society for Information Science, pp. 727–740 (1999)

---

[8] www.zemanta.com

2. Budzik, J., Hammond, K.J., Birnbaum, L., Krema, M.: Beyond similarity. In: Working notes of the AAAI Workshop on AI for Web Search (2000)
3. Henzinger, M., Chang, B.-W., Milch, B., Brin, S.: Query-free news search. In: Procs. of the 12th Intl. World-Wide Web Conference, pp. 1–10 (2003)
4. Lieberman, H., Fry, C., Weitzman, L.: Exploring the web with reconnaissance agents. CACM 44(8), 69–75 (2001)
5. Manning, C.D., Raghavan, P., Schütze, H.: Introduction to Information Retrieval. Cambridge University Press, Cambridge (2008)
6. Meade, J., Costello, F., Kushmerick, N.: Inferring topic probability for just-in-time information retrieval. In: Bell, D.A., et al. (eds.) Procs. of the 17th Irish Conference on Artificial Intelligence & Cognitive Science, pp. 103–112 (2006)
7. Rhodes, B.: Using physical context for just-in-time information retrieval. IEEE Trans. on Computers 52(8), 1011–1014 (2003)
8. Rhodes, B.J.: Just-In-Time Information Retrieval. PhD thesis, Massachusetts Institute of Technology (2000)

Towards Automatic Blotch Detection for Film Restoration by Comparison of Spatio-Temporal Neighbours

Peter Gaughran, Susan Bergin, and Ronan Reilly

Department of Computer Science, National University of Ireland, Maynooth,
Co. Kildare, Ireland
{Peter.Gaughran,Susan.Bergin,Ronan.Reilly}@nuim.ie

Abstract. In this paper, a new method of blotch detection for digitised film sequences is proposed. Due to the aging of film stocks, their poor storage and/or repeated viewing, it is estimated that approximately 50% of all films produced prior to 1950 have either been destroyed or rendered unwatchable [1,2]. To prevent their complete destruction, original film reels must be scanned into digital format; however, any defects such as blotches will be retained. By combining a variation of a linear time, contour tracing technique with a simple temporal nearest neighbour algorithm, a preliminary detection system has been created. Using component labelling of dirt and sparkle the overall performance of the completed system, in terms of time and accuracy, will compare favourably to traditional motion compensated detection methods. This small study (based on 13 film sequences) represents a significant first step towards automatic blotch detection.

Keywords: blotch, detection, film, restoration, machine vision.

1 Introduction

Over time, the mechanical viewing of analogue film reels is abrasive and destructive. Even the storage of film reel archives unavoidably suffers because of chemical breakdown such as vinegar syndrome [2]. Given this eventual destruction, saving the material makes its digital conversion essential. Digital conversion also has the comparative ease of distribution of the content once it has been scanned and converted (Digital TV, Blu-ray/DVD discs, downloads). Unfortunately, while the remastering process ensures no further decay will occur, damage incurred prior to scanning will of course be retained.

Traditionally, when restoring footage, each frame of a motion picture reel must be chemically bathed. An average feature length of, for example, 2 hours (7,200 seconds) at 24 frames a second, results in approximately 173,000 frames that have to be cleaned. Specific areas per frame must also be visually identified and dealt with by hand - cleaned if *dirt* (not removed by the initial step) is present, or 'filled in' if *sparkle* is found. *Dirt* blotches are mainly caused by dust or dirt that has adhered to the film stock over time and result in 'dark spots' on a frame, whereas *sparkle* is

L. Coyle and J. Freyne (Eds.): AICS 2009, LNAI 6206, pp. 114–123, 2010.
© Springer-Verlag Berlin Heidelberg 2010

caused by the abrasion of the celluloid, resulting in the silver nitrate showing through as 'bright spots' (Fig. 1 shows some examples). Both are random and single frame defects, that is, no specific instance of dirt or sparkle will appear at the same co-ordinates in a preceding or following frame. It should be noted that line scratches are different in that they manifest as vertical lines, and over several frames will remain in approximately the same spatial position [3]. As a result of this property, line scratches are suitable for detection by the means proposed here.

Fig. 1. A sample frame from *Duck and Cover* (1951). Some examples of dirt are enclosed in the squares, while sparkle is encircled.

Given the time consuming nature of traditional restoration, it is extremely expensive and labour intensive. It is possible to digitally restore the material using various intelligent and/or signal processing algorithms. These algorithms seek to improve the subjective visual quality of the individual frames. Whether digital or more traditionally analogue, an entire film restoration system is usually composed of scene segmentation, flicker correction, blotch and scratch detection and removal, image stabilization and (perhaps most controversially) noise reduction[1]. Of these stages, it is the detection of dirt and sparkle blotches that is the focus of this study.

Industrial software exists (such as AlgoSoft, Amped and DIAMANT) – but the means of detection and success rate are unpublished; however, peer assessment and cinematic critique has not been favourable [4]. Previous academic research includes detection of dirt and sparkle by means of motion estimation and 3D autoregressive

---

[1] Film grain – small grains of a metallic silver halide derivative - may show when projecting a reel if enough photons hit when recording. Many directors deliberately shoot in such a way as to enhance this effect, yet some restoration algorithms remove it. For more information, see [5] *American Cinematographer, Post Focus,* May 2008.

modelling – in particular, the JOMBADI (Joint Model BAsed Detection and Interpolation) algorithm [6]. The JOMBADI approach attempts to combine blotch detection and repair in a single step; a statistical model of the frame is created and motion vectors randomly adjusted until a predicted (reconstructed) frame is reached (based on either prediction error or maximum number of iterations). This results in either very high computational loads and/or lack of accuracy.

Global Motion Segmentation for blotch detection has also been attempted – using this technique, blotches are detected as 'areas' of pixels that do not adhere to *any* parametric global interframe transformation model [7]. Being exhaustive, this also results in a high computational load, and is subject to the accuracies, inaccuracies and possible contradictions of the various transformation models employed.

Czúni *et al.* have implemented DIMORF - a neural network for semi automatic detection coupled with an XML database to minimise false positives (by meta tagging incorrect finds in a single frame, all other such instances can be ignored if found in subsequent frames) [8]. As such, DIMORF aspires more to being a semi-automatic detection and indexing software system.

The detection method proposed here is composed of two stages; firstly a single frame is deconstructed into separate components, secondly, these components are then compared with their immediate (if any) temporal neighbours. In order to begin the detection process a chosen frame is converted to two binary images (one based on the original frame for dirt detection, the other an inverted copy, for detecting sparkle). To achieve this goal with minimal loss of component information, local thresholding is applied to the source frame. This thresholding process is outlined in the following section, with the means of blotch detection in single and multiple frames in described Section 3. Section 4 details the experimental setup and results, and Section 5, future work.

2   Preliminary Isolation

In order to separate potential blotches from other objects within a frame, two processes are applied :- (i) local thresholding, and (ii) contour tracing.

2.1 Local Thresholding

Also known as *dynamic* or *adaptive* thresholding [9], local thresholding is used to isolate (but not identify) individual components of objects within the selected frame. Instead of a global threshold applied to all pixels, this operation changes the threshold dynamically across the frame. Developed for industrial use when uneven lighting conditions prevented the segmentation of a lighter foreground object from its background, local thresholding gives binary image output by analysing each pixel with respect to its local neighbourhood. The mean of this neighbourhood is calculated and if the current pixel is black (*i.e.*, an object pixel) it is thresholded to white if the difference between the calculated mean and the current pixel value is lower than that of a user defined offset.

The value of this offset will depend on a variety of factors, including, but not limited to, film grain, differing illumination between scenes and possibly motion.

Fig. 2. The original frame, left, and the same frame after it has been locally thresholded

The values employed in this study were obtained from frame based training sets that were manually derived by the first author. (This manual process is an extremely time-consuming and difficult one, requiring thorough examination of each sequence frame by frame.) These values could then be used across frame sequences containing live action or animation, with differing illumination but were shot on the same film stock (i.e., the same level of grain). Future work will concentrate on the automatic generation of this offset. Figure 2 gives an example of a frame before and after local thresholding. After the thresholding, a contour tracing algorithm is then applied to label all potential blotches.

2.2 A Linear-Time, Contour Tracing, Component-Labelling Algorithm

Originally designed for document analysis and recognition (DAR), the algorithm employed to label the contours and components within the generated binary images was devised by Chang *et al.*, and is shown to be faster than traditional component labelling algorithms [10]. Each component is labelled using a contour tracing technique; as polygons are fully determined by vectors, so too are components fully determined by their respective contours, and as such all component pixels can be found. High-order objects such as characters, textlines, and text regions need to be classified in order to effectively perform a task such as DAR [11], but the application of the technique to blotch detection in film sequences appears to be novel.

A frame is processed in the same manner as when it was originally scanned – line by line, left to right from top to bottom. When a contour (either internal or external) is encountered, the tracing procedure is then applied [12] and all pixels along the contour are assigned a label, e.g., L. The contour is then traced back to its starting point, and scanning resumes. Later, when L is revisited, any neighbouring black (object) pixels are also assigned the label L. Thus, while only a single pass over the entire image is required, contour points are visited more than once due to the aforementioned contour tracing procedure, but no more than a constant number of times. Once a label index has been assigned to a pixel, its value will remain unchanged. The operations can be broken down into four major steps (see Figure 3).

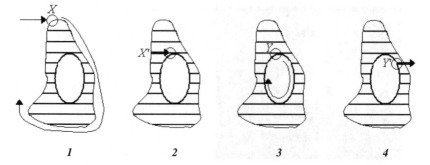

Fig. 3. The four steps of contour tracing, *1* to *4*. Each line represents the current line being scanned, and the arrows show the direction of that scan.

In Step 1 when an external contour point X is encountered for the first time, a complete trace of the contour is performed until a return to X. A label is then assigned to X and all points along that contour. Step 2 shows what occurs when a labelled external contour point X' is encountered. The scan line is followed to find all subsequent black pixels (if they exist) and all are then assigned the same label. In Step 3, if an internal contour point Y is encountered for the first time, it is assigned the same label as the external contour of the same component. The internal contour containing Y is then traced, and its contour points are all assigned the same label. Finally, Step 4 dictates that when a labelled internal contour point, Y', is encountered, all subsequent black pixels along the same scan line (if they exist) are then assigned the same label. Two separate passes of this algorithm are required, one to generate a set of potential dirt blotch candidates, the other, a set of potential sparkle. The four steps are then repeated until all components in the image have been labelled.

3   Blotch Detection

3.1   Single Frame

Once the two sets of possible blotches (one for dirt, the other for sparkle) have been generated for a given frame by application of local thresholding and contour tracing, the process of isolating genuine blotches can begin. Figure 4 shows an example of a subsection of a frame that has been thresholded to begin detection of dark blotches, for dirt.

The vast majority of object pixels will, of course, be genuine, and not at all representative of defective blotches. In order to separate and reduce false positives from potentially genuine candidates, a set of criteria has been devised.

- According to the relevant literature (and corroborating by data generated from this research to date), blotches are rarely larger than 40 * 40 pixels, at standard definition resolutions [13]
- Blotches are isolated areas of discontinuous pixel intensities
- As previously mentioned, blotches are single frame aberrations, not occurring at the same spatial coordinates over more time

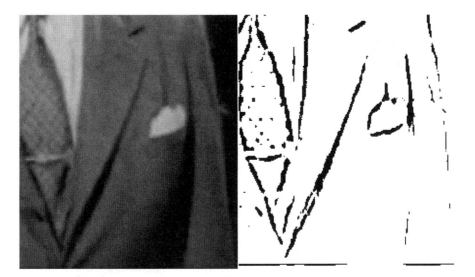

Fig. 4. On the left, close up of a frame, on the right, the locally thresholded equivalent. The adaptive threshold algorithm generates object pixels along areas of change in contrast – usually edges.

The first two criteria allow for great reduction in the number of possible blotches when using a single frame (larger values than 40 * 40 pixels may certainly be used, but the resultant set of single frame blotch candidates will necessarily be larger.) To further reduce the number of possible blotches, an approach similar to the Simplified Ranked Order Difference (SROD) detector [14] is used. A customly laid-out neighbourhood of *n* approximately equidistant points just outside the external contour of the blotch under investigation are selected (see Figure 5). Standard morphological neighbourhoods are impossible to use given the irregular shape of the blotches. The selected values are then compared to the mean grayscale value of the blotch as it appears in the original frame. If greater than half of the values selected are beyond a 'similarity of intensity' threshold, the blotch is marked; if less, the blotch is likely to be a false positive. (If the value of *n* chosen is even and the result an even split, the average of all *n* values is compared to the threshold.) Of the 13 film sequences (from 3 different films stocks of similar age) tested to date, the application of the first two criteria checks results in a reduction of the dirt and sparkle 'per-frame' supersets by an average of 53%, with less than 2 blotch detection failures (from an average of 16 actual blotches) per frame. In addition, these undetected blotches could be considered minor in terms of size, and also in terms of visual discontinuity; when compared with the surrounding pixel intensities, the unfound blotches usually measured less than half of the difference of their grayscale mean and their other dirt/sparkle set equivalents in the same frame. For the remaining blotches, their classification may be further determined by applying the third criteria; exploration of a given blotch's temporal neighbour, in a preceding and/or following frame.

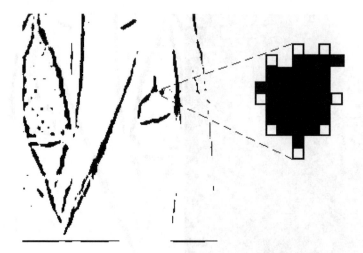

Fig. 5. Close up of a blotch with a neighbourhood of $n = 8$ (represented by the blank squares). The points are calculated by radiating out from the approximate centre of the blotch until the border has been reached, and then incremented by one.

3.2 Multiple Neighbouring Frames

In order to exploit the single frame, non-recurrence property of dirt and sparkle blotches, it is important to note that the digital frames being used must be representative of the original frame rate that the film was shot at, usually 24 progressive frames a second [15]. Altered frame rates of scanned film material can result in analogue single frame blotches becoming multiple frame digital counterparts (frame rate alteration is usually performed for television broadcast, and varies on the location depending on PAL/NTSC etc). The aim of this part of the process is to

Fig. 6. The thresholded image on the left is the first frame in a given film sequence, the image on the right, its immediate temporal neighbour. Even purely visual inspection reveals the remarkable degree of similarity between the images. The rate of motion is not high in this sequence, however, and thus is not to be considered indicative of all film sequences.

further reduce the remaining potential sets of dirt and sparkle blotches, by comparing the sets with their nearest neighbours. Given the standard twenty four frames-per-second shooting speed of motion picture cameras, consider Figure 6.

A 'temporal location radius', based on a given blotch's Euclidean distance to its temporal neighbours, is then applied to each of the inter-frame blotches, *i.e.*, a permitted radius for the movement of a selected blotch based on the rate of change detected between frames, similar to instance based machine learning algorithms such as k-nearest neighbour [16]. A simple frame subtraction of the frame under investigation, f, from its neighbours $f + 1$ and $f - 1$ respectively can give a false impression of the rate of change due to film grain, minor illumination changes etc.; however, using the thresholded counterparts of f, $f - 1$ and $f + 1$ yields a more accurate result. If the rate of change between frames is small or large, the radius is set accordingly. By implementing this stage of the process, the numbers of potential dirt and sparkle blotch candidates are reduced by a further 18%, on average.

4 Experimental Setup and Results

While ample standard definition test footage is widely available from online resources such as the Prelinger Archives (http://www.archive.org/details/prelinger), and the accessibility of high definition footage becoming more common, independent benchmark footage is difficult to obtain, perhaps because of the proprietary, often copyrighted nature of the material. Consequently, the results presented in Table 1 are generated by direct comparison of the blotches detected by the system with the user annotated versions of the same film sequences. The 13 sequences that have been annotated to date represent the beginning of a much larger library that will be compiled. Given that each annotated sequence was between 2 and 5 seconds long, at 24 frames a second, an average of 100 images per sequence was visually analysed by the first author both singly and in groups of three to generate accurate data for testing purposes. Over time, with improvements in software based on the initial findings of this work, the generation of new (and larger) test data will become less involved.

The sequences were chosen as they originate from the beginning or end of a film reel, usually the most damaged sections. All of the five chosen sequences were 30 frames long, with 28 frames examined starting at frame 2 and ending at 29, allowing each frame to have a preceding and following neighbour. Based on the above results, genuine dirt blotch detection averaged 66.8%, and genuine sparkle, 62.6%. Four of the five sequences were well illuminated scenes, possibly explaining the lower result for sparkle detection as the average pixel intensity was high. The detection of false positives for both dirt and sparkle at present still appears to be randomly distributed, with no apparent connection between the instances discovered to date. True negatives vary greatly in number depending on the frame in question and the content of the footage, effectively resulting in everything else in the image not identified as a blotch. As such, while it is possible to calculate sensitivity, specificity is meaningless. The mere presence of false positives *may* not prove problematic, however, as replacement

Table 1. Comparison of blotch detection hit-rate with user generated data, from 5 chosen film sequences.

Film Sequence	Dirt Blotches Detected	False Positives	False Negatives	Num. of Actual Dirt Blotches
1	23	5	9	32
2	54	10	39	93
3	64	8	23	97
4	38	4	13	51
5	42	9	25	67

Film Sequence	Sparkle Blotches Detected	False Positives	False Negatives	Num. of Actual Sparkle Blotches
1	45	12	23	68
2	49	17	37	86
3	41	10	27	68
4	22	7	10	32
5	39	13	25	64

of missing frame data (incorrectly perceived as missing or actual) is ultimately dependent on whatever reconstruction method(s) will be employed. In conclusion, the techniques as implemented here represent a substantial first step towards automatic blotch detection, and the results significant enough (given the traditional, time consuming alternative) to warrant further research.

5 Future Work

The work completed to date has used limited samples of film stock, most of which originates from public domain archives of the 1950s. Footage from different eras and using different frame rates would make for an interesting application. Likewise, the availability of such footage is usually in standard definition – the acquisition of high definition (2K, 4K and 8K) material to suitably test the scaling of the algorithm would be highly desirable.

The automatic generation of the offsets used at the local thresholding stage and the differences of the mean grayscale intensities, as well as the selection of the value of n for the custom, border based neighbourhood would be advantageous, as would the inclusion of a locally generated temporal location radius; currently this value is global across the frame. (In many instances, whole areas of a frame sequence remain relatively static, with motion occurring in specific spatial areas.) Other blotch characteristics based on the contour geometry generated by the algorithm from Section 1.2 could be taken into consideration; perhaps the application of several machine learning algorithms could be implemented and their results compared.

References

1. Kurreck, I.H.: Diploma-Thesis Untersuchung zur Restaurierung der Sprossenschrift von Lichtton-aufzeichnungen durch digitale Bildverarbeitung, University of Applied Sciences Wiesbaden (2000)
2. Harris, R.A.: Preservation: Why Are Films and Videos Disappearing? American Film Institute, Washington (February 1993)
3. Gullu, M.K., Urhan, O., Erturk, S.: Scratch Detection via Temporal Coherency Analysis and Removal Using Edge Priority Based Interpolation. In: IEEE International Symposium on Circuits and Systems (ISCAS 2006), pp. 4591–4594 (2006)
4. Krebs, J.: Creating the Video Future, Sound & Vision Magazine (November 2004)
5. American Cinematographer, Post Focus (May 2008)
6. Kokaram, A.C.: Advances in the detection and reconstruction of blotches in archived film and video. In: Digital Restoration of Film and Video Archives (Ref. No/049), pp. 71–76. IEEE, Los Alamitos (2001)
7. Komatsu, T., Saito, T.: Detection and Restoration of Film Blotches Using Global motion Segmentation. In: ICIP 1999, vol. III, pp. 479–483 (1999)
8. Czúni, L., Hanis, A., Kovács, L., Kránicz, B., Licsár, A., Szirányi, T., Kas, I., Kovács, G., Manno, S.: Digital Motion Picture Restoration System for Film Archives (DIMORF). SMPTE Motion Imaging Journal 113, 170–176 (2004)
9. Shapiro, L.G., Stockman, G.C.: Computer Vision. Prentice Hall, Englewood Cliffs (2000)
10. Chang, F., Chen, C., Lu, C.: A Linear Time Component Labelling Algorithm Using Contour Tracing Technique. Computer Vision and Understanding 93(2), 206–220 (2004)
11. Chang, F.: Information From Document Images: Problems and Solutions. International Journal of Document Analysis Recognition, Special Issues Document, Anal. Office Syst. 4, 46–55 (2001)
12. Haig, T.D., Attikiouzel, Y.: An Improved Algorithm for Border Following of Binary Images. In: Proceedings of IEE European Conference on Circuit Theory Design, pp. 118–122 (1989)
13. Kokaram, A.: Motion Picture Restoration, ch. 6. Springer, Heidelberg (1998)
14. Gullu, M.K., Urhan, O., Erturk, S.: Blotch Detection and Removal for Archive Film Restoration. AEU - International Journal of Electronics and Communications 62(7), 534–543 (2008)
15. Brownlow, K.: Silent Films: What Was the Right Speed? Sight and Sound, 164-167 (Summer 1980)
16. Garcia, V., Debreuve, E., Barlaud, M.: Fast K Nearest Neighbor Search Using GPU. In: Proceedings of Computer Vision and Pattern Recognition Workshops (CVPRW), pp. 1–6 (June 2008)

Analysis of the Effect of Unexpected Outliers in the Classification of Spectroscopy Data

Frank G. Glavin and Michael G. Madden

College of Engineering and Informatics,
National University of Ireland, Galway, Ireland
frank.glavin@gmail.com, michael.madden@nuigalway.ie

Abstract. Multi-class classification algorithms are very widely used, but we argue that they are not always ideal from a theoretical perspective, because they assume all classes are characterized by the data, whereas in many applications, training data for some classes may be entirely absent, rare, or statistically unrepresentative. We evaluate one-sided classifiers as an alternative, since they assume that only one class (the target) is well characterized. We consider a task of identifying whether a substance contains a chlorinated solvent, based on its chemical spectrum. For this application, it is not really feasible to collect a statistically representative set of outliers, since that group may contain *anything* apart from the target chlorinated solvents. Using a new one-sided classification toolkit, we compare a One-Sided k-NN algorithm with two well-known binary classification algorithms, and conclude that the one-sided classifier is more robust to unexpected outliers.

Keywords: One-Sided, One-Class, Classification, Support Vector Machine, k-Nearest Neighbour, Spectroscopy Analysis.

1 Introduction

1.1 One-Sided Classification

One-sided classification (OSC) algorithms are an alternative to conventional multi-class classification algorithms. They are also referred to as single-class or one-class classification algorithms, and differ in one vital aspect from multi-class algorithms, in that they are only concerned with a single, well-characterized class, known as the target or positive class. Objects of this class are distinguished from all others, referred to as outliers, that consist of *all* the other objects that are not targets. In one-sided classification, training data for the outliers may be either rare, entirely unavailable or statistically unrepresentative.

Over the past decade, several well-known algorithms have been adapted to work with the one-sided paradigm. Tax [1] describes many of these one-sided algorithms and notes that the problem of one-sided classification is generally more difficult than that of conventional classification. The decision boundary in the multi-class case has the benefit of being well described from both sides with

L. Coyle and J. Freyne (Eds.): AICS 2009, LNAI 6206, pp. 124–133, 2010.

appropriate examples from each class being available, whereas the single-class case can only support one side of the decision boundary fully, in the absence of a comprehensive set of counter-examples. While multi-class (including binary or two-class) algorithms are very widely used in many different application domains, we argue that they are not always the best choice from a theoretical perspective, because they assume that all classes are appropriately characterized by the training data. We propose that one-sided classifiers are more appropriate in these cases, since they assume that only the target class is well characterized, and seek to distinguish it from any others. Such problem domains include industrial process control, document author identification and the analysis of chemical spectra.

1.2 Spectroscopic Analysis

Raman spectroscopy, which is a form of molecular spectroscopy, is used in physical and analytical chemistry. It involves the study of experimentally-obtained spectra by using an instrument such as a spectrometer [2]. According to Gardiner [3], Raman spectroscopy is a well-established spectroscopic technique which involves the study of vibrational and rotational frequencies in a system. Spectra are gathered by illuminating a laser beam onto a substance under analysis and are based on the vibrational motion of the molecules which create the equivalent of a chemical fingerprint. This unique pattern can then be used in the identification of a variety of different materials [4].

1.3 Machine Learning Task

In this work, we consider the task of identifying materials from their Raman spectra, through the application of both one-sided and multi-class classification algorithms. Our primary focus is to analyse the performance of the classifiers when "unexpected" outliers are added to the test sets. The spectra are gathered from materials in pure form and in mixtures. The goal is to identify the presence or absence of a particular material of interest from its spectrum. This task can be seen as an "open-ended" problem, as having a statistically representative set of counter-examples for training is not feasible, as has been discussed already.

In particular, we consider the application of separating materials to enable the safe disposal of harmful solvents. Chemical waste that is potentially hazardous to the environment should be identified and disposed of in the correct manner. Laboratories generally have strict guidelines in place, as well as following legal requirements, for such procedures. Organic solvents can create a major disposal problem in organic laboratories as they are usually water-immiscible and can be highly flammable [5]. Such solvents are generally created in abundance each day in busy laboratories. Differentiating between chlorinated and non-chlorinated organic solvents is of particular importance. Depending on whether a solvent is chlorinated or not will dictate how it is transported from the laboratory and, more importantly, what method is used for its disposal [6]. Identifying and labeling such solvents is a routine laboratory procedure which usually makes the disposal a straightforward process. However, it is not unlikely that the solvents could be accidentally contaminated or inadvertently mislabeled. In such circumstances it would be beneficial to have an analysis method that would correctly identify whether or not a particular solvent was chlorinated.

We have carried out several experiments for this identification using both one-sided and multi-class classification algorithms in order to analyse the effect of adding "unexpected" outliers to the test sets.

2   Related Research

Madden and Ryder [7] explore the use of standard multi-class classification techniques, in comparison to statistical regression methods, for identifying and quantifying illicit materials using Raman spectroscopy. Their research involves using dimension reduction techniques to select some features of the spectral data and discard all others. This feature selection process is performed by using a Genetic Algorithm. The predictions can then be made based only on a small number of data points. The improvements that can be achieved by using several different predictor models together were also noted. This would come at the cost of increased computation but was shown to provide better results than using just one predictor by itself.

O'Connell et al. [8] propose the use of Principal Component Analysis (PCA), support vector machines (SVM) and Raman spectroscopy to identify an analyte[1] in solid mixtures. In this case, the analyte is acetaminophen, which is a pain reliever used for aches and fevers. They used near-infrared Raman spectroscopy to analyse a total of 217 samples, some of which had the target analyte present, of mixtures with excipients[2] of varying weight. The excipients that were included were sugars, inorganic materials and food products. The spectral data was subjected to first derivative and normalization transformations in order to make it more suitable for analysis. After this pre-treatment, the target analyte was then discriminated using Principal Component Analysis (PCA), Principal Component Regression (PCR) and Support Vector Machines. According to the authors, the superior performance of SVM was particularly evident when raw data was used for the input. The importance and benefits of the pre-processing techniques was also emphasized.

Howley [9] uses machine learning techniques for the identification and quantification of materials from their corresponding spectral data. He shows how using Principal Component Analysis (PCA) with machine learning methods, such as SVM, could produce better results than the chemometric technique of Principal Component Regression (PCR). He also presents customized kernels for use with spectral analysis based on prior knowledge of the domain. A genetic programming technique for evolving kernels is also proposed for when no domain knowledge is available.

---

[1] An analyte is a substance or chemical constituent that is determined in an analytical procedure.

[2] An excipient is an inactive substance used as a carrier for the active ingredients of a medication.

3   A Toolkit for One-Sided Classification

In the course of our research, we have developed a one-sided classification toolkit written in Java. It is a command line interface (CLI) driven software package that contains one-sided algorithms that may be chosen by the user at runtime and used to create a new classifier based on a loaded data set and a variety of different adjustable options. Both experiment-specific and classifier parameter options can be set. The toolkit was designed to carry out comprehensive and iterative experiments with minimal input from the user. The resulting classifiers that are generated can be saved and used at a later stage to classify new examples. The user can set up many different runs of an experiment, each differing by an incremented random number seed that shuffles the data for every run before it is broken up into training and testing sets. Results are printed to the screen as they are calculated; these include the classification error, sensitivity, specificity and confusion matrix for each run or individual folds.

4   Data Sets and Algorithms Used

4.1   Primary Data Set

The primary data set that we used for these experiments was compiled in earlier research, as described by Conroy *et al.* [6]. It comprises of 230 spectral samples that contain both chlorinated and non-chlorinated mixtures. According to the authors, the compilation of the data involved keeping the concentrations of the mixtures as close as possible to real life scenarios from industrial laboratories. Twenty five solvents, some chlorinated and some not, were included; these are listed in Table 1.

Table 1. A list of the various chlorinated and non-chlorinated solvents used in the primary data set and their grades. (Source: Conroy *et al.* [6]).

Solvent	Grade	Solvent	Grade
Acetone	HPLC	Cyclopentane	Analytical
Toluene	Spectroscopic	Acetophenol	Analytical
Cyclohexane	Analytical & Spect.	n-Pentane	Analytical
Acetonitrile	Spectroscopic	Xylene	Analytical
2-Propanol	Spectroscopic	Dimethylformanide	Analytical
1,4-Dioxane	Analytical & Spect.	Nitrobenzene	Analytical
Hexane	Spectroscopic	Tetrahydrofuran	Analytical
1-Butanol	Analytical & Spect.	Diethyl Ether	Analytical
Methyl Alcohol	Analytical	Petroleum Acetate	Analytical
Benzene	Analytical	Chloroform	Analytical & Spect.
Ethyl Acetate	Analytical	Dichloromethane	Analytical & Spect.
Ethanol	Analytical	1,1,1-trichloroethane	Analytical & Spect.

Table 2. Summary of chlorinated and non-chlorinated mixtures in the primary data set. (Source: Howley [9]).

	Chlorinated	Non-chlorinated	Total
Pure Solvents	6	24	30
Binary Mixtures	96	23	119
Ternary Mixtures	40	12	52
Quaternary Mixtures	12	10	22
Quintary Mixtures	0	7	7
Total	154	76	230

Several variants of the data set were created, which differed only by the labeling of the solvent that was currently assigned as the target class. In each of these variants, all instances not labeled as targets were labeled as outliers. These relabeled data sets were used in the detection of the specific chlorinated solvents: Chloroform, Dichloromethane and Trichloroethane. As an example of the data, the Raman spectrum of pure Chloroform, a chlorinated solvent, is shown in Fig. 1. Other samples from the data set consist of several different solvents in a mixture which makes the classification task more challenging. A final separate data set was created such that all of the chlorinated solvents were labeled as targets. This is for carrying out experiments to simply detect whether a given mixture is chlorinated or not.

4.2 Secondary Data Set

For our Scenario 2 experiments (see Section 5.1), we introduce 48 additional spectra that represent outliers that are taken from a different distribution to those that are present in the primary dataset. These samples are the Raman spectra of various laboratory chemicals, and none of them are chlorinated solvents nor are they the other materials that are listed in Table 1. They include materials such as sugars, salts and acids in solid or liquid state, including Sucrose, Sodium, Sorbitol, Sodium Chloride, Pimelic Acid, Acetic Acid, Phthalic Acid and Quinine.

4.3 Algorithms Used

We carried out the one-sided classification experiments using our toolkit. The conventional classification experiments were carried out using the Weka [10] machine learning software.

We have chosen a One-Sided k-Nearest Neighbour (OkNN) algorithm and two conventional classification algorithms; namely, k-Nearest Neighbour, that we refer to as Two-Class KNN, and a Support Vector Machine (SVM) that we will refer to as Two-Class SVM.

The OkNN algorithm we use is based on one described by Munroe and Madden [11]. The method involves choosing an appropriate threshold and number of neighbours to use. The average distance from a test example 'A' to its m nearest

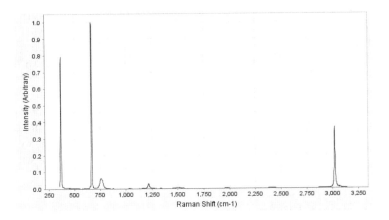

Fig. 1. The Raman Spectrum of a sample of 100% pure Chloroform

neighbours is found and this is called 'D1'. Then, the average distance of these neighbours to their own respective k nearest neighbours is found and called 'D2'. If 'D1' divided by 'D2' is greater than the threshold value, the test example 'A' is rejected as being an outlier. If it is less than the threshold, then it is accepted as being part of the target class.

5   Description of Experiments

5.1   Scenarios Considered

Two scenarios are described in our experiments, as described next.

Scenario 1: "Expected" Test Data Only. In this scenario, the test data is sampled from the same distribution as the training data. The primary dataset is divided repeatedly into training sets and test sets, with the proportions of targets and outliers held constant at all times, and these internal test sets are used to test the classifiers that are built with the training datasets.

Scenario 2: "Unexpected" and "Expected" Test Data. In this scenario, we augment each test dataset with the 48 examples from the secondary data set that are *not* drawn from the same distribution as the training dataset. Therefore, a classifier trained to recognise any chlorinated solvent should reject them as outliers. However, these samples represent a significant challenge to the classifiers, since they violate the standard assumption that the test data will be drawn from the same distribution as the training data; it is for this reason that we term them "unexpected".

This second scenario is designed to assess the robustness of the classifiers in a situation that has been discussed earlier, whereby in practical deployments of classifiers in many situations, the classifiers are likely to be exposed to outliers that are not drawn from the same distribution as training outliers. In fact, we contend that over the long term, this is inevitable: if we know *a priori* that the outlier class distribution is not well characterized in the training data, then we must accept that sooner or later, the classifier will be exposed to data that falls outside the distribution of the outlier training data.

It should be noted that this is different from *concept drift*, where a target concept may change over time; here, we have a static concept, but over time the weaknesses of the training data are exposed. Of course, re-training might be possible, if problem cases can be identified and labeled correctly, but we concern ourselves with classifiers that have to maintain robust performance without re-training.

5.2   Experimental Procedure

The data sets, as described earlier, were used to test the ability of each algorithm in detecting the individual chlorinated compounds. This involved three separate experiments for each algorithm, to detect Chloroform, Dichloromethane and Trichloroethane. A fourth experiment involved detecting the presence of any chlorinated compound in the mixture.

All spectra were first normalized. A common method for normalizing a dataset is to recalculate the values of the attributes to fall within the range of zero to one. This is usually carried out on an attribute-by-attribute basis and ensures that certain attribute values, which differ radically in size from the rest, don't dominate in the prediction calculations. The normalization carried out on the spectral data is different to this in that it is carried out on an instance-by-instance basis. Since each attribute in an instance is a point on the spectrum, this process is essentially rescaling the height of the spectrum into the range of zero to one.

For each experiment, 10 runs were carried out with the data being randomly split each time into 67% for training and 33% for testing. The splitting procedure from our toolkit ensured that there was the same proportion of targets and outliers in the training sets as there was in the test sets. The same data set splits were used for the one-sided classifier algorithms and the Weka-based algorithms, to facilitate direct comparisons.

A 3-fold internal cross validation step was used with all the training sets, to carry out parameter tuning. A list of parameter values was passed to each classification algorithm and each, in turn, was used on the training sets, in order to find the best combination that produced the smallest error estimate. It must be emphasized that we only supplied a small amount of different parameters for each algorithm and that these parameters used were the same for all of the four variants of the data set. The reason for this was that our goal was not to tune and identify the classifier with the best results overall but to notice the change in performance when "unexpected" outliers were added to the test set.

For the One-Sided kNN algorithm, the amount of nearest neighbours (m) and the amount of their nearest neighbours (k) was varied between 1 and 2. The threshold values tried were 1, 1.5 and 2. The distance metric used was Cosine

Similarity. For the Weka experiments, the Two-Class kNN approach tried the values 1,2 and 3 for the amount of nearest neighbours. The Two-Class SVM varied the complexity parameter C with the values of 1,3 and 5. The default values were used for all of the other Weka parameters.

5.3   Performance Metric

The error rate of a classification algorithm is the percentage of examples from the test set that are incorrectly classified. We measure the average error rate of each algorithm over the 10 runs to give an overall error estimate of its performance. With such a performance measure being used, it is important to know what percentage of target examples were present in each variant of the data set. This information is listed in Table 3 below.

Table 3. Percentage of target examples in each variant of the *primary* data set

Dataset	Targets	"Expected" Outliers	Target Percent
Chlorinated or not	154	76	66.95%
Chloroform	79	151	34.34%
Dichloromethane	60	170	26.08%
Trichloroethane	79	151	34.34%

6   Results and Analysis

The results of the experiments carried out are listed in Table 4, Table 5, and Table 6 below. Each table shows the overall classification error rate and standard deviation (computed over 10 runs) for each algorithm, for both of the scenarios that were tested.

It can be seen that while the conventional multi-class classifiers perform quite well in the first scenario, their performance quickly begins to deteriorate once the "unexpected" outliers are introduced in Scenario 2. The One-Sided kNN's performance is generally worse than the multi-class approach in Scenario 1. As described in Section 1.1, the decision boundary for the multi-class classifiers have the benefit of being well supported from both sides with representative training examples from each class. In such a scenario, the multi-class algorithms essentially have more information to aid the classification mechanism and, therefore, would be expected to out-perform the one-sided approach.

In detecting whether or not a sample is chlorinated, the average error rate of the Two-Class kNN increased by 28.87% and the Two-Class SVM increased by 33.57% in Scenario 2. In contrast with the two-class classifiers, the One-Sided kNN is seen to retain a consistent performance and the error is actually decreased by 2.24%. When the algorithms are detecting the individual chlorinated solvents, the same pattern in performance can be seen. The multi-class algorithms' error rates increase, in some cases quite radically, in the second scenario. The One-Sided kNN manages to remain at a more consistent error rate and, in all cases, the overall error rate is reduced somewhat.

Table 4. Overall average error rate for two-class kNN in both scenarios

Two-Class kNN	Scenario 1.	Scenario 2.
	Error % (std. dev.)	Error % (std. dev.)
Chlorinated or not	6.49 (2.03)	35.36 (3.65)
Chloroform	22.59 (6.93)	39.44 (7.37)
Dichloromethane	11.94 (4.89)	16.24 (3.49)
Trichloroethane	23.24 (5.10)	25.68 (4.27)

Table 5. Overall average error rate for two-class SVM in both scenarios

Two-Class SVM	Scenario 1.	Scenario 2.
	Error % (std. dev.)	Error % (std. dev.)
Chlorinated or not	4.67 (1.95)	38.24 (2.19)
Chloroform	11.68 (4.01)	37.2 (2.39)
Dichloromethane	8.70 (4.37)	11.68 (3.52)
Trichloroethane	11.03 (3.47)	30.08 (2.50)

Table 6. Overall average error rate for one-sided kNN in both scenarios

One-Sided kNN	Scenario 1.	Scenario 2.
	Error % (std. dev.)	Error % (std. dev.)
Chlorinated or not	10.90 (4.5)	8.66 (3.07)
Chloroform	26.10 (3.43)	16.37 (2.46)
Dichloromethane	12.98 (3.23)	7.95 (1.94)
Trichloroethane	20.77 (3.46)	12.59 (2.07)

It should be noted that our experiments are not concerned with comparing the relative performances of a one-sided classifier versus the multi-class classifiers. Rather, we analyse the variance between the two scenarios for each individual classifier and demonstrate the short-comings of the multi-class approach when it is presented with "unexpected" outliers. Our results demonstrate the one-sided classifier's ability to robustly reject these outliers in the same circumstances.

7   Conclusions and Future Work

Our research demonstrates the potential drawbacks of using conventional multi-class classification algorithms when the test data is taken from a different distribution to that of the training samples. We believe that for a large number of real-world practical problems, one-sided classifiers should be more robust than multi-class classifiers, as it is not feasible to sufficiently characterize the outlier concept in the training set. We have introduced the term "unexpected outliers" to signify outliers that violate the standard underlying assumption made by multi-class classifiers, which is that the test set instances are sampled from the same distribution as the training set instances. We have shown that, in such circumstances, a one-sided classifier can prove to be a more capable and robust alternative. Our future work will introduce new datasets from different domains and also analyse other one-sided and multi-class algorithms.

Acknowledgments. The authors are grateful for the support of Enterprise Ireland under Project CFTD/05/222a. The authors would also like to thank Dr. Abdenour Bounsiar for his help and valuable discussions, and Analyze IQ Limited for supplying some of the Raman spectral data.

References

1. Tax, D.M.J.: One-Class Classification, PhD Thesis. Delft University of Technology (2001)
2. Hollas, J.M.: Basic Atomic and Molecular Spectroscopy. Royal Society of Chemistry (2002)
3. Gardiner, D.J., Graves, P.R., Bowley, H.J.: Practical Raman Spectroscopy. Springer, New York (1989)
4. Bulkin, B.: The Raman Effect: An Introduction. John Wiley, New York (1991)
5. Harwood, L.M., Moody, C.J., Percy, J.M.: Experimental Organic Chemistry: Standard and Microscale. Blackwell Publishing, Malden (1999)
6. Conroy, J., Ryder, A.G., Leger, M.N., Hennessey, K., Madden, M.G.: Qualitative and quantitative analysis of chlorinated solvents using Raman spectroscopy and machine learning. In: Opto-Ireland 2005, vol. 5826, pp. 131–142 (2005)
7. Madden, M.G., Ryder, A.G.: Machine Learning Methods for Quantitative Analysis of Raman Spectroscopy Data. In: International Society for Optical Engineering (SPIE 2002), vol. 4876, pp. 1130–1139 (2002)
8. O'Connell, M.L., Howley, T., Ryder, A.G., Leger, M.N., Madden, M.G.: Classification of a target analyte in solid mixtures using principal component analysis, support vector machines and Raman spectroscopy. In: Opto-Ireland 2005, vol. 5826, pp. 340–350 (2005)
9. Howley, T.: Kernel Methods for Machine Learning with Application to the Analysis of Raman Spectra. PhD Thesis. National University of Ireland, Galway (2007)
10. Witten, I.H., Frank, E.: Data Mining: Practical machine learning tools and techniques, 2nd edn. Morgan Kaufmann, San Francisco (2005)
11. Munroe, D.T., Madden, M.G.: Multi-Class and Single-Class Classification Approaches to Vehicle Model Recognition from Images. In: AICS 2005, Portstewart (2005)

Just Say It: An Evaluation of Speech Interfaces for Augmented Reality Design Applications

Nicholas Hanlon, Brian Mac Namee, and John Kelleher

DIT AI Group, School of Computing,
Dublin Institute of Technology, Dublin, Ireland
firstname.lastname@dit.ie

Abstract. Design has been one of the most successful application areas for *augmented reality* (AR) technology. However, because of the *head-mounted-displays* typically used in immersive AR applications users are not able to use traditional interface modalities such as keyboards and mice. *Speech interfaces* offer an attractive solution to this problem. Using an interior design application this paper describes an evaluation experiment which shows that speech interfaces are an attractive control solution for AR design applications.

1 Introduction

Augmented reality (AR) techniques have been particularly successful in design applications [1]. Mixing real and virtual objects within the field of view of a user offers the opportunity to visualise proposed environments. However, a problem arises in AR design applications, and in all immersive AR applications. Since users typically wear a *head-mounted-display* (HMD) they are not free to use common interface devices such as keyboards or mice due to the restricted field of view. *Speech interfaces* offer an attractive control solution for such applications.

Using a bespoke AR interior design application this paper evaluates the suitability of speech interfaces for AR design applications. The contribution of the paper is that it demonstrates that a speech interface based control solution works well for this application. From this we extrapolate that speech interfaces are worth pursuing for AR design applications in general.

To ground the evaluation presented in the paper, section 2 gives an overview of AR technology, existing AR systems for design, speech interfaces, and AR systems that use speech interfaces. Section 3 then describes our speech-controlled AR interior design system, paying particular attention to the *frame-and-slot* [2] semantic representation used, and the finite-state-machine used for parsing utterances. The evaluation of the speech interface for this application is presented in section 4. Finally, section 5 presents conclusions and outlines future work.

2 Background

Augmented reality (AR) applications augment video images of the real world with virtual objects rendered to appear as if they exist in the real world. This

L. Coyle and J. Freyne (Eds.): AICS 2009, LNAI 6206, pp. 134–143, 2010.

is achieved by calculating the positions of known objects within video images of the real world and positioning virtual objects relative to these, a process known as *registration*. Registration is most commonly achieved using *fiducial markers* [3] which are special tags that are easily identified within a video frame. The distinctive black square and symbol visible in Fig. 1(a) is a typical example. The square border is used to calculate the orientation of the marker relative to the camera, from which a rendering engine can calculate a transformation to position virtual objects relative to the marker. As a user changes their viewing position these transformations are recalculated so that virtual objects always appear to remain in the correct position with respect to the real scene. The symbols on the fiducial markers uniquely identify each one.

In the most common viewing solution for immersive AR applications the user views their environment using a *head-mounted display* (HMD) (a Trivisio ARVision 3D HMD (www.trivisio.com) is used in this work). A *video-see-through* HMD is composed of two cameras and two small monitors which are fixed over the eyes of the wearer. The wearer does not view the real world directly, but rather sees a feed from one of the cameras on the screen in front of each of their eyes. In this way virtual objects can be placed within the scenes that are viewed by the wearer.

From the beginnings of AR research the potential to use the technology in design applications was identified - empty rooms could be furnished with virtual furniture [4,5], or planned buildings could be viewed at their proposed sites [6,7]. The contribution of this work is not a novel interior design application, but the use of a speech interface to control such an application. When using a HMD, common interaction modalities (e.g. keyboard and mouse) are not suitable as the user is not able to see either peripherals or their own hands. The use of a speech interface solves this problem. Using speech as an interface requires solving two problems: *automatic speech recognition* (ASR) [2] and *natural language understanding* (NLU) [8]. These are two very different problems.

The goal of ASR is to map from an acoustic voice signal to a string of words. As a general problem (automatically mapping from any speaker, speaking on any topic, in any environment, to a correct transcription of what they have said) ASR is far from being solved. However, in more restricted domains - e.g. where a system has been trained to a particular speaker's voice, or where the topic of spoken language has been restricted - ASR has developed into a technology that is mature enough to be used by general computer users with relatively little training. Indeed, ASR has matured to a stage where modern operating systems include ASR as an optional interface modality (e.g. Windows Vista).

The goal of NLU is to map natural language into a formal semantic representation that is designed to be used by a computer. The main problems faced by NLU are the variation in natural language (i.e. the same thing can be said in multiple ways) and ambiguity (i.e. a particular utterance may be used to convey several different meanings depending on the context of the utterance and the goals of the speaker). As with ASR, NLU as a general problem is far from being solved. However, following in the *microworlds* tradition (e.g. SHRDLU [9]), it is possible to develop NLU components for specific well defined domains.

Because of the difficulties outlined above, the use of speech interfaces in AR applications has not been particularly widespread, although there are some interesting examples. Irwati et al [10] describe a multi-modal interface to an AR system which uses both speech and gestural information, while the SEAR system [11] is a hands-free AR system used by pipe-inspection technicians that allows limited natural language dialogues between technicians and the system. Because of this lack of research attention the use of speech interfaces in AR applications is a promising research area. The next section will describe the AR interior design application that we have built to examine the use speech interface based control solutions in AR design applications.

3   A Speech-Controlled AR Design Application

The purpose of this application is to allow an interior designer stand within an empty room and virtually experiment with different furnishings and decoration viewed through a HMD. By using a speech interface base control solution the user will not be tied to a mouse and keyboard but will be free to move within the space and so view it from any perspective. Rather than using a real full-size room, a table-top mockup featuring a floor and two walls (as shown in Fig. 1(a)) is used. A single fiducial marker is placed on the floor of the room so that it can be located when viewed through a HMD. The open source ARToolkit API [3] is used for fiducial marker recognition. Once the marker has been recognised, the mock-up room is augmented with floor and wall coverings (the positions of which are based on predefined dimensions of the mock-up room) and any virtual objects that have been added to the scene. The floor of the room is divided into a square grid layout and the positions of virtual objects are stored on this grid. Fig. 1(b) shows the room after augmentation. While the AR and rendering components of the system are basic, the speech interface warrants detailed discussion.

The system's speech interface consists of two major components: an *automatic speech recognition* (ASR) and a *natural language understanding* (NLU) component. The ASR component was developed using the Microsoft Speech SDK 5.1 (www.microsoft.com/speech). Current ASR systems are not currently capable of automatically transcribing any speaker speaking about any topic. There are two common ways in which this limitation is addressed: training systems to recognise particular speakers, or limiting the allowed vocabulary. Rather than requiring that our system be trained for every new speaker, the vocabulary of words that the ASR system tries to recognize was limited. This was deemed appropriate as the domain of this system is relatively well-defined, in terms of the types of objects that the user will refer to and the types of actions they will wish the system to perform.

This custom vocabulary of the system consisted of verbs, nouns, adjectives and adverbs. The verbs in the system's vocabulary were: DELETE, PLACE, ADD, ROTATE, UNDO, REPEAT, AGAIN, DEBUG, CANCEL, EXIT, MOVE, RESET, PAINT,

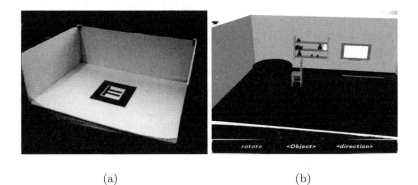

(a)   (b)

Fig. 1. (a) The mock-up room created for the application before augmentation and (b) the room wih augmentations and feedback given to the user on utterances so far

SHOW, HIDE, SAVE, LOAD. The nouns in the vocabulary were: TABLE, LAMP, STOOL, CHAIR, SOFA, BED, TV, LIGHT, CURVE-CHAIR, SHELF, WALL, FLOOR, GROUND, and the numbers ONE, TWO, ..., NINE. The adjectives the system could recognise were: GREEN, DARK-BLUE, RED, WHITE, BLACK, PURPLE, OR-ANGE, YELLOW, LEFT, RIGHT, FORWARDS, and BACKWARDS. Finally, the system could also recognise the adverbs YES, and NO.

It should be noted that there are no *structural* or *closed-class* words (e.g. determiners, prepositions etc.) in the vocabulary of the ASR system. This means that if the user inputs ADD A CHAIR the ASR system will ignore the indefinite A and simply return the sequence of strings ADD CHAIR. There were several reasons why it was decided to exclude structural words from the vocabulary of the system. Firstly, it was not felt that dropping these words from the input would adversely affect the ability of the system to interpret the semantics of the commands it was designed to handle. Secondly, it enabled us to reduce the vocabulary of the system to its bare essentials. As noted previously, this reduction increases the accuracy of the ASR component in recognising what has been said. However, more importantly, the exclusion of these short structural words from the ASR vocabulary also helps to alleviate the issue of background noise being picked up as input by the ASR system. Finally, excluding these words simplified the parsing of the input by the NLU system; simply put, the shorter the string the easier it is to parse.

The output of the ASR component is a sequence of strings where each string is a word in the custom vocabulary. This sequence of strings is passed to the NLU component where each string is mapped to a command instruction that the system carries out.

The NLU component uses a *frame-and-slot* [2] semantic representation. This means that each command input by the user is converted into a frame structure that contains several slots for information regarding how the command should be carried out. For example, an input such as *paint wall black* corresponds to the following filled out frame: ACTION: PAINT | OBJECT: WALL | COLOUR: BLACK.

The set of frames used by the system is: [ACTION + OBJECT], [ACTION + OBJECT + DIRECTION], [ACTION + OBJECT + COLOUR], [ACTION + FILENAME], [ACTION].

The NLU component generates these semantic representations by parsing the input using a *domain specific semantic grammar*. The rules for the grammar are defined below (note that each rule in this grammar is augmented with semantic attachments that specify how the components of the input map to the slots in the frame being constructed):

- S → DELETE | PLACE | ADD + TABLE | LAMP | STOOL | CHAIR | SOFA | BED | TV | LIGHT | CURVE-CHAIR | SHELF | FLOOR : [ACTION + OBJECT]
- S → ROTATE | MOVE + TABLE | LAMP | STOOL | CHAIR | SOFA | BED | TV | LIGHT | CURVE-CHAIR | SHELF + LEFT | RIGHT : [ACTION + OBJECT + DIRECTION]
- S → PAINT + WALL | GROUND | FLOOR+ GREEN | DARK-BLUE | RED | WHITE | BLACK | PURPLE | ORANGE | YELLOW : [ACTION + OBJECT + COLOUR]
- S → SAVE | LOAD + ONE | TWO |...| NINE : [ACTION + FILENAME]
- S → UNDO | REPEAT | AGAIN | DEBUG | CANCEL | RESET | SHOW | HIDE | EXIT : [ACTION]

The language accepted by this grammar can be formally described as a *regular right linear language*: the rules in a right linear language have a single non-terminating on the right-hand side that if present must be the last symbol in the string. Because the language accepted by the grammar can be described as a regular language it can be parsed using a *finite state machine* (FSM). Fig. 2 shows the FSM used by the system to parse input. The FSM is shown as a directed graph where the arcs between the states (nodes) are labelled with the input strings that licence the FSM to transition along the arc, and the frame-slot that is filled by the value of the input string that triggered the transition.

The FSM has one start state (State 0) and two terminating states (States 7 and 8). Terminating states are indicated by a double-circle. This FSM is deterministic as its behavior during parsing is fully determined by the state it is in and the symbol it is looking at. To parse input into frames the FSM receives a sequence of strings and starts in the *Idle State* (or State 0). It then iterates through the strings in the input sequence. If the current string matches a label on one of the arcs leaving the current state then the slot indicated by the arc label is filled with the current input string; the FSM moves to the next state by crossing the arc; and parsing advances one string in the input sequence. If there is no match, then an error has occurred and the system moves to its error state, State 8. This process continues until the input sequence is empty.

If the machine transitions to the terminating State 7 it will have fully populated one of the frames accepted by the system. In such instances the FSM is said to accept the input and the frame is passed to a task queue. However, if the machine transitions to the terminating State 8 the FSM is said to reject the input. There are three ways that the machine can transition to State 8. First,

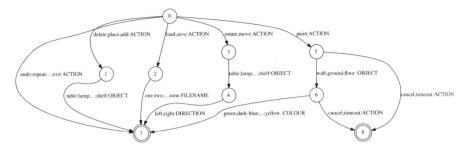

Fig. 2. The finite state machine used by the system to parse input

if the input contains the string CANCEL the FSM transitions from the current state to State 8. Secondly, if the machine runs out of input when it is in a non-terminating state it will automatically transition to State 8 after a predefined time-out interval. Finally, if the system comes across an unexpected input term (i.e. it cannot transition from its current state) it will transition to State 8 and report an error to the user. On entering State 8 the current input queue is emptied and no action takes place within the scene. On receiving new voice input from the user the system will return to State 0. Note that, although the FSM can follow a *cancel*, *time out*, or *error* transition from any non-terminating state to State 8, due to space considerations in Fig. 2 the *cancel* and *time-out* transitions are only shown from States 5 and 6.

Once a frame has been fully populated the system returns to the idle state and the frame is added to a task queue. Each filled out frame from the task queue is then converted into a function call with parameters specified. The first stage in this process is to map the string value of the ACTION slot to a numeric ID. Currently, this is done using a table lookup. Note that this mapping may map multiple ACTION slot values to the same numeric ID. This many-to-one mapping enables the system to handle the natural variation in the input that arises through users using different words to express the same function (e.g. the user may use either PLACE or ADD to add an object to the scene). The task manager uses a switch function on the numeric IDs to select the appropriate function call and passes the other slot values as parameters to the function. Each function then causes an appropriate action to take place within the scene (e.g. adding a new object, or moving an existing one).

Once an utterance by the user is recognised by the system a status-bar-like display at the bottom of the screen (shown in Fig. 1(b)) shows the slots associated with that frame to give feedback to the user. When using speech interfaces feedback is extremely important to give the user confidence that the system is responding correctly to their inputs [12]. When the system enters an error state (i.e. encounters an unexpected speech input such as a colour when an object type is expected) the text in the status bar turns red to indicate to the user that this has happened. Informal trials with a small group of users found that this status bar feedback solution was more suitable in this application than sonification-based solutions or solutions that gave additional textual feedback to the user.

The status bar found the right balance between providing sufficient information to the user and not overly interfering with their immersive experience.

The next section will describe how this system was used to evaluate the suitability of speech interfaces for AR design applications.

4   Evaluation

The evaluation experiment tasked users with furnishing and decorating a series of pre-defined rooms. In the evaluation participants were first given a short document which explained the experimental procedure (without indicating the goals of the experiment) and how to use the system. Participants were then timed trying to reproduce the four rooms shown in Fig. 3. These were presented to participants in the order shown and are of increasing complexity.

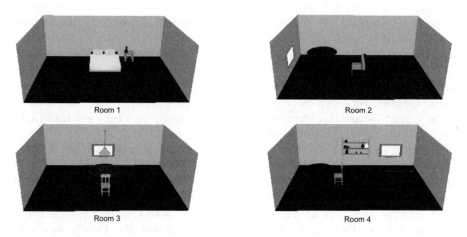

Fig. 3. The four rooms that participants in the evaluation experiment were asked to reproduce using the system

There were two versions (A and B) of the instruction script given out to participants. The versions were given randomly to participants so that half received version A (group A) and half version B (group B). Version A gave users only a list of valid commands without any explanation of them. Version B additionally gave users an explanation of each command and the correct way to use it. This was done to gauge how much instruction was required in order for participants to successfully use a speech interface. Ten participants took part in the experiment. These were a mixture of males and females with varying degrees of computer literacy. None had experience of using AR or speech interface based systems.

The primary evaluation metric used in the experiment is the time taken for participants to complete the four room layouts. The ability of participants to complete this task in reasonable time indicates the suitability of the speech interface used. Evaluating performance on a task also gives an objective measure and so is preferred over more qualitative evaluation techniques.

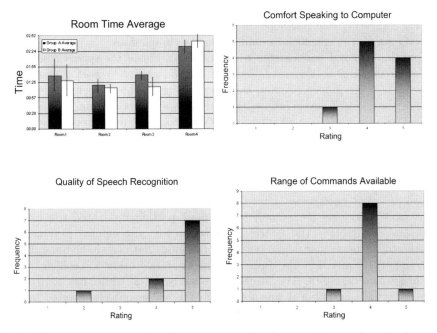

Fig. 4. The average times taken for members of each group to complete the layouts of the four evaluation rooms and histograms of participants' responses to the survey questions

Fig. 4 shows the average time taken (with standard deviations) for participants in each of the groups to complete each of the room layouts. The first observation from this graph is that in all cases participants were able to complete each room layout in under 3 minutes. In informal experiments using a conventional interface (using a keyboard and mouse) to the application it was found that 3 minutes was a reasonable estimate for the time required to complete a task of this level of complexity. A more formal experiment comparing these versions o the interface will be undertaken in the future. This first observation indicates that *a speech interface is suitable for AR design applications*, which is the main finding of this evaluation.

The second observation is that the difference between the times taken by members of group A and group B are minor - a paired two-tailed Student's t-test does not indicate a significant difference. This indicates that the instruction set did not require detailed explanation and shows that participants were intuitively able to use a speech interface.

In order to further explore these results participants were given a short survey after they had completed the experiment with their answers given on a five-point *Likert scale*. Participants were also offered an opportunity to provide open-ended comments on their experiences. Question 1 asked users to: *rate how comfortable you felt speaking to the computer, rather than using keyboard and mouse (1 = very uncomfortable, 5 = very comfortable)*. Fig. 4 shows a histogram of the responses to this question. The majority of participant responses are at the *4* and *5* levels indicating that participants were comfortable using the speech interface. This reinforces the conclusions made from the timing data.

Question 2 asked participants to: *rate the quality of the speech recognition, did it recognise your commands well or did you have to repeat yourself (1 = very bad, 5 = very good)*. Again, as shown in Fig. 4, the majority of responses were at the *4* and *5* levels indicating that the speech recognition was accurate. In their comments some participants did refer to problems in recognition when background noise was present, and one participant, who had a relatively thick accent, had difficulty in getting the system to understand a small subset of the available commands - the rating at the *2* level came from this participant.

Question 3 asked participants to: *evaluate the range of commands available to you (1 = not enough commands to control the scene, 5 = more than enough commands to control the scene)*. While most participants rated the range of commands available at the *4* level, as shown in Fig. 4, a number of issues were mentioned. In particular, some participants found that certain commands were quite repetitive and that the ability to repeat an operation a specified number of times would be useful. Also, users were surprised that while they were able to colour the walls and floor it was not possible to colour objects inserted into the scene. These would be relatively easy additions to make to the system.

5   Conclusions

The question posed in this paper is: *are speech interfaces suitable for AR design applications*. To answer this question an AR interior design application was built in which users virtually furnish and decorate a mock-up room using a speech interface. The ability of people to use this application was evaluated in an experiment in which users were asked to create given room layouts, and the time taken to do this was recorded. In this experiment all participants could use the system to lay out all of the rooms successfully in very short times. This strongly supports the use of speech interfaces for AR design applications.

The main direction for future work is increasing the sophistication of the speech interface. For example, at present only one of each object type is allowed as this removes the need to perform *reference resolution* [2]. Allowing multiple objects of each type and commands such as *move the sofa at the front to the right* would require the system to resolve the *sofa* reference to a particular sofa in the scene. This is a fundamental competence of dialogue systems and is by no means a solved problem. Understanding other similar utterances such as such as spatial references [13] and anaphoric references [14] would require a much more sophisticated dialogue understanding system. However, this system would serve as a perfect test-bed for evaluating approaches to understanding these more complex sorts of utterances.

Finally, an obvious important future development will be to deploy the system into a real room and this will be done in the very near future. The use of a full scale room will introduce a range of a new language understanding challenges as the user will be able to move around the environment viewing it from different angles, and so seemingly benign statements such as *move the sofa left* will become much more interesting as the system will have to determine, from the point of view of the user, what they mean by left.

References

1. Azuma, R., Baillot, Y., Behringer, R., Feiner, S., Julier, S., MacIntyre, B.: Recent advances in augmented reality. Computer Graphics and Applications 21(6) (2001)
2. Jurafsky, D.: Speech and Language Processing. Prentice-Hall, Englewood Cliffs (2008)
3. Kato, H., Billinghurst, M.: Marker tracking and hmd calibration for a video-based augmented reality conferencing system. In: Proc. of the 2nd IEEE and ACM International Workshop on Augmented Reality (1999)
4. Ahlers, K., Kramer, A., Breen, D., Chevalier, P.Y., Crampton, C., Rose, E., Tuceryan, M., Whitaker, R., Greer, D.: Distributed augmented reality for collaborative design applications. In: Proceedings of Eurographics 1995, pp. 3–14 (1995)
5. Kato, H., Billinghurst, M., Poupyrev, I., Imamoto, K., Tachibana, K.: Virtual object manipulation on a table-top ar environment. In: Proceedings of the IEEE and ACM International Symposium on Augmented Reality 2000, pp. 111–119 (2000)
6. Thomas, B.H.: Augmented Reality Visualisation Facilitating The Architectural Process. In: Mixed Reality in Architecture, Design And Construction. Springer, Heidelberg (2009)
7. Dunston, P.S., Wang, X.: Mixed reality-based visualization interfaces for architecture, engineering, and construction industry. Journal of Construction Engineering and Management 131(12), 1301–1309 (2005)
8. Manning, C.D., Schuetze, H.: Foundations of Statistical Natural Language Processing. MIT Press, Cambridge (1999)
9. Winograd, T.: Understanding natural language. Cognitive Psychology 3(1) (1972)
10. Irawati, S., Green, S., Billinghurst, M., Duenser, A., Ko, H.: An Evaluation of an Augmented Reality Multimodal Interface Using Speech and Paddle Gestures. In: Pan, Z., Cheok, D.A.D., Haller, M., Lau, R., Saito, H., Liang, R. (eds.) ICAT 2006. LNCS, vol. 4282, pp. 272–283. Springer, Heidelberg (2006)
11. Goose, S., Sudarsky, S., Zhang, X., Navab, N.: Speech-enabled augmented reality supporting mobile industrial maintenance. IEEE Pervasive Computing 2(1) (2003)
12. Sears, A., Jacko, J.A.: The Human-Computer Interaction Handbook: Fundamentals, Evolving Technologies, and Emerging Applications. CRC Press, Boca Raton (2008)
13. Kelleher, J., Kruijff, G.J., Costello, F.: Proximity in context: an empirically grounded computational model of proximity for processing topological spatial expression. In: Proceedings of Coling-ACL 2006, Sydney Australia (2006)
14. Modjeska, N.N.: Resolving Other-Anaphora. PhD thesis, School of Informatics, University of Edinburgh (2003)

SceneMaker:
Intelligent Multimodal Visualisation
of Natural Language Scripts

Eva Hanser, Paul Mc Kevitt, Tom Lunney, and Joan Condell

School of Computing & Intelligent Systems,
Faculty of Computing & Engineering,
University of Ulster, Magee
Derry/Londonderry BT48 7JL,
Northern Ireland
hanser-e@email.ulster.ac.uk,
{p.mckevitt,tf.lunney,j.condell}@ulster.ac.uk

Abstract. Producing plays, films or animations is a complex and expensive process involving various professionals and media. Our proposed
software system, *SceneMaker*, aims to facilitate this creative process by
automatically interpreting natural language film/play scripts and generating multimodal, animated scenes from them. During generation of
story content, SceneMaker will give particular attention to emotional aspects and their reflection in fluency and manner of actions, body posture,
facial expressions, speech, scene composition, timing, lighting, music and
camera work. Related literature and software on Natural Language Processing, in particular textual affect sensing, affective embodied agents,
visualisation of 3D scenes and digital cinematography are reviewed. In
relation to other work, SceneMaker will present a genre-specific text-to-
animation methodology which combines all relevant expressive modalities and is made accessible via web-based and mobile platforms. In
conclusion, SceneMaker will enhance the communication of creative ideas
providing quick pre-visualisations of scenes.

Keywords: Natural Language Processing, Text Layout Analysis, Intelligent Multimodal Interfaces, Affective Agents, Genre Specification,
Automatic 3D Visualisation, Affective Cinematography, SceneMaker.

1 Introduction

The production of plays or movies is an expensive process involving planning,
rehearsal time, actors and technical equipment for lighting, sound and special
effects. It is also a creative act which requires experimentation, visualisation
of ideas and their communication between everyone involved, e.g., playwrights,
directors, actors, cameramen, orchestra, managers and costume and set design-
ers. We are developing a software system, *SceneMaker*, which will assist in this
production process. SceneMaker will provide a facility to test and pre-visualise

L. Coyle and J. Freyne (Eds.): AICS 2009, LNAI 6206, pp. 144–153, 2010.
© Springer-Verlag Berlin Heidelberg 2010

scenes before putting them into action. Users input a natural language (NL) text scene and automatically receive multimodal 3D visualisations. The objective is to give directors or animators a reasonable idea of what a scene will look like. The user can refine the automatically created output through a script and 3D editing interface, accessible over the internet and on mobile devices. Thus, SceneMaker will be a collaborative tool for script writers, animators, directors and actors, sharing scenes online. Such technology could be applied in the training of those involved in scene production without having to utilise expensive actors and studios. Alternatively, it could be used for rapid visualisation of ideas and concepts in advertising agencies.

SceneMaker will extend an existing software prototype, CONFUCIUS [1], which provides automated conversion of single natural language sentences to multimodal 3D animation of characters' actions and camera placement. SceneMaker will focus on the precise representation of emotional expression in all modalities available for scene production and especially on human-like modelling of body language and genre-sensitive art direction. To achieve this, SceneMaker will include new tools for text layout analysis of screenplays or play scripts, commonsense and affective knowledge bases for context understanding, affective reasoning and automatic genre specification. This research focuses on three research questions: How can emotional information be computationally recognised in screenplays and structured for visualisation purposes? How can emotional states be synchronised in presenting all relevant modalities? Can compelling, life-like and believable animations be achieved?

Section 2 of this paper gives an overview of current research on computational, multimodal and affective scene production. In section 3, the design of SceneMaker is discussed. SceneMaker is compared to related multimodal work in section 4 and section 5 discusses conclusions and future work.

2   Background

Automatic and intelligent production of film/theatre scenes with characters expressing emotional states involves four development stages:

1. Detecting personality traits and emotions in the film/play script
2. Modelling affective 3D characters, their expressions and actions
3. Visualisation of scene environments according to emotional findings
4. Development of a multi-modal user interface and mobile application.

This section reviews state-of-the-art advances in these areas.

2.1   Detecting Personality and Emotions in Film/Play Scripts

All modalities of human interaction express personality and emotional states, namely voice, word choice, gestures, body posture and facial expression. In order to recognise emotions in text and to create life-like characters, psychological theories for emotion, mood, personality and social status are translated into computable methods, e.g., Ekman's 6 basic emotions [2], the Pleasure-Dominance-Arousal model (PAD) [3] with intensity values or the OCC model (Ortony-Clore-Collins) [4] with cognitive grounding and appraisal rules. Word choice is a useful indicator for the personality of a story character, their social situation, emotional state and attitude. Different approaches to textual affect sensing are able to recognise explicit affect words such as keyword spotting and lexical affinity [5], machine learning methods [6], hand-crafted rules and fuzzy logic systems [7] and statistical models [6]. Common knowledge based approaches [8,9] and a cognitive inspired model [10] include emotional context evaluation of non-affective words and concepts. The unified writing style and strict formatting of screenplays and play scripts eases the machine parsing of scripts and facilitates the detection of semantic context information for visualisation. The prose of scene descriptions focuses on what is audible and visible. Through text layout analysis of capitalisation, indentation and parentheses, elements such as dialog, location, time, present actors, actions and sound cues can be visually recognised and directly mapped into XML-presentations [11].

2.2   Modelling Affective Embodied Agents

Research aiming to automatically model and animate virtual humans with natural expressions faces challenges not only in automatic 3D character manipulation/transformation, synchronisation of face expressions, e.g., lips and gestures with speech, path finding and collision detection, but furthermore in the refined sensitive execution of each action. The exact manner of an affective action depends on intensity, fluency, scale and timing and impacts on the viewer's interpretation of the behaviour. Various scripting languages specifically cater for the modelling of the detected emotions and affective behaviour characteristics.

Non-verbal behaviour of avatars is automatically modelled from conversational text with the Behaviour Expression Animation Toolkit (BEAT) [12]. Based on the analysis of linguistics and context of dialogue scripts appropriate Multimodal Presentation Mark-up Language (MPML) [13] annotations are automatically added to model speech synthesis, facial and body animations of 3D agents. SCREAM (Scripting Emotion-based Agent Minds) [14] is a web-based scripting tool for multiple characters which computes affective states based on the OCC-Model [4] of appraisal and intensity of emotions, as well as social context. ALMA [15] (a Layered Model of Affect) implements AffectML, an XML based modelling language which incorporates the concept of short-term emotions, medium-term moods and long-term personality profiles. The OCEAN personality model [16], Ekman's basic emotions [2] and a model of story character roles are combined through a fuzzy rule-based system [7] to decode the meaning of scene descriptions and to control the affective state and body language of the characters. The high-level control of affective characters in [7] maps personality and emotion output to graphics and animations. Postural values for the four main body areas, head, trunk, upper and lower limbs, manipulate the shape, geometry and motion of the character model based on animation techniques for believable characters [17] considering physical characteristics of space, timing, velocity, position, weight and portion of the body. Embodied Conversational Agents (ECA) are capable of real-time face-to-face conversations with human users or other agents, generating and understanding NL and body movement. The virtual human, Max [18], engages museum visitors in small talk. Max listens while users type their input, reasons about actions to take, has intention and goal plans, reacts emotionally and gives verbal and non-verbal feedback. Greta [19] is modelled as an expressive multimodal ECA. The Affective Presentation Markup Language (APML) defines her facial expressions, hand and arm gestures for different communicational functions with varying degrees of expressivity (manner). The behaviours are synchronised with the duration of speech phonemes.

Multimodal annotation coding of video or motion captured data specific to emotion collects data in publicly available facial expression or body gesture databases [20]. The captured animation data can be mapped to 3D models, which is useful for instructing characters precisely on how to perform desired actions.

2.3   Visualisation of 3D Scenes and Virtual Theatre

Visual and acoustic elements involved in composing a virtual story scene, the construction of the 3D environment or set, scene composition, automated cinematography and the effect of genre styles are addressed in complete text-to-visual systems such as SONAS [21], WordsEye [22], CONFUCIUS [1] and ScriptViz [25], and the scene directing system, CAMEO [27]. SONAS constructs a three-dimensional virtual town scenario according to the verbal descriptions of a human user. Besides information on the location, scene visualisation requires consideration of the positioning and interaction of actors and objects, the camera view, light sources and audio like background noises or music. WordsEye depicts non-animated 3D scenes with characters, objects, actions and environments. A database of graphical objects holds 3D models, their attributes, poses, kinematics and spatial relations in low-level specifications. In CONFUCIUS, multimodal 3D animations of single sentences are produced. 3D models perform actions, dialogues are synthesised and basic cinematic principles determine camera placement.

Cinematography can assist in conveying themes and moods in animations. Film techniques are automatically applied to existing animations in [23]. Reasoning about plot, theme, character actions, motivations and emotions, they follow cinematic rules which define appropriate placement and movement of camera, lighting, colour schemes and the pacing of shots. A high-level synchronised Expression Mark-up Language (EML) [24] integrates environmental expressions like cinematography, illumination and music as a new modality into the emotion synthesis of virtual humans. ScriptViz renders 3D scenes from NL screenplays immediately during the writing process, extracting verbs and adverbs to interpret events and states in sentences. The time and environment where a story takes place, the theme the story revolves around and the emotional tone of films, plays or literature classify different genres with distinguishable presentation styles. Commonly, genres are categorised into, e.g., action, comedy, drama, horror and romance. Genre is reflected in the detail of a production, exaggeration and fluency of movements, pace (shot length), lighting, colour and camerawork. These parameters are responsible for viewer perception, inferences and expectations and thus for an appropriate affective viewer impression. Cinematic principles in different genres are investigated in [26]. Dramas and romantic movies are slower paced with longer dialogues, whereas action movies have rapidly changing, shorter shot length. Comedies tend to be presented in a large spectrum of bright colours, whereas horror films adopt mostly darker hues. The automatic 3D animation production system, CAMEO, incorporates direction knowledge, like genre and cinematography, as computer algorithms and data to control camera, light, audio and character motions. A system which automatically recommends music based on emotion is proposed in [28]. Associations between emotions and music features in movies are discovered by extracting chords, rhythm and tempo of songs.

2.4   Multimodal Interfaces and Mobile Applications

Technological advances enable multimodal human-computer interaction in the mobile world. The system architecture and rendering can be placed on the mobile device itself or distributed from a server via wireless broadband networks. SmartKom Mobile [29] deploys the multimodal system, SmartKom, on mobile devices. The user interacts with a virtual character through dialogue. Supported modalities include language, gesture, facial expression and emotions carried through speech emphasis. Script writing tools assist the writing process of screenplays or play scripts, like the web-based FiveSprockets [30] or ScriptRight [31] for mobile devices. The Virtual Theatre Interface project [32] offers a web-based user interface to manipulate actors' positions on stage, lighting and audience view points.

The wide range of approaches, presented here, to modelling emotions, moods and personality aspects in virtual humans and scene environments along with first attempts to deploy multi-modal agents on mobile devices provide a sound basis for SceneMaker.

3   Design of SceneMaker

Going beyond the animation of explicit events, the software prototype, Scene-Maker will use Natural Language Processing (NLP) methods for screenplays to automatically extract and visualise emotions, moods and film/play genre. Scene-Maker will augment short 3D scenes with affective influences on the body language of actors and environmental expression, like illumination, timing, camera work, music and sound automatically directed according to the genre style.

3.1   Architecture of SceneMaker

SceneMakers's architecture is shown in Fig. 1. The main component is the *scene production module* including modules for understanding, reasoning and multimodal visualisation situated on a server. The *understanding module* performs

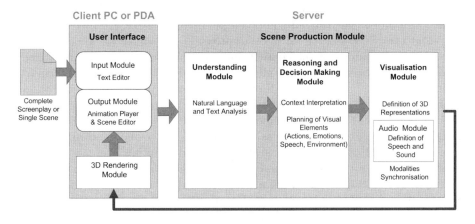

Fig. 1. Architecture of SceneMaker

natural language processing and text layout analysis of input text. The *reasoning module* interprets the context based on common, affective and cinematic knowledge bases, updates emotional states and creates plans for actions, their manners and representation of the set environment. The *visualisation module* maps these plans to 3D animation data, selects appropriate 3D models from the graphics database, defines their body motion transitions, instructs speech synthesis, selects sound and music files from the audio database and assigns values to camera and lighting parameters. The visualisation module synchronises all modalities into an animation manuscript. The online user interface, available via desktop computers and mobile devices, consists of two parts. The input module provides assistance for film and play script writing and editing and the output module renders the 3D scene according to the manuscript and allows manual scene editing to fine-tune the automatically created animations.

3.2   Implementation of SceneMaker

Multimodal systems automatically mapping text to visuals face challenges in interpreting human language which is variable, ambiguous, imprecise and relies on common knowledge between the communicators. Enabling a machine to understand a natural language text involves feeding the machine with grammatical structures, semantic relations and visual descriptions to be able to match suitable graphics. Existing software tools fulfilling sub-tasks will be modified, combined and extended for the implementation of SceneMaker. For the interpretation of input scripts, SceneMaker will build upon the NLP module of CONFUCIUS [1], but a pre-processing tool will first decompose the layout structure of the input screenplay/play script. The syntactic knowledge base parses input text and identifies parts of speech, e.g., noun, verb, adjective, with the Connexor Part of Speech Tagger [33] and determines the constituents in a sentence, e.g., subject, verb and object, with Functional Dependency Grammars [34]. The semantic knowledge base (WordNet [35] and LCS database [36]) and temporal language relations will be extended by an emotional knowledge base, e.g., WordNet-Affect [37], and context reasoning with ConceptNet [9] to enable an understanding of the deeper meaning of the context and emotions. In order to automatically recognise genre, SceneMaker will identify keyword co-occurrences and term frequencies and determine the length of dialogues, sentences and scenes/shots. In SceneMaker, the visual knowledge of CONFUCIUS, such as object models and event models, will be related to emotional cues. CONFUCIUS' basic cinematic principles will be extended and classified into expressive and genre-specific categories. EML [24] is a comprehensive XML-based scripting language to model expressive modalities including body language and cinematic annotations. Resources for 3D models are H-Anim models [38] which include geometric or physical, functional and spatial properties. For speech generation from dialogue text, the speech synthesis module used in CONFUCIUS, FreeTTS [39], will be tested for its suitability in SceneMaker with regard to mobile applications and the effectiveness of emotional prosody. An automatic audio selection tool, as in [28], will be incorporated for intelligent, affective selection of sound and music according the theme and mood of a scene.

Test scenarios will be developed based on screenplays of different genres and animation styles, e.g., drama films, which include precise descriptions of set layout and props versus comedy, which employs techniques of exaggeration for expression. The effectiveness and appeal of the scenes created in SceneMaker will be evaluated against hand-animated scenes and existing feature film scenes. The functionality and usability of SceneMaker's components and the GUI will be tested in cooperation with professional film directors, comparing the process of directing a scene traditionally with actors or with SceneMaker.

4   Relation to Other Work

Research implementing various aspects of modelling affective virtual actors, narrative systems and film-making applications relates to SceneMaker. CONFUCIUS [1] and ScriptViz [25] realise text-to-animation systems from natural language text input, but they do not enhance visualisation through affective aspects, the agent's personality, emotional cognition or genre specific styling. Their animations are built from well-formed single sentences and they do not consider the wider context. SceneMaker will facilitate animation modelling of sentences, scenes or whole scripts. Single sentences require more reasoning about default settings and more precision will be achieved from collecting context information from longer passages of text. SceneMaker will introduce text layout analysis to derive semantic content from the particular format of screenplays/play scripts. Emotion cognition and display will be related to commonsense knowledge. No previous storytelling system controls agent behaviour through integrating all of personality, social status, narrative roles and emotions. Only EML [24] combines multimodal character animation with film making practices based on an emotional model, but it does not consider personality types or genre. CAMEO [27] is the only system relating specific cinematic direction, for character animation, lighting and camera work, to the genre or theme of a given story, but genre types are explicitly selected by the user. SceneMaker will introduce a new approach to automatically recognise genre from script text with keyword co-occurrence, term frequency and calculation of dialogue and scene length. SceneMaker will bring all relevant techniques together to form a software system for believable affective computational animation production from NL scene scripts. SceneMaker will present a web/mobile based user interface for directors or animators to directly edit scenes.

5   Conclusion and Future Work

The software system, SceneMaker, contributes to believability and artistic quality of automatically produced animated, multimedia scenes. SceneMaker, which automatically visualises affective expressions of screenplays, aims to advance knowledge in the areas of affective computing, digital storytelling and expressive multimodal systems. Existing systems solve partial aspects of NLP, emotion modelling and multimodal storytelling. Thereby, we focus on semantic interpretation of screenplays or play scripts, the computational processing of emotions, virtual agents with affective behaviour and expressive scene composition including emotion-based audio selection. In relation to other work, SceneMaker will incorporate an expressive model for multiple modalities, including prosody, body language, acoustics, illumination, staging and camera work. Emotions will be inferred from context. Genre types will be automatically derived from the scene scripts and influence the design style of output animations. The 3D output will be editable on mobile devices. SceneMaker's mobile, web-based user interface will assist directors, drama students, writers and animators in the testing of their ideas. Accuracy of animation content, believability and effectiveness of expression and usability of the interface will be evaluated in empirical tests comparing manual animation, feature film scenes and real-life directing with SceneMaker. In conclusion, SceneMaker will automatically produce multimodal animations with heightened expressivity and visual quality from screenplay or play script input.

References

1. Ma, M.: Automatic Conversion of Natural Language to 3D Animation. Ph.D. Thesis, School of Computing and Intelligent Systems, University of Ulster (2006)
2. Ekman, P., Rosenberg, E.L.: What the face reveals: Basic and applied studies of spontaneous expression using the facial action coding system. Oxford University Press, Oxford (1997)
3. Mehrabian, A.: Framework for a Comprehensive Description and Measurement of Emotional States. Genetic, Social, and General Psychology Monographs 121(3), 339–361 (1995)
4. Ortony, A., Clore, G.L., Collins, A.: The Cognitive Structure of Emotions. Cambridge University Press, Cambridge (1988)

5. Francisco, V., Hervás, R., Gervás, P.: Two Different Approaches to Automated Mark Up of Emotions in Text. In: Sattar, A., Kang, B.-h. (eds.) AI 2006. LNCS (LNAI), vol. 4304, pp. 101–114. Springer, Heidelberg (2006)

6. Strapparava, C., Mihalcea, R.: Learning to identify emotions in text. In: Proceedings of the 2008 ACM Symposium on Applied Computing, SAC 2008, pp. 1556–1560. ACM, New York (2008)

7. Su, W.-P., Pham, B., Wardhani, A.: Personality and Emotion-Based High-Level Control of Affective Story Characters. IEEE Transactions on Visualization and Computer Graphics 13(2), 281–293 (2007)

8. Liu, H., Lieberman, H., Selker, T.: A model of textual affect sensing using real-world knowledge. In: Proceedings of the 8th International Conference on Intelligent User Interfaces, IUI 2003, pp. 125–132. ACM, New York (2003)

9. Liu, H., Singh, P.: ConceptNet: A practical commonsense reasoning toolkit. BT Technology Journal 22(4), 211–226 (2004)

10. Shaikh, M.A.M., Prendinger, H., Ishizuka, M.: A Linguistic Interpretation of the OCC Emotion Model for Affect Sensing from Text. In: Affective Information Processing, pp. 45–73. Springer, London (2009)

11. Choujaa, D., Dulay, N.: Using screenplays as a source of context data. In: Proceeding of the 2nd ACM International Workshop on Story Representation, Mechanism and Context, SRMC 2008, pp. 13–20. ACM, New York (2008)

12. Cassell, J., Vilhjálmsson, H.H., Bickmore, T.: BEAT: the Behavior Expression Animation Toolkit. In: Proceedings of the 28th Annual Conference on Computer Graphics and interactive Techniques SIGGRAPH 2001, pp. 477–486. ACM, New York (2001)

13. Breitfuss, W., Prendinger, H., Ishizuka, M.: Automated generation of non-verbal behavior for virtual embodied characters. In: Proceedings of the 9th International Conference on Multimodal Interfaces, ICMI 2007, pp. 319–322. ACM, New York (2007)

14. Prendinger, H., Ishizuka, M.: SCREAM: scripting emotion-based agent minds. In: Proceedings of the First International Joint Conference on Autonomous Agents and Multiagent Systems: Part 1, AAMAS 2002, pp. 350–351. ACM, New York (2002)

15. Gebhard, P.: ALMA - Layered Model of Affect. In: Proceedings of the 4th International Conference on Autonomous Agents and Multiagent Systems, AAMAS 2005, pp. 29–36. Utrecht University. ACM, Netherlands, New York (2005)

16. De Raad, B.: The Big Five Personality Factors. In: The Psycholexical Approach to Personality. Hogrefe & Huber (2000)

17. Thomas, F., Johnson, O.: The Illusion of Life: Disney Animation, pp. 47–69. Abbeville Press/Hyperion (1981, reprint 1997)

18. Kopp, S., Allwood, J., Grammer, K., Ahlsen, E., Stocksmeier, T.: Modeling Embodied Feedback with Virtual Humans. In: Wachsmuth, I., Knoblich, G. (eds.) ZiF Research Group International Workshop. LNCS (LNAI), vol. 4930, pp. 18–37. Springer, Heidelberg (2008)

19. Pelachaud, C.: Multimodal expressive embodied conversational agents. In: Proceedings of the 13th Annual ACM International Conference on Multimedia, MULTIMEDIA 2005, pp. 683–689. ACM, New York (2005)

20. Gunes, H., Piccardi, M.: A Bimodal Face and Body Gesture Database for Automatic Analysis of Human Nonverbal Affective Behavior. In: 18th International Conference on Pattern Recognition, ICPR, vol. 1, pp. 1148–1153. IEEE Computer Society, Washington (2006)

21. Kelleher, J., Doris, T., Hussain, Q., Nualláin, S.Ó.: SONAS: Multimodal, Multi-User Interaction with a Modelled Environment. In: Spatial Cognition, pp. 171–184. John Benjamins Publishing Company, Amsterdam (2000)
22. Coyne, B., Sproat, R.: WordsEye: an automatic text-to-scene conversion system. In: Proceedings of the 28th Annual Conference on Computer Graphics and Interactive Techniques, pp. 487–496. ACM Press, Los Angeles (2001)
23. Kennedy, K., Mercer, R.E.: Planning animation cinematography and shot structure to communicate theme and mood. In: Proceedings of the 2nd International Symposium on Smart Graphics, SMARTGRAPH 2002, vol. 24, pp. 1–8. ACM, New York (2002)
24. De Melo, C., Paiva, A.: Multimodal Expression in Virtual Humans. In: Computer Animation and Virtual Worlds 2006, vol. 17 (3-4), pp. 239–348. John Wiley & Sons Ltd, Chichester (2006)
25. Liu, Z., Leung, K.: Script visualization (ScriptViz): a smart system that makes writing fun. In: Soft Computing, vol. 10(1), pp. 34–40. Springer, Heidelberg (2006)
26. Rasheed, Z., Sheikh, Y., Shah, M.: On the use of computable features for film classification. IEEE Transactions on Circuits and Systems for Video Technology 15, 52–64 (2005)
27. Shim, H., Kang, B.G.: CAMEO - camera, audio and motion with emotion orchestration for immersive cinematography. In: Proceedings of the 2008 international Conference on Advances in Computer Entertainment Technology, ACE 2008, vol. 352, pp. 115–118. ACM, New York (2008)
28. Kuo, F., Chiang, M., Shan, M., Lee, S.: Emotion-based music recommendation by association discovery from film music. In: Proceedings of the 13th Annual ACM international Conference on Multimedia, MULTIMEDIA 2005, pp. 507–510. ACM, New York (2005)
29. Wahlster, W.: Smartkom: Foundations of Multimodal Dialogue Systems. Springer, Heidelberg (2006)
30. FiveSprockets, http://www.fivesprockets.com/fs-portal
31. ScriptRight, http://www.scriptright.com
32. Virtual Theatre Interface, http://accad.osu.edu/research/virtual_environment_htmls/virtual_theatre.htm
33. Connexor, http://www.connexor.eu/technology/machinese
34. Tesniere, L.: Elements de syntaxe structurale. Klincksieck, Paris (1959)
35. Fellbaum, C.: WordNet: An Electronic Lexical Database. MIT Press, Cambridge (1998)
36. Lexical Conceptual Structure Database, http://www.umiacs.umd.edu/~bonnie/LCS_Database_Documentation.html
37. Strapparava, C., Valitutti, A.: WordNet-Affect: an affective extension of WordNet. In: Proceedings of the 4th International Conference on Language Resources and Evaluation, LREC 2004, vol. 4, pp. 1083–1086 (2004)
38. Humanoid Animation Working Group, http://www.h-anim.org
39. FreeTTS 1.2 - A speech synthesizer written entirely in the JavaTM programming language, http://freetts.sourceforge.net/docs/index.php

The Enhanced Ranked List

Cathal Hoare and Humphrey Sorensen

Computer Science Department,
University College Cork,
Ireland
{hoare,sorensen}@cs.ucc.ie

Abstract. Currently information-seeking interfaces treat each separate search query and result as a sequence of unrelated singletons rather than as a sequence of actions that inform one another as part of an information-seeking task. In order to successfully complete their search goals, the user must formulate and order their queries by applying a search strategy to the information problem. In reality, users often lack a feedback mechanism between disparate parts of the strategy. The objective of this paper is to explore how document sets can be used in pairs to explicitly support session-based information exploration.

1 Introduction

The Enhanced Ranked List (ERL) allows users to explore an information space and identify salient points within it over the course of an information seeking session. A pair of document sets are presented to the user - one shows the ranked results of the current query while the other maintains a list of artifacts of interest for the duration of the query session. These landmark artifacts can then be used as the basis of further queries; this form of interaction promotes creation of queries that are informed by previous search cycles in the session. This paper will describe the metaphor behind the interface before outlining the application's implementation and architecture. An evaluation of ERL will then reveal how the average gain of participants was higher for users of ERL when compared to those using a single ranked list; this improvement is shown to be because of the tendency of the ERL users to use information discovered in previous query cycles.

It is intended that ERL be used for exploratory search [9] - that is, search that persists over at least several cycles and is made up of several interlinked information needs. This type of search is undertaken in all walks of life, from medical researchers [4] to college students writing a report. Many of these searchers do not receive formal instruction on how to search and depend on self-taught ad-hoc strategies that are often sub-optimal[1]. While it is necessary to note and collate

---

[1] D. M. Russell's "How do Google Searchers Behave?" Last retrieved on 20 April 2009 from http://dmrussell.googlepages.com/HowdoGooglesearchersbehave-PCDStanfo.pdf

L. Coyle and J. Freyne (Eds.): AICS 2009, LNAI 6206, pp. 154–163, 2010.
© Springer-Verlag Berlin Heidelberg 2010

relevant information artifacts - the authors and others [12] have observed various strategies including paper and electronic lists and notes, bookmarks and the use of tabs on browsers - many users rely on memory. A significant body of research has highlighted the need to marshal solutions to search sub-goals and to allow exploration continue from these information landmarks. Markey [11] discusses the various ways that an information problem can morph and develop during a search session and makes recommendations for interface components that handle these changes. Bates [1] and Blake et al [5] make several recommendations for integrated features that interfaces should support to allow development of informed queries. Common commercial efforts have, to-date been limited. Applications such as Google Notebook[2] and Microsoft OneNote[3] provide the ability to record and annotate items of interest. However, the types of artifacts that can be recorded is limited, and while aggregated content can be searched, individual items cannot be directly used as queries. Several approaches to guiding user strategy over the duration of a search session have been developed within the research community. These include facetted-search [6] - organizing results into meaningful contextual groups, strategy portals [3] - provision of critical search procedures within specific domains and recommender systems [2] - providing feedback in the form of query expansion or links to specific documents.

2   The Enhanced Ranked List

TheEnhanced-Ranked List (ERL) Interface is shown in Fig. 1, where typical facts are enlarged. It is designed to support a wide range of search types, from simple lookup searches to complex exploratory search tasks of indefinite duration. The interface is made up of four distinct regions. The traditional query field, labelled 1 in Fig. 1, is the starting point for each search session. It supports full Boolean query syntax; this syntax is based on Google's format. On submitting a query, a result header, labelled 2, provides metadata for both the query and the result set. The result set returns a list of results - ten results per page. Each result shows a header (labelled 3), first line of the document, document metadata and a set of contextual operations relevant to the document type. The header can be clicked on to open the document in a new tab, or moused over to provide a popup of the document in-situ on the results page. The format of the result is intentionally formatted in the Google style to provide a sense of familiarity to users of the application. Some of the contextual operations act on the documents; while the *similar documents* (labelled 4) operation uses the document as query that searches the entire document collection. Other contextual actions provide interaction with the *fact list.*

The *remember this* action, labelled 5, allows a user to add a document to the *fact list* - titled *things that I remembered on the interface.* Items added to the list persist for the duration of the browsing session or until the user clears the list (labelled 6). It is the contention of this paper that facts improve the usefulness

---

[2] http://www.google.com/notebook/
[3] http://office.microsoft.com/en-us/onenote/default.aspx

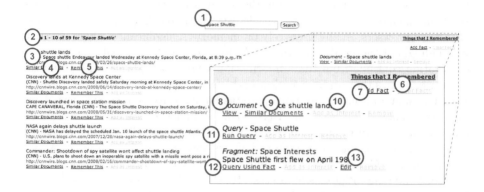

Fig. 1. The ERL Interface

of ranked lists when finding a solution extends over several cycles of seeking, either because of the complexity of the task or because of an inability to express a suitable query due to a lack of knowledge about the topic.

To solve these issues, three types of facts are implemented by the interface. Besides documents, both queries and user-defined/metadata facts can be added as items in the fact list. Document facts can be added to the fact list in one of two ways. The first involves dragging the result onto the list; the user can also click on the *remember this* contextual action (labelled 5). As a result, on the fact list, a range of contextual actions (labelled 8) are available, including *view* (to view the document), *similar documents* (to invoke a search of the entire collection for similar documents, labelled 9) and *add to interests* (in order to persist the result beyond the current search session, labelled 10). Document facts can also be removed from the list. Query facts represent entire result sets. They are added as a fact by dragging the result set description (labelled 2) onto the fact list. This type of fact has three associated contextual actions including *run query* (labelled 11) which reruns the query. Query facts can also be added as an interest and can be removed from the fact list. User facts are used to capture information relevant to the user's current context, or to capture metadata about a particular document or class of documents. They are created by clicking *add fact* (labelled 7). This type of query can be used as a query (labelled 12). Seekers can use this type of fact to record significant authors, important dates and relevant links. User facts can be edited as new information becomes available (labelled 13). All facts can be annotated to note its context and significance.

Several other features are implemented by the interface. User interests that persist for periods longer than a query session are also catered for. A user can mark any type of fact as an *interest*. The details of these facts are recorded by the server and can be imported back into the application at a later date. Interests can also be published as an online report in the form of an automatically generated wiki page. This page can be shared with other collaborating researchers. The interface also employs popup document previews. When a user passes a mouse

Table 1. Table of tasks undertaken in evaluation

Task 1
Record as many documents as possible while avoiding non-relevant documents about news articles outlining air safety issues and accidents that occurred during training in the US Air Force.
Task 2
Record as many documents as possible while avoiding non-relevant documents about news articles outlining civilian air accidents listed in the news archives that were caused by engine failure.

over a document in either the ranked list or fact list a popup display of the document's content appears. Keywords used in a query are highlighted on this popup. These features were not used in the evaluation described later and are mentioned here to complete the interface description.

The server architecture is implemented in two parts, a document crawler and a client server for retrieval. The architecture has been applied to several sources including RSS news feeds and Wikis such as Wikipedia[4]. This paper describes experiments conducted with news feeds. The systems content is indexed using the Lucene information retrieval engine[5]. The retrieval module is responsible for managing user interests and queries. Queries are submitted via a servlet that uses Lucene to generate a result set. This result set is wrapped in XML and passed to the client. A servlet also provides an interface onto the server to manage user interests.

The client is implemented using Adobe Flash[6] and OpenLaszlo[7]. This technology was chosen to provide Rich Internet Application (RIA) style functionality with a browser independent technology.

3   Evaluation Methodology and Execution

An evaluation of ERL was conducted to determine if it encourages users towards a more complete strategy that consisted of search cycles that were informed by previous cycles. The evaluation was carried out by a group of 12 subjects; the group was drawn from a wide range of professions and ranged between the ages of 19 and 36 years of age. All considered themselves proficient at search. The users were chosen at random from a list of responders to an email invitation to participate. A test collection of news articles was harvested over the later half of 2008. During this time, six questions were formulated and during the six months of harvesting, documents that were relevant to the questions, shown in Table 1, were used as tasks in the evaluation; each user carried out both tasks - using a

---

[4] http://www.wikipedia.org
[5] http://lucene.apache.org
[6] http://flash.adobe.com
[7] http://www.openlaszlo.org

Results for Task 1

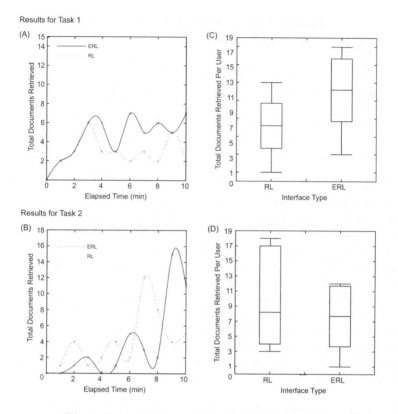

Results for Task 2

Fig. 2. Enhanced Ranked List Evaluation Results

standard ranked list for one and ERL for the other. Users, tasks and interface were matched randomly, while the order of interface usage was also randomized.

For each task, each user was given ten minutes to retrieve as many documents as possible. The screen of each user was recorded using the iShow[8] software package, while the scene around each user was also recorded on digital camcorder. Document interactions on the interface were also logged. In completion of the two tasks, each user was also interviewed. Analysis was completed by examining the relationship between documents retrieved, documents viewed, facts created and queries submitted. Each user conducted the evaluation on a machine equipped with a $2\,Ghz$ dual-core processor, $2\,Gb$ of RAM, a 19' screen and standard keyboard and mouse.

4   Analysis of Information Gain

This analysis of the evaluation begins by examining the rate at which relevant documents were retrieved by each interface for each task. Having shown a general

---

[8] http://www.shineywhitebox.com/home/home.html

improvement in this rate for users exploring unfamiliar domains using ERL, the authors will show that this improvement is due to the *fact list* and its tendency to guide users towards using informed queries.

For the purposes of this paper, gain means the number of relevant documents retrieved. The gain achieved for each task is presented from two perspectives. The first - corresponding to parts (A) and (B) of Fig. 2 - shows cumulative gain over time for the two tasks undertaken; gain in this case is the number of relevant documents retrieved. Parts (C) and (D) of Fig. 2 show the distribution of gain for individual subjects.

The gain for task one is shown in Fig. 2 Part (A). For this task, ERL immediately matches the Ranked List (RL), and after three minutes quickly out performs it. This was an interesting result, as users considered Task 1 a more difficult task. All stated that they knew little about military aviation and began querying with a set of simple queries. The performance gain by ERL was made through the use of contextual queries from queries from documents added to the fact list.

This pattern is particularly evident for task two (Fig. 2 Part (B)). It is thought that this was because searchers demonstrated a greater knowledge of the domain, recalling several recent civilian air accidents that had featured in the media - particularly Spanair in Madrid and the British Airways crash at Heathrow - and used those as the basis for their initial queries. While both interfaces demonstrated a continuous increase, towards the end ERL began to show an increased rate of gain (minutes 8 to 10 on Part (B)). These results suggest that ERL provides a greater benefit to users facing a topic with which they are not familiar.

When total gain distributed across the sample population is examined (Fig. 2 Parts (C) and (D)), the immediate impression is of the range of gain achieved. In both tasks, the minimum gain is zero to two documents retrieved irrespective of which interface was used. These users demonstrated *incredulous repetitions*[11] - that is, repeated modification of queries to the point that the goal of the *perfect query* supersedes that of the *perfect result*. While vigorous query refinement was undertaken, it was never informed by the content of previous results; rather, result set characteristics, such as number of documents returned, were used to guide query development. Users with low gain also demonstrated *query loyalty*, a term coined by the authors to describe the tendency to believe that the query has returned a correct result. It was characterized by continuously looking at the next page of results rather than attempting to refine the query to promote documents of interest. The sample also revealed a number of excellent searchers, again, irrespective of the interface used. These users also used a range of structured strategies. This is apparent in the RL plot for Task 2 (Fig. 2 Part (D)); a minority (3) drove the gain made by the upper quartile higher even though the mean for users of the interface was significantly lower.

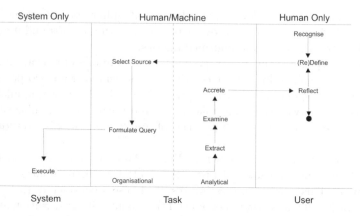

Fig. 3. Re-arranged General Model

5   The Relationship between Gain and User Strategy

Overall, gain achieved by users of RL is distributed evenly. The difference between the highest/lowest gain and upper/lower quartiles is regular, irrespective of task. A significant pattern emerges when the distribution of gain is examined for the Enhanced Ranked List (ERL). In this case, the upper quartile and mean is closer to the largest gain achieved and the lower quartile is further from the lowest gain achieved. This pattern can be observed in both tasks. The pattern indicates that the ERL interface helps users to achieve gain approaching that of the best performing user. It will be shown that this is because users are encouraged to use a more productive search strategy by the features of ERL.

Examining users' actions as they conducted the evaluation tasks required modeling of their actions. This allows comparison of actions across interfaces and between users. A general seeking model, described by Marchionini [10], details processes conducted at a query cycle level. This model was chosen to show user actions due to its ability to express user actions both over an individual cycle and over a series of cycles when it is combined with time series data. For the sake of identifying the authors' area of interest - the interaction between the system and the user - the general model is re-arranged as shown in Fig. 3. The user is made directly responsible for query execution. The user is informed by the system in four processes - source selection, query definition, result examination and information extraction. The authors add an extra process - *accrete* to include any action, such as note-taking or annotation, which externalize learning during a search cycle.

For this paper, the model was adjusted to take account of limitations in the experiment; specifically, source selection and query creation were grouped as a single task as there was just one source. Only transitions in the model that could be observed - those in the user/system category - were considered.

Transitions were drawn as follows; each time a new query was initiated from the search field, the transition between formalize query and examine was strengthened. Contextual queries from either results or facts caused strengthening of both transitions between accrete, examine or extract and formalize query, and formalize query and examine. If a user submits a query without examining any results, then the examine-reflect transition was strengthened, while the examine-formalize query transition was strengthened if information derived from the result set was used as a Boolean query or similar document search is used from a result. If a result was added to the fact list, then the examine-accrete transition was strengthened. Finally, if one or more documents are viewed, the examine-extract transition was strengthened. A similar set of transitions exist from the extract and accrete states. The extract state is reached when a document identified in the examine state is read, while the accrete state is reached when a document, result or user fact is added to the fact list.

A transition map showing transitions made during the evaluation is shown in parts (A) and (B) of Fig. 4. Each transition is shown as a percentage of the total number of transitions made. The results are statistically significant $(t = 4.5, df = 10, .001 \leq P \leq .0005)$ and for a 90% confidence level the error rate was ± 5.11. The most common transition on both interfaces is reflect-formalize query. RL scores 87% on this transition, while ERL scores 76.4%. This implies that using ERL, there is a greater tendency to formulate queries from information discovered in the examine (0% RL, 5.3% ERL), extract (12.7% RL, 5.1% ERL) and accrete (13.8% ERL) states. These transitions can only be made if information from a result set informs the query. In the ERL interface, pearls - over 90% of pearls were documents, with some user facts, and only one result set fact - were dominant when creating informed queries.

A model of all transitions made by the user who achieved the highest gain during the evaluation is shown in Parts C (RL) and Part D (ERL) of Fig. 4. This person, an experienced searcher, achieved excellent results irrespective of the interface used. Both searchers are characterized by a particularly high percentage of transitions that provide feedback to new searches - 33% of queries were informed by previous searches in RL while the corresponding figure for ERL was 36.7%. This user used the fact list to organize his search, gaining a broad view of the topic using terms known a-priori and new terms discovered during the search. During this time documents that were added as facts were used as starting points for new searches by invoking contextual searches. This user effectively used *user facts* to marshal information learned during the search period. Terms and phrases that were unrelated in the result set were grouped together as new concepts and used to invoke new queries.

Comparing the average model of usage for RL (Part (A) of Fig. 4) to the corresponding Highest Gain Model for RL reveals a significantly different set of user actions. The rate of query abandonment is significantly higher (87% for average user verses 66% for user with the highest gain), while the rate of feedback is significantly lower (12.7% for average verses 33% for highest). When the average model of usage for the enhanced ranked list (Part (B) of Fig. 4) is compared to the ERL model in Part (D) of the same figure, the differences, while still significant, are not as pronounced. The rate of feedback achieved in

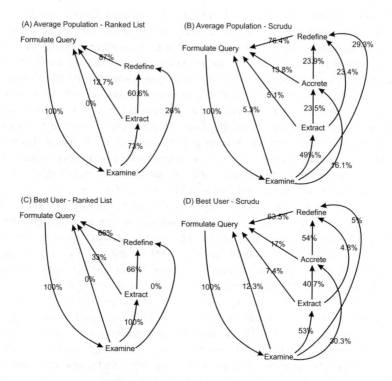

Fig. 4. Model Development for Highest Gain (above) verses Average Gain (below)

the average model is significantly larger (24.2% for the average verses 36.7% for user with highest gain). While the feedback occurs across all three feedback transitions (examine to formalize, extract to formalize and accrete to formalize) in the highest gain model, the average model saw most feedback originating on the accrete to formalize transition, that is, through queries that originated from the *facts list*.

While the users achieving the highest or lowest gain are not influenced by the ERL, the average user follows a model closer to that of the best performing user when the ERL interface is employed. Furthermore, it has been shown that the feature implemented to support the pearl growing strategy - the *facts list* - is the key component that caused this improvement.

6   Conclusions and Future Work

This paper has shown that with a few disarmingly simple modifications, the ranked list can be used to support session based information tasks. The rate of retrieval of relevant documents was shown to increase when using ERL, particularly for unfamiliar domains. Furthermore, users tended to use beneficial search strategies - such as creating informed queries - that elevated the performance of the average user. There remain a number of issues which the authors intend to address. The evaluation did not address the uptake of ERL features. In order to address this deficit, a new version of the interface is to be released *into the wild* - that is, employed on an interface that users happen upon and use in a natural seeking environment. In addition to this survey, tests similar to those reported herein will be undertaken with a bigger sample population and in specific domains to understand the benefits of ERL with greater acuity.

Finally, exploration of the potential applications of the user models developed herein is being undertaken. It is hoped that the strategies employed by the least successful searchers - those exhibiting signs of *incredulous repetitions* and *query loyalty* - can be identified dynamically, and a recommender system which offers advice on *how* to search rather than *what* to search can be developed.

References

1. Bates, M.J.: The design of browsing and berrypicking techniques for the online search interface. Online Review 13(5), 407–424 (1989)
2. Belkin, N.J.: Helping people find what they don't know. Communications of the ACM 43(8), 58–61 (2000)
3. Bhavnani, S.K., Bichakjian, C.K., Johnson, T.M., Little, R.J., Peck, F.A., Schwartz, J.L., Strecher, V.J.: Strategy Hubs: Next-Generation Domain Portals with Search Procedures. In: CHI 2003, Florida, USA (2003)
4. Blake, C., Pratt, W.: Collaborative Information Synthesis I: A model of information behaviors of scientists in medicine and public health. Journal of the American Society for Information Science and Technology 57(13), 1740–1749 (2006)
5. Blake, C., Pratt, W.: Collaborative Information Synthesis II: Recommendations for Information Systems to Support Synthesis Activities. Journal of the American Society for Information Science and Technology 57(14), 1888–1895 (2006)
6. Hearst, M.: Clustering versus Facetted Categories for Information Exploration. Communications of the ACM 49(4), 59–61 (2006)
7. Jansen, B.J., Spink, A., Saracevic, T.: Real life, real users, and real needs: A study and analysis of user queries on the web. Information Processing & Management 36(2), 207–227 (2000)
8. Joho, H., Jose, J.M.: Slicing and Dicing the Information Space using local contexts. In: Information Interaction in Context (IIiX), Copenhagen, Denmark (2006)
9. Marchionini, G.: Exploratory Search: From Finding to Understanding. Communications of the ACM 49(4), 41–46 (2006)
10. Marchionini, G.: Information seeking in electronic environments. Cambridge University Press, New York (1995)
11. Markey, K.: Twenty-Five Years of End-User Searching, Part 2: Future Research Directions. Journal of the American Society for Information Science and Technology 58(8), 1123–1130 (2007)
12. Morris, D., Morris, M.R., Venolia, G.: SearchBar: A Search-Centric Web History for Task Resumption and Information Re-finding. In: CHI 2008, Florence, Italy (2008)

A Prediction Market for Toxic Assets*

Alan Holland**

Cork Constraint Computation Centre,
Department of Computer Science,
University College Cork,
Cork, Ireland

Abstract. We propose the development of a prediction market to provide a form of collective intelligence for forecasting prices for "toxic assets" to be transferred from Irish banks to the National Asset Management Agency. Such a market allows participants to assume a stake in a security whose value is tied to a future event. We propose that securities are created whose value hinges on the transfer amount paid for loans from the agency to a bank. In essence, bets are accepted on whether the price is higher or lower than a quoted figure. The prices of securities indicate expected transfer costs for toxic assets. Prediction markets offer a proven means of aggregating distributed knowledge pertaining to estimates of uncertain quantities and are robust to strategic manipulation. We propose that a prediction market runs in parallel to a pricing procedure for individual assets conducted by the government agency. We advocate an approach whereby prices are chosen as a convex combination of the agency's internal estimate and that of the prediction market. We argue that this will substantially reduce the cognitive burden for the government agency and improve the accuracy, speed and scalability of pricing. This approach also offers a means of empowering both property experts and non-experts in a cost-effective and transparent manner.

1 Introduction

Ireland is currently suffering a severe economic crisis. A large number of impaired property loans from Irish banks to developers lies at the heart of the problem. These loans were primarily made to support the acquisition of land banks or the development of residential and commercial properties. Following the collapse in market confidence and property prices, most of these loans are not likely to be repaid in full. The Irish Government has recently decided to set up a National Asset Management Agency (NAMA) whose objective is to acquire "toxic assets" from Irish banks on a mandatory basis so that they are removed from the balance sheet of banks at an agreed price. The NAMA is charged with acquiring these loans so that banks can remove uncertainty from their balance sheet, attract capital from elsewhere and continue to lend to businesses so that non-property related industries can access credit once more. There are three key challenges faced by this agency.

* This work is funded by Enterprise Ireland (grant number PC/2008/0367).
** The author wishes to thank all 35 traders who participated in the prediction market for fictional assets. The author is also grateful to David Pennock, Brian Lucey and Karl Whelan for their comments on a preliminary version of this paper.

L. Coyle and J. Freyne (Eds.): AICS 2009, LNAI 6206, pp. 164–173, 2010.

1. It is necessary to determine a *price* for these assets in the absence of a liquid property market and price signals so that the government can break-even or realise a profit in five to fifteen years time.
2. A *scalable* pricing mechanism that can expedite the asset transfer process for thousands of impaired assets without compromising on accuracy is desirable. Given the large number of properties that are dispersed across Ireland and other countries that require valuation, it is imperative that any approach can be rapidly expanded to deal with the enormous volume of troubled loans.
3. The pricing mechanisms need to be *transparent* so that it is clear to all tax-payers that no preferential treatment is being offered to any party and the process does not suffer from political interference.

The most pressing challenge is the determination of a fair price because there is a degree of urgency surrounding the transfer of assets so that banks can resume lending as soon as possible. The European Commission issued guidelines to governments regarding the purchase of impaired assets [3] (Section 5.5). The Commission is opposed to state-aid but does allow for purchasing assets above current market prices in these extenuating circumstances when potential buyers have little or no access to loan facilities. A communication states that

"...*the value attributed to impaired assets in the context of an asset relief program (the 'transfer value') will inevitably be above current market prices in order to achieve the relief effect. To ensure consistency in the assessment of the compatibility of aid, the Commission would consider a transfer value reflecting the underlying long-term economic value (the 'real economic value') of the assets, on the basis of underlying cash flows and broader time horizons, an acceptable benchmark indicating the compatibility of the aid amount as the minimum necessary. Uniform hair-cuts applicable to certain asset categories will have to be considered to approximate the real economic value of assets that are so complex that a reliable forecast of developments in the foreseeable future would appear* **impracticable**." Paragraph 40 of [3].

The Commission tentatively suggests that a "hair-cut" approach may have to be considered because certain asset classes have complex associated valuation problems and valuing the vast portfolio may be impracticable. A fair price should reflect the long-term economic value of these assets when they are resold in five to fifteen years time when access to credit has resumed and sales are conducted in an orderly manner. The quest to predict the future resale value and hence what should be paid now is extremely challenging. When speaking about predicting future events in general Bragues claims that, "*a potential solution to this epistemological conundrum has emerged through mass collaboration*" [2]. Prediction markets realise this vision by allowing participants to purchase a stake in a security whose value is tied to a future event. The fluctuating prices offer a continuously updated probability estimate of the likely outcome of the event. The key argument that we posit in this paper is that a more accurate and scalable pricing mechanism can be made practicable even for complex asset classes by leveraging the "wisdom of crowds" via a prediction market.

Organisation. Section 2 outlines possible approaches that may be considered by the NAMA when determining prices. Section 3 discusses our proposed extension to the individualised valuation approach. Section 4 addresses implementation considerations. Section 5 discusses possible extensions including the ability to optimise the value of a portfolio of assets by determining dependencies between assets and finding super- or sub-additive valuations. Section 6 concludes.

2   Existing Possible Approaches

In the absence of liquidity in the property market, the NAMA has a limited choice of options in terms of determining a fair price for assets. It is desirable to determine a price that will offer at least a break-even return not alone to save the taxpayer from punitive losses but also because deliberate over-payment constitutes state-aid and is against EU regulations. If the banks require additional capital, besides the payments for toxic assets in the form of government bonds, this may be conducted via alternative means such as nationalisation. The government is hopeful, however, that removing the risk associated with these assets may attract third party investors to provide additional capital that can support lending.

2.1   The "Hair-Cut" Approach

This involves bundling property classes according to various key attributes. For example, green-field sites on the edge of small towns may constitute a bundle. The NAMA may then determine the price for each asset to be the original selling price for which the loan was taken and then applying an arbitrary percentage reduction on this in order to determine the sale price. This is a crude approach with the advantage that it is quick and not labour intensive. The disadvantage is that it is liable to be very inaccurate and may leave the taxpayer with an extremely heavy financial burden if too much is paid for these assets. Its inaccuracy stems from the fact that the price paid for the property during the period of irrational exuberance is the key parameter in determining its price now. The wild variance in over-payments within the same property categories will be propagated if this approach is applied.

  The variance in values for assets that fall within the same class can be enormous. For example, some green field sites were bought without planning permission or residential/commercial zoning as though this was a formality. It is not possible to discount their value to agricultural levels based on this alone but it may be an indication of over-payment. Some assets may have strategic potential for valuable construction projects in future years. A crude "hair-cut" approach is, in-effect, a hopeful estimate that the aggregate value of the respective properties when resold in five to fifteen years time will approximately recover the monies spent now.

2.2   Multiple Competing Privately Managed Funds

Bebchuk proposes the idea of providing funds to competing privately managed funds for acquiring troubled assets in America [1]. It is argued that this approach would ensure that the government subsidy is kept to a minimum and aligns participants incentives with that of the taxpayer. In some ways it is a superior approach to that described previously because it crucially gives an incentive to firms for information discovery regarding the underlying property valuations. Vital information regarding attributes that influence the resale value of the property including employment statistics, demographics *etc* will be considered by many competing firms, thus leveraging a wider knowledge base.

However, when smaller firms enter a market for assets whose long-term value has a large degree of uncertainty, these firms have a lower tolerance for risk than a single organisation with a much larger budget. It would lead to avoidance of the riskier assets and competition for the most attractive properties. In the context of the Irish property market, there are many high risk properties that require the intervention of an agent whose attitude to risk is almost completely neutral. Furthermore, there is a lack of privately managed funds with any interest in acquiring Irish assets. Another difficulty is that the approach suffers from the winner's curse effect, given the common value of the asset [8]. Firms are likely to decrease their bids in the expectation that if they win the auction for the loan, their estimate was the most optimistic. This would increase the likelihood of under-payment and negate the desirable relief-effect to banks.

2.3   Individualised Property Valuation Approach

Using this approach, the NAMA would solicit services from a large number of property and valuation experts. These experts would use their knowledge and experience to apply the most appropriate pricing methodologies for each property in turn. For example, complex assets such as semi-completed residential estates will require a different valuation mechanism than commercial office buildings. This is extremely problematic for a number of reasons. The pricing methodologies tend to be time-consuming and require inspections and analysis of related properties. It would be necessary for the NAMA to issue contracts to thousands of valuers in order to complete the pricing phase in a timely manner. Specialist expertise would be required in many geographic regions and across classes of properties such as agricultural land, quarries, entertainment venues and restaurants and retail space.

This process is also not incentive compatible. If valuers perceive a benefit to their business in the taxpayer overpaying for assets, then the NAMA has no means of ensuring that the reported value is a true reflection of their belief. This mechanism may thus lead to spurious valuations. It may also lead to public opposition because the pricing process is not transparent and there is no independent means of anomaly detection.

For each property category, an expert valuer would use an appropriately tailored valuation methodology [9]. The valuation of each property involves the examination of many attributes and thus a large cognitive burden. Hence, the European Commission suggested that although this approach is desirable it may be impracticable [3]. We argue here that it is practicable with the aid of a prediction market.

3   Our Approach: Individualised Pricing Coupled with a Prediction Market

In order to address the shortcomings of an exhaustive individualised property valuation approach, we suggest that a prediction market be initiated so that distributed knowledge among property experts (and even non-experts) can be shared in a manner that incentives the revelation of large volumes of information. This market would run alongside the internal individualised valuation process conducted by the NAMA. Invited participants in the market will be offered an opportunity to wager on the transfer price that is determined for assets under review. This provides a means of leveraging "the wisdom of crowds" and improving the accuracy of fair price predictions in the absence of a liquid property market. Such an automated mechanism for price prediction offer scalability and a clear incentive for the NAMA to determine prices that are aligned with public/market opinion. This addresses some of the criticisms regarding transparency and accountability leveled at the NAMA by various commentators [4,12].

We advocate that the prediction market is operated on a public-access basis but with additional incentives for registered experts in property valuation to participate. Given the ease with which scalability can be provided, it is difficult to justify the exclusion of members of the public should they feel confident about their ability to decide the long-term economic value of any relevant properties. A fully inclusive prediction market is more politically acceptable, more accurate and also more robust to efforts at manipulation.

3.1 Key Benefits of Prediction Markets

A key advantage of prediction markets over other approaches to intelligence gathering (e.g. surveys) is that they provide incentives for truthful revelation of beliefs [13]. If prediction markets are used as inputs into future decisions, this may provide a countervailing incentive to trade dishonestly to manipulate market prices. However, Hanson and Oprea demonstrated that such attempts at manipulation are destined to fail because other participants have a greater incentive to counteract such efforts [6]. An important role for prediction markets is that potential profits offer an incentive for information discovery. The aggregated finding of all such efforts at information discovery would provide a strong indication to the NAMA as to the markets expectation regarding the fair price that will be paid. Another major benefit is speed; it has been shown that prediction markets respond quickly to new information [10]. Furthermore they are accurate. Some of the behavioural anomalies that are witnessed in surveys (e.g. extremist candidates perform better in secret ballot elections than in pre-election surveys) can be removed or dramatically reduced. Prediction markets for events such as political elections are widely regarded as more accurate than survey techniques [5].

3.2 Increasing Market Liquidity

An active prediction market with many trades is more likely to produce accurate results. Firstly, it is important to inform potential market participants about the existence of the market. Secondly it is important to incentivise participation.

We would envisage that in a real deployment, actual cash would be utilised as a currency. In order to boost liquidity, it would be beneficial for registered members of the property valuation sector be offered "free bets" that can only be liquidated once the money was wagered a fixed number of times. Valuers, therefore, have an incentive to participate and maximize their returns by betting on property assets about which they are most knowledgeable. The market should also be open to members of the public so that they can open accounts, deposit money and then commence trading. They would have an incentive to participate if they perceive that other traders are either over- or under-estimating the price that the NAMA will pay for the properties. This would act as a deterrent to any coalition of auctioneers or valuers who attempted to artificially inflate the price of properties.

3.3   Leveraging the Prediction Market to Reduce the NAMA's Cognitive Burden

For the prediction market to be truly useful, it needs to accelerate the valuation process for the NAMA and improve pricing accuracy. Given the impracticability of attempting to conduct a thorough valuation process for every property we now suggest a means by which the NAMA can optimally leverage prediction markets results.

We advocate an approach whereby the NAMA spreads its cognitive resources thinly across all properties and attempts to estimate the value of properties in the knowledge that there will be a relatively large degree of inaccuracy. We suggest that a convex combination of the values decided upon internally and those suggested by the prediction market would then be selected as a final price. This approach incorporates the prediction markets opinion as an endogenous variable within the NAMA pricing process. The less cognitive resources expended by the agency on a specific asset, the more likely it is that market participants believe the quoted price won't differ significantly from the announced actual payment. This leads to a deceleration in the rate of convergence.

It is well known that increased liquidity in prediction markets leads to more accurate estimates [11]. Therefore, it would be wise for the NAMA to focus more cognitive re-sources upon markets that received less attention. This may be modeled as a resource allocation optimization problem for the agency that has incentive to focus on assets that received less attention in the prediction market. By commiting to this strategy, the author conjectures that relative levels of liquidity in various markets indicate an equi-librium in a congestion game that reflects the markets opinion regarding the uncertainty of asset valuations. A market that has received many trades is congested and, there-fore, focus switches to other markets that received less cognitive effort. Ceteris paribus, participants are attracted to markets that are likely to receive more attention from the NAMA.

3.4   Deployment Considerations

For a real prediction market to function successfully the following items would be nec-essary. Firstly, it would be necessary to know the properties that are under scrutiny before prices are announced. Secondly, temporal consideration are important for the correct functioning of the market. It is important for market participants to know a cut-off date by which it will become public knowledge how much was paid for cer-tain assets. Thirdly, in order to encourage liquidity it would be advisable to offer "free bets", say EUR1,000 each, to invited participants from the property valuation field. It is not strictly necessary that the NAMA finance this incentive. It is also necessary to impose restrictions on cashing ones credits and insistence on wagering each free Euro a fixed number of times would provide a mechanism for engaging participants. Finally, it is necessary that a tailored prediction market software platform be secure and robust.

Fortunately, Ireland has one of the world's leading prediction market makers based in Dublin called Intrade. It would be wise to leverage such expertise in the event of financing and deploying a prediction market of this kind.

4 Prototype

Several software providers offer a service whereby subscribers can create and manage online prediction markets. We describe a prototype that we created for several fictional properties.[1] We prepared a prediction marketplace using software developed by Inkling Incorporated. We listed nine fictional properties and described their key attributes. The properties were as follows:

- a vacant commercial office building in Sandyford, Dublin,
- a hotel set on fifteen acres in Donnybrook, Dublin 4,
- an apartment complex in Salthill, Galway,
- a car showroom in west Dublin,
- a golf resort in the Algarve, Portugal,
- an apartment complex in Cork,
- an unfinished residential estate in Mullingar, Co. Westmeath (see Figure 4),
- a twenty-acre residentially zoned field beside Cavan town,
- a ten-acre residentially zoned field in Oranmore, Co. Galway.

Market participants were asked a question of the form "*Sandyford commercial office building; what will the NAMA pay for this property?*". Participants can register for free, using a pseudonym if desired, and receive $5,000 in virtual currency to make bets on the transaction price that the agency will pay for the loan received to construct this property.

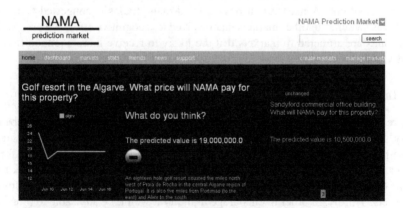

Fig. 1. Homepage for prediction market prototype

---

[1] The system can be viewed at https://nama.inklingmarkets.com.

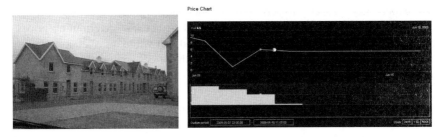

(a) Fictional unfinished residential estate in Mullingar

(b) Prediction markets price evolution for Mullingar property

Fig. 2. Unfinished estate in Mullingar

The initial price is an arbitrary guess made by the market operator. Market participants can choose to wager on the agreed price being higher or lower than the current threshold (Fig. 2(b)). They can choose how much to invest in that decision, Figures 3(a) and 3(b). Participants are more inclined to enter markets pertaining to securities about which they were most knowledgeable. This would probably involve studying assets in their vicinity. In this manner, knowledge aggregation on a grand scale is fully automated.

(a) Higher/lower choice

(b) Investment amount indicating confidence

Fig. 3. Trading decisions

For our prototype we promoted the fictional market via email and blog postings. An email was forwarded to all staff in UCC inviting them to participate in the market. Secondly, messages were posted to boards.ie, irisheconomy.ie and thepropertypin.com inviting participation with a link to a preliminary paper on the subject [7]. The market was active for just over two weeks and thirty five traders registered. There were 150 trades in that period and the predicted prices stabilised in the final four days for all properties. Most participants were either academics from UCC or professionals from the property sector who viewed the posting on thepropertypin.com. The prediction market also has a leader-board of the best performing traders and several participants remarked on how well they were performing relative to others. So competitive instincts can also act as an incentive for participation.

An experienced property expert from an auctioneering and valuation firm agreed to act as a price-setter in the absence of the NAMA actually determining prices for these properties. Unsurprisingly, the expert warned that without inspections and more detailed information regarding property histories, the prices are merely indicative. This is not a problem for the experiment, instead it is a feature of the challenges as they exist in reality. We developed this prototype in order to illustrate a process of valuation and how both members of the public and property experts can participate in a transparent market that can help to establish a more accurate valuation. We are not attempting to prove prediction market accuracy. There is ample extant literature that has proven this fact [11]. Moreover, the NAMA itself is not likely to engage in exhaustive complex valuations for many properties so heuristic methods will be adopted in reality in any case. The prediction market closed on Monday June 15th and at the time of writing the property expert had not completed his valuations. Due to this and space constraints we leave a more detailed analysis of this experiment for future work.

5   Possible Extensions

It is possible to set up more complex contracts that depend on the outcome of more than one event in a *combinatorial prediction market*. This offers insight into the dependencies or correlation between events. For example, multiple nearby properties may display super- or sub-additive valuations. The overall value may be enhanced if the assets are complementary. For example, adjacent properties may offer access to a road or other resources that increase the overall value of the combination. It is important that such synergies are captured if possible. In the case where asset values are sub-additive, it may be preferable to demolish one property and resell the other. The necessary queries (i.e. combinatorial markets) will need to be decided using heuristics based on proximity or adjacency.

A desirable bespoke element of a tailored solution would include geographical browsing of assets that are close to a participants location. Other desiderata include a complete specification of the NAMAs proposed methodology for estimating asset values. This would aid participants understanding of the goals of the NAMA in price determination in order to pre-empt their deliberation and costly knowledge discovery.

6   Discussion and Conclusion

We presented a novel application of prediction markets for property valuation. Furthermore, it is the first time, to the best of the author's knowledge, that it has been suggested to be used to predict an endogenous event. The NAMA has not yet announced any pricing methodology and some of the key ideas in this paper were forwarded to the agency when they issued a request for proposals.

We acknowledge that the individualised pricing approach is a formidable task and completing all such valuations whilst following conventional best practice is impracticable in its own right. However, when participants in a prediction market understand that this is the objective of the NAMA, the focal point of the game for each participant is to estimate this figure. It is therefore possible to transfer the cognitive burden from the agency to market participants by using "the wisdom of crowds" as a key input in this process. This complementary online prediction market would enhance the accuracy, speed and scalability of pricing toxic assets when conducted in parallel to an individualised property valuation methodology whose objective is to identify the long-term economic value of assets. It would also offer transparency and a voice to the general public who wish to have an input in this matter. Our key claim is that the NAMA the problem of valuation is immense and complex but is manageable with the aid of a prediction market. It deserves consideration as an complementary approach for price-setting. There is little to lose but much to gain in adopting this approach.

References

1. Bebchuk, L.A.: Buying troubled assets. Yale Journal on Regulation 29 (2009) (forthcoming)
2. Bragues, G.: Prediction markets: The practical and normative possibilities for the social production of knowledge. Episteme 6, 91–106 (2009)
3. European Commission: Communication from the commission on the treatment of impaired assets in the community banking sector (2009), http://ec.europa.eu/competition/state_aid/legislation/impaired_assets.pdf
4. Gurdgiev, C., Lucey, B.: What's wrong with NAMA (April 2009), http://trueeconomics.blogspot.com/2009/04/whats-wrong-with-nama.html (Unedited version of article in Business and Finance) (April 23)
5. Hanson, R.: Combinatorial information market design. Information Systems Frontiers 5(1), 107–119 (2003)
6. Hanson, R., Oprea, R.: Manipulators increase information market accuracy, mimeo, George Mason University (2005)
7. Holland, A.: A prediction market for toxic assets prices. arXiv:0905.4171v1 [cs.CE] (May 2009)
8. Kagel, J.H., Levin, D.: The winners curse and public information in common values auctions. American Economic Review 76, 894–920 (1986)
9. Pagourtzi, E., Assimakopoulos, V., Hatzichristos, T., French, N.: Real estate appraisal: A review of valuation methods. Journal of Property Investment and Finance 21(4), 383–401 (2003)
10. Snowberg, E., Wolfers, J., Zitzewitz, E.: Partisan impacts on the stockmarket: Evidence from prediction markets and close elections, mimeo, University of Pennsylvania (2006)
11. Surowiecki, J.: The Wisdom of Crowds. Anchor, New York (August 2005)
12. Whelan, K.: Panel discussion. RTE Primetime, April 30 (2009)
13. Wolfers, J., Zitzewitz, E.: Prediction markets. In: Durlauf, S.N., Blume, L.E. (eds.) The New Palgrave Dictionary of Economics. Palgrave Macmillan, Basingstoke (2008)

Learning without Default: A Study of One-Class Classification and the Low-Default Portfolio Problem

Kenneth Kennedy[1], Brian Mac Namee[1], and Sarah Jane Delany[2]

[1] School of Computing,
Dublin Institute of Technology, Dublin, Ireland
[2] Digital Media Centre,
Dublin Institute of Technology, Dublin, Ireland
kenneth.kennedy@dit.ie, brian.macnamee@comp.dit.ie,
sarahjane.delany@dmc.dit.ie

Abstract. This paper asks at what level of class imbalance *one-class classifiers* outperform *two-class classifiers* in credit scoring problems in which class imbalance, referred to as the *low-default portfolio problem*, is a serious issue. The question is answered by comparing the performance of a variety of one-class and two-class classifiers on a selection of credit scoring datasets as the class imbalance is manipulated. We also include *random oversampling* as this is one of the most common approaches to addressing class imbalance. This study analyses the suitability and performance of recognised two-class classifiers and one-class classifiers. Based on our study we conclude that the performance of the two-class classifiers deteriorates proportionally to the level of class imbalance. The two-class classifiers outperform one-class classifiers with class imbalance levels down as far as 15% (i.e. the imbalance ratio of minority class to majority class is 15:85). The one-class classifiers, whose performance remains unvaried throughout, are preferred when the minority class constitutes approximately 2% or less of the data. Between an imbalance of 2% to 15% the results are not as conclusive. These results show that one-class classifiers could potentially be used as a solution to the low-default portfolio problem experienced in the credit scoring domain.

1 Introduction

Financial institutions use quantitative *credit scoring* models to assist in the decision of whether or not to grant credit to a credit applicant. The term "credit scoring" is used to describe the process of determining the likelihood that applicants will default on their loan repayments [1]. The outcome of this process results in assigning credit applicants into one of two classes: *accept* (likely to repay or the positive class) and *reject* (likely to default or the negative class). Predictive variables extracted from application forms, externally supplied data and existing own-company records allow credit scoring models to yield an estimate of *probability of default* [2]. This decision to accept or reject an applicant for credit is taken by comparing the estimated probability of default with a suitable threshold [2]. Credit scoring models can be divided into two types: (i) *Application scoring* - credit scoring which deals with new applicants and; (ii) *Behavioural*

L. Coyle and J. Freyne (Eds.): AICS 2009, LNAI 6206, pp. 174–187, 2010.

scoring - credit scoring based on managing existing accounts. This study is confined to application scoring. Credit scoring is used inter-changeably with the term application scoring throughout.

A particular difficulty with building credit scoring models is that the data used to build models is historical data detailing the performance of customers granted credit in the past (i.e. did they or did they not default?). However, the vast majority of customers do not default and so the number of defaulters represented in training sets is typically very low. Furthermore, when defaults do occur they tend to be cyclical, for example a recession can result in a cluster of defaults occurring. This leads to the *low-default portfolio problem* and means that credit scoring datasets are usually heavily imbalanced. A banking industry workgroup [3] report that among the seven largest UK banks, 32% of retail exposures secured by residential properties will suffer from insufficient default data to give a satistically significant estimate. According to the Council of Mortgage Lenders (CML)[1], in the UK for the second quarter of 2009 there were 11,400 cases of possession, equivalent to one mortgage in 1,000. Apart from the academic challenges that arise from the low-default portfolio problem, it is also of considerable practical importance. Even a small improvement of a fraction of a percent in the accuracy of credit scoring might translate into significant future saving [1,4].

Previously Lee and Cho [5] reported that with 5% or lower minority class data, one-class classifiers outperform two-class classifiers. It should be noted that this study used support vector-based classifiers only and the performance of the one-class classifiers on real world datasets was optimised using training data from both classes. A similiar study by the same authors [6] found that one-class classifiers trained on one-class only are prefered with 1% or lower minority class data. Raskutti and Kowalczyk [7] use two high dimensional real world datasets and reported that with approximately 3% or lower minority class data, the performance of one-class support vector machine (SVM) [8] surpassed that of the two-class SVM [9].

In this paper we will compare *one-class classification* (OCC) methods with more common two-class classification approaches on three credit scoring datasets over a range of class imbalance ratios. The purpose of this study is to determine at what level of class imbalance the performance of OCC methods outrank the performance of two-class approaches. To the best of our knowledge, no attempt has been made to examine one-class classifiers as a solution to the low-default portfolio problem. The remainder of this paper is organised as follows: a short overview of credit scoring is given in Section 2, followed by a discussion of classification techniques in Section 3. Section 4 describes the classification performance criteria of the experiments and then evaluates classifier performance. Section 5 presents conclusions and future work.

2   Credit Scoring

The recent subprime mortgage crisis in the USA has caused some companies the loss of billions of dollars due to customers' defaults. Effective credit risk assessment is now

---

[1] The Council of Mortgage Lenders is an industry body whose members are banks, building societies and other lenders who together undertake around 98% of all residential mortgage lending in the UK. There are 11.1 million mortgages in the UK, with loans worth over £1.2 trillion.

recognised as a crucial factor to gaining a competitive advantage which can help financial institutions to grant credit to creditworthy customers and reject non-creditworthy customers. According to the CML, UK gross mortgage lending for the second quarter of 2009 was estimated to total £33,902 million. It is therefore legitimate to conclude that a small improvement in the accuracy of credit scoring has positive financial consequences. Another practical consideration is Basel II regulation [10]. Under this accord, using the internal ratings based (IRB) approach, financial institutions calculate their own risk parameters (e.g. probability of default) in order to calculate risk weighted assets. The risk weighted assets help determine the minimum capital requirements that the banks are required to retain, and act as a buffer against unexpected losses. Using the IRB approach, financial institutions can create credit scoring models more customised to certain risk sensitivities. Such legislation serves to increase the importance of credit scoring whilst creating new challenges.

Many classification techniques have been used for credit scoring [11], some of which include traditional statistical methods such as logistic regression; non-parametric statistical methods, such as k-nearest neighbour; and sophisticated methods such as neural networks.

3 Classification Techniques

This section lists the classifiers used in our study. The following two-class classifiers were assessed: (i) Logistic regression[2]; (ii) Naïve Bayes [13][2]; (iii) Artificial neural network using a multilayer perceptron (MLP)[3]; and (iv) Support Vector Machines [9] as they have been shown to perform well when applied to credit scoring problems in the past [11]. For all of the two-class classifiers a cut-off score is applied to the classifier output score, data instances above the cut-off are assigned to the positive class and those with scores below to the negative class.

3.1 One Class Classification

One-class classifiers are constructed to recognise a target class from all other classes. Other synonymous terms used in the literature also include: *outlier detection* [14], *novelty detection* [15], *concept learning* [16] and *data description* [17]. One-class classifiers can be categorised into three types:(i) *density-based*; (ii) *boundary-based* and; (iii) *reconstruction-based*. In all three types, two distinct elements can be identified. The first element is a measure for the distance $d(z)$ or resemblance $p(z)$ of an object z to the target class. The second element is a user-defined threshold, θ, on this distance or resemblance. New objects are accepted when the distance to the target class is less than the value of θ or when the resemblance is greater than the value of θ. OCC methods differ in their definition of $p(z)$ or $d(z)$, and in their optimisation of thresholds with respect to the training set [18]. A comprehensive review of OCC methods and techniques is available in [19,20]. In the current study we select five common OCC techniques: Gaussian and

---

[2] See [12] for further details on the use of this technique in credit scoring.
[3] See [4] for further details on the use of artificial neural networks in credit scoring.

Naïve Parzen (density-based types), Support Vector Data Description (SVDD) and k-Nearest Neighbour (k-NN) (boundary-based types), and k-means (reconstruction-based type).

Gaussian Model [18]: This method assumes that the data is distributed according to the normal (Gaussian) distribution. The mean and covariance matrix is estimated from the data, and instances located in the two tails are considered outliers. A user-defined parameter r can be used to add regularisation to the estimated covariance matrix.

Naïve Parzen [18]: This technique is a simplification of the Parzen density estimator inspired by the Naïve Bayes approach [21]. A Parzen density is estimated for each separate feature dimension, and the probabilities are multiplied to give the final target probability [21].

Support Vector Data Description [18,22]: The SVDD separates the data of interest from different classes by placing a hypersphere around the class of objects that are represented by the training set from all other possible objects in the object space. The hypersphere is defined by a centre a and a radius R. The aforementioned threshold, θ, can be supplied to allow the hypersphere model of the SVDD to reject a fraction of the training objects, which sufficiently decreases the volume of the hypersphere. The boundaries of the hypersphere can be made more flexible by introducing kernel functions of user-defined width.

k-NN [18]: k-NN finds the distance of a test object x to its k-th nearest neighbour in the training set, the distance from this nearest neighbour to its k-th nearest neighbour in the training set is also found. Based on the quotient between these distances and an appropriate threshold value, x may either be rejected as being an outlier, or accepted as being part of the target class.

k-means [18]: k-means clustering is one of the simplest reconstruction methods. In order to perform k-means clustering for OCC, it is assumed that the data is clustered and can be described by a set of prototype vectors. To classify a new object, its distance to all the prototypes is measured and averaged. This is used to score the extent to which it is an outlier.

3.2 Evaluation Experiment

The aim of the evaluation is to compare the performance of one-class classifiers with two-class classifiers and assess whether one-class classifiers can successfully identify defaulters, and at what level of class imbalance their performance is superior to that of the two-class classifiers. This section describes the datasets, and the evaluation measures and methodology. Finally, experimental results are presented and discussed.

3.3 Datasets

Three real-world datasets are used in our experiments: the Australian[4], Japanese[5] and German[6] credit datasets, all of which are available from the UCI Repository of Machine Learning Databases [23]. Table 1 describes the characteristics of the datasets.

---

[4] http://archive.ics.uci.edu/ml/datasets/Statlog+(Australian+Credit+Approval)
[5] http://mlr.cs.umass.edu/ml/datasets/Japanese+Credit+Screening
[6] http://archive.ics.uci.edu/ml/datasets/Statlog+(German+Credit+Data)

The class ratio of accept instances to reject instances is included. The Australian credit dataset consists of 307 instances of creditworthy applicants and 383 instances of non-creditworthy applicants. The Japanese dataset describes credit card application approval. After deleting the data with missing attribute values, there are 653 instances, with 357 instances granted credit and 296 instances refused credit. The German credit scoring data is imbalanced to a greater extent, consisting of 700 creditworthy applicants and 300 non-creditworthy applicants. In all cases the variables used describe important features of a customer such as credit history, personal information and details of the credit requested. The numeric features of all three datasets are normalised.

Table 1. Characteristics of the datasets used in the experimentation

Dataset	# Classes	Accept:Reject	# Nominal features	# Numeric features	# Boolean features
Australian	2	45:55	6	8	0
Japanese	2	55:45	6	6	3
German	2	70:30	7	13	0

3.4 Assessment Measures

To assess the classification results we count the number of true positive (TP), true negative (TN), false positive (FP) (classified as positive, but actually negative) and false negative (FN) (classified as negative, but actually positive) examples in a given test set. We use *Sensitivity*, *Specificity*, as used by Baesens et al. [11], and the *harmonic mean* of both of these scores to measure the classification quality of all classifiers used in our study. Sensitivity is calculated as: $\frac{TP}{TP+FN}$ and measures the proportion of positive (accept) examples that are predicted to be positive. Specificity, calculated as: $\frac{TN}{TN+FP}$, measures the proportion of negative (reject) examples that are predicted to be negative. As per Hoff et al. [24], in order to provide a suitable composite measure of sensitivity and specificity we employ the harmonic mean, which corresponds to a particular adaptation of the F-measure [25].

$$Harmonic\ Mean = \frac{2 * Sensitivity * Specificity}{Sensitivity + Specificity} \qquad (1)$$

3.5 Experimental Procedure

Each dataset was divided into training, validation and testing data by stratified random sampling, in which there were 55% training, 15% validation and 30% testing examples per dataset. The process of training, validation and testing was conducted 10 times, the average results are reported. Initially for all three datasets the two-class classifiers were trained on the training data, the validation data was used to tune the model and eventually their performance was assessed on the test data. The sensitivity, specificity and harmonic mean were recorded. Then for all three datasets, the number of negative instances in the training dataset was randomly reduced by 10%. It is necessary to balance the datasets in order to avoid biasing the classifier towards the majority class. To achieve this random oversampling was performed on the remaining data instances of the negative class. The validation and test sets remained unchanged throughout this process. The classifiers were retrained and reassessed on the test dataset. This process was repeated until the number of negative examples in the training set reached zero.

While simplistic, random oversampling has performed well in empirical studies (e.g. Batista et al. [26]) even when compared to other, more complicated oversampling methods [27]. As oversampling only replicates existing data instances, it can be argued that it does not add any actual data to the dataset [5,27]. Figure 1 illustrates the effect of not oversampling the minority class on the Australian dataset. Without balancing the training set, the performance of the two-class classifiers (particularly the SVMs) deteriorates. The Naïve Bayes classifier trained on the Australian and Japanese dataset proved to be an exception. Oversampling actually weakened the performance of the Naïve Bayes classifier to a small degree, as illustrated in Figure 1. After training, there is a possibility that the Naïve Bayes classifier is overfitting, fitting the training data well, but performing poorly on unseen data.

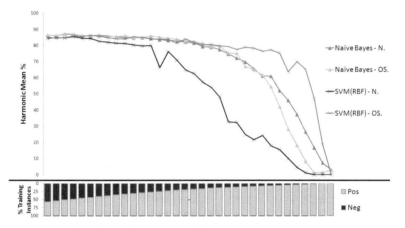

Fig. 1. Australian Harmonic Mean: % of available Training Instances. A comparison of oversampling (OS) and no oversampling (N).

The Data Description toolbox[7] is an open source Matlab library of one-class classifiers and was used to implement the OCC techniques used in this study. When training the one-class classifiers only data from one class was employed, the positive class (creditworthy applicants). The validation data (consisting of two-classes) was used to tune the models and their performance was assessed on the test data. For the one-class k-means classifier the number of clusters was fixed at 10. For the one-class k-NN classifier the number of neighbours was set to 10. This figure was selected in keeping with Baesens et al. [11], who used 10-NN two-class classifier. The one-class Naïve Parzen classifier required no parameter tuning. The SVDD used the Gaussian kernel (default setting).

---

[7] http://ict.ewi.tudelft.nl/~davidt/dd_tools.html

All the two-class classifiers were implemented using Weka [28] release 3.6.0. The Naïve Bayes classifier used a supervised discretisation algorithm to convert numeric attributes to nominal attributes. The logistic regression classifier was optimised for the ridge value in the log-likelihood. The neural net was implemented using a multi-layer perceptron (MLP). The number of hidden neurons was defined as (*#attributes* + *classes*)/2. The MLP was optimised using the rate of learning. The SVM was implemented using Lib-SVM [29] using a radial basis function (RBF) kernel and adopted a grid search mechanism to tune the width γ of the RBF kernel and the cost parameter C. Results for a SVM using a linear kernel are also included.

4   Results and Discussion

Table 2 displays the performance of the the the two-class classifiers across the datasets. The classifiers have been trained on data containing: all of the available defaulters (100%); one-fifth of the available defaulters (20%) and so on until none of the defaulters are used (0%). The deterioration in the two-class classifiers is largely due to their inability to correctly identify the increasingly rare defaulters. Eventually, in almost all cases, their sensitivity rate hits 100% because in the absence of defaulters they identify all test set instances as non-defaulters. Of the two-class classifiers, based on the harmonic mean across the range of all class imbalances, there is very little to distinguish the performance of logistic regression, SVM with RBF kernel and SVM with linear kernel, as exemplified in Table 2. Overall, the SVM linear kernel performs fractionally better than logistic regression followed closely by the SVM with RBF kernel. However it should be

Table 2. Sensitivity, specificity and harmonic mean (HM) using the Logistic Regression (LR), Naïve Bayes (NB), MLP, SVM RBF kernel (SVM-R), and SVM Linear kernel (SVM-L) classifiers. Best performing HM for each dataset is underlined.

Dataset	Classifier	100% Sens	Spec	HM	20% Sens	Spec	HM	10% Sens	Spec	HM	5% Sens	Spec	HM	0% Sens	Spec	HM
Aus	LR	83.88	88.21	85.93	84.05	82.70	83.12	87.25	75.76	80.91	86.57	66.48	75.02	100	0	0
	NB	81.28	92.26	86.38	84.96	83.34	84.00	89.73	65.03	75.20	95.47	27.57	42.02	99.38	1.59	3.09
	MLP	81.10	89.61	85.05	90.41	83.43	86.62	90.71	79.15	84.25	90.18	67.64	75.97	100	0	0
	SVM-R	83.27	87.13	85.04	85.84	77.99	81.45	83.47	72.92	77.44	85.58	68.22	75.33	100	0	0
	SVM-L	91.27	85.18	88.04	90.28	85.66	87.78	88.48	81.47	84.62	89.06	70.94	78.07	100	0	0
Jap	LR	84.99	82.72	83.69	88.26	74.08	80.37	89.42	69.77	78.28	90.57	65.02	75.38	100	0	0
	NB	89.49	79.75	84.23	91.58	71.54	80.16	95.68	44.14	60.13	99.71	6.00	10.99	100	0.70	1.37
	MLP	85.26	87.25	86.07	89.17	75.78	81.57	92.09	61.95	72.84	97.24	37.46	52.96	100	0	0
	SVM-R	84.42	87.95	85.99	87.59	83.38	85.13	88.31	72.10	78.96	88.42	63.10	72.90	100	0	0
	SVM-L	81.63	93.23	86.99	85.76	83.74	84.45	88.38	74.49	80.27	90.32	58.57	70.17	100	0	0
Ger	LR	72.98	69.18	70.93	78.39	53.99	63.59	81.54	47.07	59.31	88.39	27.59	41.29	100	0	0
	NB	75.12	66.19	70.22	85.38	37.16	50.50	96.09	9.61	17.18	99.07	2.13	4.04	99.95	0.31	0.62
	MLP	75.73	57.75	64.22	84.77	34.52	46.62	91.10	24.12	37.58	84.70	24.40	22.79	100	0	0
	SVM-R	73.32	68.11	70.43	74.21	56.65	63.83	77.89	44.94	54.36	82.27	30.85	43.02	100	0	0
	SVM-L	72.62	69.46	70.89	71.84	54.17	61.28	76.20	47.01	57.30	85.21	27.54	39.43	100	0	0

noted that this is a generalised logistic regression model and financial institutions typically have at their disposal methods to increase and extend its accuracy and flexibility [30]. The Naïve Bayes performs worst of the two-class classifiers.

Table 3 displays the results of the selected one-class classifiers. Overall, the Gaussian and Naïve Parzen models appear to perform best. Both of these models are density-based methods. This approach is known to work very well when a good probability model is assumed and the sample size is sufficiently large [18]. Excluding the Gaussian one-class classifier, the performance of the one-class classifiers on the Australian dataset is rather ordinary. There are a number of factors that might contribute to this. Two customers with similar characteristics can easily belong to different classes [31]. Also, credit scoring datasets are typically very noisy [11], particularly the Australian dataset [32].

Table 3. Sensitivity, specificity and harmonic mean (HM), along with standard deviation, for the one-class classifiers. Best performing HM for each dataset is underlined.

Classifier	Australian			Japanese			German		
	Sens	Spec	HM	Sens	Spec	HM	Sens	Spec	HM
Gaussian	74.43	82.43	77.77 (2.97)	74.03	76.46	74.77 (3.03)	57.05	59.38	56.76 (3.15)
Naïve Parzen	59.02	71.10	63.52 (3.81)	77.26	74.39	75.48 (1.81)	58.90	50.44	53.08 (4.24)
k-NN(10)	66.53	68.25	65.78 (3.14)	71.33	63.66	66.73 (3.35)	59.38	54.45	56.03 (2.13)
k-means(10)	67.24	66.45	64.56 (3.86)	66.13	64.88	64.23 (2.60)	61.69	53.54	56.54 (2.43)
SVDD	60.85	70.87	65.17 (3.82)	67.48	60.62	61.78 (4.75)	65.72	47.27	53.69 (3.57)

Figures 2, 3 and 4 display the test set harmonic mean of all 10 classifiers for each of the datasets. The rate of training set transformation, in terms of the number of positive and negative instances, is displayed as a percentage bar beneath each harmonic mean graph. It is evident from Figures 2, 3 and 4 that initially the two-class classifiers outperform the one-class classifiers. However, as the number of defaulters are gradually removed from the training sets the performance of the two-class classifiers begins to deteriorate. As the one-class classifiers are trained using only non-defaulters their performance remains constant throughout.

The crossover in performance between the best one-class classifier and worst two-class classifier indicates the point where two-class classifiers generally outperform one-class classifiers. This crossover point occurs when the minority class constitutes approximately 14%, 11% and 20% of the training set data respectively for the Australian, Japanese and German data. These figures suggest that two-class classifiers outperform one-class classifiers when the minority class constitutes, on average, 15% or more of the training set data.

The crossover in performance between the best two-class classifier and the worst one-class classifier indicates the point where one-class classifiers generally outperform two-class classifiers. With the Australian and Japanese test sets, this crossover occurs when the minority class constitutes approximately 2% of the training set data. As the German dataset begins with a positive:negative ratio of 70:30, the harmonic mean of the two-class classifiers declines quickest of all three datasets. This crossover occurs

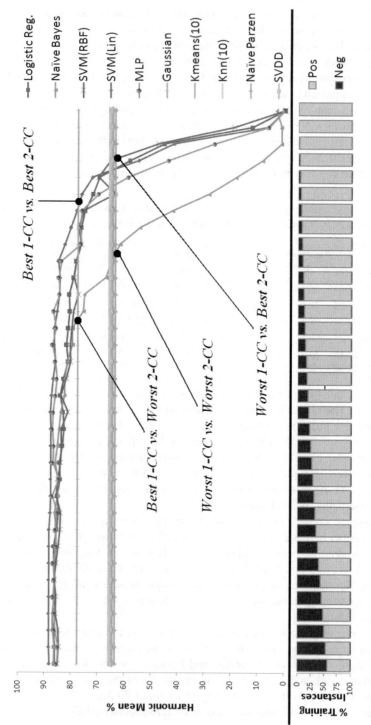

Fig. 2. Australian Harmonic Mean: % of Available Training Instances. Crossover points of best/worst one-class classifier (1-CC) and two-class classifier (2-CC) are also identified.

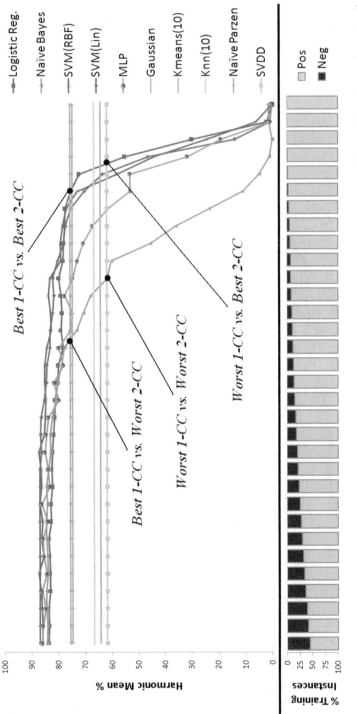

Fig. 3. Japanese Harmonic Mean: % of available Training Instances. Crossover points of best/worst one-class classifier (1-CC) and two-class classifier (2-CC) are also identified.

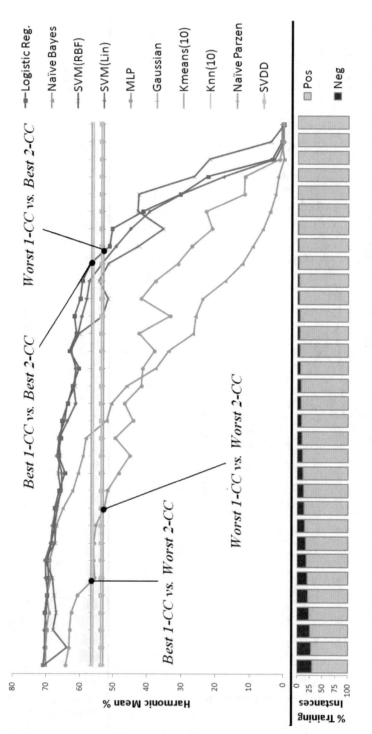

Fig. 4. German Harmonic Mean: % of available Training Instances. Crossover points of best/worst one-class classifier (1-CC) and two-class classifier (2-CC) are also identified.

for this dataset when the minority class constitutes approximately 3% of the training set data. These figures indicate that one-class classifiers generally outperform two-class classifiers when the minority class data represents 2% of the training set data. This suggests that two-class classification methods are relatively robust to imbalanced data and that OCC methods should only be considered in the most extreme cases.

With minority class data of between 2% and 15% the distinction between OCC and two-class classification methods is less clear cut. However, the crossover between the best one-class classifier and best two-class classifier on the Australian test set occurs when the training set is comprised of approximately 5% minority class data. For the Japanese test set, the crossover between the best one-class classifier and best two-class classifier occurs when the training set is approximately 4% minority class data. The crossover between the best one-class classifier and best two-class classifier on the German test set occurs when the training set is 3% minority class data. Therefore with approximately 4% or less minority class data, one-class classifiers, under certain conditions, can be considered ahead of two-class classifiers.

5   Conclusions

This study asked at what level of class imbalance the performance of OCC techniques outperform two-class classification techniques for credit scoring problems. Class imbalance is a particularly important issue in credit scoring applications due to the low-default portfolio problem. The experiments were conducted using three real-world credit scoring datasets. It was found that, initially, the two-class classifiers outperform the one-class classifiers. However as the the rate of class imbalance increases and the performance of the two-class classifiers falls off.

With 2% or lower minority (reject or negative class) class data, one-class classifiers are more accurate than two-class classifiers. Conversely, with 15% or higher minority class data, two-class classifiers clearly outperform one-class classifiers. With an imbalance between 2% and 15% minority class data, the results are not as conclusive, however with 4% or lower minority class data, certain one-class classifiers outperform two-class classifiers. Therefore we can conclude that one-class classifiers offer a viable solution to the low-default portfolio problem when the class imbalance is severe, and so warrant further research as a solution to the low-default portfolio problem.

For the two-class classifiers, the harmonic mean of the sensitivity and specificity was calculated assuming a default cut-off value on the classifier's output. This may, however, not be the most appropriate threshold to use for more skewed datasets as some classifiers have a tendency to always predict the majority class yielding 100% sensitivity and 0% specificity. However, by applying random oversampling this concern was alleviated to some degree.

In a future experiment we will use a validation set to determine the optimal cut-off threshold for each classifier at each level of class imbalance. A two-dimensional graph called the receiver operating characteristic (ROC) curve is commonly used, particularly with class imbalance, to present the results of two-class classifiers. However, a debate exists on the appropriate application of ROC curves [33]. When a large skew in the class distribution occurs, ROC curves sometimes provide an overly optimistic view of an algorithm's performance [34]. Furthermore, ROC curves can be unreliable in the case of severe class imbalance [35]. Cost curves [36] could also be used and a comparison between the suitability of both measures should be discussed.

Despite the absence of defaulters from the training set, one-class classifiers proved successful at identifying defaulters. Conversely, having been trained exclusively on non-defaulters, one-class classifiers performance at identifying the creditworthy cases was rather unremarkable. This leads to an obvious direction of future research: investigating the performance of classifier ensembles consisting of a combination of several one-class and two-class classifiers whose classification decisions are computed based on various aggregation methods.

Finally, there are many other factors that influence the low-default portfolio problem, such as the size of the data, data fragmentation and the complexity of the inputs to name a few [37,38]. The low-default portfolio problem needs to be analysed with respect to them.

Acknowledgment

The authors would like to thank Pádraig Cunningham for his remarks and suggestions.

References

1. Hand, D.J., Henley, W.E.: Statistical classification methods in consumer credit scoring: a review. Journal of the Royal Statistical Society, Series A, 523–541 (1997)
2. Verstraeten, G., den Poel, D.V.: The impact of sample bias on consumer credit scoring performance and profitability. Journal of the Operational Research Society 56, 981–992 (2004)
3. Joint British Bankers Asc, London Investment Banking Asc, Intl. Swaps, Derivatives Asc Industry Working Group.: The irb approach for low default portfolios (ldps)- recommendations of the joint bba, liba, isda industry working group. BBA, LIBA, ISDA Working Paper (2004)
4. West, D.: Neural network credit scoring models. Computers and OR 27, 1131–1152 (2000)
5. Lee, H., Cho, S.: The novelty detection approach for different degrees of class imbalance. In: King, I., Wang, J., Chan, L.-W., Wang, D. (eds.) ICONIP 2006. LNCS, vol. 4233, pp. 21–30. Springer, Heidelberg (2006)
6. Lee, H., Cho, S.: Focusing on non-respondents: Response modeling with novelty detectors. Expert Systems with Applications 33, 522–530 (2007)
7. Raskutti, B., Kowalczyk, A.: Extreme re-balancing for SVMs: a case study. ACM SIGKDD Explorations Newsletter 6, 60–69 (2004)
8. Scholkopf, B., Platt, J.C., Shawe-Taylor, J., Smola, A.J., Williamson, R.C.: Estimating the support of a high-dimensional distribution. Neural computation 13, 1443–1471 (2001)
9. Vapnik, V.: The nature of statistical learning theory. Springer, New York (1995)
10. Bank for Intl. Settlements: Basel II: intl. convergence of capital measurement and capital standards: a revised framework. BIS (2004)
11. Baesens, B., Gestel, T.V., Viaene, S., Stepanova, M., Suykens, J., Vanthienen, J.: Benchmarking state-of-the-art classification algorithms for credit scoring. JORS 54, 627–635 (2003)
12. Thomas, L.C., Oliver, R.W., Hand, D.J.: A survey of the issues in consumer credit modelling research. Journal of the Operational Research Society 56, 1006–1015 (2005)
13. Duda, R.O., Hart, P.E.: Pattern classification and scene analysis (1973)

14. Ritter, G., Gallegos, M.T.: Outliers in statistical pattern recognition and an application to automatic chromosome classification. Pattern Recognition Letters 18, 525–540 (1997)
15. Bishop, C.M.: Novelty detection and neural network validation. IEE Proceedings-Vision, Image and Signal processing 141, 217–222 (1994)
16. Japkowicz, N., Myers, C., Gluck, M.: A novelty detection approach to classification. In: Proceedings of the Fourteenth Joint Conference on Artificial Intelligence (1995)
17. Tax, D.M.J., Duin, R.P.W.: Support vector domain description. Pattern Recognition Letters 20, 1191–1199 (1999)
18. Tax, D.: One-class classification. Unpub. doc/dis. Delft University of Technology (2001)
19. Hodge, V., Austin, J.: A survey of outlier detection methodologies. AI Rev. 22, 85–126 (2004)
20. Chandola, V., Banerjee, A., Kumar, V.: Anomaly detection: A survey. ACM, New York (2009)
21. Tax, D.M.J., Duin, R.P.W.: Characterizing one-class datasets. In: Proceedings of the 16th Annual Symposium of the Pattern Recognition Assoc. of S. Africa, pp. 21–26 (2005) (Citeseer)
22. Tax, D.M.J., Duin, R.P.W.: Support vector data description. ML 54, 45–66 (2004)
23. Asuncion, A., Newman, D.: UCI machine learning repository. University of California, Irvine, School of Information and Computer Sciences (2007)
24. Hoff, K.J., Tech, M., Lingner, T., Daniel, R., Morgenstern, B., Meinicke, P.: Gene prediction in metagenomic fragments. BMC Bioinf. 9, 217 (2008)
25. Rijsbergen, C.J.V.: Information Retrieval. Butterworths, London (1979)
26. Batista, G.E., Prati, R.C., Monard, M.C.: A study of the behavior of several methods for balancing machine learning training data. ACM SIGKDD Explrs. Newsl. 6, 20–29 (2004)
27. Liu, A., Ghosh, J., Martin, C.: Generative oversampling for mining imbalanced datasets. In: Proceedings of the 2007 International Conference on Data Mining, DMIN, pp. 25–28 (2007)
28. Witten, I.H., Frank, E.: Data Mining: Practical Machine Learning Tools and Techniques with Java Implementations, pp. 265–320. Morgan Kaufmann Publishers, San Francisco (2000)
29. Chang, C.C., Lin, C.J.: LIBSVM: a library for support vector machines
30. Ong, C.S., Huang, J.J., Tzeng, G.H.: Building credit scoring models using genetic programming. Expert Systems with Applications 29, 41–47 (2005)
31. Hand, D.J.: Consumer credit and statistics. Statistics in Finance, 69–81 (1998)
32. Quinlan, J.R.: Simplifying decision trees. Machine Intel. 27, 234 (1987)
33. Elkan, K.: Invited talk- the real challenges in data mining- a contrarian view (2003)
34. Davis, J., Goadrich, M.: The relationship between precision-recall and ROC curves. In: Proc of the 23rd Intl. Conf. on ML, pp. 233–240. ACM, New York (2006)
35. Elazmeh, W., Japkowicz, N., Matwin, S.: Evaluating misclassifications in imbalanced data. In: Fürnkranz, J., Scheffer, T., Spiliopoulou, M. (eds.) ECML 2006. LNCS (LNAI), vol. 4212, pp. 126–137. Springer, Heidelberg (2006)
36. Drummond, C., Holte, R.C.: Explicitly representing expected cost: An alternative to ROC representation. In: Proc. of 6th ACM SIGKDD, pp. 198–207. ACM, New York (2000)
37. Japkowicz, N., Stephen, S.: The class imbalance problem: A systematic study. Intelligent Data Analysis 6, 429–449 (2002)
38. Weiss, G.M.: Mining with rarity. ACM SIGKDD Explorations Newsletter 6, 7–19 (2004)

A Survey of Recent Trends in One Class Classification

Shehroz S. Khan and Michael G. Madden

College of Engineering and Informatics,
National University of Ireland Galway, Ireland
{shehroz.khan,michael.madden}@nuigalway.ie

Abstract. The One Class Classification (OCC) problem is different from the conventional binary/multi-class classification problem in the sense that in OCC, the negative class is either not present or not properly sampled. The problem of classifying positive (or target) cases in the absence of appropriately-characterized negative cases (or outliers) has gained increasing attention in recent years. Researchers have addressed the task of OCC by using different methodologies in a variety of application domains. In this paper we formulate a taxonomy with three main categories based on the way OCC has been envisaged, implemented and applied by various researchers in different application domains. We also present a survey of current state-of-the-art OCC algorithms, their importance, applications and limitations.

Keywords: One Class Classification, Outlier Detection, Support Vector Machines, Positive and Unlabeled Data.

1 Introduction

Conventional multi-class classification algorithms aim to classify an unknown object into one of several pre-defined categories. A problem arises when the unknown object does not belong to any of those categories. In one-class classification [1][2], one of the classes (referred to as the positive class or target class) is well characterized by instances in the training data. For the other class (non-target), it has either no instances at all, very few of them, or they do not form a statistically-representative sample of the negative concept.

To motivate the importance of one-class classification, let us consider some scenarios. One-class classification can be relevant in detecting machine faults, for instance. A classifier should detect when the machine is showing abnormal/faulty behaviour. Measurements on the normal operation of the machine (positive class training data) are easy to obtain. On the other hand, most faults will not have occurred so one will have little or no training data for the negative class. As another example, a traditional binary classifier for text or web pages requires arduous pre-processing to collect negative training examples. For example, in order to construct a homepage classifier [3], collecting sample of homepages

L. Coyle and J. Freyne (Eds.): AICS 2009, LNAI 6206, pp. 188–197, 2010.
© Springer-Verlag Berlin Heidelberg 2010

(positive training examples) is relatively easy, however collecting samples of non-homepages (negative training examples) is very challenging because it may not represent the negative concept uniformly and may involve human bias.

The outline of the paper is as follows. In Section 2 we compare OCC and multi-class classification problems. In Section 3 we propose a taxonomy for the study of OCC and present current state-of-the-art survey of some of the major research contributions under the proposed taxonomy. Section 4 concludes our presentation with summary of the research work in OCC and guidelines for future research.

2   OCC vs. Multi-class Classification

In a conventional multi-class classification problem, data from two (or more) classes are available and the decision boundary is supported by the presence of example samples from each class. Moya et al. [4] originate the term One-Class Classification in their research work. Different researchers have used other terms to present similar concepts such as Outlier Detection [5], Novelty Detection [6] or Concept Learning [7]. These terms originate as a result of different applications to which OCC has been applied.

The drawbacks that are encountered in the conventional classification problems, such as the estimation of error rates, measuring the complexity of a solution, the curse of dimensionality, the generalization of the method, and so on, also appear in OCC, and sometimes become even more prominent.

As stated earlier, in OCC tasks, the negative data is either absent or limited in its distribution, so only one side of the classification boundary can be determined definitively by using the data. This makes problem of one-class classification harder than the problem of conventional multi-class / binary classification. The task in OCC is to define a classification boundary around the positive (or target) class, such that it accepts as many objects as possible from the positive class, while it minimizes the chance of accepting non-positive (or outlier) objects. Since only one side of the boundary can be determined, in OCC, it is hard to decide, on the basis of just one class how tightly the boundary should fit in each of the directions around the data. It is also harder to decide which attributes should be used to find the best separation of the positive and non-positive class objects. In particular, when the boundary of the data is long and non-convex, the required number of training objects might be very high. Hence it is to be expected that one-class classification algorithms will require a larger number training instances relative to conventional multi-class classification algorithms [2].

3   Taxonomy and Review of OCC Work

Based on reviewing past research that has been carried out in the field of OCC by using different algorithms, methodologies and application domains, we propose a taxonomy with three broad categories for the study of OCC problems. The taxonomy can be summarized as (see Fig. 1):

(a) *Availability of Training Data:* Learning with positive data only (or with a limited amount of negative samples) or learning with positive and unlabeled data
(b) *Methodology Used:* Algorithms based on One Class Support Vector Machines (OSVMs) or methodologies based on algorithms other than OSVMs
(c) *Application Domain Applied:* OCC applied in the field of text/document classification or in other application domains

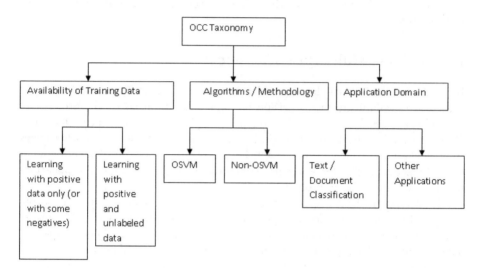

Fig. 1. Proposed Taxonomy for the Study of OCC Techniques

The proposed categories are not mutually exclusive, so there may be some overlapping among the research carried out in each of these categories. However, they cover almost all of the major research conducted using the concept of OCC in various contexts and application domains. The key contributions in most OCC research fall into one of the above-mentioned categories.

3.1   Availability of Training Data

OCC problems have been studied extensively under three broad frameworks:

1. Learning with positive examples only
2. Learning with positive examples and some amount of poorly distributed negative examples
3. Learning with positive and unlabeled data

The last category has recieved much research interest among the text/document classification community [8][9][10] that will be discussed in detail below in Section 3.3.

Tax and Duin [11][12] and Scholkopf et al.[13] have developed algorithms based on support vector machines to tackle the problem of OCC using positive examples only (refer to Section 3.2). The main idea behind these strategies is to construct a decision boundary around the positive data so as to differentiate the outliers (non-positives) from the positive data.

For many learning tasks, labeled examples are rare, whereas numerous unlabeled examples are easily available. The problem of learning with the help of unlabeled data given a small set of labeled examples is studied by Blum and Mitchell [14] by using the concept of co-training for text classification. The co-training setting can be applied when a data set has natural separation of its features. Co-training algorithms incrementally build basic classifiers over each of these feature sets. They show that under the assumptions that each set of features is sufficient for classification, and the feature sets of each instance are conditionally independent, given the class, PAC (Probably Approximately Correct) learning [15] guarantees on learning from labeled and unlabeled data. Muggleton [16] presents a theoretical study in the Bayesian framework where the distribution of functions and examples are assumed to be known. Skabar [17] describes the use of feed-forward neural network to learn a classifier from a data set consisting of labeled positive examples along with a corpus of unlabeled examples containing positive and negative samples.

3.2 Algorithm Used

OSVM. The one-class classification problem is often solved by estimating the target density [4], or by fitting a model to the data support vector classifier [18]. Tax and Duin [11][12] seek to solve the problem of OCC by distinguishing the positive class from all other possible patterns in the pattern space. Instead of using a hyper-plane to distinguish between two classes, a hyper-sphere is found around the positive class data that encompasses almost all points in the data set with the minimum radius. This method is called the Support Vector Data Description (SVDD). Thus training this model has the possibility of rejecting some fraction of the positively-labeled training objects, when this sufficiently decreases the volume of the hyper-sphere. Furthermore, the hyper-sphere model of the SVDD can be made more flexible by introducing kernel functions. Tax [2] considers a Polynomial and a Gaussian kernel and found that the Gaussian kernel works better for most data sets. A drawback of this technique is that they often require a large data set; in particular, in high dimensional feature spaces, it becomes very inefficient. Also, problems may arise when large differences in density exist. Objects in low-density areas will be rejected although they are legitimate objects.

Scholkopf et al. [13][19] present an alternative approach to the above mentioned work of Tax and Duin on OCC using a separating hyper-plane. The difference between theirs and Tax and Duins approach is that instead of trying to find a hyper-sphere with minimal radius to fit the data, they try to separate the surface region containing data from the region containing no data. This is achieved by constructing a hyper-plane which is maximally distant from origin, with all data points lying on the opposite side from the origin and such that the margin is positive. Their paper proposes an algorithm that computes a binary function that returns +1 in small regions (subspaces) that contain data and -1 elsewhere. The data is mapped into the feature space corresponding to the kernel and is separated from the origin with maximum margin. They evaluate the efficacy of their method on the US Postal Services data set of handwritten digits and show that the algorithm is able to extract patterns which are very hard to assign to their respective classes and a number of outliers were identified.

Manevitz and Yousef [20] propose a different version of the one class SVM which is based on identifying outlier data as representative of the second class. The idea of this methodology is to work first in the feature space, and assume that not only is the origin the second class, but also that all data points close enough to the origin are to be considered as noise or outliers. The vectors lying on standard sub-spaces of small dimension (i.e. axes, faces, etc.) are treated as outliers. They evaluate their results on Reuters Data set[1] and the results are worse than the OSVM algorithm presented by Scholkopf et al. [19].

Classifiers are commonly ensembled to provide a combined decision by averaging the estimated posterior probabilities. When Bayes theorem is used for the combination of different classifiers, under the assumption of independence, a product combination rule can be used to create classifier ensemble. The outputs of the individual classifiers are multiplied and then normalized (also called the logarithmic opinion pool [21]). In OCC, as the information on the non-positive data is not available, in most cases, the outliers are assumed to be uniformly distributed and the posterior probability can be estimated. Tax [2] mentions that in some OCC methods, distance is estimated instead of probability for one class classifier ensembling. Tax observes that the use of ensembles in OCC improves performance, especially when the product rule is used to combine the probability estimates.

Yu [22] proposes an OCC algorithm with SVMs using positive and unlabeled data, and without labeled negative data, and discusses some of the limitations of other OCC algorithms [1][3][13][20]. Yu comments that in the absence of negative examples, OSVM requires a much larger amount of positive training data to induce an accurate class boundary.

Non-OSVMs. Ridder et al. [23] conduct an experimental comparison of various OCC algorithms, including: (a) Global Gaussian approximation; (b) Parzen density estimation; (c) 1-Nearest Neighbor method; and (d) Gaussian approximation (combines aspects of (a) and (b)). Manevitz and Yousef [24] trained a simple neural network to filter documents when only positive information is available. To incorporate the restriction of availability of positive examples only, they used a three-level feed forward network with a "bottleneck".

DeComite et al. [25] modify the C4.5 decision tree algorithm [26] to get an algorithm that takes as input a set of labeled examples, a set of positive examples, and a set of unlabeled data, and then use these three sets to construct the decision tree. Letouzey et al. [27] design an algorithm which is based on positive statistical queries (estimates for probabilities over the set of positive instances)

---

[1] http://www.daviddlewis.com/resources/testcollections/reuters21578

and instance statistical queries (estimates for probabilities over the instance space). They design a decision tree induction algorithm, called POSC4.5, using only positive and unlabeled data. They present experimental results on UCI data sets[2] that are comparable to the C4.5 algorithm.

Wang et al. [28] investigate several one-class classification methods in the context of Human-Robot interaction for face and non-face classification. Some of the noteworthy methods used in their study are: (a) SVDD; (b) Gaussian data description; (c) KMEANS-DD; (d) Principal Component Analysis-DD. In their experimentation, they observe that SVDD attains better performance than the other OCC methods they studied.

3.3 Application Domain Used

Text Classification. Traditional text classification techniques require an appropriate distribution of positive and negative examples to build a classifier; thus they are not suitable for this problem of OCC. It is of course possible to manually label some negative examples, though that it is labour-intensive and a time consuming task. However the core problem remains, that it is difficult or impossible to compile a set of negative samples that provides a comprehensive characterization of everything that is 'not' the target concept, as is assumed by a conventional binary classifier.

The ability to build classifiers without negative training data is useful in a scenario when one needs to extract positive documents from many text collections or sources. Liu et al. [29] propose a method (called Spy EM) to solve this problem in the text domain. It is based on Naïve Bayesian classification (NB) and the Expectation Maximization (EM) algorithm [30]. The main idea of the method is to first use a technique to identify some reliable / strong negative documents from the unlabeled set. It then runs EM to build the final classifier. Yu et al. [3][31] propose an SVM-based technique called PEBL (Positive Example Based Learning) to classify Web pages with positive and unlabeled pages. Once a set of strong negative documents is identified, SVM is applied iteratively to build a classifier. PEBL is sensitive to the number of positive examples and gives poor results when they are small in number. Li and Liu [9] propose an alternative method that extracts negative data from the unlabeled set using the Rocchio method [32] . Although the second step also runs SVM iteratively to build a classifier, there is a key difference in selection of the final classifier. Their technique selects a "good" classifier from a set of classifiers built by SVM, while PEBL does not. It is shown theoretically by Liu et al. [29] that if the sample size is large enough, maximizing the number of unlabeled examples classified as negative while constraining the positive examples to be correctly classified will produce a good classifier. Liu et al. [8] develop a benchmarking system called LPU (Learning from Positive and Unlabeled data)[3] and also propose an approach based on a biased formulation of SVM that allows noise (or error) in

---

[2] http://www.ics.uci.edu/ mlearn/MLRepository.html
[3] http://www.cs.uic.edu/ liub/LPU/LPU-download.html

positive examples. They experiment on Reuters data set and Usenet articles by Lang [33] and conclude that biased-SVM approach outperforms other existing two-step techniques.

Peng et al. [34] present a text classifier from positive and unlabeled documents based on Genetic Algorithms (GA). They perform experiments on the Reuters data set and compare their results against PEBL [31] and OSVM, and show that their GA based classification performs better. Koppel et al. [35] study the "Authorship Verification" problem where only examples of writings of a single author are given and the task is to determine if a given piece of text is or is not written by this author. They test their algorithm on a collection of twenty-one 19th century English books written by 10 different authors and spanning a variety of genres. They obtain overall accuracy of 95.7% with errors almost equally distributed between false positives and false negatives.

Denis et al. [36] introduce a Naïve Bayes algorithm and shows its feasibility for learning from positive and unlabeled documents. The key step in their method is in estimating word probabilities for the negative class because negative examples were not available. This limitation can be overcome by assuming an estimate of the positive class probability (the ratio of positive documents in the set of all documents). In practical situations, the positive class probability can be empirically estimated or provided by domain knowledge. Their results on the WebKB data set[4] show that error rates of Naïve Bayes classifiers obtained from positive examples trained with enough unlabeled examples are lower than error rates of Naïve Bayes classifiers obtained from labeled documents.

Other Application Domains. OSVMs have been successfully applied in a wide variety of application domains such as Handwritten Digit Recognition [1][2][19], Information Retrieval [20], Face Recognition Applications [28][37], Medical Analysis [38], Bioinformatics [39][40], Spam Detection [41], Anomaly Detection [42][43], Machine Fault Detection [44]. Compression neural networks for one-sided classification have been used in many application areas, including detecting Mineral Deposits [17]. Wang and Stolfo use one-class Naïve Bayes to detect Masquerade Detection [45] in a network and show that less effort in data collection is required with comparable performance as that of a multi-class classifier. Munroe and Madden [46] present a one class k-nearest neighbor approach for vehicle recognition from images and showed that the results are comparable to that of standard multi-class classifiers.

4   Conclusions and Future Work

The goal of One-Class Classification is to induce classifiers when only one class (the positive class) is well characterized by the training data. In this paper, we have presented a survey of current state-of-the-art research work using OCC. We observe that the research carried out in OCC can be broadly presented by three different categories or areas of study, which depends upon the availability

[4] http://www-2.cs.cmu.edu/afs/cs.cmu.edu/project/theo-20/www/data/

of training data, classification algorithms used and the application domain investigated. Under each of these categories, we further provide details of commonly used OCC algorithms. Although the OCC field is becoming mature, still there are several fundamental problems that are open for research, not only in describing and training classifiers, but also in scaling, controlling errors, handling outliers, using non-representative sets of negative examples, combining classifiers and reducing dimensionality.

Classifier ensembles have not been exploited very much for OCC problems, and techniques such as boosting and bagging deserve further attention. Another point to note here is that in OSVMs, the kernels that have been used mostly are Linear, Polynomial, Gaussian or Sigmoidal. We suggest it would be fruitful to investigate some more innovative forms of kernel, for example Genetic Kernels [47], that have shown greater potential in standard SVM classification. In the case where abundant unlabeled examples and some positive examples are available, researchers have used many two-step algorithms (as have been discussed in Section 3.3). We believe that a Bayesian Network approach to such OCC problems would be an interesting exercise.

This survey provides a broad insight into the study of the discipline of OCC. Depending upon the data availability, algorithm use and application, appropriate OCC techniques can be applied and improved upon. We hope that this survey will provide researchers with a direction to formulate future novel work in this field.

References

1. Tax, D., Duin, R.: Uniform object generation for optimizing one-class classifiers. J. Machine Learning Research 2, 155–173 (2001)
2. Tax, D.: One Class Classification. PhD thesis, Delft University of Technology (2001)
3. Yu, H., Han, J., Chang, K.C.C.: Positive-example based learning for web page classification using svm. In: Proc. Eighth International Conference on Knowledge Discovery and Data Mining (KDD 2002), pp. 239–248 (2002)
4. Moya, M., Koch, M., Hostetler, L.: One-class classifier networks for target recognition applications. In: Proceedings World Congress on Neural Networks, pp. 797–801 (1993)
5. Ritter, G., Gallegos, M.: Outliers in statistical pattern recognition and an application to automatic chromosome classification. Pattern Recognition Letters 18, 525–539 (1997)
6. Bishop, C.: Novelty detection and neural network validation. IEEE Proceedings on Vision, Image and Signal Processing, Special Issue on Applications of Neural Networks 141(4), 217–222 (1994)
7. Japkowicz, N.: Concept-Learning in the absence of counterexamples: An autoassociation-based approach to classification. PhD thesis, New Brunswick Rutgers, The State University of New Jersey (1999)
8. Liu, B., Dai, Y., Li, X., Lee, W., Yu, P.: Building text classifiers using positive and unlabeled examples. In: Proceedings of the 3rd IEEE International Conference on Data Mining (ICDM 2003) (2003)

9. Li, X., Liu, B.: Learning to classify texts using positive and unlabeled data. In: 18th International Joint Conf. on Artificial Intelligence (IJCAI 2003), pp. 587–594 (2003)

10. Lee, W., Liu, B.: Learning with positive and unlabeled examples using weighted logistic regression. In: Proceedings of the 20th International Conference on Machine Learning (ICML 2003) (2003)

11. Tax, D., Duin, R.: Data domain description using support vectors. In: Proc. ESAN 1999, Brussels, pp. 251–256 (1999)

12. Tax, D., Duin, R.: Support vector domain description. Pattern Recognition Letters 20, 1191–1199 (1999)

13. Scholkopf, B., Williamson, R., Smola, A., Taylor, J., Platt, J.: Support vector method for novelty detection. In: Solla, S.A., Leen, T., Muller, K. (eds.) Neural Information Processing Systems, pp. 582–588 (2000)

14. Blum Mitchell, T.: Combining labeled and unlabeled data with co-training. In: Proceedings of 11th Annual conference on Computation Learning Theory, pp. 92–100. ACM Press, New York (1998)

15. Valiant, L.: Theory of the learnable. ACM 27(11), 1134–1142 (1984)

16. Muggleton, S.: Learning from the positive data. Machine Learning (2001)

17. Skabar, A.: Single-class classifier learning using neural networks: An application to the prediction of mineral deposits. In: Proceedings of the Second International Conference on Machine Learning and Cybernetics, vol. 4, pp. 2127–2132 (2003)

18. Burges, C.J.C.: A tutorial on support vector machines for pattern recognition. Data Mining and Knowledge Discovery 2(2), 1–47 (1998)

19. Scholkopf, B., Williamson, R., Smola, A., Taylor, J.: Sv estimation of a distributions support. In: Advances in Neural Information Processing Systems (1999)

20. Manevitz, L.M., Yousef, M.: One-class svms for document classification. Journal of Machine Learning Research 2, 139–154 (2001)

21. Benediktsson, J., Swain, P.: Consensus theoretic classification methods. IEEE Transactions on Systems, Man and Cybernetics 22(4), 688–704 (1992)

22. Yu, H.: Single-class classification with mapping convergence. Machine Learning 61(1), 49–69 (2005)

23. de Ridder, D., Tax, D., Duin, R.: An experimental comparison of one-class classification methods. In: Proceedings of the 4th Annual Conference of the Advacned School for Computing and Imaging, Delft (1998)

24. Manevitz, L., Yousef, M.: Document classification on neural networks using only positive examples. In: Proc. of 23rd Annual International ACM SIGIR Conference on Research and Development in Information Retrieval, pp. 304–306 (2000)

25. De Comite, F., Denis, F., Gillerson, R., Letouzey, F.: Positive and unlabeled examples help learning. In: Watanabe, O., Yokomori, T. (eds.) ALT 1999. LNCS (LNAI), vol. 1720, pp. 219–230. Springer, Heidelberg (1999)

26. Quinlan, J.R.: C4.5: Programs for Machine Learning. Morgan Kaufmann, San Mateo (1993)

27. Letouzey, F., Denis, F., Gilleron, R.: Learning from positive and unlabeled examples. In: Algorithmic Learning Theory, 11th International Conference, Sydney, Australia (2000)

28. Wang, Q., Lopes, L.S., Tax, D.J.: Visual object recognition through one-class learning. In: International Conference on Image Analysis and Recognition, pp. 463–470 (2004)

29. Liu, B., Lee, W., Yu, P., Li, X.: Partially supervised classification of text documents. In: Proc. of ICML (2002)

30. Dempster, A.P., Laird, N.M., Rubin, D.: Maximum likelihood from incomplete data via the em algorithm. Journal of the Royal Statistical Society (1977)
31. Yu, H., Han, J., Chang, K.: PEBL: Web page classification without negative examples. IEEE Transactions on Knowledge and Data Engineering 16(1) (2004)
32. Rocchio, J.: Relevant feedback in information retrieval. In: Salton, G. (ed.) The SMART retrieval system- experiments in automatic document processing, NJ, Englewood Cliffs (1971)
33. Lang, K.: Newsweeder: Learning to filter netnews. In: ICML 1995 (1995)
34. Peng, T., Zuo, W., He, F.: Text classification from positive and unlabeled documents based on ga. In: Proc. of VECPAR 2006, Brazil (2006)
35. Koppel, M., Schler, J.: Authorship verification as a one-class classification problem. In: Proceedings of the twenty-first International Conference on Machine learning, Alberta, Canada, vol. 69 (2004)
36. Denis, F., Gilleron, R., Tommasi, M.: Text classification from positive and unlabeled examples. In: 9th International Conference on Information Processing and Management of Uncertainty in Knowledge-Based Systems (2002)
37. Zeng, Z., Fu, Y., Roisman, G.I., Wen, Z., Hu, Y., Huang, T.S.: One-class classification for spontaneous facial expression analysis. In: Proceedings of the 7th International Conference on Automatic Face and Gesture Recognition, pp. 281–286 (2006)
38. Gardner, B., Krieger, A.M., Vachtsevanos, G., Litt, B.: One-class novelty detection for seizure analysis from intracranial eeg. Journal of Machine Learning Research 7, 1025–1044 (2006)
39. Spinosa, E.J., de Carvalho, A.C.P.L.F.: SVMs for novel class detection in bioinformatics. In: Brazilian Workshop on Bioinformatics, pp. 81–88 (2004)
40. Alashwal, H.T., Deris, S., Othman, R.M.: One-class support vector machines for protein-protein interactions prediction. International Journal Biomedical Sciences 1(2), 120–127 (2006)
41. Sun, D., Tran, Q., Duan, H., Zhang, G.: A novel method for chinese spam detection based on one-class support vector machine. Journal of Information and Computational Science 2(1), 109–114 (2005)
42. Li, K., Huang, H., Tian, S., Xu, W.: Improving one-class svm for anomaly detection. In: Proceedings of the second international conference on machine learning and cybernetics, pp. 2–5 (November 2003)
43. Perdisci, R., Gu, G., Lee, W.: Using an ensemble of one-class svm classifiers to harden payload-based anomaly detection systems. In: Sixth International Conference on Data Mining, pp. 488–498 (2006)
44. Shin, H.J., Eom, D.W., Kim, S.S.: One-class support vector machines: an application in machine fault detection and classification. Computers and Industrial Engineering 48(2), 395–408 (2005)
45. Wang, K., Stolfo, S.J.: One class training for masquerade detection. In: ICDM Workshop on Data Mining for Computer Security (2003)
46. Munroe, D.T., Madden, M.G.: Multi-class and single-class classification approaches to vehicle model recognition from images. In: Proc. AICS 2005: Irish Conference on Artificial Intelligence and Cognitive Science, Portstewart (2005)
47. Howley, T., Madden, M.G.: An evolutionary approach to automatic kernel construction. In: Kollias, S.D., Stafylopatis, A., Duch, W., Oja, E. (eds.) ICANN 2006. LNCS, vol. 4132, pp. 417–426. Springer, Heidelberg (2006)

Steady State RF Fingerprinting for Identity Verification: One Class Classifier versus Customized Ensemble

Barnard Kroon[1], Susan Bergin[1], Irwin O. Kennedy[2],
and Georgina O'Mahony Zamora[1]

[1] Department of Computer Science,
National University of Ireland
Maynooth, Co. Kildare, Ireland
[2] Bell Laboratories,
Alcatel-Lucent,
Blanchardstown Industrial Park,
Dublin 15, Ireland

Abstract. Mobile phone proliferation and increasing broadband penetration presents the possibility of placing small cellular base stations within homes to act as local access points. This can potentially lead to a very large increase in authentication requests hitting the centralized authentication infrastructure unless access is mediated at a lower protocol level. A study was carried out to examine the effectiveness of using Support Vector Machines to accurately identify if a mobile phone should be allowed access to a local cellular base station using differences imbued upon the signal as it passes through the analogue stages of its radio transmitter. Whilst allowing prohibited transmitters to gain access at the local level is undesirable and costly, denying service to a permitted transmitter is simply unacceptable. Two different learning approaches were employed, the first using One Class Classifiers (OCCs) and the second using customized ensemble classifiers. OCCs were found to perform poorly, with a true positive (TP) rate of only 50% (where TP refers to correctly identifying a permitted transmitter) and a true negative (TN) rate of 98% (where TN refers to correctly identifying a prohibited transmitter). The customized ensemble classifier approach was found to considerably outperform the OCCs with a 97% TP rate and an 80% TN rate.

Keywords: Machine Learning, Classification, Ensemble Classifiers, Support Vector Machines, One Class Classifiers.

1 Introduction

The increase in broadband penetration and mobile phone proliferation allows for the deployment of Femto cellular base stations directly into the home, allowing the owners to make mobile calls using their broadband connection. The reception area from a Femto cell would however allow external traffic to access the

L. Coyle and J. Freyne (Eds.): AICS 2009, LNAI 6206, pp. 198–206, 2010.
© Springer-Verlag Berlin Heidelberg 2010

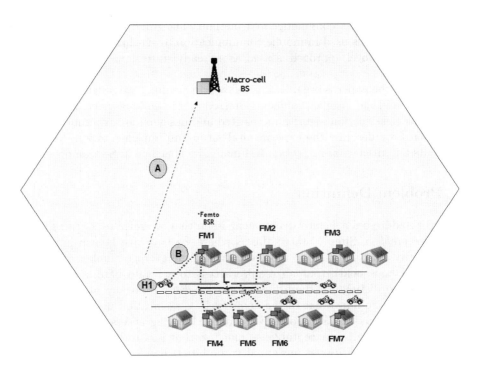

Fig. 1. Example Femto Deployment

base station, which results in an increase in authentication traffic to determine their access rights. This increase can be exponential and runs the serious risk of overloading the cellular service provider's authentication backend[1]. Figure 1 shows the deployment of Femto stations FM1 through FM7 within the larger macro cell serviced by base station BS. Passing mobiles, such as H1, will rapidly establish connections between the Femto cells and the macro cell. Each connection requires an authentication request. Using local authentication on the Femto itself without a need to access the authentication server would relieve this possible problem. Filters, power amplifiers, inductors, capacitors, PCB materials and soldering used in the manufacture of a transmitter all imbue unique characteristics onto the transmitted signal, and using these differences a transmitter can be identified using Radio Frequency (RF) fingerprinting. The 3GPP UMTS standard recommends the uniquely identifying IMSI (International Mobile Subscriber Identifier) should not be sent in plain text over the air. We discuss this and other motivating aspects of the problem in more depth in papers published previously by the authors[2,3].

There are typically two ways of identifying RF signal sources, transient state analysis and steady state analysis[4]. Transient state analysis is more commonly used and operates by detecting transient state signals which are generated as a transmitter is powered up for the first time. In data communications different communicating entities have limited common signal portions and as such steady state analysis is a less commonly used method. The Random Access Channel (RACH) preamble is used in mobile communication to synchronize communication and in our novel approach is used as a steady state signal common to all transmitters.

The rest of the paper is organized as follows. In Section 2 we provide the problem context and the specific problem addressed in this work. Section 3 describes the various classification algorithms selected and designed for experimentation. In Section 4 we describe the experimental setup and implementation, followed by results and discussion in Section 5. Finally, we conclude in Section 6.

2   Problem Definition

This work addresses a Femto deployment issue that we refer to as the *five in the house problem*. Simply stated this is where we have five known handsets, (the quantity is assumed to be representative of the average number of mobile phones in a household), that all require access to a Femto base station. The challenge is to distinguish these five known handsets from any other handset which might come into range of the Femto cell. Classification under these specific conditions has two additional constraints. Denying access to a permitted handset is completely unacceptable, so much so that it is to be avoided even if it means allowing additional unwanted (prohibited) handsets onto the Femto. These prohibited handsets will later be denied by the traditional authentication measures. This adds the requirements that the true positive (TP) rate must be as close to 100% as possible, where TP refers to correctly identifying that the handset belongs to the house and should be allowed access to the Femto base station. Additionally, although of lesser importance, a high true negative (TN) rate must be achieved where TN refers to correctly identifying where a handset does not belong to the house and should be refused access.

Previous work on RF fingerprinting has focussed mainly on identifying different mobile phone handsets by manufacturer and by model[2,3]. While this work is relevant, the approach used is not sufficient for the *five in the house problem*.

3   Classification

In this Section we describe a number of different approaches to tackling the *five in the house* classification problem. All approaches are based on the Support Vector Machine, so we start in Section 3.1 by providing an overview of a Support Vector Machines and in Section 3.2 we describe an alternative set of classifier implementations.

3.1   Support Vector Machines

Support Vector Machines (SVMs) are a relatively recent set of supervised machine learning algorithms that have been shown to have either equivalent or significantly better generalization performance than other competing methods on a wide range of classification problems [5]. They can be used to classify linearly separable data using the original input space or non-linearly separable data by mapping to a higher dimensional feature space in which a linear separator can be found.

In a typical binary classification problem composed of a training dataset $\{(\mathbf{x_1},y_1),(\mathbf{x_2},y_2),...,(\mathbf{x_m},y_m)\}$ where $\mathbf{x_i} \in \Re_\mathbf{d}$ and $y_i \in \{\pm1\}$, SVMs seek a solution to the following Lagrangian optimization function:

$$W(\alpha) = \sum_{i=1}^{m} \alpha_i - \frac{1}{2} \sum_{i,j=1}^{m} \alpha_i \alpha_j y_i y_j K(\mathbf{x}_i, \mathbf{x}_j) \tag{1}$$

subject to the following constraints

$$C \geq \alpha_i \geq 0 \quad \forall i \qquad and \qquad \sum_{i=1}^{m} \alpha_i y_i = 0. \tag{2}$$

C is an optional parameter that controls the trade off between allowing training errors and forcing rigid margins. That is, it represents a soft margin that allows some misclassifications which can be beneficial in noisy datasets. Where a soft margin is not allowed, the constraint is simply $\alpha_i \geq 0$. K represents the kernel function and numerous choices exist, including linear, Polynomial and Radial Basis Functions (RBF). RBF SVMs are currently the most popular choice of non-linear SVM and are implemented in this study[5,6]. Once an optimal solution is found, the decision function for a new point $\mathbf{z}$ is given by

$$f(\mathbf{z}) = sign \left(\sum_{i=1}^{m} y_i \alpha_i K(\mathbf{x}_i, \mathbf{z}) + b \right). \tag{3}$$

$\mathbf{z}$ is a training example, b is the bias and non-zero α_i values represent support vectors, the points that lie closest to the hyperplane.

The 'One-against-one' [7] multiclass approach is implemented in this study as it has been shown to have comparable if not better generalized accuracy than alternative techniques and requires considerably less training time [8], [9]. The method consists of constructing an SVM for each pair of classes. Thus for a problem with n classes $n(n-1)/2$ SVMs are trained to distinguish between the samples of one class form the samples of another class. For an unknown pattern, each SVM votes for one class and the class with the highest number of votes is chosen.

SVM One Class Classifiers (OCCs) operate on a different principle. Whilst traditional classifiers are trained on 2 or more classes, OCCs are only trained on a single class of samples (positive samples) and attempt to learn the unique features of this class so that it can accurately identify an unseen sample of this class as distinct from a sample of any other class. OCC distinguish between the trained class and other samples by identifying the other samples as outliers in the distribution described by the training set.

3.2   SVM Classifier Implementations

The SVM and OCC SVM implementation utilized in this study are the implementations provided by the libSVM library[10]. However not all of the functionality required in this study was implemented in the library and the following Section describes the changes in methodology that were used.

While an SVM typically outputs only the predicted class of an unknown sample, it can be enhanced to also output a Probability Density (PD) estimate. The estimates are based on the distance each test point is from the separating hyperplane, the further the point is from the hyperplane, the higher the probability it belongs in the class [11].

It has already been shown that standard RBF kernel SVMs have a high accuracy distinguishing between different transmitters[2]. Using this knowledge coupled with the PD estimates allows us to use these classifiers on the *five in the house problem*. It was found that if the SVM was shown a handset present in the training set, a positive sample, the PD showed a high Standard Deviation (SD). Conversely if the SVM was shown an unknown handset, one not present in the training set, the PD showed a low SD. To take advantage of this difference in SD between known and unknown samples a number of different composite classifiers were constructed using the RBF SVM as a base. While these classifiers are all multi-class classifiers, they are trained only on the handsets that it is to recognize. When the classifier is tested it is shown both positive samples and negative samples. It has also been shown that handsets of the same model can be harder to distinguish than handsets of a different model[2,3]. The Tiered, Weighted and Double classifiers are constructed in such a way as to potentially allow one of the sub-classifiers to avoid having multiple identical handsets, or if unavoidable at least favor one over the other.

Single Classifier. The Single classifier is an RBF SVM, using the PD output to determine classification. Because this is a RBF SVM at least 2 handsets are required in the training set in order for the classifier to attempt to distinguish between them.

Tiered Classifier. The Tiered Classifier is slightly more complex in construction, but follows the basic principle of the Single classifier. If presented with n handsets, it consists of n RBF SVM classifiers each trained on unique group of $n - 1$ handsets. As an example, if presented with handsets A, B and C then the three classifiers are each trained on the only one of the sets (A and B), (A and C) and (B and C).

This classifier requires at least 3 handsets in the training set, as each sub-classifier is effectively a Single classifier requiring a minimum 2 handsets. The resulting PD output by each sub-classifier is summed per label and then normalized to sum to 1 again before classification is made.

Weighted Tiered Classifier. The Weighted Tiered (Weighted) Classifier is constructed similarly to the Tiered Classifier, but uses weights to assign greater importance to a particular class. In each sub-classifier one unique class is weighted as more important than the rest. This means handsets A, C and B respectively in the training sets (A and B), (A and C) and (B and C) from the Tiered Classifier example will be the weighted handsets.

Double Weighted Classifier. Following the same principle as the Weighted Classifier, the Double Weighted Classifier (Double) weights a unique pair of handsets in each classifier as more important than the rest. At least 4 handsets are required to construct this classifier, as each sub-classifier requires at least 1 class not weighted otherwise it would effectively be identical to a Tiered classifier.

4   Experimental Setup and Implementation

The RACH preambles, representing the handsets, used in the classification tasks were captured in an anechoic chamber using a Rhode and Schwarz FSQ26 signal analyzer at 20MSamples/s. An Alcatel-Lucent 2100 MHz UMTS base station, transmitting on very low power (less than 100mW), with a modified software load was used. The modified software ensured that:

1. The base station never responded to the RACH preambles thus ensuring the handset would continue the transmission of the RACH preamble ramp sequence, simplifying RACH transmission capture.
2. Modified system information blocks (SIBs), used by the UMTS standard to configure handset operation, allow us to restrict the handset to only use a single RACH preamble signature and scrambling code meaning every RACH preamble transmission contains the same digital Inphase/Quadrature (I/Q) content.

Sixty nine handsets of varied manufacturer and model were used and approximately 1200 RACH preambles captured per handset. We extracted 177 features using the frequency domain binning algorithm described in [3].

These captured RACH preambles were used in two classification tasks using the SVM OCC setup. In the first experiment 69 OCC SVMs were each trained on data from a single handset. Then they were tested using preamble samples from all 69 handsets to determine how accurately each classifier could identify individual handsets. The second experiment was to verify the results from the first experiment and to ascertain how the OCC responded to multiple handsets in the training set. Five classifiers were trained to identify 5 handsets, as opposed to only 1 handset in the first experiment, and then were again used to distinguish between the known handsets and a selection of the unknown handsets.

The third experiment used the ensemble classifiers. For each classification task the number of known handsets, referred to here as positive samples, was selected at random from a normal distribution with mean 5, representing the number of handsets present in the *five in the house problem*. The width of the distribution was chosen such that at least 2 and at most 8 handsets were chosen[1]. A test set was also chosen for each classification task, consisting of random samples

---

[1] The resulting distribution had a standard deviation on 1.23.

from between 10 and 69 handsets were selected as the test set, which included at least one of the training handsets. Each of the custom classifiers was trained and tested using identical training and test sets, taking into account that the Double classifier required at least 4 different handsets in the training set, and the Tiered and Weighted classifiers require at least 3 handsets in the training set.

5   Results and Discussion

The results from the two different types of classifiers are quite different. Initially the output from the OCC looks exceedingly good with an average accuracy of 98% across the classifiers. A more detailed analysis of these results, specifically focussing on TP and TN, shows that while a high TN rate of 98% is achieved the more important TP rate is exceedingly low at 50%. Table 1 outlines the performance of the OCC (accuracy, TP and TN) as well as the associated standard deviation values. This discrepancy between the accuracy and TP and TN rates stem from the unbalanced nature of the data. Approximately 98.5% of the data presented to any of the classifiers consisted of prohibited handsets, whereas only the remaining 1.5% were permitted handsets.

Table 1. Experiment 1: Single Handset One Class Classifier Results Summary

	Average	Maximum	Minimum	Standard Deviation	Median
Accuracy	97.76%	99.28%	90.14%	0.01	97.99%
True Positive	49.03%	56.70%	39.72%	0.03	48.75%
True Negative	98.48%	99.9986%	90.66%	0.01	98.72%

The second experiment further validated the previous results. The five classifiers obtained similar accuracies to the individual classifiers, specifically: 93%, 95%, 91%, 91% and 86%. The TP and TN rates remained consistent as can be seen in Table 2. These results show that the use of OCC SVMs aren't ideally suited to the *five in the house problem*.

The third experiment with the ensemble RBF SVM classifiers showed promise as the threshold, based off the SD, determining classification could be directly modified. Table 3 shows the resulting TP and TN rates associated with different

Table 2. Experiment 2: Five in the House One Class Classifier Results Summary

	True Positive	True Negative
Experiment 1	48%	96%
Experiment 2	47%	98%
Experiment 3	48%	94%
Experiment 4	45%	95%
Experiment 5	50%	89%

Table 3. Custom Classifier Potential Thresholds

Threshold	TP	TN
0.05	1.0000	0.0001
0.10	1.0000	0.1483
0.15	0.9977	0.5798
0.20	0.9962	0.6447
0.25	0.9894	0.6794
0.30	0.9705	0.7121
0.35	0.9402	0.7472
0.40	0.8735	0.7855
0.45	0.0000	1.0000
...	...	...
0.95	0.0000	1.0000

Table 4. Custom Classifier Results Summary

Classifier	Average		Standard Deviation		Tests
	True Positive	True Negative	True Positive	True Negative	
Single	96.77%	79.13%	0.031	0.115	636
Tiered	93.63%	84.89%	0.051	0.079	825
Weighted 10	93.41%	85.33%	0.052	0.086	845
Weighted 100	93.41%	85.29%	0.053	0.088	845
Double 10	93.07%	85.75%	0.053	0.074	766
Double 100	93.05%	85.77%	0.053	0.074	765

threshold values for the PD SD where any value higher than the threshold is classified as a known handset, and any lower as unknown. These results are the combined average of all the ensemble classifiers over a total of approximately 1200 experiments in total.

The threshold values between 0.15 and 0.35 are broadly in line with the requirements of the *five in the house problem*, as per Section 2, and as such 0.25 was chosen as the threshold value that would be used in the classifiers. The results from the third experiment, using only the chosen threshold, are outlined in Table 4 which shows the averages for the different classifier rates as well as their associated standard deviations and the number of tests run using that classifier.

It should be noted that the Single classifier has a higher TP rate than all the other ensemble classifiers, and that the spread on these is also lower, as evidenced by the lower standard deviation. While the associated TN rate is lower than the other classifiers', the difference in performance shows that the Single classifier is overall a better classifier. An ANOVA test, with $p = 0.01$, confirms this difference as being statistically significant.

The performance difference is partly due to the smoothing effect experienced when combining the output from the different sub-classifiers resulting in a less pronounced difference in SD for these ensemble classifiers. The net result is that any advantage gained from the construction of these classifiers is negated by this. The Single classifier also has the added benefit that it is the easiest to implement.

6   Conclusion

We have described the *five in the house problem*, a telecommunications Femto cell system problem, and experimentally investigated a number of machine learning classifier solutions. Statistically verified experimental results show that a Single Classifier, a custom ensemble classifier based on the Probability Density output from a Support Vector Machine, achieves the best results. Based on 636 tests, the Single Classifier achieves the best combination of True Positive and True Negative results, 97% and 79% respectively. The result offers great encouragement for more research, including the possibility of combining the results from multiple RACH preambles to further improve accuracy.

References

1. Ho, L., Claussen, H.: Effects of user-deployed, co-channel femtocells on the call drop probability in a residential scenario. In: IEEE International Symposium on Personal (September 2007)
2. O'Mahony Zamora, G., Bergin, S., Kennedy, I.O.: Using support vector machines for passive steady state rf fingerprinting. In: International Joint Conferences on Computer, Information, and Systems Sciences, and Engineering (2008)
3. Kennedy, I.O., Scanlon, P., Buddhikot, M.: Passive steady state rf fingerprinting: A cognitive technique for scalable deployment of co-channel femto cell underlays. In: Proceedings IEEE Conference on Dynamic Spectrum Access Networks (October 2008)
4. Gerdes, R., Daniels, T., Mina, M., Russell, S.: Identification via analog signal fingerprinting: A matched filter approach. In: ISOC Network and Distributed System Security Symposium (2006)
5. Burges, C.: A tutorial on support vector machines for pattern recognition. Knowledge Discovery and Data Mining 2(2), 121–167 (1998)
6. ScholKopf, B., Smola, A.J.: Learning with Kernels: Support Vector Machines, Regularization, Optimization, and Beyond. MIT Press, Cambridge (2002)
7. Knerr, S., Personnaz, L., Dreyfus, G.: Single-layer learning revisited: a stepwise procedure for building and training a neural network. Neurocomputing: Algorithms, Architectures and Applications (1990)
8. Hsu, C.-W., Lin, C.-J.: A comparison of methods for multiclass support vector machines. IEEE Transactions on Neural Networks 13(2), 415–425 (2002)
9. Milgram, J., Cheriet, M., Sabourin, R.: 'one against one' or 'one against all': Which one is better for handwriting recognition with svms? In: Tenth International Workshop on Frontiers in Handwriting Recognition (2006)
10. Chang, C.-C., Lin, C.-J.: LIBSVM: a library for support vector machines (2001), Software available at http://www.csie.ntu.edu.tw/~cjlin/libsvm
11. Platt, J.: Probabilistic outputs for support vector machines and comparison to regularized likelihood methods. In: Advances in Large Margin Classifiers, pp. 61–74 (2000)

An Analysis of Order Dependence in k-NN

David McSherry and Christopher Stretch

School of Computing and Information Engineering,
University of Ulster, Coleraine BT52 1SA, Northern Ireland
{dmg.mcsherry, ct.stretch}@ulster.ac.uk

Abstract. In classification based on k-NN with majority voting, the class assigned to a given problem is the one that occurs most frequently in the k most similar cases (or instances) in the dataset. However, different versions of k-NN may use different strategies to select the cases on which the solution is based when there are ties for the kth most similar case. One strategy is to break ties for the kth most similar case based on the ordering of cases in the dataset. We present an analysis of the order dependence introduced by this strategy and its effects on the algorithm's performance.

Keywords: classification, k-NN, instance-based learning, case-based reasoning.

1 Introduction

An algorithm widely used for classification learning in pattern recognition, instance-based learning, case-based reasoning (CBR), and data mining is "k-nearest neighbor" (k-NN) [1-5]. In k-NN with majority voting, the approach to combining class labels on which we focus in this paper, the class assigned to a target problem is the one that occurs most frequently in the k most similar cases (or instances) in the dataset. However, different versions of k-NN may differ in the strategy used to construct the "retrieval set" of cases on which the solution is based when there are ties for the kth most similar case. One strategy for dealing with ties for the nearest neighbor in 1-NN is to assign the class that occurs most frequently among the tied cases to the target problem [1]. A similar strategy used in some versions of k-NN is to include all ties for the kth most similar case in the retrieval set (e.g., [2, 6-8]).

Another strategy is to break ties for the kth most similar case, thus ensuring the retrieval of exactly k cases (e.g., [6-7]). One way to break ties for the kth most similar case is to give priority to tied cases that appear first in the dataset. In this paper, we investigate the order dependence introduced when case ordering is used to break ties in this way (i.e., different solutions for different orderings of cases in the dataset) and its effects on the algorithm's performance. Of course, ties for the kth most similar case can instead be broken randomly, although the inconsistency that this introduces (i.e., different solutions for identical problem descriptions) may be an important factor when k-NN is used for routine problem solving (e.g., in a CBR system).

In Sections 2 and 3, we present our analysis of order dependence in k-NN when case ordering is used to break ties for the kth most similar case. While the study of order effects in incremental learning is concerned with the order in which instances

L. Coyle and J. Freyne (Eds.): AICS 2009, LNAI 6206, pp. 207–218, 2010.
© Springer-Verlag Berlin Heidelberg 2010

are presented to an incremental learner [9], our analysis examines the effects of case ordering in the dataset, for a given tie-breaking strategy, on the performance of a lazy learner (i.e., k-NN). Also in the context of lazy learning, it is worth noting that the solutions provided by a CBR system may depend on the order in which problems are presented to the system [10], although this is not an issue that we consider in our analysis. An important role in our analysis is played by the notion of *similarity layers* (i.e., sets of equally similar cases) in k-NN [11]. For example, with case ordering used to break ties for the kth most similar case, the k-NN retrieval set can differ only in the cases that it includes from a similarity layer that we refer to as the *critical* similarity layer. Our empirical results and conclusions are presented in Sections 4 and 5.

2   Order Dependence in k-NN

Our analysis focuses on $k^{(ord)}$-NN, a version of k-NN with majority voting in which case ordering is used to break ties for the kth most similar case, thus ensuring the retrieval of exactly k cases. First we present a formal definition of the $k^{(ord)}$-NN retrieval set in which the role of case ordering is made explicit. We then examine the structure of the retrieval set in terms of similarity layers [11] and identify conditions in which the $k^{(ord)}$-NN solution for a given problem is certain to be order independent.

Dataset Structure. We assume the existence of at least k cases in the dataset, where each case C consists of a problem description and a solution. The problem description is a list of features $\{a_1 = v_1, ..., a_m = v_m\}$, where $a_1, ..., a_m$ are the attributes in the dataset and $v_i \in domain(a_i) \cup \{missing\}$ for $i = 1$ to m, where $domain(a_i)$ is the set of possible values of a_i. For $i = 1$ to m, we denote by $\pi_i(C)$ the value of a_i in C. The solution is a class label, which we denote by $class(C)$.

Query Representation. A query describes a problem to be solved as a list of problem features $Q = \{a_1 = v_1, ..., a_m = v_m\}$, where $a_1, ..., a_m$ are the attributes in the dataset and $v_i \in domain(a_i) \cup \{unknown\}$ for $i = 1$ to m. We say that Q is a *full-length* query if $\pi_i(Q) \in domain(a_i)$ for $i = 1$ to m, where $\pi_i(Q)$ is the value of a_i in Q.

Antecedents of a Case. For any case C, we define:

$$antecedents(C) = \{C^* : ord(C^*) < ord(C)\} \tag{1}$$

where $ord(C)$ is one more than the number of cases that appear before C in the dataset. For example, if C_1 and C_2 are the 1st and 2nd cases in the dataset, then $ord(C_1) = 1$, $ord(C_2) = 2$, $antecedents(C_1) = \varnothing$, and $antecedents(C_2) = \{C_1\}$.

Competitors of a Case. We assume the existence of a similarity measure $Sim(C, Q)$ that is used to rank the available cases in order of decreasing similarity to a given query Q. However, our results are equally applicable to distance measures with only minor changes in terminology. For any case C and query Q, we define:

$$more\text{-}similar(C, Q) = \{C^* : Sim(C^*, Q) > Sim(C, Q)\} \tag{2}$$

$$equally\text{-}similar(C, Q) = \{C^* : Sim(C^*, Q) = Sim(C, Q)\} \tag{3}$$

$$equally\text{-}similar\text{-}antecedents(C, Q) = equally\text{-}similar(C, Q) \cap antecedents(C) \tag{4}$$

$$competitors(C, Q) = more\text{-}similar(C, Q) \cup equally\text{-}similar\text{-}antecedents(C, Q) \tag{5}$$

The $k^{(ord)}$-NN Retrieval Set. A case contributes to the $k^{(ord)}$-NN solution for a given problem if and only if it has less than k competitors. That is, for any case C and query Q, the $k^{(ord)}$-NN retrieval set for Q is:

$$r(k^{(ord)}\text{-}NN, Q) = \{C : |competitors(C, Q)| < k\} \tag{6}$$

In $5^{(ord)}$-NN, for example, if the 4 most similar cases are followed by 3 equally similar cases, then only one of the 3 equally similar cases can have less than 5 competitors.

The $k^{(ord)}$-NN Solution. The class assigned to a given problem in $k^{(ord)}$-NN is the one that occurs most frequently in the retrieval set. If two or more classes occur with equal frequency in the $k^{(ord)}$-NN retrieval set, then the one that occurs most frequently in the dataset as a whole is selected as the solution in our experiments.

Similarity Layers. As illustrated in Fig. 1 for a binary classification task, a given query Q partitions the dataset into similarity layers $L_0, ..., L_n$ such that for $i = 0$ to $n - 1$, all cases in L_i are equally similar to Q and more similar than any case in L_{i+1} [11]. More formally, we define the similarity layers for a given query Q to be the sets of equally similar cases:

$$L_0 = \{C : more\text{-}similar(C, Q) = \emptyset\} \tag{7}$$

and

$$L_i = \{C : more\text{-}similar(C, Q) = \bigcup_{j=0}^{i-1} L_j\} \tag{8}$$

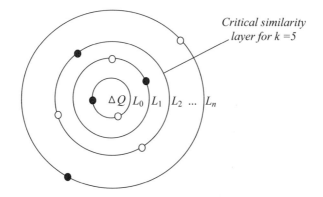

Fig. 1. Similarity layers for an example query. The classes in the dataset are Class 1 (filled circles) and Class 2 (unfilled circles).

for all $i \geq 1$ such that the set of cases on the right-hand side of (8) is non-empty. In Fig. 1, the query is shown as a triangle and cases are shown as filled circles (Class 1) or unfilled circles (Class 2).

Critical Similarity Layer. We will refer to the outermost similarity layer that contributes to the $k^{(ord)}$-NN retrieval set for a given query Q as the *critical* similarity layer for Q. For the example query in Fig. 1, the critical similarity layers for $k = 1, 3$, and 5 are L_0, L_1, and L_2 respectively.

Lemma 1. *The critical similarity layer for a given query Q in $k^{(ord)}$-NN is the innermost similarity layer L_i such that $\sum_{j=0}^{i} |L_j| \geq k$.*

Proof. If $|L_0| \geq k$, then for any $i > 0$ and $C \in L_i$, $|competitors(C, Q)| \geq |more\text{-}similar(C,$
$Q)| = \sum_{j=0}^{i-1} |L_j| \geq |L_0| \geq k$ and so $C \notin r(k^{(ord)}$-NN$, Q)$. It follows that L_0 is the only similarity layer that contributes to the $k^{(ord)}$-NN retrieval set, and must therefore be the critical similarity layer for Q as required. If $|L_0| < k$, and L_i is the innermost similarity layer such that $\sum_{j=0}^{i} |L_j| \geq k$, then $i \geq 1$. Thus if C_1 is the first case in the dataset such that $C_1 \in L_i$, then $|competitors(C_1, Q)| = |more\text{-}similar(C_1, Q)| = \sum_{j=0}^{i-1} |L_j| < k$. It follows that $C_1 \in r(k^{(ord)}$-NN$, Q)$, and therefore that L_i contributes to the $k^{(ord)}$-NN retrieval set. On the other hand, for any $i' > i$ and $C_2 \in L_{i'}$, it can be seen that $|competitors(C_2,$
$Q)| \geq |more\text{-}similar(C_2, Q)| \geq \sum_{j=0}^{i} |L_j| \geq k$, and so $C_2 \notin r(k^{(ord)}$-NN$, Q)$. It follows that L_i is the outermost similarity layer that contributes to the $k^{(ord)}$-NN retrieval set, and thus the critical similarity layer for Q as required.   □

Lemma 2. *If L_0 is the critical similarity layer for a given query Q in $k^{(ord)}$-NN, then $r(k^{(ord)}$-NN$, Q) \subseteq L_0$. Otherwise, $L_j \subset r(k^{(ord)}$-NN$, Q)$ for $j = 0$ to $i - 1$, and $|r(k^{(ord)}$-NN$, Q) \cap L_i| = k - \sum_{j=0}^{i-1} |L_j|$, where L_i is the critical similarity layer for Q.*

Proof. If L_0 is the critical similarity layer for Q, then no other similarity layer contributes to the k-NN retrieval set, and so $r(k^{(ord)}$-NN$, Q) \subseteq L_0$ as required. Now suppose that $i > 1$, where L_i is the critical similarity layer for Q, and let C_0 be the first case in the dataset such that $C_0 \in r(k^{(ord)}$-NN$, Q) \cap L_i$. For any j from 0 to $i - 1$ and $C_1 \in L_j$, we know that $Sim(C_1, Q) > Sim(C_0, Q)$, and so $competitors(C_1, Q) = more\text{-}similar(C_1, Q)$ $\cup$ $equally\text{-}similar\text{-}antecedents(C_1, Q) \subset more\text{-}similar(C_0, Q) \subseteq more\text{-}similar(C_0, Q)$ $\cup$ $equally\text{-}similar\text{-}antecedents(C_0, Q) = competitors(C_0, Q)$. Thus $|competitors(C_1, Q)|$ $< |competitors(C_0, Q)| < k$, and so $C_1 \in r(k^{(ord)}$-NN$, Q)$. We have now established that $L_j \subseteq r(k^{(ord)}$-NN$, Q)$ for $j = 0$ to $i - 1$. As L_i also contributes to $r(k^{(ord)}$-NN$, Q)$, the containment can be seen to be strict for $j = 0$ to $i - 1$. As L_i is the only other similarity layer that contributes to $r(k^{(ord)}$-NN, $Q)$, it also follows as required that $|r(k^{(ord)}$-NN, $Q)$

$$\cap L_i| = k - \sum_{j=0}^{i-1} |L_j|.$$ □

Order Dependence. It follows from Lemma 2 that for any ordering of cases in the dataset, the $k^{(ord)}$-NN retrieval set for a given query Q can differ only in the cases it includes from the critical similarity layer. Nevertheless, the $k^{(ord)}$-NN solution for the example query in Fig. 1 is order dependent for $k = 1, 3$, and 5. For example, the $5^{(ord)}$-NN retrieval set must include one of the 3 cases from L_2, the critical similarity layer for $k = 5$. If the case shown as a filled circle in L_2 is selected, the $5^{(ord)}$-NN solution for Q will be Class 1, while if one of the cases shown as unfilled circles is selected, the solution will be Class 2. However, the $k^{(ord)}$-NN solution for a given query need not be order dependent.

Theorem 1. *The $k^{(ord)}$-NN solution for a given query Q is order independent if there exists $i \geq 0$ such that $k = \sum_{j=0}^{i} |L_j|$.*

Proof. If there exists $i \geq 0$ such that $k = \sum_{j=0}^{i} |L_j|$, then L_i is the innermost similarity layer for Q such that $\sum_{j=0}^{i} |L_j| \geq k$, and therefore the critical similarity layer for Q by Lemma 1. Moreover, if $k = |L_0|$, then for any $C \in L_0$, $|competitors(C, Q)| \leq |L_0| - 1 = k - 1 < k$, and so $C \in r(k^{(ord)}$-NN, $Q)$. With L_0 as the critical similarity layer for Q, it is also clear that no other similarity layer can contribute to $r(k^{(ord)}$-NN, $Q)$, and so $r(k^{(ord)}$-NN, $Q) = L_0$. It follows as required that the $k^{(ord)}$-NN retrieval set is the same for any ordering of cases in the dataset. If $k = \sum_{j=0}^{i} |L_j|$ where $i > 0$, then for any $C_1 \in L_i$, $|competitors(C_1, Q)| \leq \sum_{j=0}^{i-1} |L_j| + |L_i| - 1 = k - 1 < k$, so $C_1 \in r(k^{(ord)}$-NN, $Q)$. It follows that the $k^{(ord)}$-NN retrieval set includes all cases from L_i, the critical similarity layer for Q. As the $k^{(ord)}$-NN retrieval set can differ only in the cases it includes from the critical similarity layer by Lemma 2, this is enough to ensure that the $k^{(ord)}$-NN solution is the same for any ordering of cases in the dataset.   □

Theorem 2. *The $k^{(ord)}$-NN solution for a given query Q is order independent if all cases in the critical similarity layer for Q have the same class label.*

Proof. We know from Lemma 2 that the $k^{(ord)}$-NN retrieval set for a given query Q can differ only in the cases it includes from the critical similarity layer for Q. If all cases in the critical similarity layer for Q have the same class label, it follows that the frequencies of competing classes in the $k^{(ord)}$-NN retrieval set must be the same for any ordering of cases in the dataset. Consequently, the $k^{(ord)}$-NN solution for Q must also be the same for any ordering of cases in the dataset.   □

Conditions for Order Independence. In general, neither of the conditions identified in Theorems 1 and 2 is a *necessary* condition for a $k^{(ord)}$-NN solution to be order independent. For example, the $k^{(ord)}$-NN solution for the query in Fig. 1 is order independent for $k = 7$, although not all cases in the critical similarity layer (L_2) have the same class label. If similarity layer L_3 (not shown in Fig. 1) contains one representative of Class 1 (filled circles) and two of Class 2, then the $k^{(ord)}$-NN solution for $k = 9$ will be order independent (i.e., Class 2) even though neither of the conditions in Theorems 1 and 2 is satisfied. In Theorem 3, we identify a necessary and sufficient condition for the $1^{(ord)}$-NN solution for a given query to be order independent. As we show in Section 4, this enables the percentage of problems for which the solution is order dependent in $1^{(ord)}$-NN to be estimated for a given dataset and similarity measure with no need to compare solutions for different case orderings.

Lemma 3. *In* $1^{(ord)}$-NN, *the critical similarity layer for any query* Q *is* L_0, *and* $r(1^{(ord)}$-NN, $Q) = \{C\}$, *where* C *is the first case in the dataset such that* $C \in L_0$.

Proof. Let C_1 be the first case in the dataset such that $C_1 \in L_0$. It can be seen that $|competitors(C_1, Q)| = 0$ and also that $C_1 \in competitors(C_2, Q)$ for any $C_2 \neq C_1$. As C_1 is the only case such that $|competitors(C_1, Q)| < 1$, it follows that $r(1^{(ord)}$-NN, $Q) = \{C_1\}$. As the only similarity layer that contributes to the $1^{(ord)}$-NN retrieval set, L_0 is the critical similarity layer for Q as required.   □

Theorem 3. *The* $1^{(ord)}$-NN *solution for a given query* Q *is order independent if and only if all cases in the innermost similarity layer have the same class label.*

Proof. We know from Lemma 3 that the critical similarity for any query Q in $1^{(ord)}$-NN is L_0, and that $r(1^{(ord)}$-NN, $Q) = \{C_1\}$, where C_1 is the first case in the dataset such that $C_1 \in L_0$. Thus if all cases in L_0 have the same class label, then the $1^{(ord)}$-NN solution for Q must be the same for any ordering of cases in the dataset. Conversely, if it is not true that all cases in L_0 have the same class label, then there exists $C_2 \in L_0$ such that $class(C_2) \neq class(C_1)$. The $1^{(ord)}$-NN solution for Q can thus be changed from $class(C_1)$ to $class(C_2)$ by moving C_2 to the top of the dataset.   □

Nominal and Discrete Attributes. Our analysis in this section makes no assumption about the similarity measure used to construct the $k^{(ord)}$-NN retrieval set. However, in similarity measures for datasets with numeric attributes, it is not unusual for most cases to have different similarity scores. We also know from Theorem 2 that the $k^{(ord)}$-NN solution for a given query can be order dependent only if the critical similarity layer contains more than one case. We can therefore expect order dependence to be a common occurrence only in datasets in which all the attributes are nominal or discrete. In Section 3, we identify conditions in which the number and sizes of the similarity layers for a given query can be determined in advance for such datasets.

3   Similarity Layer Size

Focusing in this section on datasets in which all the attributes are nominal or discrete, we identify conditions in which the number and sizes of the similarity layers can be determined in advance for a given query. Below we define the similarity measure used in our analysis, and also in the experiments reported in Section 4. When applied to datasets in which all the attributes are nominal or discrete, as in the following discussion, we will refer to it as the "matching features" (MF) similarity measure. Also in this case, we will refer to the similarity layers for a given query Q as the MF similarity layers for Q. Note that we assume all attributes to be equally weighted in our analysis.

Similarity Measure. For any dataset with attributes $a_1, ..., a_m$, we define:

$$Sim(C, Q) = \frac{1}{m} \times \sum_{i=1}^{m} sim_i(C, Q) \tag{9}$$

where for each $i = 1$ to m such that a_i is numeric:

$$sim_i(C, Q) = 1 - \frac{|\pi_i(C) - \pi_i(Q)|}{\max(a_i) - \min(a_i)} \text{ if } \pi_i(C), \ \pi_i(Q) \in domain(a_i) \tag{10}$$

$$sim_i(C, Q) = 0 \text{ if } \pi_i(C) = \text{missing or } \pi_i(Q) = \text{unknown} \tag{11}$$

and for each $i = 1$ to m such that a_i is nominal or discrete:

$$sim_i(C, Q) = 1 \text{ if } \pi_i(C) = \pi_i(Q) \tag{12}$$

$$sim_i(C, Q) = 0 \text{ if } \pi_i(C) \neq \pi_i(Q) \tag{13}$$

Complete Dataset. We say that a dataset is *complete* if all attributes are nominal or discrete and every combination of their values is represented by at least one case in the dataset. In practice, most datasets have much fewer cases than needed for completeness, and completeness may not be achievable because of dependencies between features in a given dataset. Nevertheless, completeness is an important special case in our analysis of similarity layer size.

Lemma 4. *In a complete dataset with attributes $a_1, ..., a_m$, the MF similarity layers for any full-length query Q are $L_0, ..., L_m$ where $L_i = \{C : Sim(C, Q) = \frac{m-i}{m}\}$ for $i = 0$ to m.*

Proof. A case's description can fail to match a full-length query Q on 0, 1, ..., or m attributes. In the MF similarity measure, this gives rise to $m + 1$ distinct similarity scores, and thus $m + 1$ distinct similarity layers, none of which can be empty if the dataset is complete. It can also be seen that for $i = 0$ to m, L_i is the set of cases that fail to match Q on i of the m attributes in the dataset and no other attributes, thus having a similarity score of $\frac{m-i}{m}$ according to the MF similarity measure.   □

Minimally Complete Dataset. We say that a complete dataset is *minimally complete* if no two cases have the same description and there are no missing values in the data-set. In Theorem 4, we show that the number and sizes of the MF similarity layers in a minimally complete dataset are the same for any full-length query. For a dataset that is complete but not minimally complete, the coefficients identified in the theorem are *lower bounds* for the sizes of the MF similarity layers.

Theorem 4. *In a minimally complete dataset with attributes a_1, ..., a_m, the sizes of the MF similarity layers L_0, L_1, ..., L_m for any full-length query Q are the coefficients of x^0, x^1, ..., x^m in the expansion of $P(x) = (1 + r_1x)(1 + r_2x)$ ... $(1 + r_mx)$, where $r_j = |domain(a_j)| - 1$ for $j = 1$ to m.*

Proof. We know from Lemma 4 that the MF similarity layers for any full-length query Q in a complete dataset are L_0, L_1, ..., L_m where each L_i is the set of cases that fail to match Q on i of the m attributes in the dataset and no other attributes. If the dataset is also minimally complete, then there can be only one case that matches Q exactly. Thus $| L_0 | = 1$, which is also the coefficient of x^0 in the expansion of $P(x)$. Now for any $i \in \{1, ..., m\}$ and $S \subseteq \{1, ..., m\}$ such that $| S | = i$, the number of possi-ble case descriptions that fail to match Q on the i attributes with indices in S and no other attributes is:

$$pr(S) = \prod_{j \in S} (|domain(a_j)| - 1) = \prod_{j \in S} r_j \qquad (14)$$

Moreover, the number of possible case descriptions that fail to match Q on any set of i attributes and no other attributes is the sum of all such products arising from the ^mC_i subsets of $\{1, ..., m\}$ of size i. As the dataset is minimally complete, each such case description is represented by a single case in the dataset. By definition, each of these cases has a similarity score of $\frac{m-i}{m}$ and so belongs to similarity layer L_i by Lemma 4. Also, any other case must have a higher or lower similarity score and so cannot be-long to L_i. It can also be seen that $pr(S) = \prod_{j \in S} r_j$ is one of the products that contrib-ute to the coefficient of x^i in the expansion of $P(x)$. In fact, the coefficient of x^i is the sum of all such products arising from the ^mC_i subsets of $\{1, ..., m\}$ of size i. It follows as required that $| L_i |$ is the coefficient of x^i in the expansion of $P(x)$ for $i = 0$ to m.   □

The Contact Lenses Dataset. One example of a minimally complete dataset is the Contact Lenses dataset [12-13]. Attributes in the dataset and their numbers of values are age (3), spectacle prescription (2), astigmatism (2), and tear production rate (2). It follows from Theorem 4 that the sizes of the MF similarity layers L_0, L_1, L_2, L_3, and L_4 for any full-length query Q are the coefficients of x^0, x^1, x^2, x^3, and x^4 in $P(x) = (1 + 2x)(1 + x)(1 + x)(1 + x) = 1 + 5x + 9x^2 + 7x^3 + 2x^4$, namely 1, 5, 9, 7, and 2. It can thus be seen from Theorem 1 that the solution for any full-length query in $k^{(ord)}$-NN based on the MF similarity measure is order independent for $k = 1, 6, 15, 22,$ and 24.

Binary Attributes. In a minimally complete dataset with m binary attributes, we know from Theorem 4 that the sizes of the MF similarity layers L_0, L_1, ..., L_m for any full-length query Q are the coefficients of x^0, x^1, ..., x^m in $P(x) = (1 + x)^m$. It follows from the binomial theorem that $| L_i | = {}^mC_i$ for $i = 0$ to m. If $m = 10$, for example, then the sizes of the MF similarity layers are 1, 10, 45, 120, 210, 252, 210, 120, 45, 10, and 1.

4   Empirical Study

Our empirical study investigates the effects of using case ordering to break ties for the kth most similar case on the accuracy of k-NN. We also assess the degree of order dependence of $1^{(ord)}$-NN (as defined in Section 4.1) for a selection of datasets. The datasets used in our experiments, all of which are available from the UCI Machine Learning Repository [13], are:

- Breast Cancer (286 cases, 9 attributes, 2 classes)
- Voting Records (435 cases, 16 attributes, 2 classes)
- Post Operative (90 cases, 8 attributes, 3 classes)
- Lymphography (148 cases, 18 attributes, 4 classes)
- Dermatology (366 cases, 34 attributes, 6 classes)

The similarity measure used in our experiments is described in Section 3. All attributes in the selected datasets are nominal or discrete, with the exception of Dermatology, which has one numeric attribute (Age). There are missing values only in Breast Cancer, Voting Records, and Dermatology. Except where otherwise stated, we use the same ordering of cases as in the original UCI dataset in our experiments.

4.1   Order Dependence in $1^{(ord)}$-NN

We know from Theorem 3 that the $1^{(ord)}$-NN solution for any query is order independent if and only if all cases in the innermost similarity layer (ISL) have the same class label. This enables the *degree* of order dependence of $1^{(ord)}$-NN (i.e., the percentage of queries for which the solution is order dependent) to be estimated for a given dataset and similarity measure with no need to compare the results it produces for different orderings of cases in the dataset. In this section, we present the results of such an experiment on the Breast Cancer dataset [13] in which we also investigate the size of the ISL for simulated queries. We also estimate the degree of order dependence of $1^{(ord)}$-NN when applied to each of the other datasets.

We temporarily remove each case in turn from the Breast Cancer dataset and use its description as a simulated query to rank the remaining cases in order of decreasing similarity according to the MF similarity measure (Section 3). For each such query, we record the size of the ISL and whether or not all cases in the ISL have the same class label. Fig. 2 shows the ISL sizes and their relative frequencies among the 286 simulated queries in the experiment.

With an average size of 3.2 cases, the ISL contains a single case for less than 40% of queries. The proportion of ISLs of each size that contain cases with more than one class label can be seen from the shaded portion of each bar in the graph. For example,

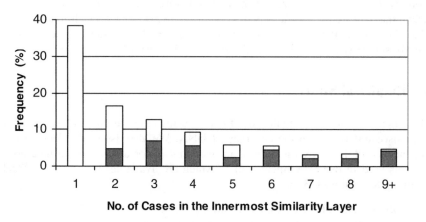

Fig. 2. Size of the innermost similarity layer (ISL) for simulated queries in the Breast Cancer dataset [13]. The proportion of ISLs of each size that contain cases with more than one class label can be seen from the shaded portion of each bar in the graph.

there are cases with conflicting class labels in more than half of the ISLs that contain 4 cases. In summary, the ISL contains cases with more than one class label for 94 of the 286 queries in the experiment. This provides an estimate of 33% for the degree of order dependence of $1^{(ord)}$-NN when applied to the Breast Cancer dataset with retrieval based on the MF similarity measure.

The estimated degrees of order dependence of $1^{(ord)}$-NN for all 5 datasets are shown in Table 1. For the datasets with only nominal or discrete attributes, the percentage of simulated queries for which the $1^{(ord)}$-NN solution is order dependent ranges from 8% to 47%. In contrast, no occurrence of order dependence was detected among the simulated queries in the Dermatology dataset (the only dataset with a numeric attribute). Finally, it is worth noting that the degree of order dependence of $1^{(ord)}$-NN, though dependent on the similarity measure, is independent of the ordering of cases in a given dataset.

Table 1. Estimated degree of order dependence of $1^{(ord)}$-NN for each dataset

Breast Cancer	Voting Records	Post Operative	Lymphography	Dermatology
33%	8%	47%	20%	0%

4.2 Effects of Order Dependence on the Accuracy of $k^{(ord)}$-NN

Our investigation of the effects of order dependence on the accuracy of $k^{(ord)}$-NN is based on *leave-one-out* cross validation [14]. In this approach, each case is temporarily removed from the dataset and its description is presented as a problem to be solved by an algorithm to be evaluated using the remaining cases as a training set. The percentage of such leave-one-out trials in which the class predicted by the algorithm is correct (i.e., the same as in the left-out case) is used to estimate the algorithm's accuracy on unseen problems. For each dataset, Table 2 shows the accuracy achieved by $k^{(ord)}$-NN for $k = 1$ to 5 with both the original (O) and reverse (R) ordering of cases in the dataset. The highest levels of accuracy achieved for each dataset are shown in bold.

Table 2. Accuracy of $k^{(ord)}$-NN on the selected datasets with the original (O) and reverse (R) orderings of cases in the dataset. The best accuracy results for each dataset are shown in bold.

Dataset		$k = 1$	$k = 2$	$k = 3$	$k = 4$	$k = 5$
Breast Cancer	O:	72.7	72.7	**73.4**	73.1	**73.4**
	R:	58.0	67.1	62.6	69.9	60.5
Voting Records	O:	93.1	92.6	93.1	**93.6**	93.1
	R:	91.5	92.9	92.9	93.3	92.9
Post Operative	O:	56.7	70.0	64.4	**71.1**	68.9
	R:	50.0	67.8	58.9	**71.1**	64.4
Lymphography	O:	78.4	80.4	79.7	79.7	81.8
	R:	79.1	77.7	**83.8**	81.1	81.8
Dermatology	O:	94.3	95.6	96.4	96.4	**97.3**
	R:	94.3	96.2	96.2	96.4	97.0

The effects of order dependence on the accuracy of $k^{(ord)}$-NN appear to be greatest in the Breast Cancer dataset, with reductions in accuracy of up to 20% when the ordering of cases in the dataset is reversed. In contrast, there are only slight differences, if any, in the levels of accuracy achieved by $k^{(ord)}$-NN when the ordering of cases in the Dermatology dataset is reversed. This finding is consistent with our expectation that the presence of one or more numeric attributes in a dataset may help to reduce the impact of order dependence in $k^{(ord)}$-NN. The effects of order dependence are also noticeable in the Post Operative dataset, with reductions in the accuracy of $k^{(ord)}$-NN for most values of k when the ordering of cases in the dataset is reversed. As shown by the results for Lymphography, the accuracy of $k^{(ord)}$-NN may increase for some values of k and decrease for others when the ordering of cases in a given dataset is reversed.

5   Conclusions

Our analysis of k-NN when case ordering is used to break ties for the kth most similar case suggests that the resulting order dependence is likely to have most effect on the algorithm's performance in datasets with only nominal or discrete attributes. For example, its accuracy on the Breast Cancer dataset [13] with case ordering used to break ties was reduced by up to 20% when the ordering of cases in the dataset was reversed. Other contributions of our analysis include a necessary and sufficient condition for a 1-NN solution to be order independent when case ordering is used to break ties. This enables the degree of order dependence of 1-NN to be assessed for a given dataset (e.g., 33% for Breast Cancer) with no need to compare solutions for different orderings of cases in the dataset.

Acknowledgement. Thanks to Matjaz Zwitter and Milan Soklic for providing the Breast Cancer and Lymphography datasets in the UCI Machine Learning Repository.

References

1. Cover, T.M., Hart, P.E.: Nearest Neighbor Pattern Classification. IEEE Transactions on Information Theory 1, 21–27 (1967)
2. Ripley, B.D.: Pattern Classification and Neural Networks. Cambridge University Press, Cambridge (1996)
3. Mitchell, T.M.: Machine Learning. McGraw-Hill, New York (1997)
4. Aha, D.W.: The Omnipresence of Case-Based Reasoning in Science and Application. Knowledge-Based Systems 11, 261–273 (1998)
5. Wu, X., Kumar, V., Quinlan, J., Ghosh, J., Yang, Q., Motoda, H., McLachlan, G., Ng, A., Liu, B., Yu, P., Zhou, Z.-H., Steinbach, M., Hand, D., Steinberg, D.: Top 10 Algorithms in Data Mining. Knowledge and Information Systems 14, 1–37 (2008)
6. Brooks, A.D.: knnflex: A More Flexible KNN, `http://cran.r-project.org/web/packages/knnflex`
7. R Development Core Team: A Language and Environment for Statistical Computing. R Foundation for Statistical Computing, Vienna, Austria (2009)
8. Zhua, M., Chena, W., Hirdes, J., Stolee, P.: The K-Nearest Neighbor Algorithm Predicted Rehabilitation Potential Better than Current Clinical Assessment Protocol. Journal of Clinical Epidemiology 60, 1015–1021 (2007)
9. Langley, P.: Order Effects in Incremental Learning. In: Reimann, P., Spada, H. (eds.) Learning in Humans and Machines: Towards an Interdisciplinary Learning Science. Elsevier, Oxford (1995)
10. Leake, D., Whitehead, M.: Case Provenance: The Value of Remembering Case Sources. In: Weber, R.O., Richter, M.M. (eds.) ICCBR 2007. LNCS (LNAI), vol. 4626, pp. 194–208. Springer, Heidelberg (2007)
11. McSherry, D.: Diversity-Conscious Retrieval. In: Craw, S., Preece, A.D. (eds.) ECCBR 2002. LNCS (LNAI), vol. 2416, pp. 219–233. Springer, Heidelberg (2002)
12. Cendrowska, J.: PRISM: an Algorithm for Inducing Modular Rules. International Journal of Man-Machine Studies 27, 349–370 (1987)
13. Asuncion, A., Newman, D.J.: UCI Machine Learning Repository. University of California, Irvine, School of Information and Computer Sciences (2007)
14. Kohavi, R.: A Study of Cross-Validation and Bootstrap for Accuracy Estimation and Model Selection. In: 14th International Joint Conference on Artificial Intelligence, pp. 1137–1143. Morgan Kaufmann, San Mateo (1995)

Norm Convergence in Populations of Dynamically Interacting Agents

Declan Mungovan, Enda Howley, and Jim Duggan

Department Of Information Technology,
National University Of Ireland, Galway
firstname.secondname@nuigalway.ie

Abstract. Agent Based Modelling (ABM) is a methodology used to study the behaviour of norms in complex systems. Agent based simulations are capable of generating populations of heterogeneous, self-interested agents that interact with one another. Emergent norm behaviour in the system may then be understood as a result of these individual interactions. Agents observe the behaviour of their group and update their belief based on those of others. Social networks have been shown to play an important role in norm convergence. In this model[1] agents interact on a fixed social network with members of their own social group plus a second random network that is composed of a subset of the remaining population. Random interactions are based on a weighted selection algorithm that uses an individual's path distance on the network. This means that friends-of-friends are more likely to randomly interact with one another than agents with a higher degree of separation. Using this method we investigate the effect that random interactions have on the dissemination of social norms when agents are primarily influenced by their social network. We discover that increasing the frequency and quality of random interactions results in an increase in the rate of norm convergence.

1 Introduction

Normative behaviour, or norms, can be defined as a set of conventions or behavioural expectations that people in a population abide by. They help maintain one's popularity within a group and ensure that individuals can productively cooperate with one another. Ignoring social norms, or conventions, can lead to negative repercussions for individuals including being ostracised from a group. Social norms present a balance between individual freedom on the one hand and the goals of the society on the other [22]. Conventions play an important role in creating a framework in which agents can structure their actions to help reduce social friction. There are two types of social norm conventions: top-down and bottom up. Top-down norms represent laws that are enforced on the population [9]. Bottom up conventions, such as shaking hands when introducing oneself, represents emergent behaviour from within the group. In this scenario agents,

---

[1] The support of Science Foundation Ireland is gratefully acknowledged.

L. Coyle and J. Freyne (Eds.): AICS 2009, LNAI 6206, pp. 219–230, 2010.

acting in their own self interest, choose which action to take based upon their interactions with others in the population. This is the type of social norm conversion that we investigate in this paper. Agents use locally available information to determine their selection of social norms.

ABM specifies a population as a collection of interacting, self-interested agents, where macroscopic behaviour is explained by the interaction of different individuals over time. Using this approach we can explain system-wide characteristics as emergent behaviour emanating from individual interactions of the agents.

The proposal we present in this paper is that an agent is unlikely to change its immediate social network of acquaintances very much. An individual in the population will, generally speaking, have the same wife, boss, friend etc. from one day to the next. They will, however, have a series of random ad hoc interactions with members of the general public. We recognise, however, that not all random interactions are the same. One is more likely to randomly meet one's next door neighbours best friend than a complete stranger. To account for this we bias random interactions based on the social distance that separates agents in the network. We then run a number of experiments that test the importance of the frequency and quality of these random interactions. We aim to discover at what point random interactions will influence the emergence of a global conventions. Specifically, we we aim to:

1. Design an algorithm that selects a random individual based on their social distance in the network.
2. Test the random interaction conditions that are most important in determining the emergence of a global convention on a population of agents.

The rest of the paper is structured as follows; Section 2 presents an introduction to previous work in the area of norm convergence and social networks. Section 3 gives a description of the formal model used to define the agent based simulator and an explanation of how the simulator was designed and implemented. Section 4 presents the experimental results. Finally, in Section 5 we outline our conclusions and possible future work.

2   Related Research

2.1   Norm Emergence

Agent-based Modelling (ABM) has been used in recent years as a method of studying social norms [15] [5] [2]. Savarimuthu et al. [18] generated a network of agents whose topology changes dynamically. Agents initially randomly collide on a 2D grid and then proceed to form social networks. Villatoro et al. [21] investigate the effect that network topology has on the emergence of norms. They simulate agents interacting on a lattice and scale free network. They found that highly clustered networks resulted in norm convergence in a shorter time. Conte et al. [2] and Walker et al. [22] describe a framework on integrating concepts of Multi Agent Systems with normative behaviour and how both disciplines interact. A considerable amount of the literature has studied the effects of norm emergence in populations that are fully connected and interact in a random fashion [19] [22]. The network that agents interact on, however, has been shown to play a significant role on the dynamics of diffusion [12][21][18]. Most of this work has dealt with static networks that are generated at initialisation time and do not change for the duration of the simulation. There have, however, been some attempts to frame research within the bounds of dynamic networks [18].

2.2   Social Networks

The type of network that an agent interacts on can play an important role on the dynamics of diffusion [17]. Networks can be envisioned as a series of nodes, N, that each have k links to other nodes. Depending on the network type, $k \geq 0$. In the next section we give an overview of different network types that agents can interact on.

Random Network. The *Random Graph* of Erdős and Rényi is one of the most widely studied models of a network [4]. However, it differs from real networks in that it lacks network clustering or transitivity [16]. The network consists of N nodes randomly connected to one another. The probability of a connection between two nodes is fixed where: $p_c = k/(N-1)$ and k = average number of links per person. Figure 1 shows an example of a simple random network where $k = 1.5$ and $N = 8$ and $p_c = 0.21$. Notice in that it is possible for some nodes on the network to be completely disconnected from the rest.

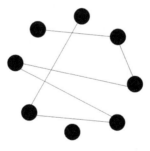

Fig. 1. Random Network

Small World Social Networks. The idea of *Small World Networks* first gained widespread popularity with Stanley Milgram's small-world study of large and sparse networks [14]. Watts et al. later describe these networks as being formed by rewiring the edges of regular lattices with probability p_w [24] . Small World Networks are highly clustered, yet have length scaling properties equivalent to the expectations of randomly assembled graphs [23]. Notice in Fig. 2(a) that the link with the dashed line has been re-wired to another part of the network. This creates an instant shortcut to distant nodes. Small world graphs span

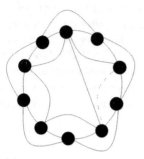 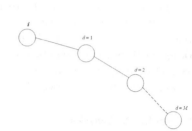

(a) Small World Network   (b) Path Distance from Node

Fig. 2.

the gap between ordered lattices and random graphs. Note that when $p_w = 1$, then all links are randomly assigned and the network becomes a random network. Lee et al. [13] investigated the effect that changing the value of p_w has on the emergence of a winner take all outcome in product adoption. They discovered that as p_w is increased the chance of a winner take all outcome becomes more likely. This is because as the value of p_w gets closer to one the network starts to become more like a random network. This prevents localized cliques of products from existing. An analysis of a number of real world human networks [25] [20] [3] [1] have shown that they form small world networks.

Clustering Coefficient. The clustering coefficient of a vertex in a graph is a measure of the proportion of neighbours of that vertex that are neighbours of one another [23]. The more sparse and random a network is the lower the clustering. For node i the value of the clustering coefficient , c_i, is calculated as described in equation 1 where ε_i is the total number of edges between the neighbours of node i and k_i is the total number of neighbours of node i.

$$c_i = \frac{2\varepsilon_i}{k_i(k_i - 1)} \tag{1}$$

Path Length. The Maximum Path Length (MPL), Fig. 2(b), is the maximum number of steps required to get to the furthest node, or nodes, on the network. Dijkstra's algorithm [26] uses a breadth first search to traverse the network and discover the shortest path to each agent. The average shortest path length is the average number of steps along the shortest paths for all possible pairs of network nodes. It is a measure of the how quickly information etc. can diffuse through the network. Studies have shown that random and small world networks show a low average path length [7] [23].

Dynamic Networks. Fenner et al. [6] describe a stochastic model for a social network. Individuals may join the network, existing actors may become inactive and, at a later stage, reactivate themselves. The model captures the dynamic nature of the network as it evolves over time. Actors attain new relations according to a preferential attachment rule that weights different agents according to their degree[2].

2.3   Randomness in Agent Based Modeling

Agent based modelling (ABM) has a number of advantages over classical game theory approaches. Firstly, ABMs are capable of implementing Monte Carlo[3] type stochastic iterations of a complex system. Izquierdo et al. [10] highlight the fact that any computer model is in fact, due to its very nature, deterministic. However, we can use pseudo-random number generators to simulate random variables within the model and generate an artificial Monte Carlo generator. The pseudo-random number generator is an algorithm that takes in a random input seed value and generates a result that approximates a random number. This property allows us to simulate randomness that is present in real world systems. In this fashion, an agent based simulation that provides the same input variables but implements a level of randomness can produce, sometimes, significantly different outcomes. A key challenge of analysing an ABM is in identifying an appropriate set of state variables.

We can see from the section that norm emergence is heavily influenced by the individuals that an agent meets in the network. Real world interactions are dynamic, this is a feature we aim to capture in this paper.

3   Model Design

The following section describes formally the decision making rules agents use to choose random interactions and the actions they take based on their observations. Agents receive a utility from observing the norms that have been adopted by the other individuals it encounters. Agents interact with s members of their social network and r randomly selected agents. Initially nodes are set to having adopted either social convention j or k. Nodes interact with a period drawn randomly from an exponential distribution with mean duration $\epsilon_i = 3$. This models the fact that all agents don't update their norm selection simultaneously. An agent, i, will chose to adopt norm j if the utility it observes from adopting this norm is greater than the utility it would receive from adopting convention k as defined in 2.

$$u_{i,t}^j > u_{i,t}^k \qquad (2)$$

The utility that agents receive from each norm is defined in 3. This is divided into the utility communicated from its direct neighbours, $D_{i(t-1)}^j$, plus the utility it receives from the random interactions it makes, $R_{i(t-1)}^j$.

---

[2] The degree of an agent is the number of acquaintances it has in its social network.
[3] A Monte Carlo algorithm relies on repeated random sampling to compute their results.

$$u_{i,t}^j = \alpha D_{i(t-1)}^j + \beta R_{i(t-1)}^j \tag{3}$$

Where α is the weighting placed on an agent interacting with the members of its own social network and β is the weighting of interactions taking place with random members of the agents network. The higher the β value the more importance agents place on random interactions. The direct network effects are defined in 4 where n is the total number of nodes on the network and $\theta_{h(t-1)}^j = 1$ if agent h has adopted social convention j.

$$D_{i(t-1)}^j = \sum_{h=1}^n \mu_{ih}\theta_{h(t-1)}^j \qquad \mu_{ih} \begin{cases} 1 \text{ if } i \text{ is an acquaintance of } h \\ 0 \text{ otherwise} \end{cases} \tag{4}$$

Similarly we define the random network effects in 5 where n is the total number of nodes on the network and $\omega_{h(t-1)}^j = 1$ if agent h has adopted social convention j.

$$R_{i(t-1)}^j = \sum_{h=1}^n \phi_{ih}\omega_{h(t-1)}^j \qquad \phi_{ih} \begin{cases} 1 \text{ if } i \text{ has a random interaction with } h \\ 0 \text{ otherwise} \end{cases}$$

$$\tag{5}$$

Agents interact with random members of the population using a Weighted Random Interaction (WRI) algorithm based on their distance from others on the network. We use a modified version of Zipf's law 6 to calculate a nodes weight. The probability of agent i, with Maximum Path Distance (MPD) of M, randomly interacting with agent h having a path distance of d from i is equal to:

$$p_{ih}(d) = \frac{\dfrac{1}{(d-1)^\lambda}}{\sum_{m=1}^{M-1}\left(\dfrac{1}{m^\lambda}\right)} \qquad d \geq 2 \tag{6}$$

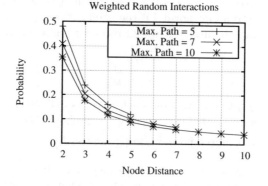

Fig. 3. Weighted Random Interactions

Where λ is the exponent that characterises the distribution. For the experiment carried out in this paper we set $\lambda = 1$. Note the condition that d $\geq$ 2 as a node is assumed to interact with members of its social network ($d = 1$). It can be seen from 6 [8] that the distribution is normalised and the frequencies sum to 1 as expressed in 7.

$$\sum_{d=2}^{M-1} p_{ih}(d) = 1 \tag{7}$$

The graph shown in Fig. 3 shows the distance probability distribution of three different nodes with Maximum Path Distance (MPD) ranging from 5 to 10. We can see from the diagram that agents with a lower path distance are more likely to interact than ones with a higher path distance.

4   Results

In all the simulations conducted, a population of 1000 agents in a small world configuration with average degree of 10 was generated. Initially all nodes are randomly given one of two norms. All the results shown are the average of 1000 different simulations. A new Small World network was generated for each simulation. Initially each agent on the network maps its social distance from every other agent. We used Dijkstra's algorithm [11] to calculate the MPL for each node. Every time an agent interacts it generates a new set of ad hoc random interactions based on the WRI algorithm described above. We conducted four different experiments using the model described in Section 3. In Experiment 1 we simply vary the rewiring probability of the network and investigate the effect of norm convergence. Experiment 2 introduces random interactions taking place over the core small world network. We study the effect on norm convergence by varying both the value for the strength of random interactions, β, and the number of random interactions that an agent has, r. Experiment 3 and Experiment 4 both explore the level of norm convergence over time.

4.1   Experiment 1: Varying Rewiring Probability

Fig. 4 shows the effect of norm convergence when the rewiring probability is changed. We observe that the probability of all agents converging on a common norm is increased when the value of p_w is increased. This is similar to the finding of Lee et al. [13] in the domain of product adoption mentioned earlier. While increasing the value of p_w results in an increase in norm convergence, it reduces the level of clustering in the network. Real world human networks have high levels of clustering so this means that increasing p_w is unrealistic. In the next three experiments we maintain a core, highly clustered, small world network but introduce ad hoc random interactions that the agents have with others in the population.

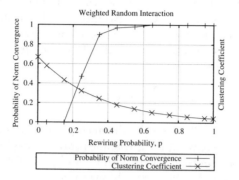

Fig. 4. Probability of Norm Convergence varying p

4.2   Experiment 2: Adding Random Interactions

In this experiment a small world network is created with a rewiring probability of $p_w = 0.05$ and $\alpha = 1$ as shown in Table 1. As we have seen in Fig. 4 norm convergence will not happen when p_w is at this level. In Fig. 5 we observe the effect of norm convergence when agents are allowed to interact with randomly selected individuals on the network who are not part of their social network. We vary both the value agents place on random interactions, β, and the number of random interactions that they have, r. The number of random interactions starts at 0 and is increased by a value of 2 until it reaches 16. The strength of random interactions, β, is increased from 0 to 1. When β equals 1 then agents place the same strength on interactions with random members of the populations as on their own social network.

Table 1. Simulation Experiment Variables

N	α	p_w	k_i	ϵ_i	Number of Norms
1000	1.0	0.05	10	3	2

Fig. 5 shows a snap show of the level of norm convergence over a series of different time steps. In Fig. 5(a) when $t = 100$ the level of norm convergence is high when both β and the number of random interaction are high. Norm convergence fails to occur when both the strength and quantity of random interactions is too low. Indeed, when agents are having up to 8 random interactions but those occurrences only carry a weight of 0.1 of random interactions then norm emergence will not occur. Increasing the number of random interaction or increasing the strength of these interactions results in norm emergence. From Fig. 5 we can see that if $\beta > 0.5$ and the number of random interactions $r > 6$ then norm convergence is guaranteed. If agents have the same number of random interactions as members of their social network, or $s = r = 10$, then β only

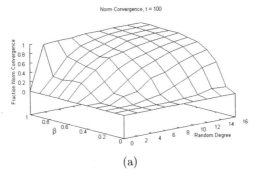

(a)

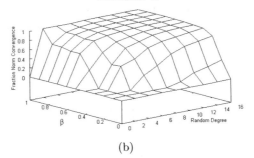

(b)

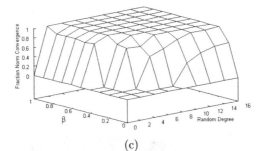

(c)

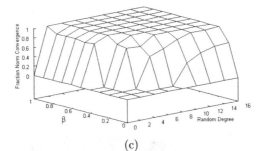

(d)

Fig. 5. Norm Convergence over Time

needs to be 0.2 to almost guarantee norm convergence. Interestingly, allowing agents to interact beyond ∼ 300 time steps has little impact on the level of norm convergence. This experiment shows that random interactions with members of a nodes social network plays an important role in norm convergence.

4.3   Experiment 3: Varying Random Interactions

In Fig. 6 we set the level of $\beta = 0.1$ and increment the number of random interactions. We can see that there is no norm convergence when the time is less than approximately 50 or the number of random interactions is less than 10. We can see that once the population overcomes this threshold level of random interactions then there is a steady increase in the number of simulations resulting in convergence. The graph appears to be a series of terraces because the random degree is increased in steps of 2.

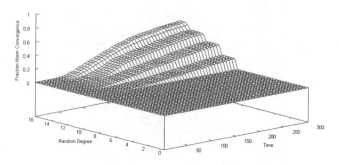

Fig. 6. Level of Norm Convergence over Time Varying Random Degree

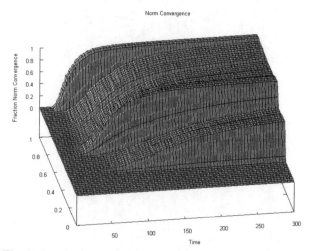

Fig. 7. Level of Norm Convergence over Time Varying Beta

4.4 Experiment 4: Varying the Level of β

In this final experiment we set the level of random interactions to 4, $\alpha = 1$ and incremented the level of β. We can see from Fig. 7 that there are several jumps in norm convergence when we increase the level of β. Specifically, when $\beta \leq 0.2$ then none of the simulations converge to a common norm. When $\beta \geq 0.5$ then all the simulations converge to a common norm. We can also see that that when $0.2 \leq \beta \leq 0.3$ then some norm emergence does occur but at a much slower rate.

5 Conclusions

The aim of this paper was to construct a more realistic network of agent inter-actions that might help explain the emergence of norms in society. We defined an algorithm that uses a nodes social distance on the network to calculate its chance of interacting with a random member of the population. We have demon-strated the importance that random agents can have on the emergence of social norms. Particularly our research demonstrates how norms can rapidly take hold in environments were agents interact heavily with random individuals outside their social network. This would perhaps be analogous to people in a large city interacting with lots of random individuals versus residents of a rural area that mostly meet members of their own social network. Our results from Section 4 highlight that norm convergence is dependant on both the frequency and quality agents place on random interactions.

References

1. Baum, J.A.C., Shipilov, A.V., Rowley, T.J.: Where do small worlds come from? Ind. Corp. Change 12(4), 697–725 (2003)
2. Conte, R., Falcone, R., Sartor, G.: Introduction: Agents and norms: How to fill the gap? Artificial Intelligence and Law 7(1), 1–15 (1999)
3. Davis, G.F., Yoo, M., Baker, W.E.: The Small World of the American Corporate Elite, 1982-2001. Strategic Organization 1(3), 301–326 (2003)
4. Erdos, P., Reyni, A.: On the evolution of random graphs. Publ. Math. Inst. Hungar. Acad. Sci. 4(5), 17–61 (1961)
5. Luck, M., López, F.L.y., d'Inverno, M.: A normative framework for agent-based sys-tems. Computational & Mathematical Organization Theory 12(2), 227–250 (2006)
6. Fenner, T., Levene, M., Loizou, G., Roussos, G.: A stochastic evolutionary growth model for social networks. Comput. Netw. 51(16), 4586–4595 (2007)
7. Fronczak, A., Fronczak, P., Holyst, J.A.: Average path length in random networks (2002)
8. Gabaix, X.: Zipf's law for cities: An explanation*. Quarterly Journal of Eco-nomics 114(3), 739–767 (1999)
9. Goldfarb, B., Henrekson, M.: Bottom-up versus top-down policies towards the com-mercialization of university intellectual property. Research Policy 32(4), 639–658 (2003)
10. Izquierdo, L.R., Izquierdo, S.S., Galán, J.M., Santos, J.I.: Techniques to understand computer simulations: Markov chain analysis. Journal of Artificial Societies and Social Simulation 12(1), 6 (2009)

11. Johnson, D.B.: A note on dijkstra's shortest path algorithm. J. ACM 20(3), 385–388 (1973)
12. Kittock, J.: Emergent conventions and the structure of multi–agent systems. In: Lectures in Complex systems: The Proceedings of the 1993 Complex Systems Summer School. Santa Fe Institute Studies in the Sciences of Complexity Lecture Volume VI, Santa Fe Institute, pp. 507–521. Addison-Wesley, Reading (1995)
13. Lee, E., Lee, J., Lee, J.: Reconsideration of the Winner-Take-All Hypothesis: Complex Networks and Local Bias. Management Science 52(12), 1838–1848 (2006)
14. Milgram, S.: The small world. Psychology Today 2, 60–67 (1967)
15. Mukherjee, P., Sen, S., Airiau, S.: Norm emergence under constrained interactions in diverse societies. In: AAMAS 2008: Proceedings of the 7th International Joint Conference on Autonomous Agents and Multiagent Systems. International Foundation for Autonomous Agents and Multiagent Systems, Richland, SC, pp. 779–786 (2008)
16. Newman, M.E.J.: Random graphs as models of networks (2002)
17. Rahmandad, H., Sterman, J.: Heterogeneity and network structure in the dynamics of diffusion: Comparing agent-based and differential equation models. Management Science 54(5), 998–1014 (2008)
18. Savarimuthu, B.T.R., Cranefield, S., Purvis, M., Purvis, M.: Norm emergence in agent societies formed by dynamically changing networks. In: IAT 2007: Proceedings of the 2007 IEEE/WIC/ACM International Conference on Intelligent Agent Technology, Washington, DC, USA, pp. 464–470. IEEE Computer Society, Los Alamitos (2007)
19. Shoham, Y., Tennenholtz, M.: On social laws for artificial agent societies: Off-line design. Artificial Intelligence 73, 231–252 (1995)
20. Verspagen, B., Duysters, G.: The small worlds of strategic technology alliances. Technovation 24(7), 563–571 (2004)
21. Villatoro, D., Malone, N., Sen, S.: Effects of interaction history and network topology on rate of convention emergence. In: Proceedings of 3rd International Workshop on Emergent Intelligence on Networked Agents (2009)
22. Walker, A., Woolridge, M.: Understanding the emergence of convensions in multi agent systems. In: Proceedings of the First International Conference on Multi-Agent Systems (ICMAS 1995), vol. (1), pp. 384–389 (1995)
23. Watts, D.J.: Small worlds: The dynamics of networks between order and randomness. Princeton University Press, Princeton (1999)
24. Watts, D.J., Strogatz, S.: Collective dynamics of 'small-world' networks. Nature, 440–442 (1998)
25. Watts, D.J.: Networks, dynamics, and the small-world phenomenon. American Journal of Sociology 105(2), 493–527 (1999)
26. Benjamin Zhan, F., Noon, C.E.: Shortest Path Algorithms: An Evaluation Using Real Road Networks. Transportation Science 32(1), 65–73 (1998)

A Comparison of Word Similarity Measures for Noun Compound Disambiguation

Paul Nulty and Fintan Costello

School of Computer Science and Informatics,
University College Dublin,
Dublin 4, Ireland
{paul.nulty,fintan.costello}@ucd.ie

Abstract. Noun compounds occur frequently in many languages, and the problem of semantic disambiguation of these phrases has many potential applications in natural language processing and other areas. One very common approach to this problem is to define a set of semantic relations which capture the interaction between the modifier and the head noun, and then attempt to assign one of these semantic relations to each compound. For example, the compound phrase *flu virus* could be assigned the semantic relation *causal* (the virus causes the flu); the relation for *desert wind* could be *location* (the wind is located in the desert). In this paper we investigate methods for learning the correct semantic relation for a given noun compound by comparing the new compound to a training set of hand-tagged instances, using the similarity of the words in each compound. The main contribution of this paper is to directly compare distributional and knowledge-based word similarity measures for this task, using various datasets and corpora. We find that the knowledge based system provides a much better performance when adequate training data is available.

Keywords: noun compounds, word similarity, semantic classification, disambiguation.

1 Introduction

A noun compound is a noun phrase in which the head noun is modified by another noun, for example *flu virus* or *desert wind*. Noun compounds occur frequently in many languages, and the problem of semantic disambiguation of these phrases has many potential applications in natural language processing and other areas. Search engines which can identify the relations between nouns may be able to return more accurate results. Hand-built ontologies such as WordNet at present only contain a few basic semantic relations between nouns, such as hypernymy and meronymy. If the process of discovering semantic relations from text were automated, more links could quickly be built up. Machine translation and question-answering are other potential applications. Noun compounds are very common in English, especially in technical documentation and neologisms,

L. Coyle and J. Freyne (Eds.): AICS 2009, LNAI 6206, pp. 231–240, 2010.

while Latin languages tend to favour prepositional paraphrases instead of direct compound translation. To translate compound phrases effectively, knowing the semantic relation that holds between the two nouns is important [1]. Although noun compounds containing three or more nouns are common, in this paper we only consider compounds comprised of two nouns.

One very common approach to this problem is to define a set of semantic relations which capture the interaction between the modifier and the head noun, and then attempt to assign one of these semantic relations to each noun compound. For example, the phrase flu virus could be assigned the semantic relation causal (the virus causes the flu); the relation for desert wind could be location (the wind is located in the desert). There is no consensus as to which set of semantic relations best captures the differences in meaning of various noun phrases. Work in theoretical linguistics has suggested that noun-noun compounds may be formed by the deletion of a predicate verb or preposition [2]. However, whether the set of possible predicates numbers 5 or 50, there are likely to be some examples of noun phrases that fit into none of the categories and some that fit in multiple categories.

In this paper we investigate methods for learning the correct semantic relation for a given noun compound by comparing the new compound to a training set of hand-tagged instances. As with all supervised learning approaches, the quality of the system depends on a method of measuring the similarity between a new instance and instances in the training set. The main contribution of this paper is to directly compare distributional and knowledge-based word similarity measures for this task.

2   Noun Compound Similarity

In this paper, we will focus on word similarity measures, i.e., methods for comparing the semantic similarity of two words, rather than two pairs of words. Semantic similarity between pairs of nouns is known as *relational similarity* [3]. Some previous approaches to noun compound disambiguation have used relational similarity measures.

2.1   Relational Similarity

Relational similarity is a measure of the similarity of the semantic relation that occurs in two pairs of words. For example, consider the noun pairs *street, traffic* and *riverbed, water. street* and *riverbed* are not highly similar words, and neither are *water* and *traffic*; however, there is a high similarity in the relationship between the pair of words in each case, i.e., water flows along a riverbed, and traffic flows along a street. Relational similarity may be measured using distributional methods by searching a large corpus for sentences in which both parts of a noun compound occur together [3].

To do this, it is necessary to find instances in the corpus where both constituents of the noun compound occur within a narrow window. Certain lexical patterns which occur between two nouns may give a good indication of the semantic relation that holds between the nouns[4]. For example, to compare the compounds *street traffic* and *river water*, a large corpus is used to find strings such as *traffic in the street* or *traffic along the street*. These contexts can then be compared to the contexts for *river water*; which may include similar or identical contexts, for example *water in the river, water flows in the river*. Then, without ever directly comparing the words in the compounds, the similarity of the compounds can be judged by the similarity of the strings occurring in their mutual contexts.

The contexts do not directly indicate a particular semantic relation, but they may be used to estimate the relational similarity between the pairs of words, which can then be used, with a training set, to assign a semantic relation to noun-compounds [5,6]. One drawback of this approach is that it is not always possible to find many occurrences of both constituents within a short window, even using a very large corpus.

2.2   Lexical Similarity

Rather than using relational similarity, we are interested in how well the simpler method of comparing the similarity of the constituents of the compounds directly can work. To illustrate our method, we will consider an ideal example. Given a new noun compound *morning exercise*, which we wish to disambiguate, we may compare this compound to those in our training set of hand-tagged examples, and assign it the semantic relation of the compound which it is most similar to, based on the similarity of its constituent nouns. For this example, the most similar compound in our set might be *summer sport*, which has the relation *temporal* (i.e. the modifier indicates the time period in which the activity described by the head takes place). The similarity score is based on the sum of the similarities of *summer* and *morning*; and *sport* and *exercise*.

2.3   Knowledge Based Measures

Knowledge-based word similarity measures work by measuring the distance between two words in a hand-crafted hierarchical knowledge base such as Cyc, Roget's thesaurus or Wordnet. Wordnet is a rich lexical database in which word senses are connected according to their hypernyms and hyponyms, with abstract concepts such as *physical object* and *living entity* near the top of the hierarchy, and more specific terms such as *dog* and *Labrador* below these entries. Each node in the hierarchy corresponds to a word sense or *synset*, rather than an actual token.

There are several similarity measures available which are designed to work using the Wordnet hierarchy. The simplest kind, PATH, counts the number of nodes in the path between the two words in the tree. The inverse of this count is the similarity between the two words. Another kind, LIN, uses this count and also the information content of the nodes, which may be inferred from a separate corpus or from Wordnet itself [7]. We discuss these further in the experiments section.

2.4 Distributional Measures

Distributional measures of word similarity work by comparing the contexts in which each of the words occurs in a corpus. The simplest method of comparing contexts is known as the 'bag-of words' approach. Given two words, $w1$ and $w2$, all words which occur within a certain window, n, of $w1$ in a corpus are collected. These words are then compared with a similar 'bag-of-words' collected for $w2$, and the frequencies of words common to the contexts of both $w1$ and $w2$ are used to calculate the word similarity.

More recent approaches use parsed corpora to include some syntactic information about co-occurrence contexts of words. [14] describes a method for measuring the semantic similarity between two words based on the grammatical relationships which they are found to share in a corpus. The similarity between words is expressed as the sum of the frequencies of arguments to grammatical relations which are shared among both words. The similarity measure also specifies that the sum is weighted by the the probability of a particular argument occurring, so very common words are not given an unduly high weight. The implementation of this method will be discussed further in the following section.

For the experiments in this paper, we chose to use the UKWAC corpus. UKWAC is a very large corpus (over 2 billion tokens) of English text obtained by crawling the .uk web domain. It is annotated with part-of-speech tagging and is lemmatized. The corpus was searched through the Sketch Engine interface [11], which provides an API to many corpora, returning the grammatical relations with which a given word is most associated. Examples of our implementation of the similarity measure proposed in [14] in conjunction with the UKWAC corpus are discussed in the experiments section.

3 Experiments

The motivation for our experiments is investigate which word similarity measure works best for the task of disambiguating noun compounds. One advantage of the word similarity approach over relational similarity is that it does not require the system to have seen instances where both the head and modifier of the compound have occurred in the same sentence in a corpus. Instead, the distributional information about both the head and modifier, separately, is compared with that of the training instance and combined to measure the semantic distance between the compounds.

For all experiments, the classification was carried out using a nearest-neighbor technique, with leave-one-out cross-validation. This means that the semantic relation predicted for each noun-compound in the dataset is the relation of the compound which it is most similar to from the rest of the dataset.

3.1 Datasets

We use two datasets in our experiments. The first dataset was created by Nastase and Szpakowicz [8] and used in experiments by [3]. The data consists of 600 noun-modifier compounds. Of the 600 examples, four contained hyphenated modifiers,

Table 1. Examples of noun compounds and semantic relations from the Nastase and Szpackowicz dataset

Semantic Relation	Example compounds	Proportion of data
causal	flu virus, onion tear	.18
temporal	summer travel, morning class	.09
spatial	desert wind, home remedy	.12
participant	mail sorter, blood donor	.41
quality	rice paper, picture book	.20

Table 2. Examples of noun compounds and semantic relations from the O'Seaghdha dataset

Semantic Relation	Example compounds	Proportion of data
be	steel knife	.13
have	street name,	.14
in	forest hut,	.21
inst	rice cooker,	.19
actor	honey bee,	.16
about	fairy tale	.17

for example test-tube baby. These were excluded from our dataset. The data is labeled with two different sets of semantic relations: one set of 30 relations with fairly specific meanings and another set of 5 relations with more abstract relations. Table 1 shows the five relations and some examples. For our research we are particularly interested in noun-noun combinations. Of the 596 examples in the dataset, 325 are clearly noun-noun combinations, e.g. picture book, rice paper, while in the remainder the modifier is an adjective, for example warm air, heavy storm. We used only the noun-noun combinations in our experiments, as this is the focus of our research. Because of the relatively small size of the noun-noun data, we did not experiment with the finer-grained semantic relations, as this subdivision leaves a sparse and unbalanced dataset.

Table 1 lists the five semantic relations, example compounds for each relation, and the proportion of examples in the dataset tagged with each relation.

The second dataset we use is a set of 1443 noun compounds annotated with a set of six semantic relations created by O'Seaghdha [9]. This dataset consists of noun sequences extracted from the British National Corpus. Any compounds which were initially tagged by annotators as having an unknown, lexicalised or non-compositional meaning were discarded from an initial set of 2000 compounds. The remaining compounds were each classified with one of 6 semantic relations. The relations, examples, and the distribution of each relation are presented in Table 2.

The full collection and annotation process for this dataset is fully described in [9].

3.2   Wordnet Experiments

Word similarity can be judged in a number of ways, as discussed in section two. For the Wordnet experiments, we use the position of words in the Wordnet hypernym hierarchy as the measure of similarity.

A number of issues arise when using this measure. Firstly, Wordnet is a database of word senses, or *synsets*, rather than tokens or lemmas. Most words can have more than one sense, and the sense distinctions in Wordnet are quite fine-grained. Since we are attempting to disambiguate the compound out of context, the best available method of choosing the correct sense is to assign to each word its most frequent sense. The most-frequent-sense baseline is currently not out-performed by modern contextless word sense disambiguation systems [10].

Secondly, there are a number of possible measures to calculate the difference between two nodes on the hypernym tree. Six Wordnet-based measures are implemented in the python Natural Language Tool Kit (NLTK) [12]. Based on previous work [13] we chose to experiment with four of these. The PATH routine simply counts the number of edges between the two word senses in the Wordnet hierarchy. LCH counts the edges between the senses and also takes into account how deep each of the senses is in the hierarchy. WUP counts the edges between the senses, their depth in the hierarchy, and also the depth of their least common subsumer (deepest common ancestor). The LIN measure, also described in [14], calculates similarity based on the information content of the two Wordnet senses and their least common subsumer. The information content metric is computed using the Brown corpus.

Initially, to compute the similarity of two compounds we simply add the similarity of the heads and the similarity of the modifiers, i.e.:

sim(A,B)= sim(ModifierA, ModifierB)+sim(HeadA,HeadB).

We also experimented with using the product of the word similarities as the compound similarity. To return to our ideal example, the compounds *morning exercise* and *summer sport* should be judged highly similar by the Wordnet measures since *summer* and *morning* share a common ancestor (*time-period*) within just two edges of the Wordnet tree, and *sport* and *exercise* also have a nearby common ancestor (*activity*).

We report accuracy and f-score as our evaluation metrics. Accuracy is simply the percentage of examples which were classified with the correct semantic relation, out of the total number of examples in each dataset. F-score is a more complex measure which balances for different relation class sizes. Table 3 shows results for the Nastase and Szpakowicz dataset, table 4 results for the O'Seaghdha and Copestake dataset. Although the second dataset has 6 rather than 5 possible semantic relations, the majority class backoff baseline is actually lower, since this dataset is more balanced.

3.3   UKWAC Experiments

For comparison with the Wordnet knowledge base, we chose the UKWAC corpus as the source for our distributional similarity measures. The UKWAC (UK Web

Table 3. Results obtained using Wordnet similarity metrics on the Nastase and Sz-packowicz dataset

Similarity Metric	Sum or Product	Accuracy	F-Score	majority class baseline
LCH	*	.416	.411	.41
LCH	+	.416	.413	.41
Lin	*	**.453**	.448	.41
Lin	+	.447	**.470**	.41
PATH	+	.432	.440	.41
WUP	+	.436	.423	.41

Table 4. Results obtained using Wordnet similarity metrics on the O'Seaghdha dataset

Similarity Metric	Sum or Product	Accuracy	F-Score	majority class baseline acc
LCH	*	.498	.488	.21
LCH	+	**.501**	**.491**	.21
Lin	*	.474	.467	.21
Lin	+	.491	.484	.21
PATH	+	.497	.486	.21
WUP	+	.492	.483	.21

as Corpus) is a large corpus of English documents collected by crawling the .uk web domain [15]. The corpus was constructed by starting out with a seed set of URLs from a variety of domains, and crawling to collect more documents. HTML and other web-noise was stripped from the documents using systems developed for the CLEANEVAL 2007 task. Although there are some biases introduced by using a web-derived corpus, the UKWAC was chosen because its size (more than 2 billion tokens) should allow for detection of even rare grammatical relations among rare words.

In order to implement the similarity measure discussed in [14], we needed to extract grammatical relations from the sentences in the corpus. This was facilitated by the Sketch Engine resource, a web-based corpus query tool [11]. A part-of-speech tagged version of the UKWAC is indexed by this tool, which runs a shallow parser over a target sentence and returns a 'word sketch' containing grammatical relations and their arguments.

The Sketch Engine was queried using a python interface to their web-based javascript API. We retrieved and stored locally the word sketches for each noun involved in one of the compounds in the datasets, and compared the grammatical relation arguments of the constituent nouns for our experiments. To illustrate with an example, for the noun compounds *morning exercise* and *summer sport*, *morning* and *summer* both occur as the subjects of the following verbs: *follow (57.52), wake (53.6), rain (31.12), start (26.63), come (25.01), work (23.97)*.

The mutual information scores returned by the Sketch Engine system, (displayed after each verb), are summed to give a score of the similarity between the two words.

Table 5. Results obtained using distributional similarity metrics on the Nastase and Szpackowicz dataset

Grammatical Relation	product or sum	Accuracy	F-Score	Baseline
subjectof	*	.412	.326	.41
objectof	*	.452	.420	.41
andor	*	.470	**.468**	.41
combined	*	**.490**	.449	.41

Table 6. Results obtained using distributional similarity metrics on the O'Seaghdha dataset

Grammatical Relation	product or sum	Accuracy	F-Score	majority class baseline
subjectof	*	.343	.314	.21
objectof	*	**.430**	.418	.21
andor	*	.416	.404	.21
combined	*	.422	**.439**	.21

Again, the system was tested using leave-one-out cross validation. We experimented using the grammatical relations *subject, object, conjunction* (and/or) and a combination of all these. For this method, we found that using the product, rather than the sum, of the similarities of the components gave better results.

4 Discussion

The best results obtained from both the knowledge-based and distributional word similarity measures are presented in Table 7. In some cases, the ranking of the systems evaluated by f-score is not the same as their ranking by accuracy. f-score is a per-class evaluation measure; the macro-averaged f-score (sum of f-score for each category divided by number of categories) compensates for bias which could be introduced if the number of examples in each class is unnaturally balanced, since it gives equal weight to all classes [3]. To calculate the f-score for each class, we compute precision and recall individiually for each class. F-score is the harmonic mean of precision and recall. However, if the true proportion of compounds per class is close to that of our sample datasets, accuracy is the most relevant measure for applications.

Both measures perform above the majority class baseline for both datasets. The Wordnet-based system clearly achieves the best results on the O'Seaghdha dataset. For the Nastase dataset, the results are less clear. The Wordnet system achieves a better accuracy, while the corpus system achieves a better f-score. It may be that the results are less clear-cut on the second dataset because it is smaller and more unbalanced than the O'Seaghdha set. To test this, we repeated the experiments which achieved best results on the second dataset, while limiting the available data to 325 randomly chosen instances.

Table 7. Best results on each dataset using the Wordnet-based and distributional similarity measures

Condition	Dataset	Accuracy	F-Score	majority class baseline
Wordnet LCH	O'Seaghdha	**.501**	**.491**	.21
Corpus Object.	O'Seaghdha	.433	.418	.21
Corpus Comb.	O'Seaghdha	.422	.439	.21
Wordnet LIN	Nastase	.447	**.470**	.41
Corpus andor	Nastase	.470	.468	.41
Corpus Comb.	Nastase	**.490**	.449	.41

Table 8. Best results on the full O'Seagdha dataset (Accuracy 1443) and a reduced subset of that dataset (Accuracy325)

Condition	Dataset	Accuracy1443	Accuracy325	Baseline
Wordnet LCH	O'Seaghdha	.501	.429	.21
Corpus Object.	O'Seaghdha	.433	.402	.21
Corpus Comb.	O'Seaghdha	.422	.411	.21

The results (Table 8) show that the Wordnet based method is clearly able to take advantage of the larger dataset better than corpus-based system. However, our implementation of the distributional similarity method could possibly be improved by experimenting with different corpora and different methods of comparing word contexts.

5   Conclusion

We directly compared knowledge-based and distributional word similarity measures for the task of semantically disambiguating noun compounds. We experimented with different measures of Wordnet similarity and different parameters for the corpus similarity technique described in [14] using a very large, web-derived corpus.

Both measures achieved performance well above baseline on both datasets. The results suggest that, given enough data, the Wordnet measure produces better results, even without any word-sense-disambiguation beyond the most-frequent sense heuristic.

Experiments on a random subset of the larger dataset indicates that the Wordnet measure can take advantage of more training data better than the distributional method. Given the availability of large, hand-tagged training sets, the ease of querying resources such as Wordnet quickly, and the expensive nature of indexing and searching gigaword corpora to obtain distributional features, our results suggest that the knowledge based approach is more efficient when lexical similarity is used for disambiguation.

References

1. Johnston, M., Busa, F.: Qualia structure and the compositional interpretation of compound. In: Proceedings of the ACL SIGLEX Workshop on Breadth and Depth of Semantic Lexicons (1996)
2. Levi, J.: The Syntax and Semantics of Complex Nominals. Academic Press, New York (1978)
3. Turney, P.D., Waterman, M.S.: Similarity of Semantic Relations. Computational Linguistics 32(3), 379–416 (2006)
4. Hearst, M.A.: Automatic Acquisition of Hyponyms from Large Text Corpor. In: Proceedings of Conf. Computational Linguistics (COLING 1992) (1992)
5. Seaghdha, O'.D., Copestake, A.: Using Lexical and Relational Similarity to Classify Semantic Relations. In: Proceedings of the 12th Conference of the European Chapter of the Association for Computational Linguistics (EACL 2009), Athens, Greece (2009)
6. Nakov, P., Heast, M.: Solving Relational Similarity Problems using the Web as a Corpus. In: Proceedings of the 46th Annual Meeting of the Association for Computational Linguistics (ACL 2008), Columbus, OH (2008)
7. Seco, N., Veale, T., Hayes, J.: An Intrinsic Information Content Metric for Semantic Similarity in WordNet. In: The proceedings of ECAI 2004, the 16th European Conference on Artificial Intelligence, Valencia, Spain. John Wiley, Chichester (2004)
8. Nastase, V., Szpakowicz, S.: Exploring noun-modifier semantic relations. In: Proceedings of the 5th International Workshop on Computational Semantics (2003)
9. Seaghdha, O'.M.: Annotating and Learning Compound Noun Semantics. In: Proceedings of the ACL 2007 Student Research Workshop, Prague, Czech Republic (2007)
10. Kolhatkar, V., Pedersen, T.: WordNet::SenseRelate:: AllWords - A Broad Coverage Word Sense Tagger that Maximimizes Semantic Relatedness. In: The Proceedings of the North American Chapter of the Association for Computational Linguistics - Human Language Technologies 2009 Conference, Boulder, CO., June 1-3 (2009)
11. Kilgarriff, A., Rychly, P., Smrz, P., Tugwell, D.: The Sketch Engine. In: Proc. of EURALEX 2004, pp. 105–116 (2004)
12. Bird, S., Loper, E.: NLTK: The Natural Language Toolki. In: Proceedings of the 42nd meeting o the ACL (Demonstration session) (2004)
13. Kim, S.N., Baldwin, T.: Automatic interpretation of noun compounds using WordNet similarity. In: Dale, R., Wong, K.-F., Su, J., Kwong, O.Y. (eds.) IJCNLP 2005. LNCS (LNAI), vol. 3651, pp. 945–956. Springer, Heidelberg (2005)
14. Lin, D.: An Information-Theoretic Definition of Similarity. In: Proceedings of the 15th International Conference on Machine Learning, Madson, WI (1998)
15. Ferraresi, A., Zanchetta, E., Bernardini, S., Baroni, M.: Introducing and evaluating ukWaC, a very large web-derived corpus of English. In: Proceedings of 4th WAC workshop, LREC, Marrakech, Morocco (2008)

An Assessment of Machine Learning Techniques for Review Recommendation[*]

Michael P. O'Mahony[1], Pádraig Cunningham[2], and Barry Smyth[1]

[1] CLARITY: Centre for Sensor Web Technologies
[2] UCD Complex and Adaptive Systems Laboratory,
School of Computer Science and Informatics, University College Dublin
{michael.p.omahony,padraig.cunningham,barry.smyth}@ucd.ie

Abstract. In this paper, we consider a classification-based approach to the recommendation of user-generated product reviews. In particular, we develop review ranking techniques that allow the most *helpful* reviews for a particular product to be recommended, thereby facilitating users to readily asses the quality of the product in question. We apply a supervised machine learning approach to this task and compare the performance achieved by several classification algorithms using a large-scale study based on TripAdvisor hotel reviews. Our findings indicate that our approach is successful in recommending helpful reviews compared to benchmark ranking schemes, and further we highlight an interesting performance asymmetry that is biased in favour of reviews expressing negative sentiment.

1 Introduction

Recommendations are now a familiar feature of many online services. They help us to navigate through complex information spaces from music (iTunes) and movies (NetFlix) to books (Amazon) and consumer electronics (BestBuy). In these scenarios, recommender systems have largely been used to suggest catalog items (songs, movies, books etc.) to users based on their learned interests, which are often derived from their past purchasing behaviour. Lately, as online services embrace the world of the *social web*, *user-generated content* is playing an increasingly important role when it comes to supporting user buying decisions. For example, many online stores now include comprehensive consumer reviews to complement product descriptions, and it is not uncommon for popular products to attract hundreds of reviews from users who are only too happy to share their thoughts and opinions. Indeed many of us use sites like Amazon, Yelp and TripAdvisor primarily for their review information, even when we are planning to make our purchases elsewhere. In the world of recommender systems, these reviews can serve as a form of *recommendation explanation* [1,2,3] and can play a key role in helping the user to better evaluate the goodness of the product suggestion.

---

[*] This work is supported by Science Foundation Ireland under Grant Nos. 07/CE/I1147 and 08/SRC/I1407.

© Springer-Verlag Berlin Heidelberg 2010

The growing volume of these reviews motivates a new recommendation challenge: namely, the recommendation of balanced and helpful reviews. Although reviews are becoming increasingly commonplace, they can vary greatly in their quality and helpfulness. For example, reviews are often biased and sometimes are contributed by self-interested parties, while others can be very balanced and insightful. For this reason, the ability to recommend helpful reviews will add considerable value to the user's online experience. While some services are addressing this by allowing users to rate the helpfulness of each review, this type of feedback can be sparse and varied, with many reviews, particularly recent ones, failing to attract any feedback.

In this paper, we focus on this review recommendation task and describe a classification-based approach to suggesting helpful reviews. Briefly, we develop a classifier capable of classifing a review as either *helpful* or *unhelpful* with some confidence and go on to show how this information can be used as the basis for ranking reviews by the predicted helpfulness during recommendation. In particular, we extend our recent work on this topic [4] by evaluating a variety of different machine learning approaches, using feature selection, on a large-scale dataset from the TripAdvisor site. We highlight some interesting properties of this task and dataset from a machine learning perspective and demonstrate the considerable benefits of a *random forest* learning technique, over more conventional Bayesian and decision tree techniques, in this particular domain. We go on to show how the resulting recommender system is capable of suggesting superior reviews, compared to a number of alternative recommendation benchmarks, and highlight an interesting recommendation performance asymmetry that is biased in favour of reviews expressing negative sentiment.

2   Review Recommendation as Classification

Reviews can vary in two dimensions – they can be either *helpful* or *unhelpful* from a reader's perspective and they can express either *positive* or *negative* sentiment in respect of the product or service in question. Importantly, TripAdvisor facilitates feedback on reviews where users can indicate whether or not they found them to be helpful. In order to distinguish the most unambiguously helpful reviews from the rest, we consider a review to be helpful if and only if 75% or more of the raters of that review have found it helpful. Each TripAdvisor review also contains a score (on a 5-point scale) which indicates the user's sentiment toward the hotel. Following the example of Amazon.com (see Figure 3), we define a positive review as any review in which a score of $\geq$ 4-stars has been assigned to the hotel, and a negative review as any review in which a score of < 4-stars has been assigned. Overall, there are significantly more helpful positive reviews in our evaluation dataset than helpful negative ones, which indicates that users are much less inclined to perceive negative reviews as helpful. We discuss this matter in detail, and its impact on our evaluation, in Section 3.2.

The main objective of this work is to rank a collection of reviews in order to present a user with a small set of positive and negative reviews that will be considered helpful. In the evaluation presented here, we assess the use of *ranking* classifiers to achieve this objective. Ranking classifiers are classifiers that assign a score rather than a class label so that an unlabeled set of examples can be ranked by degree of belonging to a class.

Thus reviews can be recommended by returning the top-ranking positive and negative reviews to the user. An obvious criterion for assessing the effectiveness of the process is to score the *enrichment* of the reviews presented, i.e. if 30% of reviews selected at random are helpful and 60% or reviews selected by the classifier are helpful, then a 2-fold enrichment is achieved.

2.1 The TripAdvisor Chicago Dataset

The dataset used for the evaluation comprises reviews of Chicago hotels gathered from the TripAdvisor service[1]. This dataset is described in detail in [4] and so only summary details are provided here. The dataset contains 17,038 reviews of 7,646 hotels by 7,399 users. All reviews in the dataset have received feedback on review helpfulness on a minimum of 5 occasions. We use this feedback as the ground truth in respect of classification and recommendation performance and reviews are labeled as either helpful or unhelpful as described above.

In gathering the data each review has been represented by 23 different features. These features are divided into four categories [4]:

- *Social network features* – the degree distribution statistics in the bipartite user-hotel graph,
- *Sentiment features* – the overall rating score and (optional) sub-scores for particluar hotel features assigned by users to hotels,
- *Content features* – review length, readability and completeness, and
- *User reputation features* – the helpfulness of reviews from users in the past.

It is important to distinguish the reputation features in particular, given that these features will not be available in situations where feedback on review help-fulness is not facilitated or is limited in quantity.

2.2 Classifier Selection and Configuration

In setting up a classification-based review selection system along the lines we propose, there are a number of issues to be considered:

- The amount of training data required for good performance should be de-termined.
- An optimal subset of the 23 features has to be selected.
- A classifier with good ranking performance on the data has to be identified.

---

[1] http://www.tripadvisor.com/

Training set size: In supervised machine learning terms a training set of over 17,000 examples is very large. In most application domains, less than a thousand examples will provide good coverage of the problem domain and the addition of new examples will not improve generalisation accuracy (i.e. accuracy on unseen examples). For this reason, we performed a cross-validation analysis to see what size of training set would offer adequate coverage. The results of this evaluation are shown in Section 3.1.

Feature Selection: While the 23 features have been chosen to be predictive of review helpfulness, there is no guarantee that some of the features are not irrelevant or redundant in the presence of some of the other features. It may be that a subset of the features are sufficient to provide good performance. Indeed for some classification techniques the presence of irrelevant features may damage performance. We have tested three feature selection techniques for identifying a good feature subset. These are feature ranking based on information gain, ranking based on variable importance derived using random forest [5] and wrapper search [6]. Somewhat surprisingly, feature selection based on information gain proved to be as effective as the others and that was the method we used.

The information gain for a feature is the reduction in entropy achieved by partitioning the data based on that feature. A simple and effective subset selection strategy is to rank the features using information gain and then, starting with the highest scoring feature, evaluate using cross-validation the performance of a classifier built with that feature. Then add the next highest ranking feature and reevaluate; repeat until no further improvements are achieved [6]. The results of this feature selection strategy on the Chicago data are shown in Section 3.1.

Classifier Selection The two criteria for selecting a good classifier for this recommendation task are that it should have good accuracy on the task and that it should be able to rank reviews in terms of expected helpfulness. In practice, probabilities or confidence scores can be produced for most classifier types and Weka[2], the toolkit used in our evaluation, can assign a 'probability' to the predictions of most classifiers it supports. The classifiers we have chosen for detailed analysis are naïve Bayes, the J48 implementation of the C4.5 decision tree algorithm, the JRip implementation of the Ripper rule learner and random forests.

It is straightforward to assign a confidence to a prediction produced by naïve Bayes because the classifier directly calculates a posterior probability on which the classification is based. JRip and J48 produce confidence scores based on the distribution of training instances classified by the rule or leaf node (in the J48 case). For example, if 10 training samples are classified by a single Ripper rule and the distribution of those samples is 7 positive and 3 negative, then that rule will assign a confidence of 0.7 to all its predictions. J48 assigns confidence scores in the same way. Clearly, if there are few rules in the Ripper model or if a decision tree is very simple, then a ranking based on these confidence scores will be very coarse. Happily this is not the case with this recommendation problem – the rulesets are large and the decision trees are bushy so the resulting ranking is

---

[2] http://www.cs.waikato.ac.nz/ml/weka/

sufficiently fine for our purposes. Given that the random forest is an ensemble of decision trees, it can also assign a confidence to all the predictions it produces.

3   Evaluation

In the previous section, we have described how a classification approach can be used for recommendation. The success of this approach will depend on the accuracy achieved by the classifiers and how this translates into the recommendation of helpful reviews. In this section, we examine these issues in the context of a large-scale study using the TripAdvisor dataset described above.

In the following sections, feature selection by information gain and the classification performance versus feature subset size experiments were performed using a randomly selected 25% of dataset instances. The training set size and recommendation experiments were performed using the remaining data. Classification performance is evaluated using area under ROC curve (AUC) [7]. AUC produces a value between 0 and 1 and is equal to the probability that a classifier will rank a randomly chosen positive instance (in our case, a helpful review) higher than a randomly chosen negative one (unhelpful review).

3.1   Classification Results

The classification performance achieved by J48 versus training set size is shown in Figure 1(a). It is surprising to note that AUC continues to improve with the addition of new data, even beyond 10,000 examples. This indicates that the relationship between review helpfulness and the predictive features is complex and that very large training sets will be required to build good models.

Figures 2(a) and 2(b) show classification performance for increasing feature subset sizes when reputation features are included and excluded, respectively.

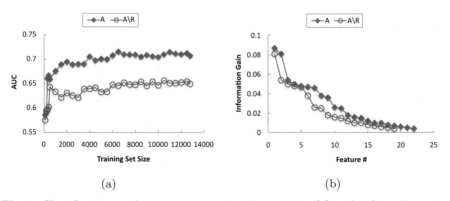

(a)   (b)

Fig. 1. Classification performance versus training set size (a) and information gain for individual features (b) when reputation features are included (labeled 'A') and excluded (labeled 'A\R')

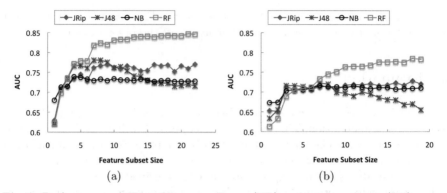

Fig. 2. Performance of JRip, J48, naïve Bayes (NB) and random forest (RF) versus feature subset size when reputation features are included (a) and excluded (b)

While classifiers trained using reputation features performed better in terms of AUC, similar trends were observed for both conditions. (We discuss reputation features in more detail in Section 3.2.).

These results indicate that J48 and to a lesser extent, naïve Bayes, were much more sensitive to a small number of optimal features than JRip or random forest. As can be seen from Figure 1(b), where information gain for individual features ranked in descending order of performance is shown, information gain declined rapidly with low values observed for the lower-ranked features. These latter features appear to be very noisy and lead to overfitting in the case of J48 and, to a lesser extent, naïve Bayes. Thus the removal of lower-ranked features improved the performance achieved by these classifiers. Interestingly, this was not the case for random forest and JRip, which proved to be robust in the presence of noisy features. Indeed, random forest can get some useful information from these noisy features with performance improving until all features are included. This is probably due to the ability of the random forest to reduce the variance component of error because it is an ensemble technique.

3.2   Recommendation Results

Ultimately, the use of classification techniques are a means to enable the recommendation of reviews to a user. The above findings indicate that reasonable classification performance has been obtained, and thus we can be optimistic that the approach can provide a basis for high quality recommendations. In this section, we evaluate the quality of these recommendations.

We adopt a form of recommendation similar to that implemented by Amazon.com, where the most helpful contrasting reviews (i.e. one positive and one negative review[3]) are presented to users side-by-side (see Figure 3). Of course this approach is limited to cases where sufficient feedback on review helpfulness has been amassed; for example, in our dataset, only 31% of all reviews were rated

---

[3] Recall from Section 2 that a positive (resp. negative) review is defined as any review in which a score of $\geq$ 4-stars (resp. $<$ 4-stars) has been assigned to the hotel.

Fig. 3. An example of the Amazon.com approach to review ranking, where the most helpful positive and negative product reviews are listed side-by-side

5 times or more. In addition, we consider two alternatives to our classification-based recommendation technique by ranking reviews by *date* (recommending the most recent positive and negative reviews) and ranking reviews at *random* (recommending a randomly selected positive and negative review).

We construct positive and negative recommendation test sets using only those hotels which have a minimum of 5 positive or negative reviews, respectively. There are 178 and 96 such hotels in the dataset, respectively. During recommendation we adopt a leave-one-out approach such that, for each test set hotel, we recommend its most helpful positive and negative reviews using classifiers which are trained on the reviews of all other hotels in the dataset.

Recommendation performance is evaluated in terms of how frequently our recommenders manage to select a review that is unambiguously helpful according to the definition given in Section 2.1; that is, a review where 75% or more of the raters of that review have found it helpful. In particular, we consider the enrichment in the percentage of helpful reviews recommended across test set hotels with respect to the random ranking scheme as described in Section 2.

We compare the enrichment provided by the two best performing classifiers from Section 3.1 – the ensemble random forest approach and the J48 decision tree. Given that random forest and J48 gave best performance using feature sets consisting of all available features and the top 8 features, respectively, we present results in Figure 4 for each classifier using both of these feature sets. Results obtained using the top 8 features are indicated by an asterisk (*).

Positive versus Negative Reviews. To begin, consider the recommendation performance that was achieved when reputation features were included. It is clear that both classifiers provided significant enrichment benefits relative to random and date-based ranking. Random forest performed the best, achieving an enrichment of 1.8 and 4 for positive and negative reviews, respectively. Similar performance was seen using the two feature subset sizes considered. As expected, J48 achieved greater enrichment using a feature subset consisting of the top 8 features, where an enrichment of 1.6 and 3.1 was achieved for positive and

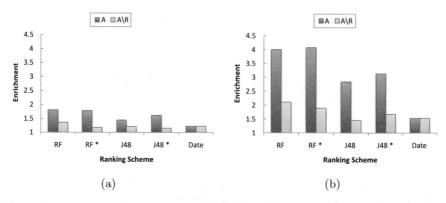

(a)   (b)

Fig. 4. Enrichment in the percentage of helpful reviews recommended with respect to the random ranking scheme for positive reviews (a) and negative reviews (b) when reputation features are included (labeled 'A') and excluded (labeled 'A\R')

negative reviews, respectively. The effect of feature subset size on the classifiers is consistent with the trends observed in Figure 2(a).

Interestingly, the classification-based approaches provided the greatest benefits in relation to the recommendation of negative reviews. As can be seen in Figure 5, the mean percentage of helpful reviews in positive and negative review test sets was 47% and 14%, respectively. Clearly, users are less inclined to find reviews expressing negative sentiment helpful, and consequently ranking such reviews by date and at random was unable to achieve good performance. Hence the need for high-performing review ranking schemes is greater for reviews expressing negative sentiment, and our results indicate that the classification-based recommenders indeed achieved particularly good enrichment for these reviews.

Reputation Features. Reputation features are designed to capture the helpfulness of reviews that individual users have authored in the past. We can therefore expect that such features are likely to exert considerable influence on recommendation performance. These features are not, however, available for all

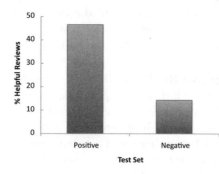

Fig. 5. Mean percentage of helpful reviews in positive and negative review test sets

reviews (because many TripAdvisor reviews receive little or no feedback). In addition, not all online services facilitate the provision of feedback on reviews, and it is therefore important to consider performance when reputation features are excluded from training instances.

When reputation features were excluded, much more modest enrichment benefits were observed from a recommendation perspective. For example, in the case of positive reviews, random forest and J48 achieved an enrichment of only 1.4 and 1.2, respectively, compared to 1.2 for ranking by date. Once again, classification performance for negative reviews was considerably better, where enrichments of 2.1, 1.7 and 1.5 were achieved for random forest, J48 and ranking by date, respectively. Thus, while the classification-based approaches have provided enrichment benefits in the absence of reputation features (and particularly so with respect to negative reviews), these results nevertheless highlight the importance of the reputation features in terms of recommendation performance.

4   Conclusions

In this paper, we have presented a classification-based approach to the recommendation of helpful product reviews. We have considered various classifiers and examined their performance in terms of training set size, feature selection, classification accuracy and the enrichment of recommended reviews with respect to benchmark ranking schemes. The learning task proved to be complex with AUC performance continuing to improve even for very large-sized training sets. JRip and random forest were robust to the presence of noisy features, while the performance of J48 in particular, and naïve Bayes to a lesser extent, improved when learning was based on feature subsets consisting of the top features as ranked by information gain. The ensemble random forest classifier provided best overall performance, and the importance of the reputation features was also discussed. The results also indicated a bias in respect of review recommendation, where the classification-based approach delivered greater enrichment for negative reviews. This finding is significant, given that such reviews are perceived as being less helpful by users, and hence the need for ranking schemes that can accurately recommend helpful reviews which express negative sentiment.

The proliferation of user-generated content continues in the world of the social web and the following related work is of interest. Recently, the effect of credibility indicators in topical blog post retrieval has been investigated [8]. Several indicators (features) were considered; for example topical consistency, regularity of posts and various measures such as spelling quality, length of post and the appropriate use of capitalisation and emoticons etc. in the text. The use of such indicators were found to significantly improve retrieval performance in [8]. Machine learning techniques were employed in [9] to classify text-based reviews from a sentiment perspective (i.e. positive versus negative reviews) using content-based feature sets. A study based on TripAvisor reviews demonstrated the effectiveness of the approach. A classification approach was also adopted in [10] to distinguish between conversational and informational questions in social

Q&A sites (e.g. Yahoo! Answers, Answerbag). In this work, features such as question category, text categorization and social network metrics were selected as the basis for classification and good performance was achieved.

In future work, we will include additional features from the above and other related work in our classification and recommendation model. We are particularly interested in developing a sufficiently rich feature set where performance does not rely as strongly on user reputation features, given that these features are not always available for particular reviews and that not all services support such feedback on reviews. In addition, we plan on applying our approach to other product review domains, e.g. Amazon.com, Hostelworld.com and blippr.com. The latter domain is of interest given that review texts are constrained to 160 characters in length, which poses additional challenges from a classification perspective.

References

1. Bilgic, M., Mooney, R.J.: Explaining recommendations: Satisfaction vs. promotion. Beyond Personalization Workshop, held in conjunction with the 2005 International Conference on Intelligent User Interfaces, San Diego, CA, USA (2005)
2. Herlocker, J.L., Konstan, J.A., Riedl, J.: Explaining collaborative filtering recommendations. In: Proceeding on the ACM 2000 Conference on Computer Supported Cooperative Work, Philadelphia, PA, USA, pp. 241–250 (2000)
3. Gretzel, U., Fesenmaier, D.R.: Persuasion in recommender systems. International Journal of Electronic Commerce 11(2), 81–100 (2006)
4. O'Mahony, M.P., Smyth, B.: Learning to recommend helpful hotel reviews. In: 3rd ACM Conference on Recommender Systems (RecSys 2009) (2009)
5. Breiman, L.: Random forests. Machine Learning 45(1), 5–32 (2001)
6. Cunningham, P.: Dimension Reduction. In: Cord, M., Cunningham, P. (eds.) Machine Learning Techniques for Multimedia: Case Studies on Organization and Retrieval, pp. 91–112. Springer, Heidelberg (2008)
7. Fawcett, T.: Roc graphs: Notes and practical considerations for researchers. Technical Report HPL-2003-4, HP Laboratories, CA, USA (2004)
8. Weerkamp, W., de Rijke, M.: Credibility improves topical blog post retrieval. In: Proceedings of the Association for Computational Linguistics with the Human Language Technology Conference (ACL 2008: HLT), June 16-18, pp. 923–931 (2008)
9. Baccianella, S., Esuli, A., Sebastiani, F.: Multi-facet rating of product reviews. In: Boughanem, M., et al. (eds.) ECIR 2009. LNCS, vol. 5478, pp. 461–472. Springer, Heidelberg (2009)
10. Harper, F.M., Moy, D., Konstan, J.A.: Facts or friends? Distinguishing informational and conversational questions in social Q&A sites. In: Proceedings of the 27th International Conference on Human Factors in Computing Systems (CHI 2009), Boston, MA, USA, pp. 759–768 (April 2009)

Buzzer – Online Real-Time Topical News Article and Source Recommender

Owen Phelan, Kevin McCarthy, and Barry Smyth

CLARITY: Centre for Sensor Web Technologies
School of Computer Science and Informatics
University College Dublin
firstname.lastname@ucd.ie

Abstract. With the increasing growth of online communication tools, as well as consumption of topical and current information from the web, there is a growing difficulty for users to keep abreast of current, relevant and interesting material. The widespread online adoption of techniques such as recommender systems has come about due to their proven ability to reduce and personalise the constituents of the information explosion. The *collective conversations* found on such services as *Twitter* are playing an increasingly useful role in monitoring current and topical trends among a large set of culturally and geographically diverse users. In this paper, we describe the ongoing development of a system that harnesses real-time micro-blogging activity such as Twitter, as a basis for promoting and influencing personalized online news and blog content. The system provides a real-time way for users to engage with content that has been influenced by popular activity of both the global community, or their own friends. We also discuss some preliminary results based on a live user evaluation.

1 Introduction

Online news sites typically contain news articles ranked by recency and the considerations of an editorial team, however little is done to present the user with topical and novel news material ranked on real-life events and conversations from the public domain. For example, a glance at any major news organization's website during and immediately after the Inauguration of U.S. President Barack Obama on the 20th of January 2009 would have prominently editorialised the event. While this event was logically deemed important enough to cover heavily, little was done by those organisations to promote it as a popular news item on the basis of explicit popularity among consumers. One disadvantage of this promotion by the major news organizations of this single event is, of course, that the many other news items of the day may be muted from public attention.

There is a long history of using techniques such as recommender systems to help users to navigate through the sea of stories that are written and published everyday [1,6]. These systems promise to promote the most relevant items to a user based on their learned or stated preferences or their previous news

L. Coyle and J. Freyne (Eds.): AICS 2009, LNAI 6206, pp. 251–261, 2010.

consumption histories, helping the user in question to keep up-to-date and to save valuable time sifting through less relevant stories. They have been used to good effect, and the recent growth of services such as the social bookmarking service *Digg*[1] demonstrate the value of collaborative filtering recommendation techniques when it comes to delivering a more relevant and compelling news service. For all the success of these systems there are some aspects of news recommendation that are not well suited, like the problem of identifying niche *topical news stories*, and by extension, content feeds themselves.

Current recommender systems are limited in their ability to identify topical stories because they typically rely on a critical mass of user consumption before such stories can be recognised. Such an example is *Google News*[2] [2], which, although a successful system, still relies on click-histories of users to provide popular items, without much consideration for the actual content itself. We have developed an early prototype system, called *Buzzer*, which takes advantage of a novel content-based approach for finding news stories among a users' set list of RSS feeds [8]. This approach harnesses a popular micro-blogging service, *Twitter*[3,5][3], as a support for promoting current and topical news items.

One of the many criticisms of Twitter's ability to present topical and current trends is that its typically unsubstantiated and unconfirmed, as opposed to formal news organisations who are libel and responsible to convey accurate information. Our approach involves using this dynamic and real-time data as a support for ranking formal sources such as user's RSS feeds in a manner other than recency. Co-occurring relevant tags between the current Twitter trends on either the public feed or among a user's friends are used as a basis for recommending content from that user's personalised list of RSS sources. The system also provides novel and personalized content from other users and a community pool of articles, as well as recommending new and relevant sources the user may not be aware of. In this paper, we describe some points on the area of news conveyance and consumption, the current state of the system, as well as several interesting points from a live user evaluation.

2   News Recommenders and Buzzer

In this section, we will discuss some aspects of how news is presented to users online, and how our proposed system builds on and differs from these. RSS (Really Simple Syndication) is a popular and important Web 2.0 technology used by a wide variety of online sites as a way to syndicate or distribute news information in the form of short-updates that can be linked back to complete stories. RSS Readers allow users to aggregate updates from many different feeds to provide a one-stop-shop to news, although as users subscribe to tens of RSS feeds this introduces a niche information overload problem [10].

---

[1] Digg - http://www.digg.com

[2] Google News - http://news.google.com

[3] Twitter - http://www.twitter.com

Online news sites such as BBC News[4] generally follow a similar structure of a typical newspaper, with columns, segments and headlines for each news element. For the most part, the content on these sites are structured to prefer and highlight the recency of content, and/or by the design of the editorial team who determine which items are worth promoting. Google News is a topically segregated aggregation of a set of feeds, with an automatic ranking strategy based on user interactions (click-histories and click-throughs)[2].

These ranking techniques are where our strategy mainly diverges from these examples. We feel that, while taking a content agnostic approach commonly found in collaborative filtering systems as found on Amazon, Digg and Google News can be useful and effective, they lack the respect for the usefulness and descriptiveness of the actual content itself in recommending *news* items to users. Collaborative filtering techniques typically involve analyzing the metadata of items themselves, without the full consideration of the items actual content. This content-agnostic approach can be a saving grace for items that are difficult to self-describe, such as photos and videos (e.g. Flickr or YouTube), however these items still typically rely on users to annotate them with descriptive text.

Our primary focus is to find a means of re-ranking content based on current topicality on super-active and dynamic social communications sites such as Twitter. This site is a so-called *micro-blogging* service that allows users to submit their own short (maximum of 140 characters) status update messages, called *tweets*, while *following* the status updates of others. Recently there has been much interest in Twitter, partly because of its popular growth [3], and also because of its ability to provide access to thoughts, intentions and activities of millions of users in real-time. Buzzer mines these tweets to discover emerging topics and breaking events, with the intention of ranking RSS news feeds so that topical articles can be effectively promoted. We have also explored extending this technique to discovering content among the pool of articles across the user-space. Another recommendation action we investigate is the recommendation of source RSS feeds themselves. This is done in a similar fashion as the article recommendations, except we take into account the feeds that the relevant articles came from. These algorithms are discussed in the following sections.

3   Example Session and User Interface

In this section, we will describe the overall user interface and some usage scenarios of the system. The user logs into the system using their Twitter login details (used by the Twitter API). The user then configures the system by providing the RSS feeds and selects a recommendation strategy that influences the types of Twitter data the system should gather. These strategies include:

1. *Public-Rank* - this strategy uses the basic technique described above but mines tweets from the public timeline (that is, the most recent public tweets across the entire Twitter user-base).

---

[4] BBC News - http://news.bbc.co.uk

Fig. 1. A screenshot of recommended articles for a given user

2. *Friends-Rank* - this strategy mines its tweets from the user's Twitter friends.
3. *Content-Rank* - this benchmark strategy does not use Twitter but instead ranks articles based on term frequency alone, by scoring articles according to the frequency of the top-100 RSS terms.

The system then collects the latest RSS and Twitter data and makes a set of recommended Buzzer feeds for that user. The system gathers the top 100 frequent co-occuring terms between the articles and the tweets contained in the users' index. This is a basis of inferring relevant and novel descriptive terms of a user, and we can use this to both search article indexes and also potentially compute simple user-user similarity scores.

The screenshot in Figure 1 shows the system's interface for recommending news items. These include the personal articles that have been computed using the user-specified content. Also shown are the recommended articles that are from the community pool of articles, that have been gathered based on the co-occuring terms searched across the pool's index. The articles in this column do not appear in the users' feeds, they are new articles that the user would not see in the primary column. A tag cloud of frequency-ranked co-occuring terms for that user are also shown, so the user can clearly see how the recommendation process occurred.

The results page also includes a standard term/frequency tag cloud that includes terms ordered and sized based on the frequency of each term. This is also useful in explaining to the user the term space that the results were derived from. For example, if the user has selected a twitter-based strategy, such as using the public feed, these terms are the co-occuring terms between the specified RSS feeds of that user, and the Twitter database. The frequency is determined based on these co-occuring terms' frequencies in the Twitter database.

Figure 2 depicts the user preference page on Buzzer. This page includes preferences such as their chosen personal RSS feeds, as well as options for their

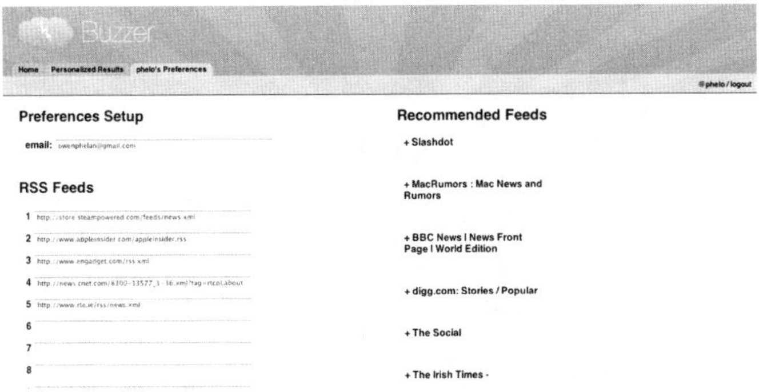

Fig. 2. A screenshot of the user preferences page, with feed recommendations in the second column that can be easily added to the user's list on the left

Twitter influences (either the public, or friends feeds, or no Twitter influence at all). More importantly, the page provides the user with a list of recommended and relevant RSS feeds, which is based on the algorithm discussed previously. The next section discusses how these feeds are generated and recommended to users in greater detail.

4   Architecture and Recommendation Methods

As already mentioned, Buzzer adopts a content-based recommendation technique, by mining content terms from RSS and Twitter feeds as the basis for article ranking. Content-based approaches to recommending news articles have proven successful in the past. For example, perhaps the earliest example of a news recommendation service, *Krakatoa Chronicle* [4] represented user profiles as a weighted vector of terms drawn from the articles that a given user liked, and matched this weighted vector against a new set of articles to produce a ranked list for presentation to the user. Similarly, Billsus and Pazzani's *News-Dude* [1] harnessed content based representations and multi-strategy learning techniques to generate short-term and long-term user profiles, as the basis for news recommendation. Although Billsus and Pazzani [7] argue that content-based approaches to finding trends and topics in news articles are difficult because of the sheer random bag-of-words unstructured nature of articles, and the complexity of natural-language processing. We bypass this consideration because our technique finds common co-occuring terms among Twitter and RSS.

The Buzzer system comprises three major components (as seen in Figure 3):

1. The *Web front-end* manages the basic user registration and login process and allows users to provide their Twitter account information and a list of RSS feeds that they wish to follow (in fact providing Twitter account information is optional since, as discussed later, Buzzer can use Twitter's *public timeline* as an alternative source of tweets, as opposed to tweets only from friends on

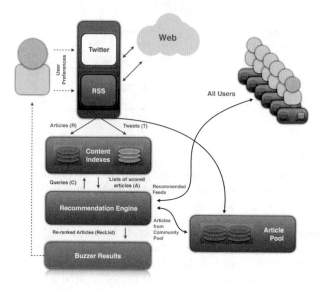

Fig. 3. High Level Architecture Diagram

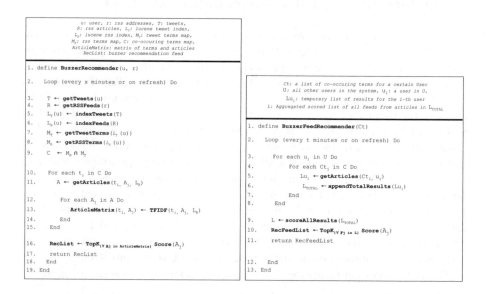

Fig. 4. Two main algorithms employed in the recommendation engine. On the left, Figure 4(a), this is the high-level description of how the user interacts and is returned feeds of article content. The algorithm on the right, Figure 4(b), shows how we recommend the feed addresses.

Twitter). The interface provides multiple feeds of personalized, community gathered and trending terms in the system's content-space.

2. The *Content Gatherer & Indexer* is responsible for mining and indexing the appropriate Twitter and RSS information, given the user's configuration settings. This component also manages the community pool of articles.

3. The *Recommendation Engine* generates a ranked list of RSS stories based on the co-occurence of popular terms within the user's RSS and Twitter indexes. It has also been extended to compute similarities among users' co-occuring terms, gather recommended feed data, and search a pooled index of the community's articles to discover new items that the case user may not subscribe to or receive.

The process by which Buzzer generates a set of ranked RSS stories is presented in detail by the algorithm in Figure 4(a). Given a user, u, and a set of RSS feeds, r, the system first extracts the latest RSS articles, R, and Twitter tweets, T and separately indexes each article and tweet to produce two *Lucene* indexes. Lucene[5] is a popular open-source search-engine tool that is suited for fast indexing and document retrieval. The resulting index terms are then extracted from these RSS and Twitter indexes as the basis to produce RSS and Twitter term vectors, M_R and M_T, respectively.

Next, we identify the set of terms, t, that co-occur in M_T and M_R; these are the words that are present in the latest tweets and the most recent RSS stories and they provide the basis for our recommendation technique. Each term, t_i, is used as a query against the RSS index to retrieve the set of articles A that contain t along with their associated TF-IDF (Term Frequency * Inverse Document Frequency) score [9] . Thus each co-occuring term, t_i is associated with a set of articles $A_1, ... A_n$, which contain t, and the TF-IDF score for t in each of $A_1, ... A_n$ to produce a matrix as shown in Figure 5. To calculate an overall score for each article we simply compute the sum of the TF-IDF scores across all of the terms associated with that article as per Equation 1. In this way, articles which contain many tweet terms with higher TF-IDF scores are preferred to articles that contain fewer tweet terms with lower TF-IDF scores.

$$Score(A_i) = \sum_{\forall t_i} element(A_i, t_i) \tag{1}$$

Finally, producing the recommendation is a simple matter of selecting the top k articles with the highest scores. Each time Buzzer gathers an individual feed from a source, the articles are copied into both the user's individual article pool, and a community pool. Each article has a differing relevance score in either pool, as their TF-IDF score changes based on the other content in the local directory with it. The algorithm outlined in Figure 4(b) describes the method by which Buzzer recommends new RSS feeds to users based on querying each other users' indexes to find new articles. Instead of returning the article data, we aggregate the article's source addresses (eg CNN, RTE, etc.), and also remove

---

[5] Apache Lucene - http://apache.lucene.org

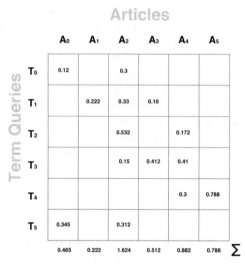

Fig. 5. Buzzer's co-occurence matrix: each cell contains the Lucene TF-IDF score (from the RSS index) of the given term in the given article

any recommended feeds the user may already be signed up to. This provides a ranked list of relevant and personalized feeds, new to the user, and influenced by the rest of the community's preferred sources.

5   User Evaluation

In order to test the validity of Buzzer to prove Twitter could be used to recommend niche/topical articles, we performed a small-scale user evaluation. The experiment involved ten participants who used a prototype system which included the basic content-based system for individual users (the community articles and feed recommendations were unavailable here). Users could use the Buzzer interface as an RSS reader or, alternatively, the Buzzer recommendation lists can be published as RSS feeds themselves and thus incorporated, as a summary feed, into the user's normal RSS reader. Each participant configured the system by providing several of their favourite RSS feeds along with their Twitter account information. The user had the ability to choose either of the recommendation strategies outlined in Section 3 (Public-Rank, Friends-Rank, Content-Rank). To begin with the users were asked explore the different types of recommendation strategies at their leisure. As a basic evaluation measure, we focused on the click-through frequency for articles across the 3 different recommendation strategies.

The results yielded interesting usage patterns. For example we found that, on average, the Twitter-based strategies resulted in between 8.3 and 10.4 click-throughs per user compared with only 5.8 article click-throughs for the content-based strategy; a relative click-through increase of between 30% and 45% for the Twitter-based strategies. We also found a preference among the users of the *Friends-Rank* recommendations compared to the recommendations derived from Twitter's Public Timeline (*Public-Rank*). This suggests that users were more likely to tune in to the themes and topics of interest of their friends over those that might be of interest to the Twitter public at large. Interestingly, however, this is at odds with the feedback provided by participants as part of a post-trial questionnaire, which indicated a strong preference for the *Public-Rank* articles; we found that 67% of users indicated a preference for *Public-Rank* recommendations compared with 22% of users indicating a preference for *Friends-Rank* recommendations. Incidentally, none of the participants favoured the *Content-rank* strategy and 11% didn't know which strategy they preferred.

Interestingly, when we compared the ratio of *Public-Rank* to *Friends-Rank* click-throughs to the number of friends the user follows on Twitter we found a correlation coefficient of -0.89, suggesting that users with more friends tend to be more inclined to benefit from the *Friends-Rank* recommendations, compared to the recommendations derived from the public timeline. Although our initial user study was preliminary, the Buzzer recommender system was well received and we found that participants preferred the Twitter-based recommendation strategies. The Buzzer feed provided the participants with interesting and topical articles which were viewed in greater detail by clicking-through to the full article.

These quantitative results, mixed with the qualitative comments gathered post-evaluation, confirmed our intuitions about the next logical steps for the system. As seen in the earlier architecture descriptions, these were integrated into the system, and we are in the process of beginning a longer-term evaluation with a significantly larger user-group to further qualify our techniques. We believe that the enhancements will improve user satisfaction by recommending a more diverse set of topical news articles as well as introducing users to new RSS feeds, to which they were previously not subscribed.

6   Discussion and Conclusions

This paper has outlined a novel system that harnesses the dynamic and descriptive power of user-generated systems such as Twitter to present users with a dynamic and personalised news article stream. A source feed recommendation technique is also described. The prototype system has been developed to show a proof of concept, along with an extensible architecture to adapt future work. We can see the Buzzer system providing considerable opportunity for further innovation and experimentation as a test-bed for real-time recommendation and user-generated data-feed analysis. As discussed, we hope to take several avenues of exploration and experimentation to discover interesting patterns and uses in and of these interesting data sources.

One of the main avenues of exploration in the next iteration of Buzzer will be to integrate collaborative filtering techniques to act as *quality* metrics for each article. One suggestion could incorporate the click-through data for each article, reputation systems for feed providers, or simple rating scales for each item. This score would be integrated into the primary content-based scoring technique described previously.

There are many ways in which the content-based recommendation technique may be improved, such as the further development and analysis of the co-occuring term content-based technique employed, as we have yet to determine if it exhibits frequency behaviors such as power-law distributions. These distributions are typically found in collaborative systems such as Flickr, where the frequencies of tags across a space of documents have a power-law curve.

The system has the potential to act as a collaborative news service, with a number of opportunities to provide additional recommendation strategies for users. These include recommending friends and potential contacts with services such as Twitter, and explore further content analysis of individual users' indexes as a different support, as well as novel new interfaces for news delivery.

The initial evaluation mentioned in this paper has yielded favourable results. Presently a second larger, more comprehensive user trial is under development to further clarify the utility of the techniques, and also to discover usage patterns in greater detail.

Acknowledgements

This work is kindly supported by Science Foundation Ireland under Grant No. 07/CE/11147 CLARITY CSET.

References

1. Billsus, D., Pazzani, M.J.: A personal news agent that talks, learns and explains. In: Proceedings of the Third International Conference on Autonomous Agents, pp. 268–275. ACM Press, New York (1999)
2. Das, A.S., Datar, M., Garg, A., Rajaram, S.: Google news personalization: scalable online collaborative filtering. In: WWW 2007: Proceedings of the 16th International Conference on World Wide Web, pp. 271–280. ACM, New York (2007)
3. Java, A., Song, X., Finin, T., Tseng, B.: Why we twitter: understanding microblogging usage and communities. In: WebKDD/SNA-KDD 2007: Proceedings of the 9th WebKDD and 1st SNA-KDD 2007 Workshop on Web Mining and Social Network Analysis, pp. 56–65. ACM, New York (2007)
4. Kamba, T., Bharat, K., Albers, M.C.: The krakatoa chronicle - an interactive, personalized, newspaper on the web. In: Proceedings of the Fourth International World Wide Web Conference, pp. 159–170 (1995)
5. Krishnamurthy, B., Gill, P., Arlitt, M.: A few chirps about twitter. In: WOSP 2008: Proceedings of the First Workshop on Online Social Networks, pp. 19–24. ACM, New York (2008)
6. Lang, K.: Newsweeder: learning to filter netnews. In: Proceedings of the 12th International Conference on Machine Learning, pp. 331–339. Morgan Kaufmann publishers Inc., San Mateo (1995)
7. Pazzani, M., Billsus, D.: Content-based recommendation systems. In: The Adaptive Web, pp. 325–341 (2007)

8. Phelan, O., McCarthy, K., Smyth, B.: Using twitter to recommend real-time topical news. In: ACM RecSys 2009, October 2009. ACM, New York (2009) (submitted)
9. Sebastiani, F., Ricerche, C.N.D.: Machine learning in automated text categorization. ACM Computing Surveys 34, 1–47 (2002)
10. Smyth, B., Cotter, P.: A personalised tv listings service for the digital tv age. Knowledge-Based Systems 13(2-3), 53–59 (2000)

An Evaluation of the GhostWriter System for Case-Based Content Suggestions

Aidan Waugh and Derek Bridge

Department of Computer Science,
University College Cork, Ireland
{a.waugh,d.bridge}@cs.ucc.ie

Abstract. The Web has many sites where users can exchange goods and services. Often, the end-users must write free-text descriptions of the goods and services they have available, or the goods and services they are seeking. The quality of these descriptions is often low. In this paper, we describe the GhostWriter system, which encourages users to write descriptions that are more comprehensive. The system makes content suggestions from a case base of successful descriptions. The paper describes a new off-line ablation study that we have carried out to evaluate the system. The results show that GhostWriter has a high success rate in making suggestions that quickly recover ablated content.[1]

1 Introduction

Trade, the exchange of goods and services, has been a feature of human existence from prehistoric times. It has evolved from simple bartering, through the introduction of money, to the development of long-distance commerce. And now the Web is allowing dis-intermediation: potential trading partners can find each other, despite being geographically distributed, and without the intervention of human intermediaries such as sales and distribution agents.

The Web contains many examples of what we will here call *Web-based exchange services*. In these services, users who have items that they wish to trade will insert descriptions into a database of items available, and search a database of items wanted; users who want items will insert descriptions into a database of items wanted, and search a database of items available. (See the left-hand side of Figure 1.) This, in high-level terms, describes the operation of classified ad services such as craigslist; on-line auction and shopping sites such as ebay; waste exchange services such as Macroom-E's Wastematchers, where the emphasis is on diverting waste products from landfill; recruitment services such as Monster; property services such as Daft.ie; and so on.[2] However, it remains a challenge to discover matches through these services.

---

[1] This research was funded by the Environmental Protection Agency of Ireland under Grant Number 2007-S-ET-5. We are grateful to Maeve Bowen and Catherine Costello of Macroom-E and wastematchers.com and to Lisa Cummins of University College Cork for their engagement in our research.

[2] www.craigslist.org; www.ebay.com; www.wastematchers.com; www.monster.ie; www.daft.ie

L. Coyle and J. Freyne (Eds.): AICS 2009, LNAI 6206, pp. 262–272, 2010.

Recommender systems, especially *case-based* recommender systems, are already successfully addressing the challenge of finding more and better matches in Web-based exchange services [10]. However, the matches these recommender systems find can only be as good as the descriptions upon which they operate. Matching is easier when descriptions have a regular structure, style or vocabulary. A corporate product catalogue that contains a relatively homogeneous set of items, each described by a domain expert, is a case in point. For example, in the catalogue of operational amplifiers sold by Analogue Devices, engineers describe the op amps using 40 strongly-typed features, e.g. the total supply voltage, which is a real-valued feature [11]. But in the kinds of Web-based exchange services that we have been describing above, these conditions generally do not hold. Items are often not homogeneous; descriptions are typically written by end-users, not by experts; there are few, if any, strongly-typed features; and there is correspondingly high reliance on free text.

In our research, we are investigating how Web-based exchange services can support end-users to write more comprehensive descriptions. We take a case-based approach. There is an obvious source of case base experience that we can exploit: successful descriptions. A successful exchange of an item through a Web-based exchange service implies not just that an item was desirable to someone, but that its description was informative enough to have initiated a transaction. Such a description forms the basis of a case in our case base.

In Section 2, we present GhostWriter, our case-based approach to making content suggestions to authors. Section 3 presents the results of an off-line evaluation of GhostWriter. Section 4 is a concluding discussion.

2   The GhostWriter System

In this section, we summarize our GhostWriter system, which makes content authoring suggestions to the user [2]. Figure 1 shows an overview of a Web-based exchange service that includes a suggestion facility of the kind we have described. The left-hand side of the figure represents a standard Web-based exchange service. But, as the right-hand side of the figure shows, we propose that the service also inserts successful descriptions into a case base. Then the service can use successful descriptions of items that are wanted to make content authoring suggestions to users who are describing wanted items, and use successful descriptions of items that are available to make content authoring suggestions to users who are describing available items.

GhostWriter is the system that we have designed and built for making these suggestions. It relies on feature extraction, which we apply in advance to successful descriptions (cases) and incrementally to the author's own description as she writes it. Up to now, our implementation, built using jColibri,[3] is suitable only for running off-line experiments. Ultimately, however, we plan to implement an Ajax client that will proactively send asynchronous requests to the server-side GhostWriter system: as the user's content grows, the client will send the new

---

[3] http://gaia.fdi.ucm.es/projects/jcolibri/

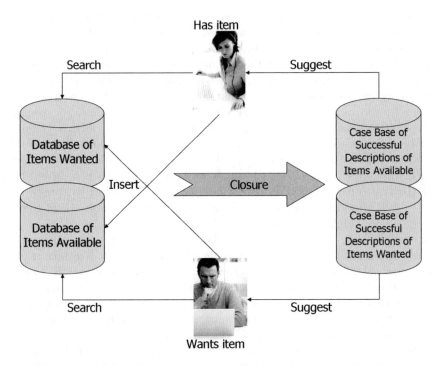

Fig. 1. A Web-based exchange service that includes a suggestion facility

content in an asynchronous HTTP request to the server; the client will update a suggestions pane with GhostWriter's responses. In this way, the user is not interrupted from her normal work, either to invoke GhostWriter or to receive its results. The user can click on a suggestion in the suggestion pane if it is close enough to her current intentions and it will be incorporated into her content, where she can edit it. More likely, the suggestions will not be close enough to what is wanted but will prompt the user to include content she hadn't thought of including. For example, if one of the suggestions is "Will deliver within a 10 mile radius", this might prompt the user to include her own delivery terms, even if these are very different from the suggested ones.

2.1 Case and New Item Representation

As mentioned, a case is a successful description. It therefore primarily consists of free text. But, as it enters the case base, we apply Feature Extraction rules. For now in our work we produce these rules manually. Each is in essence a regular expression that aims to find and extract a particular feature-value pair from the text. Hence, the rules augment each case by a set, possibly empty, of feature-value pairs. For example, we have rules for extracting an item's price, condition (e.g. excellent condition, good as new, etc.), colour, manufacturer, and so on. For example, a case might contain a free text description such as "White wooden cot with mattress...Excellent condition...Will collect". From this, we might extract quite generic feature-value pairs such as $\langle CONDITION, excellent \rangle$ and $\langle DELIVERY, Will\ collect \rangle$ and more specific ones such as $\langle COLOUR, white \rangle$ and $\langle MATERIAL, wooden \rangle$.

More formally then, a case c comprises some free text, $text(c)$, and a set of feature-value pairs, $fvs(c)$. We will denote a feature-value pair by $\langle f, v \rangle \in fvs(c)$. Note that cases do not comprise problem descriptions and solutions. There is no solution part to the cases. This is because making content authoring suggestions is in some sense a form of case completion [3]: we use cases to suggest content that the author might add to her description.

New items that the user is authoring have exactly the same representation as cases: free text and feature-value pairs. The only difference is that they grow in size, as the author adds to her content. We will denote a new item description as nid.[4]

2.2   Conversational Case-Based Suggestions

The GhostWriter approach to making content authoring suggestions to the user is inspired by Conversational Case-Based Reasoning (CCBR) [1]. In CCBR, a typical case has a problem description, comprising of a free text description and a set of question-answer pairs, and a problem solution, comprising a sequence of actions. This is very similar to our case representation, described above, except, as already mentioned, our cases have no solution component.

Aha et al.'s generic CCBR algorithm [1] starts with the user entering a free text query. Then the following repeats until the user selects a case or no further cases or questions can be suggested to the user: the system retrieves and displays a set of cases that are similar to the user's query; from these cases, the system ranks and displays a set of important but currently unanswered questions; then the user inputs more free text or answers one of the questions.

Figure 1 shows the GhostWriter approach to making content authoring suggestions. Recall that we invoke this algorithm repeatedly as the user's content grows. Each time we invoke it, it does the following:

- It initializes the result R to the empty list.
- It retrieves k_1 cases C from the case base CB, ranking them on their similarity to the user's new item description nid. In fact, we compute cosine similarity between term vectors that represent the free text descriptions, $text(nid)$ and $text(c)$ for each $c \in CB$.
- From the cases retrieved in the previous step C, we obtain up to k_2 features F. Candidates for inclusion in F are all features in each $c \in C$, after removing duplicates and any feature that is already among the features of the user's item description $fvs(nid)$, irrespective of that feature's value in $fvs(nid)$. There are many ways of ranking these candidates. At the moment we use

---

[4] We avoid the word "query", which is more common in Case-Based Reasoning, since we have found it leads to confusion.

Algorithm 1. GhostWriter's content authoring suggestion algorithm

---
Inputs: CB: case base
             nid: new item description
             k_1, k_2, k_3: number of cases, features and values, resp.

$R \leftarrow [\,]$
$C \leftarrow rank\_cases(nid, CB, k_1)$
$F \leftarrow rank\_features(C, nid, k_2)$
for each $f_i \in F$, taken in decreasing order **do**
   $V_i \leftarrow rank\_values(f_i, C, k_3)$
   insert $\langle f_i, v \rangle$ onto the end of R for each $v \in V_i$ taken in decreasing order
end for
return R

---

the simplest approach: frequency of occurrence across the cases in C. We place in F the k_2 features that have the highest frequency of occurrence.

- For each of the features obtained in the previous step $f_i \in F$, we obtain up to k_3 values for that feature V_i. Candidates for inclusion in V_i are all values for that feature in each of the cases $c \in C$, after removing duplicates. Again there are many ways to rank these candidates. At the moment, we use the original ranking of the cases C. In other words, if $c \in C$ is the highest ranked case for which $\langle f_i, v \rangle \in fvs(c)$ and $c' \in C$ is the highest ranked case for which $\langle f_i, v' \rangle \in fvs(c')$ and c has higher rank than c', then v has higher rank than v'.
- We return the ranked list of up to k_2 features, each with their ranked list of up to k_3 values, for display to the user in the suggestion pane.

When the user makes sufficient change to nid, possibly by incorporating suggestions from the suggestion pane, we run GhostWriter again to make fresh suggestions. This continues until the user is satisfied with her description and submits it to the exchange service database.

3   Experimental Evaluation

We previously reported the results of a preliminary evaluation of GhostWriter in [2]. However, there we used only one data-set and our experimental methodology had several weaknesses. Here we present the results of a new evaluation using three data-sets and an improved methodology.

One of the data-sets we use comes from the wastematchers.com waste exchange service. We scraped the other two data-sets from craigslist: one describes various computer equipment available; the other describes furniture. We summarize their characteristics in Table 1.

Unfortunately, the descriptions that we took from wastematchers.com and from craigslist, which we use in the case bases in this experiment, are not restricted to successful descriptions. Neither wastematchers.com nor craigslist

Table 1. Data-set characteristics

Data-set name	Num. cases	Avg. num. words (incl. stop-words)	Avg. num. words (excl. stop-words)	Avg. num. feature-values
wastematchers	88	6.67	4.76	0.66
craigslist-computers	68	121.26	80.00	5.00
craigslist-furniture	80	94.25	55.52	7.00

stores information about successful exchanges. In wastematchers.com, when a user deletes a description, the service shows a form that requires her to explain why the description is being deleted. She may have sold or given away the item through wastematchers.com; she may have sold or given away the item but not through the service; she may have disposed of the item (e.g. by sending it to landfill); or she may have failed to dispose of the item. At present, responses to this form allow wastematchers.com to report summary statistics. It would be a small step to retain in a case base (perhaps after expert review) descriptions of those items that were sold or given away through the service. But this has not been a characteristic of the system's existing operation. Our inability to obtain only successful descriptions may make the experimental results different from what they could be in practice.

We use a leave-one-out methodology. We temporarily remove a case from the case base, we determine what feature-values it contains, and we delete a random proportion of the feature-values. We treat this as the user's *nid*; the ablation simulates an incomplete description. We supply this *nid* to GhostWriter. GhostWriter returns an ordered set of suggestions. We randomly select one of the suggestions, where the probability of selection is greater for those suggestions that GhostWriter ranks higher. We add the selected feature-value to both the text and feature-values of the *nid*, and move on to making the next suggestion. We keep doing this until GhostWriter is unable to make further suggestions. We repeat this for each case in the case base, and we repeat the whole procedure five times to average out differences that result from random ablation.

After we add a suggested feature-value to the *nid*, we measure the similarity between the current state of the *nid* and the original case from which we created the *nid*. We measure similarity as the proportion of the ablated *features* that have been restored to the *nid*, irrespective of their *values*. In other words, we reward GhostWriter for making the right kind of suggestion (e.g. price, condition, delivery terms, etc.), even if the text of that suggestion is not the same as what was ablated. Formally, let *Ablated* be the set of ablated feature-values and let *Selected* be the set of feature-values that have been suggested, selected, and added to the *nid*, then the similarity is measured as follows:

$$\frac{|\{f : \langle f, v \rangle \in Ablated \wedge \langle f, v' \rangle \in Selected\}|}{|Ablated|} \tag{1}$$

The results are shown in Figure 2. In each graph, on the y-axis is average similarity; on the x-axis is the number of feature-values that we have added to the *nid*.

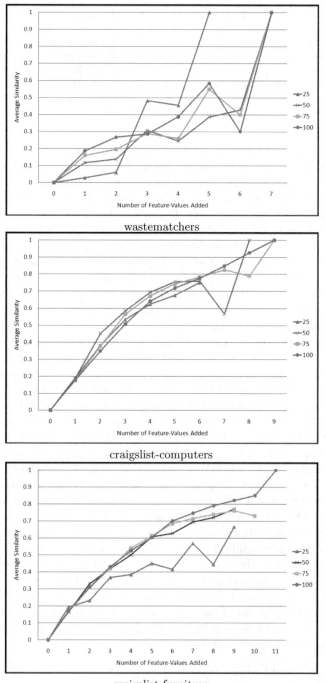

wastematchers

craigslist-computers

craigslist-furniture

Fig. 2. Average similarity at various levels of ablation as we add suggested feature-values

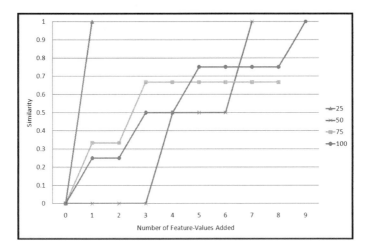

Fig. 3. Similarity at various levels of ablation as we add suggested feature-values for a single craigslist-furniture *nid*

GhostWriter was run with $k_1 = 10$ (the number of cases it retrieves), $k_2 = 2$ (the number of features it suggests), and $k_3 = 2$ (the number of values it suggests for each feature). Hence it returns up to four suggestions (two values for two features). The graphs contain different plots according to the starting amount of ablation. For example, one plot records what happens when we form the *nid* by ablating 25% of the original feature-values in the case; another plot measures what happens when there is 50% ablation; and so on.

In interpreting these results, the question is: when we add suggested feature-values to a *nid*, are we restoring some of the original features that we ablated earlier? If this is so, then the suggestions are useful ones. We also want to see that content is restored as early as possible.

The first point to explain is why the lines can fall as well as rise. For any *individual nid*, each feature-value that we add to the ablated *nid* cannot reduce similarity to the un-ablated *nid* (Equation 1). This is illustrated in Figure 3, which shows the similarity in the case of a *single nid*. The reason then that the lines in Figure 2 may fall is that each point is an average over a *different* set of *nid*s. For some *nid*s, GhostWriter may run out of suggestions much earlier than others: if the features of the retrieved cases C are all already present in the *nid*, then GhostWriter can make no fresh suggestions. So as we look at points in Figure 2 from left-to-right, each average is computed from a possibly smaller and smaller set. This can be seen in Figure 4. The percentages alongside each data point in this figure record this information. For example, on the line for 75% ablation, we were able to add two feature-value pairs to 98% of *nid*s; three to only 93%; and four to 80%.

Returning to Figure 2, we think the results are good. On average, selected suggestions do quickly recover ablated features. The lines generally climb steeply (showing that ablated features are being restored), only tailing off as the averages

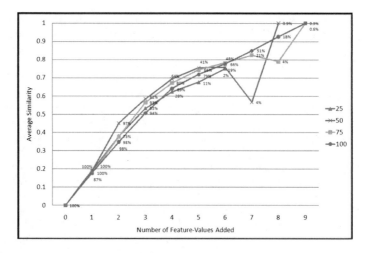

Fig. 4. Average similarity at various levels of ablation as we add suggested feature-values for craigslist-computers

are computed over smaller sets. The wastematchers plot looks much worse, but this is due to the data: as we see from Table 1, wastematchers cases have very few feature-values to begin with.

4   Conclusions and Future Work

In this paper, we have argued that the Web contains experience in the form of successful descriptions, which we can treat as cases in making suggestions to the authors of new content. We have presented our GhostWriter system, for making these suggestions, inspired by work in Conversational CBR. And we have reported results from an off-line ablation study, showing that GhostWriter can quickly restore ablated features.

We believe that GhostWriter provides a new kind of support to content authors, different from existing research. Several researchers have investigated ways of proposing completions for incomplete phrases and sentences, representative of which are [5,7]. This kind of work tends to focus on data structures for representing phrases and sentences in a way that supports fast matching with phrase and sentence prefixes. Lamontagne and Lapalme use CBR for the more challenging task of generating email replies [6]. But their work, and the work on phrase and sentence completion, is concerned with making suggestions in situations where there are 'stock responses'. We would argue that GhostWriter's task is different in nature. Its goal is to prompt the user to write a more comprehensive description. On occasion, 'stock responses' may be relevant, and the user may click on a suggestion to include it directly in her content. But just as likely, she will not accept any of the phrases (*feature-values*) that we suggest to her. Nevertheless, we hope that she will be prompted to include a phrase of her own, inspired by the *features* that we suggest. Hence, even if the use of suggestions means that descriptions more often have the same *features*, they may still be novel descriptions by virtue of not having the same *feature-values*.

In its goal, Recio-García et al's Challenger 1.0 system is more similar to our own work [8]. Their system supports the author of air incident reports. However, their texts are longer and their techniques are quite different from ours. They have no feature-value pairs and do not draw ideas from CCBR. Instead, they use standard text retrieval coupled with clustering of the results.

We envisage four main lines of future inquiry. The first, of course, is more evaluation, including comparisons with 'benchmark' systems such as the use of random suggestions, but also evaluations with real users. The second is to try some of the many ways of learning the Feature Extraction rules, see, e.g., [4]. The third is to investigate variants of the algorithm, where we would use different ways of ranking the cases, features and feature-values. In particular, we intend to replace similarity-based case retrieval by a diversity-enhanced method for retrieving the cases [9], and we might try to incorporate negative cases (unsuccessful descriptions) into the suggestion process in some way. The fourth line of inquiry, described in the next paragraph, is perhaps the most interesting.

We want to apply our approach to support the authors of *reviews* of products such as hotels and electronic goods. This introduces several new dimensions to the work. (a) The content of these reviews is probably even less predictable than the content of the descriptions in Web-based exchange services. (b) In the domain of product reviews, other users can often indicate whether they found a review to be useful or not, or whether the reviewer is trust-worthy or not. This is what we would use as a measure of whether a description is successful. It implies that the case base becomes a fuzzy set, where descriptions have different degrees of membership depending on how useful or trust-worthy people have found them to be. (c) In Web-based exchange services, an item typically has just one description. But on review sites, an item may have several reviews, and these may complement or contradict each other.

References

1. Aha, D.W., Breslow, L.A., Muñoz-Avila, H.: Conversational case-based reasoning. Applied Intelligence 14, 9–32 (2001)
2. Bridge, D., Waugh, A.: Using experience on the read/write web: The Ghostwriter system. In: Bridge, D., et al. (eds.) Procs. of WebCBR, Reasoning from Experiences on the Web, Workshop Programme at the 8th International Conference on Case Based Reasoning (2009)
3. Burkhard, H.-D.: Extending some concepts of CBR — Foundations of case retrieval nets. In: Lens, M., et al. (eds.) Case-Based Reasoning Technology: From Foundations to Applications, pp. 17–50. Springer, Heidelberg (1998)
4. Etzioni, O., Banko, M., Soderland, S., Weld, D.S.: Open information extraction from the web. Communications of the ACM 51(12), 68–74 (2008)
5. Grabski, K., Scheffer, T.: Sentence completion. In: Sanderson, M., et al. (eds.) Procs. of the 27th Annual International ACM SIGIR Conference on Research and Development in Information Retrieval, pp. 433–439. ACM Press, New York (2004)

6. Lamontagne, L., Lapalme, G.: Textual reuse for email response. In: Funk, P., González Calero, P.A. (eds.) ECCBR 2004. LNCS (LNAI), vol. 3155, pp. 234–246. Springer, Heidelberg (2004)
7. Nandi, A., Jagadish, H.V.: Effective phrase prediction. In: Koch, C., et al. (eds.) Procs. of the 33rd International Conference on Very Large Data Bases, pp. 219–230. ACM Press, New York (2007)
8. Recio-García, J.A., Díaz-Agudo, B., González-Calero, P.A.: Textual CBR in jCOL-IBRI: From retrieval to reuse. In: Wilson, D.C., Khemani, D. (eds.) Procs. of the Workshop on Textual Case-Based Reasoning, 7th International Conference on Case-Based Reasoning, pp. 217–226 (2007)
9. Smyth, B., McClave, P.: Similarity vs. diversity. In: Aha, D.W., Watson, I. (eds.) ICCBR 2001. LNCS (LNAI), vol. 2080, pp. 347–361. Springer, Heidelberg (2001)
10. Smyth, B.: Case-based recommendation. In: Brusilovsky, P., Kobsa, A., Nejdl, W. (eds.) Adaptive Web 2007. LNCS, vol. 4321, pp. 342–376. Springer, Heidelberg (2007)
11. Wilke, W., Lenz, M., Wess, S.: Intelligent sales support with cbr. In: Lenz, M., Bartsch-Spörl, B., Burkhard, H.-D., Wess, S., et al. (eds.) Case-Based Reasoning Technology. LNCS (LNAI), vol. 1400, pp. 91–113. Springer, Heidelberg (1998)

On Using Temporal Features to Create More Accurate Human-Activity Classifiers*

Juan Ye[1], Adrian K. Clear[1], Lorcan Coyle[2], and Simon Dobson[1,2]

[1] CLARITY: Centre for Sensor Web Technologies,
University College Dublin, IE
[2] Lero, The Irish Software Engineering Research Centre,
University of Limerick, IE
juan.ye@ucd.ie

Abstract. Through advances in sensing technology, a huge amount of data is available to context-aware applications. A major challenge is extracting features of this data that correlate to high-level human activities. Time, while being semantically rich and an essentially free source of information, has not received sufficient attention for this task. In this paper, we examine the potential for taking temporal features—inherent in human activities—into account when classifying them. Preliminary experiments using the PlaceLab dataset show that absolute time and temporal relationships between activities can improve the accuracy of activity classifiers.

1 Introduction

Advances in sensing technology lead to a huge amount of information being available to context-aware applications. For example, an average smartphone exposes data through accelerometers, GPS, Bluetooth, Wifi and microphones, to name but a few. There is much research into techniques to extract high-level activities from individual streams data from sensors like these [1,2,3].

In order to distinguish between various human activities, it is often necessary to consider multiple types of sensor data in aggregate. For example, combining location information, noise-level and the number of people co-located may allow us to distinguish between a *meeting* situation and a *working alone* situation. However, adding sensor infrastructure in order to distinguish between activities can be a costly process.

Time is a property of all human activities and inherent in most sensor data – almost all sensor readings are time-stamped. In this paper, we explore the effectiveness of using temporal information for classifying human activities. We hypothesise that by doing so we can create more accurate classifiers at no extra infrastructural cost.

* This work is partially supported by Science Foundation Ireland under grant numbers 07/CE/I1147, "Clarity, the Centre for Sensor Web Technologies", and 03/CE2/I303-1, "Lero: the Irish Software Engineering Research Centre".

L. Coyle and J. Freyne (Eds.): AICS 2009, LNAI 6206, pp. 273–282, 2010.
© Springer-Verlag Berlin Heidelberg 2010

Firstly, we analyse the temporal semantics of the human activities that occur in the PlaceLab dataset. This dataset records the activities of a couple living in an instrumented real-world environment for over two weeks [3]. Then, through experimentation using this dataset, we examine how effective a subset of these temporal properties and relationships are at increasing the accuracy of our activity classifiers.

The rest of this paper is organised as follows: Section 2 describes the temporal semantics of the activities in the PlaceLab dataset. In Section 3, we take a subset of the temporal features of this data and conduct some experiments to examine the effectiveness of these features in improving our classifiers. Section 4 explores some related work in the area of temporal semantics. Finally, we draw some conclusions in Section 5 and outline future directions for this research.

2   Temporal Features and Human Activities

In this section we will examine the temporal features of human activities that can be useful in improving the accuracy of activity classifiers. Temporal features of activities can be categorised as being *absolute* or *relative*. Absolute temporal features are those that exist independent of other activities, whereas relative features are those that exist in the context of other activities. We will explore these features using activity data from the PlaceLab dataset [3].

The PlaceLab is an instrumented home fitted with a large number of sensors and an audio-visual recording infrastructure. The dataset that we use in this paper was gathered in real-world conditions – a married couple moved into the PlaceLab and were encouraged to maintain their life routine as much as possible for a period of *15 days*. A third party annotated the activity categories of the married couple using the recorded video stream. These categories include (1) working (e.g., writing or using a computer); (2) leisure (e.g., watching TV); (3) meal preparation (e.g., cooking or preparing a drink); (4) cleaning (e.g., dusting or putting things away); (5) entering/leaving the PlaceLab; (6) grooming (e.g., getting dressed or undressed); (7) hygiene (e.g., toileting or bathing); and (8) eating (e.g., eating a meal or drinking).

2.1   Absolute Temporal Features

Absolute temporal features are those that exist independent of other activities. These include *physical time*, which consists of a date and time in a representation such as "2006-09-05 18:23:45", and *semantic time*, which is a symbolic representation of time such as "morning", and is abstracted from physical times. Semantic times can also be application- and person-specific. For example "lunchtime" can be between 12:00 and 13:00, during which a person routinely has their lunch. Such semantic times have been shown to be useful in predicting human activities [4].

As mentioned above, the PlaceLab activities can be classified into a set of high-level categories such as leisure and cleaning. A person's day can be segmented into continuous intervals in which the activities that are carried out are for the most part from a single high-level category [1]. We hypothesise that a person's routine will cause daily patterns to occur in the absolute temporal features of these segments. Being able to determine that some activities from one of these categories are occurring at a given time may be useful to an application, even if the actual activity cannot be determined. Therefore, as a first experiment, we will examine the potential to determine the high-level category of activities that is occurring at a given time in a person's day.

Figure 1 presents the time distribution of activity categories, including working, leisure, cleaning, entering/leaving the PlaceLab, grooming, hygiene, and eating. It illustrates the proportion of these categories at different times of the day. Each point on the x-axis corresponds to a time interval beginning at the labelled hour and ending at the following hour (e.g., 22 represents the time between 22:00 and 23:00).

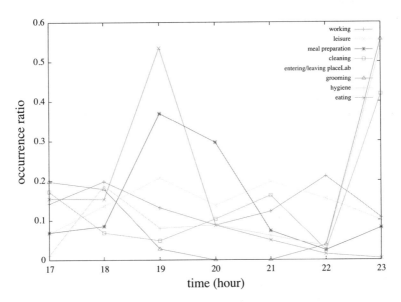

Fig. 1. Time distribution of activity categories

Even though many of the categories occur throughout the day, we can see peaks in over half of the activities during a particular hour of the day. For example, we can see that grooming mostly occurs around 17:00 and 23:00 and that eating usually takes place between 19:00 and 20:00. While these results may not be conclusive in determining the category of activities occurring, by combining the occurrence ratios from the figure with some data from sensors there is a potential to determine these categories with a high level of accuracy.

2.2 Relative Temporal Features

Relative temporal features of activities are those that exist in the context of other activities. Such features may be useful in classifying activities that do not

276   J. Ye et al.

display patterns in absolute temporal features, but can be inferred from their relationship with other activities that occurred or are occurring. For example, a person may not have a routine time for eating dinner, but they often prepare food before eating it.

Figure 1 shows a large amount of overlapping among the occurrence of the coarse-grained activity categories, so it is difficult to observe the temporal sequence between them. We will now examine a sub-set of lower-level activities, which are regarded as characteristic activities in the PlaceLab publications [3]. Figure 2 shows the probability of activities occurring before the occurrence of the activities on the x-axis. For example, there is almost 70% probability that the subject is using a computer before he uses the phone. The activities under the working and leisure categories still dominate most of the time, including "using a computer", "watching TV", and "reading". Beyond them, we can observe a few distinguishable temporal relationships; for example, "meal preparation" is likely to occur before "eating"; and "hygiene" is the activity that occurs most frequently before "grooming".

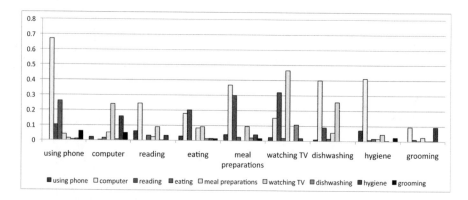

Fig. 2. Probabilities of activities occurring before the occurrence of each activity

The occurrence of activities can exhibit rich temporal semantics. Figure 3 shows the following basic temporal sequences and the compound sequences derived from them. More details can be found in [5]:

1. *overlapping* — activities a and b co-occur at some point in time; for example, a subject can watch TV and have dinner at the same time;
2. *containing* — one activity b begins after the start of, and ends before the end of, another activity a; for example, mixing and stirring food can be considered as one of the processes in cooking.
3. *preceding* — one activity a occurs before another activity b; for example, a person prepares a drink before drinking it;
4. *co-starting* — activities a and b begin at the same time;
5. *co-ending* — activities a and b end at the same time.

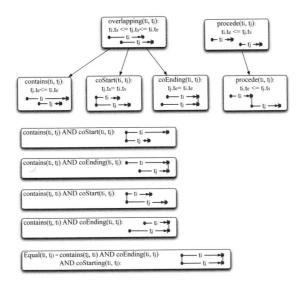

Fig. 3. Temporal semantics of activities. The starting and ending times of these activities are represented as $[t_i.t_s, t_i.t_e]$ and $[t_j.t_s, t_j.t_e]$

2.3 Time with Other Sensor Data

Time usually acts as metadata for other sensor data; that is, each sensor datum has an associated timestamp. Beyond this, further temporal semantics can be applied to sensor data so that the same sensor values can be inferred to different activities according to the time of day. For example, in a smart home where electrical current usage is monitored, high usage at 19:00 may imply that the subject is using the oven, watching TV, or using a computer; while the high usage at 02:00, when the subject is usually asleep, may suggest an electrical fault.

3   Case Study

The above section discusses the rich temporal features in human activities. Here, we demonstrate that incorporating such features into activity classifiers improves the accuracy of determining activities compared to using sensor data alone. Our experiments are carried out on the PlaceLab dataset [3].

3.1   The PlaceLab Dataset

The PlaceLab has the following types of sensors installed: infra-red motion sensors to detect motion in different rooms, object motion sensors to detect access and movement of everyday articles such as the remote control, sensors to monitor the usage of electrical current, water and gas, RFID (radio frequency identification) sensors, and switch sensors that sense the open and closed states of doors.

Since most sensors in the PlaceLab are not person-specific (except for RFID) and there are two subjects involved, this dataset has external noise, which leads to a low accuracy in activity prediction [6].

The activities that we are classifying in our experiments are the most characteristic activities of the dataset, listed in Figure 2. The activity classifier that we use is called the *situation lattice*, which is a sound mathematical model that is used to abstract and combine sensor data in a lattice structure [7]. Through a learning process, the situation lattice can build the correlation between the abstracted sensor data and the high-level activities. It supports the representation and use of domain knowledge, which allows us to incorporate temporal features in the inference process. More detail on the theoretical model, construction methodology, and inference technique can be found in [4,7].

We use the leave-one-day-out technique to evaluate the accuracy of our activity prediction. The accuracy is quantified as *F-measure*, which combines and balances sensitivity and specificity. Sensitivity is the ratio of the number of times that an activity is correctly inferred to the number of times that it is inferred. Specificity is the ratio of the number of times that an activity is correctly inferred to the number of times that it actually occurs.

3.2 Experiments

We now present two experiments: the first one explores the effectiveness of incorporating absolute temporal features, such as hour of day (from 17:00 to 24:00), into the activity classification process; and the second experiment explores the effectiveness of incorporating the following relative temporal features:

– *co-occurrence*

  • we explicitly constrain the activities that cannot co-occur according to human common sense knowledge. For example, watching TV cannot co-occur with hygiene in the bathroom. In the inference process, we remove all the activities that cannot co-occur with the activity that we have inferred with the highest probability;

  • we account for the likelihood of activities co-occurring. For example, meal preparation can sometimes co-occur with dishwashing. In the process of training the lattice, we determine the probability that any two activities will co-occur. In the inference process, we use this to predict the activities that are likely to co-occur with the activity that we have inferred with the highest probability. The following basic Bayes rule is applied: $prob(j) = prob(i) * prob(j|i)$, where $prob(i)$ is the probability of activity i occurring, $prob(j|i)$ is the probability of co-occurrence, and $prob(j)$ is the inferred probability of activity j occurring according to its co-occurrence with activity i.

– *pre-occurrence* – we account for the likelihood of an activity occurring based on the activities that occurred prior to it. Similar to the co-occurrence relationship, in the training process we determine, for each activity, the probability that any other activities occur before it. In the inference process, we use this to predict the activities that are occurring according to the activities that occurred in the previous ten minutes.

Using the above temporal features, we carried out the following experiments.

Experiment 1 : *Comparing the accuracy of activity classifiers when using temporal features compared to using other individual sensors.*
In this experiment, we evaluate the overall accuracy of each type of sensor for classifying activities. We compare this to the use of absolute time, and the combination of using absolute time and the relative temporal features described above. The results can be seen in Figure 4, where the absolute time outperforms the other sensor types by producing a higher average accuracy in predicting all activities. Moreover, the figure shows that the relative temporal features can further increase the accuracy of this classifier.

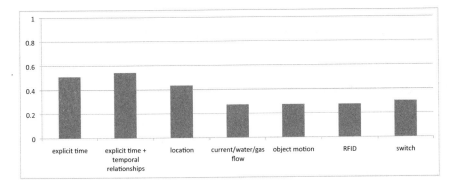

Fig. 4. Overall accuracy of predicting activities using each type of sensor

Experiment 2 : *Comparing the accuracy of activity classifiers when using all the PlaceLab sensors in aggregate, and when combining this with absolute and relative temporal features.*
In this experiment, we evaluate the accuracy of activity inference using classifiers created from the following factors:

1. all sensor types without any temporal features;
2. all sensor types including absolute time;
3. all sensor types including absolute time and the *co-occurrence* relation;
4. all sensor types including absolute time and the *pre-occurrence* relation;
5. all sensor types including absolute time, and the *co-occurrence* and *pre-occurrence* relations.

Figure 5 shows that the incorporation of temporal features improves the accuracy of inferring most activities. The most accurate classifier is the one that incorporates all of the above temporal features.

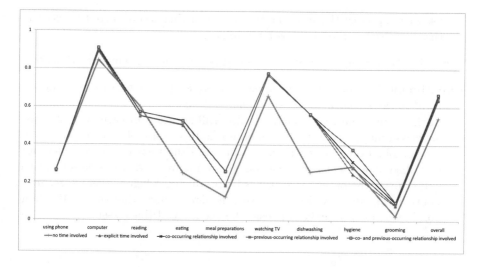

Fig. 5. Accuracy of classifiers creating using different factors

4 Related Work

In this section we describe how time has been studied elsewhere, both in terms of modelling and for use in activity recognition.

4.1 Modelling Time

Time is an important dimension of context and is inherent in every sensor reading. Most current work on modelling time is restricted to reflecting the physical nature of time, such as representation and formatting of time instants [8], and intervals. Ye *et al* [9] observe that it would be beneficial to develop a formal temporal model to exploit the features and various relationships of time.

In the GLOSS project, Dearle *et al* [10] provide an orthogonal structure to represent physical and semantic time, which is beneficial in reasoning for scheduling applications. For example, we can add an activity with a description as follows: *meeting with Erica at 4 o'clock tomorrow*. The system could then recognise that tomorrow is one day after the current date, translate it into a physical time, and then execute further actions.

SOUPA (Standard Ontology for Ubiquitous and Pervasive Applications) [8] extends the above work by exploiting diverse temporal relationships such as startsSoonerThan, startsLaterThan, startsSameTimeAs, endsSoonerThan, endsLaterThan, endsSameTimeAs, startsAfterEndOf, and endsBeforeStartOf. However, these are incomplete when compared to the temporal relationships presented in Figure 3.

4.2   Using Time

Time has been directly or indirectly involved in the treatment of uncertainty in sensor data [11,12]. Ranganathan and Niu et al describe their approach to aggregating commonly noisy, uncertain and conflicting sensor data types to determine the location of an object [11,12]. They apply an exponential decay of time to weigh each evidence source. The idea is that the fresher the evidence, the more reliable it is. Therefore, time simply acts as a measure of the reliability of other sensor data.

Partridge et al [13] study the applicability of time-use study data for ubiquitous activity-inference systems. The time-use study covers all the human activities (and other data like location) performed by the participants over a certain period, which could be a day or weeks. Partridge et al analyse how well the time-use study predicts activities using time, location, demographics, and previous activity. They argue that the study data are useful in the sense that they enable cheap and comprehensive classifiers. One of their results is that, when combined with time of day, the accuracy of activity prediction is increased up to 70%.

Hidden Markov Model (HMM) is one of the most popular techniques for activity recognition [14,15,16]. It is a statistical model in which the system being modelled is assumed to be a Markov chain that is a sequence of events. The probability of each event is dependent on the event immediately preceding it. For example, Modayil et al [15] use an interleaved HMM to predict transition probabilities better by recording the last object observed in each activity. This approach achieves very low error rates, though it requires an approximation for the inference process.

5   Conclusion and Future Work

A major challenge in sensor-rich environments is extracting high-level events, such as activities or situations, from low-level sensor data. There is much research into finding features that enable classifiers to recognise activities and distinguish them from other activities. In this paper, we have explored the effectiveness of using temporal features for this task.

We have identified absolute and relative temporal features that can be incorporated into activity classifiers to produce more accurate results at no extra infrastructural cost. We have shown through two preliminary experiments that a subset of these features do indeed produce more accurate classifiers. In the future, we will look into a formal method to model all the temporal relationships and use them in a broad range of activity classifications.

References

1. Huýnh, T., Fritz, M., Schiele, B.: Discovery of activity patterns using topic models. In: Proceedings of UbiComp 2008, South Korea, pp. 1–10 (2008)
2. Krause, A., Smailagic, A., Siewiorek, D.P.: Context-aware mobile computing: Learning context-dependent personal preferences from a wearable sensor array. IEEE Transactions on Mobile Computing 5(2), 113–127 (2006)

3. Logan, B., Healey, J., Philipose, M., Tapia, E.M., Intille, S.: A long-term evalua-tion of sensing modalities for activity recognition. In: Krumm, J., Abowd, G.D., Seneviratne, A., Strang, T. (eds.) UbiComp 2007. LNCS, vol. 4717, pp. 483–501. Springer, Heidelberg (2007)
4. Ye, J., Coyle, L., Dobson, S., Nixon, P.: Representing and manipulating situation hierarchies using situation lattices. Revue d'Intelligence Artificielle 22(5), 647–667 (2008)
5. Allen, J., Ferguson, G.: Actions and events in interval temporal logic. Journal of Logic and Computation 4(5), 531–579 (1994)
6. Coyle, L., Ye, J., McKeever, S., Knox, S., Stabeler, M., Dobson, S., Nixon, P.: Gathering datasets for activity identification. In: Proceedings of the Workshop on Developing Shared Home Behavior Datasets to Advance HCI and Ubiquitous Computing Research (colocated at CHI 2009), Boston, USA (2009)
7. Ye, J., Coyle, L., Dobson, S., Nixon, P.: Using situation lattices in sensor analysis. In: Proceedings of PerCom 2009, pp. 1–11 (2009)
8. Chen, H., Finin, T., Joshi, A.: An Ontology for Context-Aware Pervasive Comput-ing Environments. Special Issue on Ontologies for Distributed Systems, Knowledge Engineering Review 18(3), 197–207 (2004)
9. Ye, J., Coyle, L., Dobson, S., Nixon, P.: Ontology-based models in pervasive com-puting systems. The Knowledge Engineering Review 22, 315–347 (2007)
10. Dearle, A., Kirby, G.N.C., Morrison, R., McCarthy, A., Mullen, K., Yang, Y., Connor, R., Welen, P., Wilson, A.: Architectural support for global smart spaces. In: Chen, M.-S., Chrysanthis, P.K., Sloman, M., Zaslavsky, A. (eds.) MDM 2003. LNCS, vol. 2574, pp. 153–164. Springer, Heidelberg (2003)
11. Niu, W., Kay, J.: Location conflict resolution with an ontology. In: Indulska, J., Patterson, D.J., Rodden, T., Ott, M. (eds.) PERVASIVE 2008. LNCS, vol. 5013, pp. 162–178. Springer, Heidelberg (2008)
12. Ranganathan, A., Al-Muhtadi, J., Chetan, S., Campbell, R., Mickunas, M.D.: Mid-dlewhere: a middleware for location awareness in ubiquitous computing applica-tions. In: Jacobsen, H.-A. (ed.) Middleware 2004. LNCS, vol. 3231, pp. 397–416. Springer, Heidelberg (2004)
13. Partridge, K., Golle, P.: On using existing time-use study data for ubiquitous com-puting applications. In: Proceedings of the 10th International Conference on Ubiq-uitous computing, UbiComp 2008, pp. 144–153. ACM, New York (2008)
14. Hasan, M.K., Rubaiyeat, H.A., Lee, Y.K., Lee, S.: A hmm for activity recognition. In: Proceedings of ICACT 2008, vol. 1, pp. 843–846 (2008)
15. Modayil, J., Bai, T., Kautz, H.: Improving the recognition of interleaved activities. In: Proceedings of UbiComp 2008, pp. 40–43. ACM, New York (2008)
16. Piccardi, M., Perez, O.: Hidden markov models with kernel density estimation of emission probabilities and their use in activity recognition. In: Proceedings of the IEEE Conference on Computer Vision and Pattern Recognition, CVPR 2007, pp. 1–8 (2007)

Physical Activity Motivating Games

Shlomo Berkovsky, Jill Freyne, and Mac Coombe*

CSIRO Tasmanian ICT Center
GPO Box 1538, Hobart, 7001, Australia
firstname.lastname@csiro.au

1 Introduction

Contemporary lifestyle is becoming increasingly sedentary with no or little physical activity being carried out. The nature of sedentary activity is self-reinforcing, such that increasing physical and decreasing sedentary activity is difficult. We present a novel approach aimed at combating this problem in context of computer games. Rather than changing the amount of physical and sedentary activity, we propose a new game design, referred to as PLAY, MATE!, which leverages the engagement with games in order to motivate players to perform physical activity as part of playing [1]. In this demonstration we will showcase the application of the PLAY, MATE! design to the Neverball game.

2 Design and Application of PLAY, MATE!

The goal of the PLAY, MATE! game design is to change the sedentary nature of game playing to include certain aspects of physical activity. The physical activity is introduced as integral part of the game playing and the engagement of players with the game is leveraged to motivate them to perform physical activity. The motivation is achieved by modifying the following game components and aspects of interaction with the game:

- Game motivator. Players are made aware of the possibility to gain virtual game rewards in return for performing real physical activity. Also, the game is modified to motivate players to perform physical activity, such that certain game functions can be enabled and reinforced by the rewards.
- Activity interface. Players are provided with an external interface capturing the physical activity performed and converting it into virtual game rewards.

Using the above modifications, players are motivated to perform physical activity in the following way. On one hand, the game is modified such that certain functions are disabled. On the other hand, players are made aware of the fact that

* This research is jointly funded by the Australian Government through the Intelligent Island Program and CSIRO. The Intelligent Island Program is administered by the Tasmanian Department of Economic Development, Tourism, and the Arts. The authors acknowledge the contributions of Nilufar Baghaei, Dipak Bhandari, and Richard Helmer. Special thanks to Robert Kooima and the Neverball developers.

L. Coyle and J. Freyne (Eds.): AICS 2009, LNAI 6206, pp. 283–284, 2010.
© Springer-Verlag Berlin Heidelberg 2010

Fig. 1. Neverball interface (left) and accelerometer (right)

performing physical activity will gain them game related rewards: enable and re-inforce the disabled functions. A composition of these two factors, combined with engagement with the game and enjoyment of playing, motivate players to per-form physical activity. When performed, the physical activity is captured by the activity interface, processed, and converted into the game rewards, such that the disable game functions are enabled and reinforced.

We applied the PLAY, MATE! design to an open source Neverball game. In Neverball, players navigate a ball to the target point through a maze shaped surface and collect the required number of coins, while accomplishing these in a limited time (Figure 1 - left). We applied a time based motivator. The time allocated to accomplish the levels was shortened and players were made aware of the possibility to gain extra time in return for performing physical activity.

We used a compact ($42 \times 42 \times 10$ mm) and lightweight (15 gr) in-house de-veloped tri-axial accelerometer to capture player's physical activity [2]. The ac-celerometer was clipped to an elastic band and attached to the player's waist (Figure 1 - right). The acceleration signal was wirelessly transmitted 500 times per second to a USB receiver attached to the computer running Neverball. For every activity burst captured players gained one extra second in Neverball.

An empirical evaluation involving 180 players aged 9 to 12 was carried out. The results showed that (1) players performed more physical activity and de-creased their sedentary playing time, (2) girls and less skilled players performed more physical activity showing gender and gaming skills dependency, and (3) although required to perform physical activity and realistically perceiving this, players did not report a decrease in their subjective enjoyment of playing.

These results demonstrate the potential of physical activity motivating games and call for future research on user dependent applications of the PLAY, MATE! design to various games, and for a longitudinal study assessing the behavioural change caused by physical activity motivating games.

References

1. Berkovsky, S., Bhandari, D., Kimani, S., Colineau, N., Paris, C.: Designing games to motivate physical activity. In: Proceedings of the 4th International Conference on Persuasive Technology. ACM, New York (2009)
2. Helmer, R.J.N., Mestrovic, M.A., Farrow, D., Lucas, S., Spratford, W.: Smart tex-tiles: Position and motion sensing for sport, entertainment and rehabilitation. Ad-vances in Science and Technology (2008)

A Machine Learning System for Tracking Sentiment in Irish Economic News

Anthony Brew, Derek Greene, and Pádraig Cunningham

School of Computer Science & Informatics, University College Dublin
{anthony.brew,derek.greene,padraig.cunningham}@ucd.ie

Overview

Tracking sentiment in the popular media has long been of interest to media analysts and pundits. With the availability of news content via online syndicated feeds, it is now possible to automate some aspects of this process. There is also great potential to "crowdsource"[1] much of the annotation work that is required for the construction of predictive models.

Here we introduce a system that uses active machine learning techniques to monitor sentiment in economic news from popular Irish media sources. The proposed system (outlined in Figure 1) has two novel aspects. Firstly, it generates an aggregated news feed containing a diverse set of articles relevant to the Irish economy. This allows users to browse articles in their preferred news reader application, and annotate these articles as "positive", "negative" or "irrelevant" via embedded links. Secondly, the results of this manual annotation process are used to train a supervised learner that labels a much larger set of news articles. The annotation and classification trends can subsequently be tracked online[2].

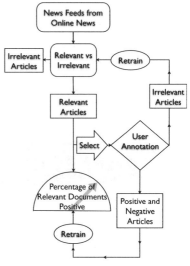

Fig. 1. Workflow of the sentiment analysis system.

Discussion: The main motivation for applying machine learning techniques in this context is to reduce the annotation effort required to train the system. For instance, the system generates online time-plots to compare the change in sentiment across news sources over time (see Figure 2). These plots reflect hundreds of articles per week, but the annotators are only asked to annotate approximately ten articles per day. The remaining articles are classified using a supervised learning system trained on the smaller set of manually annotated articles.

---

[1] Crowdsourcing is a term, sometimes associated with Web 2.0 technologies, that describes the outsourcing of a task to a large often anonymous community.

[2] See http://sentiment.ucd.ie

L. Coyle and J. Freyne (Eds.): AICS 2009, LNAI 6206, pp. 285–286, 2010.

A number of machine learning techniques are employed in the system. Firstly, articles collected from online sources are transformed to a bag-of-words representation and filtered to remove irrelevant articles (*i.e.* those not pertaining to economic news) using a Naïve Bayes classifier. Experimental evaluations show that this classification process achieves > 90% accuracy on average. From the unfiltered items, a query selection procedure chooses a diverse set of economic news stories to be manually annotated. The remainder are classified as either "positive" or "negative" by a second Naïve Bayes classifier. It is worth noting that even though the accuracy of this learner is currently not very high (about 70% on average), it is effective for producing aggregate sentiment statistics because care is taken in the training process to ensure that it is unbiased.

Another novel aspect of this problem is the availability of confidence scores on the training data, based on the distribution of user annotations. For some articles there is unanimous agreement on the sentiment of an article, while for others there is disagreement. Our evaluation has shown that this confidence information can be used in the training process to increase generalisation accuracy.

The system also provides other information regarding news sentiment, such as automatically generated lists of the most positive and negative articles, and visual "tag clouds" of terms that are most characteristic of positive and negative economic news. In the latter case weights are determined by applying Information Gain to terms occurring in positively and negatively labelled articles.

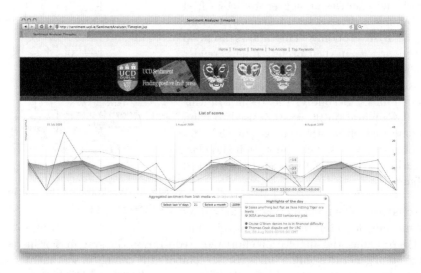

Fig. 2. A screenshot of the time-plot generated by the system, which tracks economic sentiment from the various news sources over time.

Acknowledgments. This work is supported by Science Foundation Ireland Grant Nos. 05/IN.1/I24 and 08/SRC/I140.

The Blogoduct System:
A Just-In-Time Information Retrieval Assistant for Bloggers

Ang Gao* and Derek Bridge

Department of Computer Science,
University College Cork, Ireland
ang.gao87@gmail.com, d.bridge@cs.ucc.ie

The Blogoduct System is a Just-In-Time Information Retrieval (JITIR) agent for bloggers and authors of other short documents. Blogoduct selects and extracts terms from the document (e.g. blogpost) that the user is editing, and uses these terms to formulate search engine queries. The queries are sent asynchronously to Internet search engines, and the results are aggregated and displayed alongside the user's document. Blogoduct currently provides aggregated search results from Google and Yahoo!, along with image search results from flickr.[1]

Blogoduct is a client-server webapp. Figure 1 shows, in simplified form, the Blogoduct architecture, and Figure 2 shows a screenshot of the client.

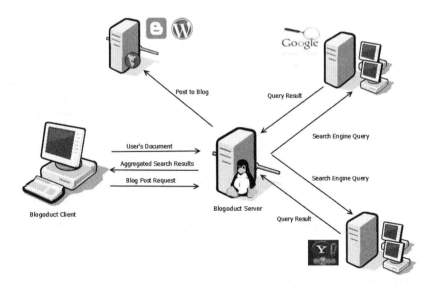

Fig. 1. The Blogoduct architecture (simplified)

---

* Supported by Science Foundation Ireland Principal Investigator Grant, 07/IN.1/I977.
[1] www.google.com; www.yahoo.com; www.flickr.com

L. Coyle and J. Freyne (Eds.): AICS 2009, LNAI 6206, pp. 287–288, 2010.

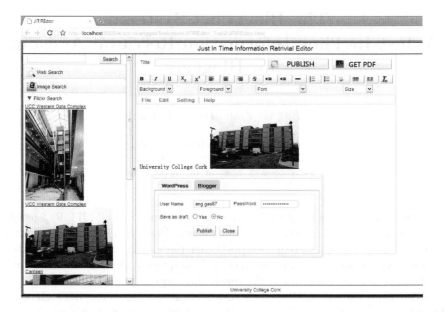

Fig. 2. A screenshot of the Blogoduct client, showing image search results and the dialog for posting to the user's blog

The client is an AJAX application. In her browser, the user sees a pane that contains a rich-text editor for creating her document, and a pane in which search results are listed. Other functionality includes: a standard search box; a search result thumbshot preview facility[2]; and a button for publishing to the user's blog.

Server-side, Blogoduct is implemented as a Java servlet. The client communicates with the Blogoduct server using GWT Remote Procedure Calls. The server receives a copy of the user's document, from which it can extract search engine queries. Ordinarily, the Blogoduct server uses Internet search engine APIs to obtain search results, in which case queries will be sets of keywords. Presently, we have implemented interfaces to the Google, Yahoo! and flickr search engines. The Google and Yahoo! results are aggregated; the flickr results are kept separate.

Blogoduct's research innovation comes in the way it extracts queries from the user's document, which uses shallow natural language processing techniques. These techniques are described in [1] (presented in the technical programme of this conference).

Reference

1. Gao, A., Bridge, D.: Using shallow natural language processing in a just-in-time information retrieval assistant for bloggers, pp. 288–289 (2009)

---

[2] Implemented using the http://thumbshots.org service

Sensing Handshakes for Social Network Development

David Haddock, Aaron Quigley, and Benoit Gaudin

University College Dublin, Lero@UCD, CASL - School of Computer Science & Informatics Belfield Office Park, Dublin 4
david.haddock@ucdconnect.ie, aaron.quigley@ucd.ie, benoit.gaudin@lero.ie

1 Introduction

Increasing ones social network and contacts currently is a manual process. Collections of business cards are exchanged or notepads are brought around to write down contact details at events such as conferences. These details are not only difficult to keep track of but the context in which the details were taken will be forgotten in time. Unfortunately business card exchange also involves more user activity subsequently in searching for the people online.

In this project we prototype a system inferring social links between people from sensed data. The system automates management of people's online social network, detecting when people meet for the first time. In order to detect such an event, we focus on handshake occurrences. Handshake detection is performed using accelerometer data from sensors placed on people's wrists. The sensors we use possess Bluetooth facility and can send data to a computer for realtime analysis or store the date for post-processing. We envisage wrist watches with such facilities would be used in a real deployment. Although such devices are not available yet, it is expected they will be in a near future as both accelerometers and Bluetooth are already available in smart phones and cameras.

The hardware we are using for this project are SHIMMER sensors which are developed by Intel. They contain a 3-axis accelerometer, Bluetooth, capability and some processing power. The software we are using for dealing with the accelerometer data signals is BioMOBIUS, which is developed by the TRIL center at University College Dublin. BioMOBIUS is an extension of the EyesWeb Graphical Development Environment developed at the University of Genoa.

The handshake detection algorithm we have developed is not only able to detect handshake-like movements from a single SHIMMER but also to cross-correlate data coming from different SHIMMERs. This allows us to eliminate other movements, which could resemble a handshake (e.g. iPod shuffling, leg scratching while sitting, white board cleaning, etc) as well as determining which two SHIMMERs are involved in one single handshake.

Our approach is explained in Section 2 and the demo that was conducted at AICS 2009 is described in Section 3.

L. Coyle and J. Freyne (Eds.): AICS 2009, LNAI 6206, pp. 289–290, 2010.

2   Handshake Detection System

Figure 1(a) shows a handshake being performed while SHIMMERs are being worn. SHIMMERs have a 3-axis accelerometer system, making it possible to detect acceleration in any direction. Because of the way SHIMMERs are worn and the specificity of a handshake gesture only one of the axes (the Y-axis, whose direction is represented by the arrows in Figure 1(a)) sends data that is relevant for handshakes. This led us to focusing on processing the signal related to the Y-axis. Figure 1(b) illustrates a signal output from the Y-axis of the SHIMMER for a handshake. The handshake detection algorithm consists of looking at individual signals first and checking whether they can be part of a handshake. Then pairs of signals are considered to check whether they are performed at the same time. This cross-correlation between the two signals can be thought as checking whether the phase and period of the two signals are similar.

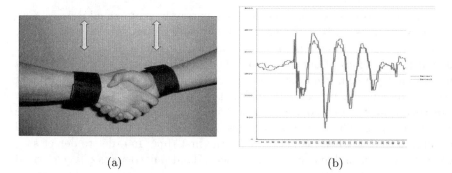

(a)   (b)

Fig. 1. A typical handshake. The X-axis corresponds to the time and the Y-axis corresponds to SHIMMER's acceleration.

3   Demo

A demo of our system was performed at AICS 2009. During this demo, each user was assigned a SHIMMER that they wore on their wrist. As users moved around the acceleration data was recorded. The recorded data was sent to a computer then read into a BioMOBIUS patch (i.e. program) which decides if a handshake actually took place. When two users shake hands, our program detects it and sends each person an email with a link to add the other on Facebook.

This demo has illustrated the ability of our system to detect handshakes when they occur and send emails accordingly. Because of hardware restrictions, it was not possible to demonstrate the ability of the system to determine the exact people involved in a handshake when several handshakes occur simultaneously. This aspect of the system will be considered in future work performing a user study.

A Decision Support System for Energy Storage Traders

Alan Holland

Cork Constraint Computation Centre,
Department of Computer Science,
University College Cork,
Cork, Ireland

We demonstrate a software application that supports energy traders in gas utilities in determining an optimal injection/withdrawal schedule for a storage facility. We employ a stochastic model for gas prices and incorporate an injection adjustment factor in our optimisation model that reflects the decisions of other agents that share space in the storage facility. The optimal injection policy is critically dependent on the pressure in the facility and thus the rates of injection and withdrawal. These adjustment factors are supplied by the store owner. This software has been deployed with several multi-national gas utilities and investment firms.

The store is typically a partially depleted gas field that can cost in the order of hundreds of millions or even billions of dollars to develop. There is, therefore, a great incentive for optimizing its utilization given the increasing volatility in gas markets. These facilities allow gas to be fed into a transmission system at times of peak demand (*e.g.* winter) or withdrawn from the grid and re-injected into the reservoir at times of low demand (*e.g.* summer). The movement of gas either into or out of the reservoir is based on "nominations" made by gas shippers as a result of demands placed on them by their end customers. Gas shippers lease portions of space and injection/withdrawal resources on an annual basis. The storage operators must be informed at the outset of each day whether they should inject or withdraw. Gas prices exhibit striking seasonality patterns where prices drop in the summer as consumption decreases and rise in the winter as temperatures drop. We model gas prices using a stochastic process and determine the expected-profit maximizing injection/withdrawal for an energy trader who wishes to decide whether to inject or withdraw gas for that day [1,2,4]. We use a linear program to solve simulated instances whose solutions are aggregated in order to determine a probalistic model of the optimal decision, be it injection or withdrawal.

We repeat the price simulations many times so that we can gain confidence in our withdrawal or injection decisions. For usability, the energy traders require a response time of at most five minutes because decisions are made early in the morning of each day with a strict deadline. The store owner estimates the pressure in the store and available injection/withdrawal capacity will fluctuate in line with the expected pressure levels. This motivates an interesting line of research that investigates the game theoretic effects of interaction between multiple agents [3].

The Monte-Carlo based approach that we employ supports robust modeling of the problem. The volatile nature of gas prices demands the inclusion of jump processes that inhibit precise numerical solution techniques. Although imperfect, this approach is very popular because it is less computationally intractable, although constraints on

L. Coyle and J. Freyne (Eds.): AICS 2009, LNAI 6206, pp. 291–292, 2010.

292   A. Holland

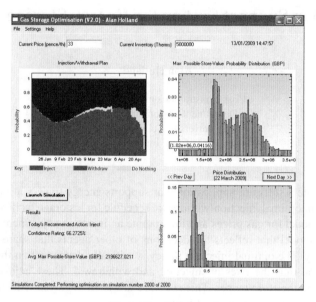

Fig. 1. User Interface

the operability of the storage facility impinge upon the speed of solving the optimal injection/withdrawal schedule for each price simulation.

The user may input the initial estimates regarding injection/withdrawal rates for future days in the remaining contract using a calendar control. These figures are supplied by the operator of the storage facility. The user can also enter the current gas price and their own inventory levels already in storage. This application allows gas utilities to optimize expected profitability by informing them of the injection/withdrawal schedule that, on average, maximizes revenue over the remaining duration of the storage contract given its capacity constraints.

The optimized schedule is displayed graphically in a color-coded manner (see Figure 1) indicating periods of injection, withdrawal and inactivity. Also, the probability distribution for ex-post profit-maximizing strategies is displayed alongside the probability distribution for future price movements. The upper bound on the expected value of the remaining storage contract is also revealed to the user once all the simulations are completed.

References

1. Holland, A.: Injection/withdrawal scheduling for natural gas storage facilities. In: Proceedings of the ACM Symposium on Applied Computing (ACM-SAC 2007) (2007)
2. Holland, A.: A decision support tool for energy storage optimization. In: Proceedings of 20th IEEE International Conference on Tools with Artificial Intelligence (ICTAI 2008) (October 2008)
3. Holland, A.: Capacitated warehouse management in multi agent environments. In: Decker, S., Sierra, C. (eds.) Proc. of 8th Int. Conf. on Autonomous Agents and Multiagent Systems (AAMAS 2009) (2009)
4. Holland, A.: Strategic interaction in ratcheted gas storage. In: Proc. of 7th IEEE International Conference on Industrial Informatics, 2009, Cardiff, Wales (June 2009)

Author Index

Printing: Mercedes-Druck, Berlin
Binding: Stein+Lehmann, Berlin